OZ CLARKE'S

WINE
HANDBOOK
1993

A Fireside Book

Published by Simon & Schuster Inc.

NEW YORK LONDON TORONTO SYDNEY TOKYO SINGAPORE

A Fireside Book
Published by Simon & Schuster Inc.
Simon & Schuster Building
Rockefeller Center,
1230 Avenue of the Americas
New York, NY 10020

Originally published in Great Britain by
Webster's Wine Price Guide Ltd,
Axe and Bottle Court, 70 Newcomen Street,
London SE1 1YT

Printed and bound in the USA

10 9 8 7 6 5 4 3 2 1

Library of Congress
Cataloging in Publication Data

Clarke, Oz.
Oz Clarke's wine handbook, 1993.
p. cm.
"A Fireside book."
Includes index.
ISBN: 0-671-79361-6
1. Wine and wine making – Dictionaries.
I. Title.   II. Title:
Wine handbook, 1993.
TP546. C53   1992
641. 2'2 – dc20

CONTENTS

FOREWORD

If I told you that I had tasted every wine recommended, let alone mentioned, in this guide, you wouldn't need a doctorate in biochemistry to realize that with the best will in the world this would be a physical impossibility. I suppose I taste as many wines in a year as almost anybody I can think of – thousands and thousands, at home and abroad, from the sublime to the frankly disgusting but I could not have produced this guide without, as they say, a little help from my friends.

The following people have contributed not only invaluable advice but also essential content to the entries in their respective areas of expertise. I cannot thank them enough for the generous spirit in which they have shared their knowledge.

Tim Atkin is one of the leaders of the new generation of writers, with a particular expertise in French wines. His contribution has been invaluable.

Kathryn McWhirter and Charles Metcalfe have rapidly established themselves as the English-speaking world's greatest experts on the wines of Spain and Portugal. I greatly appreciate their contributions.

David Gleave is one of Italy's most enthusiastic supporters and trenchant critics. With his help I think we have managed to balance the good and the bad, the old and the new in Europe's most complex and inscrutable wine nation.

We are lucky to have benefited from Giles MacDonogh's erudite knowledge of Austria, Switzerland and Germany, whose wines are undergoing a much vaunted transformation.

Huon Hooke's reputation in Australia is for incisive critical comment and scrupulous fairness in a land that boasts many wonderful wines, but a great deal of partisanship too.

Bob Campbell has a reputation as New Zealand's foremost wine critic and I am grateful for his contribution to this guide.

Larry Walker's objectivity and independence ensures we are up-to-the-minute in reporting what matters in America.

Andrew Jefford has made invaluable contributions to our sections on England, Eastern Europe, South America and South Africa.

And finally, I want to say a big thank you to my editor Fiona Holman whose attention to detail – and deadlines – made the whole enterprise come together. I couldn't have done it without her.

However, for better or for worse, this is in the end a personal guide. I have my own enthusiasms – and indeed dislikes – and these show up throughout. And I make no apology for that: I think it is positively helpful for the reader to know that there is one person's approach behind all the entries. After all, someone's got to say if a wine is good or bad and I happily shoulder that responsibility – with, as I said, a little help from my friends.

HOW TO USE THE A-Z

The A–Z section starts on page 31 and covers over 1300 entries on wines, producers, grapes and wine regions from all over the world. There are also entries on some of the more common wine-making terms, especially the ones often seen on labels.

Where relevant the entries include up-to-date vintage information and recommended producers. Detailed vintage charts with information on which wines are ready for drinking in 1993 can be found on page 268.

In the A–Z all French châteaux and domaines are listed under their individual names.

Glass Symbols These show the colour of the wine.

❙ Red wine   ⬥ Rosé wine   ♀ White wine

More than one glass indicates wines of more than one colour. The order of the colours reflects the importance of the wines in terms of volume produced. For example:

⬥ White followed by rosé wine

❙ Red followed by white wine

❙ Red followed by rosé, then white wine

Grape Symbols These identify entries on grape varieties and show the colour of the grape.

⚬ Red grape   ⚬ White grape

Star Symbols These indicate wines that are highly rated by the author.

★   A particularly good wine in its category

★★   An excellent wine in its category – worth seeking out

★★★ An exceptional, world-class wine

Cross References To help you find your way round the A–Z wine names and producers who have their own entries elsewhere in the A–Z are indicated by SMALL CAPITALS.

Special Features The A–Z section includes special 2-page features on the world's most important wine styles and grape varieties. These features include recommended vintages and producers, as well as lists of related entries elsewhere in the A–Z.

5

INTRODUCTION

The time has finally come to proclaim that the world of wine has changed irrevocably and there's no turning back. From being an elitist interest pursued by a small and privileged section of our society, wine has become one of the great levellers, one of the bonds that crosses social divides, differences of education, differences of age and sex.

How has wine changed so dramatically in these last few years? Well, let me tell you what it's been like from my vantage point in the eye of the storm. I don't come from a wine-drinking family. I didn't inherit some wonderful cellar full of ancient bottles laid down in generations past. My father's view of decent everyday wine was Yugoslavian Lutomer Riesling for the white and Hungarian Bull's Blood for the red. So when I got interested in wine I was starting from scratch. And I found it very difficult to get past scratch.

Red wine then was a fascinating but daunting world of different Bordeaux properties or Burgundy vineyards, with just an occasional intruder from Beaujolais, the Rhône or Spain. White wine was dominated by Burgundy and the Loire, with a few wines from Germany and Alsace adding spice, and an occasional sweet Sauternes topping off the selection. And that was it. When I was learning about wine, the horizons were that narrow. No wonder it was such an exclusive world and no wonder when I was offered jobs in wine I said – no thanks, there's a big wide world out there and I want to see as much of it as I can.

And see it I did. As a singer and an actor I travelled the world, and two countries, in particular, taught me an important lesson that pointed the way into the future: Australia and the USA. Wine was cheap there. Wine was wonderfully tasty there. Wine was drunk purely for pleasure by every sort of person. Wine didn't have incomprehensible names, it was called by the name of its particular grape variety, and by the name of the chap who made it. So easy. So simple, so attractive – yet so alien to what was the rule in Europe.

But Europe is now increasingly adopting what is the rule in the New World. France was the first to accept that a wine won't sell any longer simply because it has a fancy name. Italy, Spain and Germany are getting the message too: that we want flavour, we want it at a fair price, and we want to understand what we're buying through clear labelling and genuinely definable flavours and styles.

And that's what this guide is all about: I want to inform you about what is important in the modern world of wine, but not bore you with what is irrelevant or obscure. Whenever a wine is interesting, I give you some idea of its flavours, what kind of region it comes from, what kind of people make it. If a wine is important but uninteresting – I say so in no uncertain terms; you wouldn't expect anything else of me, I hope. When a wine is unimportant and uninteresting – I don't waste time on it; the space can be used to tell you more about Chardonnay and Cabernet; what's the real story in Bordeaux and Burgundy; is Chile the new buzz wine region or does Australia still have the edge; does Eastern Europe stand a chance? Yes, I know this is a pocket guide, but facts to me are pointless without opinions, and I'm an opinionated sort of fellow.

I hope the book helps you to feel part of the new world of wine. *Our* world of wine. There's never been a better time to be a wine drinker. There's never been more good wine to be tried, and it's never been as affordable as it is now. Please use this book to widen your horizons and experiences – and your pleasures – in this our Golden Age of Wine.

PICK OF THE YEAR

These are my forecasts for the trends in wine over the next year:

● We'll be drinking more Eastern European wines – the Country Reds from Bulgaria, the Cabernets from Romania and maybe even new releases from the old Soviet Republics. Hungary will continue to give us new wave whites of high quality.

● Southern France is making first rate chunky, full-flavoured reds – and one or two really attractive whites too. Their price is good. Their quality is high. We'll be drinking them.

● Spain continues to provide very good basic reds even though its more expensive examples are less reliable. So we'll drink La Mancha and Valdepeñas reds.

● From Portugal, the fruity rough-and-ready reds from Oeste and Alentejo are getting better and better. Try them.

● We'll have to stop thinking of Italy as mainly a red wine country; there are excellent snappy whites coming from the north – from Piedmont, Alto Adige and the Veneto.

● If we think of Germany solely as a supplier of Liebfraumilch it's time to think again; the 1989 and 1990 vintages are two of Germany's best ever; we should be drinking more of these too.

● California is at last beginning to produce more medium-priced wines to complement her excellent top of the range creations. These are what we'll be getting to know in 1993.

● Chile has at last cracked the code in white wine-making and the 1992s are her best ever to go with juicy Cabernet Sauvignon and Merlot reds. These we'll be drinking.

● New Zealand produces more and more tangy, fruity whites at a sky-high quality level — they're not cheap, but enjoy them.

● And, finally, Australia — will we be drinking those ripe, spicy Chardonnays, brash Shirazes, and sweetly blackcurranty Cabernets? You bet we will.

HOW WINE IS MADE

Taste a white Chardonnay from Australia and a Riesling from Germany – and they're totally different. Taste a red Beaujolais from France and a Cabernet from California – and again the flavours are totally different. This may seem to you as though I'm overstating the obvious but it's amazing how many people profess not to be able to tell the difference between wines almost as a form of inverted snobbery. Numerous factors contribute to the very different flavours of different wines. The grape variety will dramatically influence the flavour, as will the place where the grape is grown, and how the juice is then fermented, and the resulting wine then aged. And, of course, the producer may want to make red or rosé, dry white or sweet, fortified wine or sparkling wine – all different styles, all different flavours, all different methods of manufacture.

MAKING RED WINES

Squeeze all but a few very rare types of red grape and the juice that comes out is white. All the colour is in the skins – so the big difference between red and white wine-making is that for reds the colour-rich skins must go into the fermentation vat with the juice. Grape skins (like pips and stalks) also contain bitter tannins but in moderation tannin is a vital component of red wines. It gives them the extra firmness and bite that we expect of reds, and, in better wines meant for maturing, it helps preserve them as they mellow.

To avoid excessive tannin, the first step nowadays is usually to remove the grapes from the stalks, which contain particularly bitter, astringent types of tannin. If the grapes were picked by machine, the stalks will have been left on the vines. Hand-picked grapes on arrival at the winery are usually sent through a de-stalking and crushing machine, emerging as a mixture of juice, pulp, skins and pips – known as 'must' – which is pumped into the fermentation tanks.

Left to its own devices, this would soon begin to bubble away furiously as the yeasts (sometimes naturally present, sometimes added by the winemaker) convert the grape sugar into alcohol, carbon dioxide ... and heat. Modern winemakers keep a careful watch on temperature – between 25° and 28°C (77° and 82°F) is best. In wines that have become hotter than 30°C (86°F) you can often taste a jammy flavour.

Winemakers must also ensure that the skins remain in contact with the fermenting juice. Because they trap the carbon dioxide bubbles given off by the fermenting yeasts, the skins rise to the surface forming a dense mass known as the 'cap'. Winemakers of earlier times used to poke the cap down with sticks or paddles, or leap into their shallow vats and stomp the skins down with their bare feet. Nowadays, it is more often done by regularly pumping wine from the bottom of the tank and spraying it back in at the top.

It can take anything up to five weeks for all the sugar to be converted into alcohol, but from the point of view of colour, there's no need to leave the skins in for all this time. Colour and tannin are both extracted from red grape skins by the effects of heat and the gradually-forming alcohol. Winemakers looking for a softer, fruity style of red wine for drinking young will run the red juice off the skins after perhaps a week or even less, leaving the liquid to finish fermenting in another tank. For bigger, tougher wines intended for maturation, the solids stay in for longer, sometimes several weeks longer.

Once the skins and pips have been separated, they are pressed to extract the remaining dark, concentratedly tannic wine, and some or all of this may be added back to the 'free-run' wine to give it extra oomph. Now, or sometimes not until the spring when the winery warms up again, the wines undergo a 'malolactic fermentation', caused by benign bacteria, which convert sharp malic acid to softer lactic acid, making the wines taste more mellow. The wines can then be 'fined' or clarified to remove any haze or fine particles. By spring or early summer, simple young red wines can be filtered and bottled. Nouveau wines have all these processes packed into a couple of months.

Oak Gutsier reds for longer keeping may be transferred in the spring to oak barrels. How this affects the taste depends on the origin of the oak, the size of the barrel and how it was made, and how often it has already been used. Small barrels, as used in Bordeaux, and called barriques, have the most effect. New oak imparts a strong aroma and flavour of vanilla and new-sawn wood, as well as adding yet more tannin. This gives a fine wine further complexity, as well as greater aging potential. It may stay in barrel for between 6 and 18 months, regularly topped up and occasionally 'racked' – transferred off its sediment into a clean barrel – before bottling.

Carbonic Maceration Particularly aromatic, light, super-fruity red wines such as Beaujolais are made by 'whole berry' or 'carbonic' maceration. The grapes are kept whole, and placed as gently as possible into the fermenting tank. Inevitably some grapes burst, and the fermenting juice at the bottom of the tank bathes the whole grapes above in warm carbon dioxide. This makes the pulp ferment inside the grapes, producing wonderful, intensely fruity flavours and plenty of colour, while extracting very little tannin.

MAKING ROSÉ WINES

Any primary school child will tell you that you make pink by mixing white and red. But if you did that in the wine world you

9

might find yourself being prosecuted (except in Champagne, where it's legal to add a dash of local still red wine to turn your white fizz pink). Elsewhere, you have to proceed as for red wine, then run the juice off the skins when you judge the colour to be right, usually 6–24 hours after fermentation begins. From then on, you follow the white wine method.

MAKING DRY WHITE WINES

You can make white wine from red or white grapes, but most are made from white. Whatever their colour, it's important that the skins should not contaminate the juice with their tannin, as tannin makes white wines taste coarse. Usually, the grapes are de-stalked and pressed immediately, the skins being discarded. Occasionally they are gently crushed and left in a tank for a few hours' 'skin contact', since much of the flavour of some varieties (such as Chardonnay) lies in or just below the skin. The first juice off the press is the best, and good producers keep it separate. The juice must then be cleaned, by centrifuge or filter, or traditionally, by leaving it to settle for 24 hours.

Some winemakers add bought-in yeasts and yeast nutrients for a more reliable fermentation, others rely on the natural, local yeasts. Whereas red wines need highish temperatures to extract the colour, white wines are best fermented much cooler, ideally between 16° and 18°C (60° and 64°F), because low temperatures make for fresher, more aromatic whites. Once the fermentation is over (usually within about 10–15 days) the new wine is run off the sludge of dead yeasts. It is then 'fined' to clear it of any remaining hazes – often with an insoluble powdered clay called bentonite. Like reds, some whites have their acidity softened by a malolactic fermentation, but some winemakers deliberately prevent it by filtering or stunning the bacteria with sulphur dioxide, and so keep a sharper acidity in their wines. By the early months of the year following the harvest, most white wines are ready for filtering and bottling. Most are super-chilled for a few days before bottling to make them shed little white tartrate crystals, which are harmless but sometimes a cause for complaint if they turn up in the bottle.

A small number of top-notch white wines are aged for a few months in oak barrels. Indeed, a handful of top wines (often fine Chardonnays) are actually fermented in new oak barrels for especially subtle, spicy oak flavours.

MAKING SWEET WINES

Many simple, off-dry to sweetish wines (basic German wines, for example) are made by adding a little grape juice to ready-made dry wines. Wines of this sweetness can also be made – more trickily but with finer results – by stopping the fermentation just

10

before all the sugar has been converted to alcohol. But the world's finest sweet wines are made from grapes that are naturally so very sweet that the yeasts are overcome by their own alcohol long before the grape sugar has been used up. In famous sweet wine regions such as Sauternes, Germany or the Loire Valley, the grapes may become super-ripe just by concentration by the sun; but better still, if the autumn days are misty yet warm, they may be blessed with a wonderful fungus, known as 'noble rot' or *Botrytis cinerea*. Affected grapes look disgusting, but taste wonderful – the fungus sucks out the water, concentrating sugars and acids, and adding a delicious pungency.

MAKING SPARKLING WINES

Take a ready-made still wine, add a little more yeast and sugar, seal the mixture in a strong container and it will re-ferment, the trapped gas dissolving in the wine, ready to be released as fizz once you open it up. The snag is, the fine sludge of dead yeast also remains trapped, and as soon as the container is opened, the bubbles stir it up, making the wine cloudy.

For the classic 'Champagne method', the container is the bottle. Removing the fine deposit traditionally involved sticking the necks of the re-fermented bottles almost horizontally into wooden racks, and laboriously over several weeks twisting and tipping them by hand until the deposit slipped down the bottle side and on to the cork, a process called 'remuage'. Nowadays, specially developed 'agglomerating yeasts' – which clump together as they die – make the job much easier and faster, and also allow it to be done en masse, hundreds of bottles simply being rocked in large crates. Once the sediment is sitting on the cork, the neck of the bottle is frozen in a brine bath, the bottle is opened, the plug of dirty ice ejected (dégorgement), and the bottle is topped up and re-corked.

Of course it is much cheaper and less fiddly to do the second fermentation in tank, run the fizz off its sediment and bottle it under pressure. This is known as the Cuve Close or tank method. On the whole, wine producers use the Champagne method on their best wines. It gives a slightly finer, longer-lasting bubble, and often an extra touch of yeasty complexity because of prolonged contact between flavourful dead yeast and wine.

MAKING FORTIFIED WINES

Some fortified wines – such as port, Madeira or fortified Muscats – have alcohol added part way through their fermentation to kill the yeasts and preserve quite a lot of their grape sugar. Others – almost all sherries, for instance – are fermented completely until dry, and then fortified with spirit up to different degrees depending on how they are intended to age.

11

FRANCE

I've visited most of the wine-producing countries of the world by now, but the one I come back to again and again, with my enthusiasm undimmed by time, is France. The sheer range of her wine flavours, the number of wine styles, and indeed the quality differences, from very best to very nearly worst, continue to enthral me, and as each year's vintage nears, I find myself itching to leap into the car and head for the vineyards of Champagne, of Burgundy, of Bordeaux and the Loire.

CLIMATE AND SOIL

France lies between the 40th and 50th parallels north, and the climate runs from the distinctly chilly and almost too cool to ripen grapes in the far north near the English Channel, right through to the sweleteringly hot and almost too torrid to avoid grapes overripening in the far south on the Mediterranean shores. In the far north the most refined and delicate sparkling wine is made in Champagne. In the far south rich luscious dessert Muscats and fortified wines dominate. In between is just about every sort of wine you could wish for.

The factors that influence a wine's flavour are the grape variety, the soil and climate, and the winemaker's techniques. Most of the great wine grapes, like the red Cabernet Sauvignon, Merlot, Pinot Noir and Syrah, and the white Chardonnay, Sauvignon Blanc, Sémillon and Viognier find conditions in France where they can ripen slowly but reliably – and slow ripening always gives better flavours to a wine. Since grapes have been grown for over 2000 years in France, the most suitable varieties for the different soils and microclimates have naturally evolved. And since wine-making was brought to France by the Romans, generation upon generation of winemakers have refined their techniques to produce the best possible results from their different grape types. The great wines of areas like Bordeaux and Burgundy are the results of centuries of experience and of trial and error, which winemakers from other countries of the world now use and are the role models for their attempts to create good wine.

WINE REGIONS

White grapes ripen more easily than red grapes and they dominate the northern regions. Even so, the chilly Champagne region barely manages to ripen its red or white grapes on its chalky soil. But the resultant acid wine is the ideal base for sparkling wine, and the acidity of the young still wine can, with good wine-making and a few years' maturing, transform into a golden honeyed sparkling wine of incomparable finesse.

Alsace on the German border, is much warmer and drier than Champagne but still produces mainly white wines. The

German influence is evident in the fragrant but dry wine styles favoured by producers from grapes like Riesling, Pinot Gris and Gewürztraminer.

Just south-east of Paris, Chablis marks the northernmost tip of the Burgundy region, and the Chardonnay grape here produces very dry wines usually with a streak of green acidity, but nowadays with a fuller softer texture to subdue any harshness.

It's a good two hours drive further south to the heart of Burgundy – the Côte d'Or which runs between Dijon and Chagny. World-famous villages such as Gevrey-Chambertin and Vosne-Romanée (where the red Pinot Noir dominates) and Meursault and Puligny-Montrachet (where Chardonnay reigns) here produce the great Burgundies that have given the region renown over the centuries. Lesser Burgundies – but they're still good – are produced further south in the Côte Chalonnaise, while betweeen Mâcon and Lyon are the white Mâconnais wine villages and the villages of Beaujolais, famous for bright easy-going red wine from the Gamay grape.

South of Lyon in the Rhône Valley red wines begin to

dominate. The Syrah grape makes great wine at Hermitage and Côte-Rôtie in the north, while in the south the Grenache and a host of supporting grapes make full, satisfying reds of which Châteauneuf-du-Pape is the most famous. The white Viognier makes lovely wine at Condrieu and Château-Grillet in the north.

The whole of the south of France is now changing and improving at a bewildering rate. Provence and the scorched Midi vineyards are learning how to produce exciting wines from unpromising land and many of France's most tasty and most affordable wines now come under a Vin de Pays label from the south. In Roussillon the red wines are warm-spirited but good, but the sweet Muscats are better.

The south-west of France is dominated by Bordeaux, but has many other wine gems benefitting from the cooling influence of the Atlantic. Dry whites from Gascony and Bergerac can be exciting. Jurançon down in the Basque country produces remarkable sweet wines, while Madiran, Cahors and Bergerac produce good to excellent reds.

But Bordeaux is the king here. The Cabernet Sauvignon and Merlot are the chief grapes, the Cabernet dominating the production of deep reds from the Médoc peninsula and its famous villages of Margaux, St-Julien, Pauillac and St-Estèphe. Round the city of Bordeaux are Pessac-Léognan and Graves, where Cabernet and Merlot blend to produce fragrant refined reds. On the right bank of the Gironde estuary, the Merlot is most important in the plump rich reds of St-Émilion and Pomerol. Sweet whites from Sémillon and Sauvignon Blanc are produced in Sauternes, with increasingly good dry whites produced in the Entre-Deux-Mers and especially Graves and Pessac-Léognan.

The Loire Valley is the most northerly of France's Atlantic wine regions, but, since the river rises in the heart of France not far from the Rhône, styles vary widely. Sancerre and Pouilly in the east produce tangy Sauvignon whites, the centre of the river produces fizzy wine at Vouvray and Saumur, sweet wine at Vouvray and the Layon valley, red wines at Chinon and Bourgueil, and dry whites virtually everywhere, while down at the mouth of the river, as it slips past Nantes into the Atlantic swell, the vineyards of Muscadet produce one of the world's most famous but least memorable dry white wines.

CLASSIFICATIONS

France has an intricate, but eminently logical system for controlling the quality and authenticity of its wines. The system is divided into four broad classifications (in ascending order): Vin de Table, Vin de Pays, VDQS (Vin Délimité de Qualité Supérieure) and AC (Appellation Contrôlée).

Within the laws there are numerous variations, with certain

vineyards or producers singled out for special mention. The 1855 classification in Bordeaux or the Grands Crus of Alsace or Burgundy are good examples. By and large, this is a system which rewards quality. VDQS and Vin de Pays wines can be promoted to Appellation Contrôlée, for example, after a few years' good behaviour. Nonetheless, many producers have begun to find that the Vin de Pays category, which is less strict than Appellation Contrôlée, affords them greater freedom of expression. Many of the up-and-coming winemakers in the south of France are turning away from Appellation Contrôlée, which may upset the traditional balance of power in the future.

1991 VINTAGE REPORT

Vintage generalizations are difficult in France. A top-notch vintage in Bordeaux might be a lousy year in Champagne or the Rhône. The key to a successful vintage is having enough early autumn sunshine to ripen the grapes. As the 1991 vintage proved in many areas, the hard work of an entire year can be ruined by rain or a few minutes of hail at harvest time. The 1991 vintage was small compared with '90, '89 and '88, all excellent years, owing to the heavy spring frosts which damaged the vines in several areas, but it's not as bad as people claim.

The whites in Alsace and Champagne are a little green, though some pleasant Alsace has been made. Chablis is also a little green – not necessarily a bad thing in Chablis. The rest of Burgundy has done fairly well. There is a slight hint of unripeness in some of them, but the small harvest has given good wines with fairly strong personality in the Côte d'Or. Beaujolais and the whites from Mâconnais are excellent.

The northern Rhône produced good whites and reds (very good in Côte-Rôtie), the southern Rhône had a patchier time but produced some decent stuff. The South enjoyed cooler than usual conditions and produced excellent reds and good whites.

Bordeaux and the South-West were badly hit by spring frosts, and quantities of whites were way down, but the dry whites are fine, if in short supply. Sweet wines won't be a feature of 1991. The reds aren't exciting, but mostly are perfectly pleasant if a bit light, with some more serious wines made in the Haut-Médoc.

Finally the Loire Valley also suffered from frost, but the quality of the dry whites is excellent, with the reds less successful and there is not much sign of sweet wine this year.

See also ALSACE, BORDEAUX RED WINES, BORDEAUX WHITE WINES, BURGUNDY RED WINES, BURGUNDY WHITE WINES, CHAMPAGNE, CORSICA, JURA, LANGUEDOC-ROUSSILLON, LOIRE VALLEY, MIDI, PROVENCE, RHONE VALLEY, SAVOIE, SOUTH-WEST FRANCE; AND INDIVIDUAL WINES AND PRODUCERS.

ITALY

The cultivation of the vine was introduced to Italy over 3000 years ago, by the Greeks (to Sicily and the south) and by the Etruscans (to the north-east and central zones). Despite their great tradition, Italian wines as we know them today are relatively young. New attitudes have resulted, in the last 25 years or so, in a great change in Italian wine. Quality has risen, while quantity has been greatly reduced. The whole industry has been modernized, and areas like Tuscany are now among the most dynamic of any region in the world of wine.

GRAPE VARIETIES AND WINE REGIONS
Vines are grown all over Italy, stretching from the Austrian border in the north to the island of Pantelleria in the far south which is nearer to North Africa than to Sicily. The north-west, especially Piedmont, is the home of many of the best Italian red grapes, like Nebbiolo, Dolcetto and Barbera, while the north-east

(Friuli-Venezia-Giulia and Alto Adige), is more noted for the success of native white varieties like Garganega, Tocai and Ribolla, as well as imports like Pinot Grigio, Chardonnay and Sauvignon. The central Po Valley is Lambrusco country. Moving south, Tuscany is best known for its red Chianti wines from the native Sangiovese grape. South of Rome where the Mediterranean climate holds sway the traditional heavy whites and reds are gradually giving way here and there to some decent wines.

CLASSIFICATIONS

Vino da Tavola or 'table wine' means that the wine is produced either outside the existing laws, or in an area where no delimited zone exists. Both cheap basic wines and inspired innovative creations like Sassicaia and Tignanello are classified as table wines.

IGT (Indicazioni Geografiche Tipiche) is a new category, due to be introduced from the 1992 vintage, that will cover about 150 areas and should be the equivalent of French Vin de Pays.

DOC (Denominazione di Origine Controllata) is the next level up. While DOCs have imposed order on what was previously a chaotic situation, they have often recognized poor existing practices rather than enforcing improvements.

DOCG (Denominazione di Origine Controllata e Garantita) was originally conceived as a super league for those DOCs officially deemed better than run-of-the-mill, where quality would be guaranteed rather than just indicated. The only word on the label that can do this, however, is the name of the producer. Even so, DOCG has served to provide producers in zones like Barolo and Chianti with an incentive to improve quality.

1991 VINTAGE REPORT

This was a difficult vintage. Cold weather in mid-April resulted in reduced quantities almost everywhere and rain in mid-September presented many growers with problems of rot. In Piedmont quality was good for the early ripening grapes like Dolcetto and Moscato, but Nebbiolo and Barbera were affected by the late September rains. A similar story is told in the Veneto, though in Friuli some producers are proclaiming 1991 is the best vintage for whites since '86. Tuscan quality is, in some cases, as good as in '90, in others the worst in a decade. In the south, drought for the fourth consecutive year resulted in another small crop.

See also ABRUZZO, ALTO-ADIGE, CALABRIA, CAMPANIA, EMILIA, FRIULI-VENEZIA-GIULIA, LAZIO, LIGURIA, LOMBARDY, MARCHE, PIEDMONT, ROMAGNA, SARDINIA, SICILY, TRENTINO, UMBRIA, VALLE D'AOSTA, VENETO, VINO DA TAVOLA; AND INDIVIDUAL WINES AND PRODUCERS.

GERMANY

German wine has been in a state of flux for some years now. The export market is still dominated by semi-sweet Liebfraumilch-type wines, but the domestic market, only recently exposed to the drier, riper wine styles from warmer countries, now demands similar wines from Germany's growers.

GRAPE VARIETIES

The best wines come from Riesling, Scheurebe, Ruländer (also called Grauer Burgunder or Pinot Gris) and Pinot Blanc (Weissburgunder), although the widely planted Müller-Thurgau produces much of the simpler wine. Good reds can be made in the south from Pinot Noir (Spätburgunder) and Dornfelder.

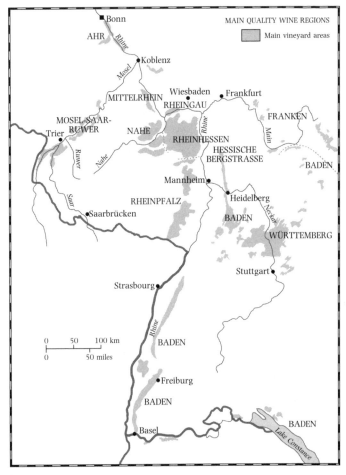

WINE REGIONS

Many of the most delectable Riesling wines come from villages such as Bernkastel, Brauneberg, Graach and Ürzig on the Mosel, and Eltville, Johannisberg and Rüdesheim in the Rheingau. The Nahe also makes superb Rieslings in the communes of Bad Kreuznach, Schloss Böckelheim and Traisen. Franken is the one place the Silvaner grape excels, often made in an earthy style. Rheinhessen is unfortunately better known for its sugary Niersteiner Gutes Domtal than it is for the excellent racy wines produced on its Rhine terraces in the villages of Nackenheim, Nierstein and Oppenheim. The Rheinpfalz is climatically similar to Alsace and has a similar potential when it comes to well-rounded, dry white (and some red) wines. Baden produces wine styles which are able to appeal to an international market increasingly reared on fuller, drier wines. In Württemberg most of the red wines are pretty inconsequential, but there are a few producers who understand the need for weight, flavour and colour in red wine-making. The other smaller wine regions make little wine and almost none is exported.

CLASSIFICATIONS

Germany's classification system is based on the ripeness of the grapes and therefore potential alcohol level.

Tafelwein (Table Wine) is the most basic term used for any low-grade blended wine.

Landwein (Country Wine) is a slightly more up-market version, linked to 17 large vineyard areas.

QbA (Qualitätswein bestimmter Anbaugebiete) is 'quality' wine from a designated region, but the grapes don't have to be very ripe, and sugar can be added to the juice to increase alcohol.

QmP (Qualitätswein mit Prädikat) or 'quality wine with distinction' is the top level. There are six levels of QmP (in ascending order of ripeness): Kabinett, Spätlese, Auslese, Beerenauslese, Eiswein and Trockenbeerenauslese.

1991 VINTAGE REPORT

After three glorious years in most of Germany's wine regions, '91 was bound to come as a slight disappointment. In the Mosel it was actually quite warm, allowing the vines to make up for some of the losses incurred during the spring frosts. Down in the Rheingau conditions were not quite so good, partially as a result of the summer drought; even so a few good wines will be made.

See also AHR, BADEN, FRANKEN, HESSISCHE BERGSTRASSE, MITTELRHEIN, MOSEL-SAAR-RUWER, NAHE, RHEINGAU, RHEINHESSEN, RHEINPFALZ, SAALE-UNSTRUT, SACHSEN, WURTTEMBERG; AND INDIVIDUAL WINE VILLAGES AND PRODUCERS.

SPAIN

From the green, damp north to the arid south, Spain has more land under vine than any other country in the world, yet because of the harsh climate, and often outmoded viticultural methods, the average grape yield in Spain is tiny.

WINE REGIONS

Galicia in the green, hilly north-west grows Spain's best, most aromatic whites. The heartland of the great Spanish reds, Rioja, Ribera del Duero and Navarra, is between the central plateau and the northern coast, Catalonia is principally white wine country (much of it sparkling Cava), though there are good reds. The central plateau of La Mancha makes mainly cheap whites, but with some attractive reds. Valencia in the south-east can rival La Mancha – for fresh, unmemorable but inexpensive reds and whites. Andalucía's specialities are the fortified wines, sherry, Montilla and Málaga.

CLASSIFICATIONS

Vino de la Tierra is Spain's equivalent of France's Vin de Pays, but so far rarely used.

DO (Denominacíon de Origen), is the equivalent of France's AC, regulating grape varieties and region of origin.

DOC (Denominacíon de Origen Calificada) is a new super-category, a step higher than DO, with rather more stringent rules. In 1991 Rioja was the first region to be promoted to DOC.

1991 VINTAGE REPORT
Catalonia had a plentiful harvest of good quality. It was exceptionally hot and dry in Rioja, Navarra and central Spain, and though quality was sound, volumes were severely down. Sherry suffered from politics as the pickers were on strike.

PORTUGAL

Portuguese consumers (and legislators) are a conservative lot, but at last things seem to be happening in this varied and attractive country, with climates that vary from the mild, damp Minho region in the north-west to sub-tropical Madeira.

WINE REGIONS
The lush, green meadows of Vinho Verde country in the Atlantic north-west give very different wine to the parched valleys of the neighbouring Douro, with a drier, more continental climate. In Bairrada and Dão soils are more important in determining the character and quality of the wines, with sandy soils in Bairrada and granite in Dão alternating and combining with clay. The Oeste and Ribatejo supply generous quantities of wine from regions either close enough to the coast to be influenced by the maritime climate, or softened by the river Tagus itself.

South of Lisbon is the Setúbal peninsula, home of some exciting table wines. The other dynamic wine region is the Alentejo, with some top-class red wines. And Madeira is unique, a volcanic island 400km (250 miles) out in the Atlantic Ocean.

CLASSIFICATIONS
Portugal is adjusting to the European quality wine system.
DOC (Denominação de Origem Controlada) The regions that were formerly classified as Região Demarcada ('demarcated region') are now known as DOC. There are 14 in all.
IPR (Indicação de Proveniência Regulamentada) is the intermediate step for 31 wine regions hoping to move up to DOC status in due course. Their wines are referred to as Vinhos de Qualidade Produzidos em Região Determinada (VQPRD).

1991 VINTAGE REPORT
The vintage was very hot and dry, resulting in a reduced yield but, helped by a little September rain, quality was good. Port is probably the best since 1985, the last declared vintage.

See also (SPAIN) ANDALUCIA, ARAGON, CASTILLA-LA MANCHA, CATALONIA, GALICIA, JEREZ Y MANZANILLA, RIOJA, NAVARRA, VALENCIA; (PORTUGAL) ALENTEJO, ALGARVE, DOURO, OESTE, PORT; AND INDIVIDUAL WINES AND PRODUCERS.

USA

America has more varied growing conditions for grapes than any other country in the world, which isn't so surprising when you consider that the 50 states of the Union cover an area larger than western Europe, and although Alaska doesn't grow grapes in the far north, Washington State does in the northwest, Texas does in the south, New York does in the north-east and even Hawaii, lost in the pounding surf of the Pacific Ocean, manages to grow grapes and make wine. Altogether over 40 states make wine of some sort or another; it ranges from pretty dire offerings which would have been better distilled into brandy or used for marinating the sirloin, to some of the greatest and most original wine flavours in the world today.

California is far and away the most important state. In its

determination to match the best red Bordeaux and white Burgundy, California proved that it was possible to take the European role models and successfully re-interpret them thousands of miles away from their home. However there is more to California than this. The Central Valley produces the majority of the simple beverage wines that still dominate the American market. Napa and Sonoma Counties north of San Francisco Bay, do produce great Cabernet and Chardonnay, but grapes like Zinfandel and Merlot are making their mark and the Carneros subregion is highly successful for Pinot Noir. In the far north Mendocino county and Lake County both produce good grapes, while south of San Francisco, in the foggy valleys that run to the sea between

Santa Cruz and Santa Barbara, exciting cool climate flavours are appearing, especially from Pinot Noir and Chardonnay.

There are those that say that much of California is too hot for producing the best table wines – and many of the critics are based in Oregon and Washington, both keen to wrest the quality crown from California. Oregon, with a decidedly cooler, but capricious climate perseveres with Pinot Noir, Chardonnay, Pinot Gris and Riesling with patchy success. Washington, so chilly and misty on the coast, actually becomes virtual desert east of the Cascade Mountains and it is here in the irrigated vineyards that superb reds and whites are being made with thrillingly focussed fruit. New Yorkers also believe that Long Island has all the makings of a classic region: this warm, temperate claw of land to the east of New York is well-suited to Merlot, Riesling and Chardonnay. Hudson Valley and the Finger Lakes can produce good wine but the winters are too cold for many classic vines. Consequently much of New York State's wine comes from hybrid vines, or the native labrusca varieties which can give flavours few people associate with fine wines.

Of the other states, Texas has the most widespread plantings of classic 'vinifera' wine varieties, but producers of excellence exist in Maryland, Virginia and Pennsylvania on the east coast, and Idaho and New Mexico in the west.

CLASSIFICATIONS
The appellation concept is very new in the US and it was only during the 1970s that a rudimentary system was established. AVA (American Viticultural Area) is a loose form of geographical classification. It merely defines a geographical or political spread of land and decrees what minimum percentage of grapes must be in the wine labelled with the AVA's name.

1991 VINTAGE REPORT
In general this is shaping up as good to very good and perhaps excellent in the major wine grape-growing states. New York had a 'textbook' growing season while Washington and Oregon had good quality fruit, despite a winter frost that cut the size of the harvest. In California a long, cool growing season meant that it was the best year for Cabernet Sauvignon since 1985. Cabernet, Zinfandel, Pinot Noir and most Chardonnay tasted in barrel in the spring of 1992 were showing very forward, accessible fruit with lots of perfume. Because of low acid levels in many parts of California it appears to be a vintage for fairly early drinking.

See also CALIFORNIA, NEW YORK STATE, OREGON, WASHINGTON STATE; AND INDIVIDUAL WINE AREAS AND WINERIES.

AUSTRALIA

Australian wine today enjoys a reputation well out of proportion to the quantity of wine produced (total output is barely one-twelfth of Italy's). While the heavy, alcoholic wines of the past are long gone, sheer volume of fruit aroma and flavour is very much the hallmark of today's styles. Production of fortified wines has plunged while sparkling wines boom and fine white and red table wines are the bread and butter.

GRAPE VARIETIES AND WINE REGIONS
Most of Australia's wine regions are concentrated in the south-east, in South Australia, Victoria and New South Wales. Hundreds of miles away in Western Australia, on approximately the same latitude, are the other important wine zones, including Margaret River and Swan Valley. Riesling, Sémillon and Shiraz have long been key varietals but now Chardonnay and Cabernet Sauvignon are the most fashionable. The use of small oak barrels for aging is important in modern reds as well as Chardonnays. Pinot Noir is yielding occasional success.

CLASSIFICATIONS
Appellation control is unknown except in the tiny regions of Mudgee and Tasmania, and there it is more a guarantee of

24

authenticity than a guide to quality. In a country so keen on inter-regional blending a system resembling France's Appellation Contrôlée would be unworkable but a new initiative, the Label Integrity Program, is being introduced. This will guarantee claims made on labels, and I would not want to see any more bureaucratic control on what goes into the bottle than this.

1992 VINTAGE REPORT

A nail-biting vintage. An unusually cool summer and autumn delayed ripening. In cool regions like Coonawarra the harvest was very late and is unlikely to produce exciting reds. However, the traditionally warm areas, like Barossa, Riverina and Riverland, benefitted greatly from the cooler ripening conditions, and some outstanding wines were made. Even the Hunter Valley which got its usual share of rainstorms at exactly the wrong moment before harvest, produced some exciting wines.

NEW ZEALAND

New Zealand's wine regions span a greater latitude than the wine regions of France and so predictably the wide range of wine styles are influenced as much by geography as they are by vintage variation or winemaker philosophy. Most reds and many Chardonnays are matured in small oak barrels but look for the words 'oak-aged' on Sauvignon Blanc labels to distinguish them from the non-oaked examples.

WINE REGIONS

Thanks to warmer ripening conditions North Island regions such as Auckland, Hawkes Bay and Martinborough are likely to make better reds and riper, fleshier whites. Gisborne makes very fleshy whites but less good reds. South Island regions such as Marlborough, Nelson, Canterbury and Central Otago produce finer-flavoured, zestier wines that tend to be fresher and more aromatic, and the whites are usually better than the reds.

1992 VINTAGE REPORT

This was one of the coolest vintages on record. Wet flowering conditions produced a low crop, especially in Chardonnay. This, and a long, cool ripening has resulted in high acid but fruity aromatic whites that could turn out extremely well, though reds may prove to be a bit severe this year.

See also (AUSTRALIA) NEW SOUTH WALES, SOUTH AUSTRALIA, VICTORIA, WESTERN AUSTRALIA; (NEW ZEALAND) AUCKLAND, CANTERBURY, CENTRAL OTAGO, HAWKES BAY, KUMEU/HUAPAI, MARLBOROUGH, MARTINBOROUGH; AND INDIVIDUAL WINERIES.

OTHER WINE REGIONS

ALGERIA The western coastal province of Oran provides three-quarters of Algeria's wine production, with Alger, just east of Oran, making up the rest. French traditions live on in the soft, but muscular wines of the Coteaux du Tlemcen, near the Moroccan border, while the dark, beefy reds of the Coteaux du Mascara in central Oran recall old-style Rhônes.

ARGENTINA The wines of the world's fourth largest producer mainly slake domestic thirst; quality-wine production for export is in its infancy here (5% only). Most vineyards are in the Mendoza region, producing mainly bulk reds but with small, important contributions from quality grapes like Cabernet, Chardonnay and Malbec. Rio Negro/Neuquén to the south, and Salta to the north, both look good for whites from Torrontés and Chardonnay, and reds from Cabernet Sauvignon, Syrah and Malbec. Look out for wines from ETCHART, Flichman, San Telmo, Torino, TRAPICHE and San Felicien (Viña Esmeralda).

AUSTRIA Much of Austria's viticulture falls either side of the country's main waterway, the Danube. Here, below the great baroque monastery of Melk, wine-making kicks off with the Wachau – the best region in Austria for dry white wines, producing great Riesling and excellent pepper-dry Grüner Veltliner. The next region along the Danube is Kamptal-Donauland, also a fine dry white wine region but with some excellent reds now being made by experimental winemakers. Other red wine regions are north and south of Vienna, the Weinviertel and the Thermenregion. Further south, on the Slovenian border, Steiermark produces modern, juicy unoaked Chardonnay (called Morillon) and Sauvignon. Burgenland in the far east produces sturdy reds and sweet whites around the Neusiedler See. See also Burgenland, Kamptal-Donauland, Steiermark, Thermenregion, Wachau, Wien.

BRAZIL Wine-making is confined to the southern tip of this huge country, and winemakers have a hard time combatting the rot that results from a generally damp sub-tropical climate. The fact that hardy labrusca and hybrid varieties still outnumber classic vinifera varieties by seven to one reflects these climatic difficulties. PALOMAS is the only serious export producer.

BULGARIA Eastern Europe's biggest success story, built mainly on the success of soft, curranty red wine. Easy-drinking renderings of the classic grape varieties (Cabernet Sauvignon, Merlot, Pinot Noir, Chardonnay, Riesling, Sauvignon Blanc), which occupy 75% of the vineyards, are the main attraction. Local red varieties, such as the plummy Mavrud, the meaty and toothsome Gamza and the deep though less common Melnik, can be good. The Dimiat can produce gentle, creamy, summer-fruit-bowl whites, while Misket (despite its name and grapy flavour, not a Muscat cousin) combines, if well handled, lively fruit with a haunting muskiness. Whites and lighter reds are mainly from the north and east (the freshest whites are those from the Black Sea coast), while richer, fuller reds come from the mountainous south and south-west. Best wineries include: (Eastern Region) KHAN KRUM, Preslav, Shumen, Varna; (Northern Region) RUSSE, SUHINDOL, Svichtov; (Southern Region) ASSENOVGRAD, Perushtitza, Plovdiv, SLIVEN, Stambolovo.

CANADA Viticulture is possible in two of Canada's southern extremities – the Okanagan valley in British Columbia and small pockets of land in Ontario. Just. It's such a close call, though, that the vast majority of Canada's vines are the hardy labrusca varieties and hybrids, with vinifera varieties inching only slowly into prominence. Inniskillin, Château des Charmes and Hillebrand Estates are the leading producers of quite good reds and whites and an occasional high class icewine.

CHILE The country has the potential to provide the world with enormous amounts of pure-tasting, bright fruity wines at an affordable price. Its vineyards have virtually no disease, ungraft-ed vines that live twice as long as their European counterparts, a hot, bright, cloudless growing season in the rain shadow of the Andes, and yet an unlimited supply of irrigation water from those same mountains. But it is so easy to exploit and abuse these vineyards that much mediocre, dilute wine has been made. Yet with the realization that if the price and the quality are right North America and northern Europe will lap up the wine, leading producers are now restricting yields, investing in stainless steel vats and new oak barrels – and making fair-priced wines of tremendous personality. Red Cabernet Sauvignon and Merlot are best, but white Chardonnay and Sauvignon are bene-fitting from reduced yields and Chile is set to play a major part in our wine drinking during the 1990s. See also Central Valley.

CHINA Despite some major Western and Japanese investment (most notably by Rémy-Martin), China's wine-producing poten-tial remains unfulfilled. Viticulture is best suited to the non-tropical northern part of the country. So far, Tsingtao Riesling and Chardonnay are the only reasonably classy wines.

CROATIA Inland Croatia produces mainly bulk whites; the best quality vineyards are on the Dalmatian coast, turning out gutsy, mouthfilling Postup, Peljesac and Faros reds.

CYPRUS The island has not had a high reputation for wine since the Crusades – when COMMANDARIA was reputedly a rich, succulent nectar worth risking your neck for. Modern Cyprus has survived on mediocre sherry-style wines and bulk shipments to the old USSR. With these markets either declining or collapsed, Cyprus, with the highest per capita grape production in the world, desperately needs to modernize to find new markets.

CZECHOSLOVAKIA The country's potential has only surfaced since the 1989 revolution. With mainly cool climate vineyards, planted with white varieties like Pinot Blanc, Muscat, Grüner Veltliner, Gewürztraminer and the strangely grapy Irsay Oliver – as well as pockets of red, a lack of a sense of direction has been the chief problem. British wine merchants involving themselves in the whole process from growing the grapes to bottling the wine are filling this gap and the future, especially for dry aromatic whites, looks bright.

ENGLAND With under 1000ha (2470 acres) of vineyards, England remains, statistically, an insignificant wine-producing nation. Yet the best English wines are unique: no other spot on earth can manage to infuse white wines with such haunting mayflower aromas and slender, graceful, willowy fruit. Every English winemaker will confirm that these are wines produced against the odds. It's not that the climate is unsuitable for vines – much of south-east England is far drier and milder than latitude would suggest. The most popular wine-making counties are Kent (Biddenden, ENGLISH VINEYARD, LAMBERHURST, STAPLE ST JAMES, Tenterden) and Sussex (BREAKY BOTTOM, CARR TAYLOR, Hidden Spring, Nutbourne Manor, St George's), with other top producers in Berkshire (THAMES VALLEY), Dorset (The Partridge), Gloucestershire (THREE CHOIRS), Oxfordshire (CHILTERN VALLEY), Somerset (Pilton Manor, WOOTTON), and Surrey (DENBIES). The problem is a predictably unpredictable weather pattern: a month or more of rain, wind and cool weather is likely at any time during the long growing season. The most successful grape varieties – the hybrid Seyval Blanc, and German-developed crosses like Schönburger, Huxelrebe, Bacchus, Kerner and Ortega – are those that can hold off disease while waiting for the last rays of October sunshine.

GREECE Best known for RETSINA, Greece still offers a depressing wine-scape. A few modern companies like Boutari, Achaia Clauss and Kourtakis are trying to make wines that are at least clean and fresh, and a few cosmopolitan estates like CHATEAU CARRAS or Gentilini do well. Pockets of quality are Naoussa and Nemea for reds and Patras and Samos for sweet wines.

HUNGARY Unfortunately the country's great wine traditions did not prosper under the Communists, but inspired wine-making by Englishman Hugh RYMAN and others, foreign investment in TOKAJI, and renewed interest in its native grape varieties is sure to make Hungary an important player during the 1990s.

ISRAEL Wine production was initiated by Baron Edmond de Rothschild at the end of the 19th century. Much is nowadays sweet red wine for Jewish family use, but excellent quality dry wines are produced at the GOLAN HEIGHTS WINERY (Gamla, Golan and Yarden labels). Carmel (based near Haifa and Tel Aviv) and Askalon's Ben Ami (Cabernet/Carignan) also produce good Cabernet-based reds.

JAPAN Some quality wines have been produced in Japan from home-grown grapes, as the wines of Château Lumière show, but much purportedly Japanese wine is produced from imported grapes, grape juice and wine sometimes, but not always, mixed with the local product.

LEBANON CHATEAU MUSAR is Lebanon's talisman of courage and quality. In this war-torn land, Musar's excellent red sounds above the conflict a clear clarion call of hope.

MEXICO This is basically brandy country, but in the far northwest some excellent reds are being made by L A Cetto.

MOLDOVA The most forward-thinking of the ex-USSR wine producers, and its Bordeaux-like, mature Rochu and Negru red wines from the Purkar winery are first-class. Straight Cabernet from the Krikova winery can also be good.

MOROCCO Traditionally known for big, rich sweet-fruited reds that found a ready blending market in France, Morocco still produces firm supple reds – Tarik and Chante Bled – as well as refreshing, but heady rosés.

ROMANIA An ancient wineland of enormous potential. It has great traditional vineyards on the Black Sea and the Moldovan border that already provide wonderful sweet wines (Murfatlar and Cotnari). The Dealul Mare winery produces rich, wild Tamaioasa and occasional sightings of Merlot, Cabernet and Pinot Noir are delicious.

SLOVENIA Many of the old Yugoslav Federation's best vineyards are found here, either on the Italian or the Austrian borders. Lutomer 'Rizling' comes from north-east Slovenia.

SOUTH AFRICA The country is waking up to the realities of the international wine market with something of a start. No-one questions the fact that South Africa has many vineyard sites that would seem to be ideal for quality wine production but it is dreadfully hampered by bureaucratic controls. Many, if not most, of the vineyards have diseases that hamper the full ripening of the grape, and few of its winemakers have as yet been able to grasp the fundamentals of what European and American wine drinkers are after, or the price they are prepared to pay.

But there is evidence of talented and forward-looking producers keen to break out of a long period of isolation and decline. Areas like Swartland, Worcester and Robertson could produce wine as good as that of Australia's Riverland or Italy's Veneto from grapes like the red Pinotage and the white Chenin, while cooler vineyards clustered round the Cape itself will be able to challenge Europe and the New World on Chardonnay, Sauvignon, Pinot Noir and Cabernet Sauvignon.

SWITZERLAND The majority of Switzerland's most interesting wines come from the French-speaking cantons of Vaud and Valais, flanking Lake Geneva and the banks of the Rhône above the lake. The German-speaking cantons do produce some pleasant, light reds and rosés usually from the Pinot Noir (Blauburgunder) grape, and easy-drinking whites from Müller-Thurgau (Rivaner). In the far south, Italian-speaking Ticino produces Merlots that range from light and juicy to really quite impressive and powerful. See also Ticino, Valais, Vaud.

TURKEY The world's fifth largest grape producer – but 97% ends up as raisins and the few remaining grapes make pretty poor reds and whites.

UKRAINE A long tradition of sparkling-wine production in Odessa can be dated back to 1896, when a member of the Roederer family established the 'Russian-French Company' to produce sparkling wines from local grapes. See also Crimea.

YUGOSLAVIA What remains of Yugoslavia now that Croatia and Slovenia have become independent is predominantly the red wine-producing part of the old federation. The Vranac grape grows full-throated bulky reds in Montenegro.

ZIMBABWE Three companies (Afdis, Monis and Philips) produce wines from grape varieties common in South Africa (Colombard, Chenin Blanc, Pinotage and Cabernet Sauvignon among others). The country's best-known wines are Philips' Flame Lily range but I have to admit I prefer the label to the grog itself.

A-Z

OF WINES, PRODUCERS, GRAPES & WINE REGIONS

In the following pages there are
over 1300 entries covering the world's top
wines, as well as leading producers, main wine
regions, grape varieties, wine terms and
classifications.

*On page 5 you will find a full explanation of
How to Use the A–Z.*

ABBOCCATO Italian term used to describe lightly sweet wine. Particularly used for off-dry ORVIETO wine.

ABFÜLLUNG German term for 'bottled by'. In general the best wines are bottled by the grower rather than a merchant, in which case the label will say Erzeugerabfüllung.

ABRUZZO *Italy* East of Rome, this region stretches from the beaches on the Adriatic coast to the mountainous Apennine interior. Main wines are the white Trebbiano d'Abruzzo DOC, usually dry and neutral, and the red Montepulciano d'Abruzzo DOC, sometimes rosé but generally a strapping, peppery red of real character.

AC/AOC (APPELLATION D'ORIGINE CONTRÔLÉE) The top category of French wines, defined by regulations covering vineyard yields, grape varieties, geographical boundaries and alcohol content. An AC guarantees the origin and, up to a point, the style of a wine, but not its quality. AC is followed in France's vinous pecking order by VDQS (Vin Délimité de Qualité Supérieure), Vin de Pays and, finally, Vin de Table.

ACACIA *Carneros AVA, California, USA* This big, black-roofed, white-walled barn on the northern shores of San Francisco Bay is one of the Carneros region's influential wineries, focusing solely on locally grown Pinot Noir and Chardonnay. The Pinot Noir ★ can be outstanding but is inconsistent. The Chardonnay is wonderfully crisp and toasty and ages beautifully, especially from the Marina vineyard ★★. Owned by the CHALONE group since 1986. Best years: 1991 90 88 87 86.

ACKERMAN-LAURANCE *Loire Valley, France* This was the first firm to make sparkling SAUMUR using the Champagne method. Today it is one of the largest producers of fizz in the area. The wines are good, inexpensive, but rarely exciting.

TIM ADAMS *Clare Valley, South Australia* Important maker of fine wine from bought-in grapes. Classic dry Riesling ★, subtly wooded Sémillon ★, and rich full-bodied Shiraz ★★ and Cabernet ★. 1990 botrytis Sémillon ★★ is super stuff, and minty, peppery Aberfeldy Shiraz ★★★ is a remarkable, and at times unnerving, mouthful of brilliance from 90-year-old vines.

ADANTI *Umbria, Italy* Located in Bevagna in central Italy, Adanti produces an astonishing range of characterful wines. The white wines, based primarily on the Grechetto grape, are tight, ripe and nutty, but the red wines, especially Sagrantino di Montefalco ★★, are the real stars – pulsating with dark, unexpected flavours. Best years: (Sangrantino)1990 88 86 85.

ADEGA Portuguese for 'winery'.

ADELAIDE HILLS *South Australia* Small, new but exciting region 30 minutes drive from Adelaide. The high altitude of the area affords a cool, moist climate ideal for fine table wines and superb sparkling wine base. Best producers: Ashton Hills, HENSCHKE, KNAPPSTEIN, PETALUMA, Shaw & Smith, Stafford Ridge.

GRAF ADELMANN *Kleinbottwar, Württemberg, Germany* Small estate which manages to produce oak-aged red wines with real colour and taste. Adelmann also makes highly rated Rieslings up to Auslese and Eiswein levels. Best years: 1990 89 88 86 79.

ADELSHEIM VINEYARD *Willamette Valley AVA, Oregon, USA* This vineyard first hit the headlines with wine labels depicting various local beauties, including the owner's wife. Since then Adelsheim has established an increasing reputation for Pinot Noir –

especially a rich Reserve ★ – and a lovely, bright, super-fresh Pinot Gris ★ that I have happy, if hazy memories of.

AGE *Rioja DOC, Rioja, Spain* Large RIOJA producer. A huge recent investment to build Rioja's largest vinification plant may improve the whole range. The Siglo Saco ★ red Crianza is their best known wine – perhaps because it comes wrapped in a hessian sack but luckily, this does not affect the taste.

AGLIANICO DEL VULTURE DOC *Basilicata, Italy* Red wine produced from the Aglianico grape grown on the steep slopes of Mt Vulture, an extinct volcano. Despite being one of Italy's most southerly DOCs, the grapes in this zone are harvested later than those in BAROLO, 1440km (900 miles) to the north, because the Aglianico grape ripens very late. The wines are tannic while young but outstandingly complex and long-lived. Best producers: D'Angelo, Paternoster.

AHR *Germany* The Ahr Valley is a largely red wine region a few miles south of Bonn. The chief grape varieties are the Spätburgunder (Pinot Noir) and the (Blauer) Portugieser. Many Ahr reds are made sweet to please the traditional market in Bonn. Sweet red wines do not find many supporters outside Germany, only Weingut J J Adenauer has achieved anything like an international reputation, and that has been won by sticking to dry wines.

AIGLE *Vaud, Switzerland* Village in the Chablais sub-region of the Swiss Vaud making white wines from the Dorin (as the locals call the Chasselas grape) and reds from the Pinot Noir. The whites with their 'flinty' bouquet are the best known; they are light and refreshing from their slight prickle. Best producers: Badoux, Landolt, Urs Saladin, Testuz.

AIRÉN Spain's – and indeed the world's – most planted white grape can make gently fruity, fresh modern whites, or thick, yellow, old-fashioned brews depending upon the skills of the winemakers. The Spanish seem to prefer the old-fashioned brews, while northern Europe definitely goes for the modern version. It grows all over the centre and south of Spain, especially in La MANCHA, VALDEPENAS and Andalucía (where it is called Lairén).

AJACCIO AC *Corsica, France*   From the west of the island around Ajaccio, this is one of the better Corsican ACs. The reds often need 2–3 years in bottle to show at their best. Best producers: Comte Péraldi★, Clos Capitoro, Dom. de Paviglia.

ALBANA DI ROMAGNA DOCG *Romagna, Italy*   In the hills south of Bologna and Ravenna, Italy's first white DOCG was a 'political' appointment that caused outrage among wine enthusiasts because of the totally unmemorable flavours of most Albana wine. Though also made dry and sparkling, the sweet version is the best. Drink young and you should be thirst-quenched, if not exactly inspired to flights of fancy. Best producers: Ferrucci, Paradiso, Zerbina.

ALBARIÑO   By far Spain's most characterful white grape. It grows in Galicia in Spain's rainy north-west, and, as Alvarinho, over the border in Portugal, in the VINHO VERDE region. When well made, Albariño wines have fascinating flavours of apricot, peach, grapefruit and Muscat grapes, refreshingly high acidity, highish alcohol – and very high prices.

ALCAMO DOC *Sicily, Italy*   One of Sicily's best dry whites. Made from the indigenous Catarratto grape grown in western Sicily, between Marsala and Palermo, it is dry, nutty and rounded. Drink young. Best producers: Castelmonte, Rapitalà, Rincione.

ALEATICO   An ancient, native Italian grape that produces sweet, after-dinner wines of quite notable alcoholic strength in Puglia, Lazio, Umbria and the Tuscan island of Elba. Changing tastes have led the wines to the brink of extinction. Best producer: Candido (delicious Aleatico di Puglia.)

ALELLA DO *Catalonia, Spain*   The city of Barcelona is fast encroaching on this tiny, hilly DO region. Alella wines, mainly white, were traditionally medium dry, but are now increasingly bone dry. Those made from Chardonnay can be good, though the unexciting Xarel-lo grape is still the main staple. Drink young. Best producers: Alta Alella, Parxet, Roura.

ALENTEJO *Portugal*   The two provinces, Alto and Baixo Alentejo, making up most of southern Portugal south and east of Lisbon, are Portugal's fastest improving red wine regions. There are eight IPR regions: Portalegre, BORBA, Redondo, Évora, REGUENGOS, Amareleja, Vidigueira (which specializes in whites) and Moura. The potential of the Alentejo is far from realized but I believe many of Portugal's finest reds will come from here. Best producers: Borba co-op★, FONSECA SUCCESSORES (Portalegre★ and Reguengos★★), Herdade de Cartuxa ★★ (Évora), Horta do Rocio (Borba), Quinta do Carmo ★★ (Borba), Redondo co-op , Reguengos de Monsaraz co-op , J P VINHOS (Moura).

ALEXANDER VALLEY AVA *California, USA* Important viticultural area centred on the Russian River from Mendocino County to middle Sonoma County. It's fairly warm with only patchy summer fog coming up the Valley from the Pacific Ocean, about 40km (25 miles) to the west. Cabernet Sauvignon is highly successful here with lovely, juicy fruit not marred by an excess of tannin. Chardonnay can also be good but doesn't give such ripe, round flavours. Best producers: Alexander Valley Vineyards, Chateau Souverain, Geyser Peak, Lyeth.

ALGARVE *Portugal* It is extraordinary that the predominantly red, feeble-flavoured wines from this holiday region should have been accorded the distinction of not one but four separate DOCs – Lagoa, Lagos, Portimão and Tavira. If I were catching a bit of sun and surf there, I'd stick to the beer.

ALIGOTÉ French grape, found almost exclusively in Burgundy, whose basic characteristic is a lemony tartness. It can make extremely nice wine, especially when made from old vines, but is generally rather dull and tart. In ripe years it can resemble a Chardonnay, especially if a little new oak is used. The best Aligoté traditionally comes from the village of Bouzeron in the Côte Chalonnaise, but other growers in the Côte d'Or are now producing more Chardonnay-like wines. Aligoté is occasionally found in the Rhône Valley and Switzerland. Best producers (Burgundy): Bachelet, COCHE-DURY★, Cogny, Confuron, Dupard, Jobard, RION.

ALLEGRINI *Valpolicella, Veneto, Italy* A small but expanding producer of increasing importance in VALPOLICELLA Classico. Refusing to produce cheap wines for the mass market, Allegrini have concentrated increasingly on quality, and especially on the single-vineyard wines, La Grola ★★, Palazzo della Torre and Fieramonte. Their Vino da Tavola La Poja ★★, made solely with the Corvina grape, has focused attention on the great potential that exists in Valpolicella. Best years: 1990 88 86 85 83.

ALOXE-CORTON AC *Côte de Beaune, Burgundy, France* An important village at the northern end of the Côte de Beaune producing mostly red wines from Pinot Noir. Its reputation is based on the two Grands Crus, CORTON (red and white) and CORTON-CHARLEMAGNE (white only). The wines from the other vineyards in Aloxe-Corton used to be some of Burgundy's tastiest at a fair price, but nowadays the reds rarely exhibit their characteristically delicious blend of ripe fruit and appetizing savoury dryness. Almost all the white wine is sold as Grand Cru; straight Aloxe-Corton Blanc is very rare. Best producers: Bize, Chandon de Briailles★, Chapuis★, Delarche★, DROUHIN, Dubreuil-Fontaine★, JADOT, LATOUR, Rafet★, Senard, TOLLOT-BEAUT★★, Voarick★. Best years: 1990 89 88 87 85 83 82 78.

ALSACE AC
Alsace, France

 Tucked away on France's eastern border with Germany, Alsace produces some of the most individual white wines of all, rich in aroma and full of ripe, distinctive flavour. To the visitor, Alsace appears the most Germanic of France's wine regions – a legacy of intermittent German occupation over the last century and a half. The food tastes German, the buildings look German and there's plenty of beer on offer. As the reputation of German wines has moved down market this perception has almost certainly restricted the popularity of Alsace wines. In their tall green bottles, they could easily be mistaken for something produced in the German Mosel-Saar-Ruwer. The irony of all this is that Alsace is proudly French. More to the point, its wines taste nothing like those from Germany. They're generally drier, richer, less acidic and more alcoholic.

Alsace is almost as far north as Champagne, but its climate is considerably warmer. The key factor is the presence of the Vosges mountains, which act as a natural barrier, protecting the vineyards from rain and westerly winds and making Alsace one of the driest places in France. In the crucial early autumn months, when the grapes are brought to full ripeness, Alsace is frequently warmer than Burgundy.

GRANDS CRUS

Since 1975 the best vineyard sites in Alsace can call themselves Grands Crus. There are around 50 of these, but the list is expanding all the time. These vineyards are restricted to one of four grapes – Riesling, Muscat, Gewürztraminer or Pinot Gris (sometimes labelled Tokay-Pinot Gris) – generally considered the finest varieties in Alsace, though Sylvaner and Pinot Blanc can produce good wines. These four are also the only grapes permitted for Vendange Tardive and Séléction de Grains Nobles, the late-picked and sometimes sweet wines which are a regional speciality. Pinot Noir, the area's only red grape, is usually confined to less well-appointed vineyards. As a result, it frequently produces wines that are closer to a rosé than a red Burgundy, although in good vintages, Alsace Pinot Noir can be excellent.

Alsace was one of the first regions to label its wines by grape variety – a practice which is now common in Australia and California, but is still frowned upon in France. Apart from Edelzwicker, which is a blend, and Crémant d'Alsace, all Alsace wines are made from a single grape variety.

See also ALSACE VENDANGE TARDIVE, CREMANT D'ALSACE, SELECTION DE GRAINS NOBLES; AND INDIVIDUAL PRODUCERS.

BEST YEARS

1990 89 88 85 83 76

BEST PRODUCERS

Edelzwicker Dopff & Irion, Klipfel, Rolly Gassmann.

Gewürztraminer Béyer, Faller, Kreydenweiss, Hugel, Ostertag, Schlumberger, Trimbach, Turckheim co-op, Zind-Humbrecht.

Muscat Théo Cattin, Dirler, Dopff & Irion, Gisselbrecht, Kuentz-Bas, Trimbach, Zind-Humbrecht.

Pinot Blanc Becker, Jos Meyer, Kreydenweiss, Rolly Gassmann, Trimbach, Turckheim co-op, Zind-Humbrecht.

Pinot Gris Blanck, Dopff & Irion, Klipfel, Rolly Gassmann, Trimbach, Zind-Humbrecht.

Pinot Noir Hugel, Turckheim co-op.

Riesling Becker, Béyer, Theo Faller, Kreydenweiss, Kuentz-Bas, Jos Meyer, Ostertag, Schlumberger, Zind-Humbrecht.

Sylvaner Pfaffenheim co-op.

ALSACE VENDANGE TARDIVE AC *Alsace, France* Vendange
Tardive means 'late-harvest'. The grapes (Riesling, Muscat,
Pinot Gris or Gewürztraminer) are picked late and almost overripe, giving higher sugar levels and therefore much more
intense, exciting flavours. The wines are usually rich and
mouthfilling and often need 5 years or more to show their personality. Best producers: Beyer★, Dopff & Irion★, HUGEL★★,
Muré★, Schlumberger★★, TRIMBACH★★, ZIND-HUMBRECHT★★★. Best
years: 1990 99 88 85 83 76. See also page 36.

ALTARE *Piedmont, Italy* Elio Altare crafts some of the most stunning of Alba's wines – outstanding Dolcetto ★★ and even finer
BAROLO ★★ and Barolo Cru Vigneto Arborina ★★★. Though a
professed modernist, his wines are intense and tannic while
young, but with clearly discernible fruit flavours, thanks largely
to tiny yields. He also makes two oak-aged wines: a Nebbiolo
and a Barbera. Best years: 1990 89 88 86 85.

ALTESINO *Brunello di Montalcino DOCG, Tuscany, Italy* Altesino
were one of the first producers in Montalcino to make a more
modern style of BRUNELLO. Their range includes a good
Brunello★★ and a superior Cru from the great hill of
Montosoli ★★, and two Vino da Tavolas, a barrique-aged
Sangiovese (Palazzo Altesi ★★) and a Sangiovese/Cabernet blend
(Alte Altesi ★★★). Best years: 1990 88 85 82.

ALTO ADIGE DOC *Alto Adige, Italy* An Italian wine with Gothic
script and German names on the label will come from the
largely German-speaking Alto Adige or Südtirol, Italy's northernmost DOC. This huge zone covers 19 different types of
wine, from grapes grown on valley floors or, ideally, steep
mountain slopes. Reds tend to be either light and perfumed
when from the Schiava grape or deep and dark if the Lagrein is
used, while whites, from grapes like Chardonnay, Riesling, Pinot
Grigio and Goldmuskateller, are usually dry, racy and fragrant.
Teutonic efficiency and Italian flair combine to make it one of
Italy's most exciting DOCs. Best producers: LAGEDER★★, St
Michael Eppan co-op, Tiefenbrunner★, Walch★.

ALVARINHO See Albariño.

AMABILE Italian for 'semi-sweet'. Generally sweeter than abboccato wines, but not so cloying as some dolce or passito styles.

AMARONE DELLA VALPOLICELLA *Valpolicella DOC, Veneto,
Italy* Amarone (literally the 'big bitter one') is a brilliantly individual, bitter-sweet style of VALPOLICELLA. It is a 'meditation wine'
for sipping at the end of a meal. Made from grapes that are ultra
sweet and shrivelled after having been dried on mats for about 5
months prior to pressing, the wines can reach up to 16% alcohol.
Though the law classifies them under RECIOTO DELLA VALPOLICELLA,
producers are adopting a less confusing terminology, calling
them simply Amarone or Amarone Classico. As with all
Valpolicella, Classico is the best. The wines can age quite easily

for 10–15 years. Best producers: ALLEGRINI★, MASI★, QUINTARELLI★.
Best years: 1990 88 86 85 83.

AMIGNE Swiss variety which is virtually limited to the region of
Vétroz in the Valais. The wine has an earthy, nutty intensity
and benefits from a few years' aging. Best producers: CAVES
IMESCH, Granges Frères (Escalier de la Dame).

AMONTILLADO See Jerez y Manzanilla DO.
AMTLICHE PRÜFUNG See Prüfungsnummer.
ANBAUGEBIET German for 'growing region' and these names will
appear on all labels. In unified Germany there now 13: Ahr,
Mosel-Saar-Ruwer, Mittelrhein, Rheingau, Nahe, Rheinhessen,
Rheinpfalz, Hessische Bergstrasse, Franken, Württemberg and
Baden. Saale-Unstrut and Sachsen are in former East Germany.

ANDALUCÍA *Spain* Fortified wines, or wines naturally so strong in
alcohol that they don't need fortifying, are the speciality of this
southern, sunbaked stretch of Spain. Apart from sherry (JEREZ Y MAN-
ZANILLA DO), there are the lesser, sherry-like wines of CONDADO DE
HUELVA DO and MONTILLA-MORILES DO, and the rich, sometimes treacly-
sweet wines of MALAGA DO. All these regions now also make some
admittedly modern, but extremely bland dry whites.

CH. L'ANGÉLUS ★★ *St-Émilion Grand Cru AC, Grand Cru Classé,
Bordeaux, France* One of the biggest and best known ST-ÉMILION
Grands Crus with an energetic owner and talented winemaker.
Increasingly good wines in the 1980s. Best years: 1990 89 88 86 85.
ANGHELU RUJU ★ *Sardinia, Italy* Produced from partly dried
Cannonau grapes grown in north-west Sardinia, the wine has a
spirity, port-like richness combined with a bitter-sweet fruit and
a burn of alcohol (thanks to its 18%) on the finish. Made only
by Sella & Mosca, it is best sipped at the end of a meal. Will age
moderately well for 3–5 years.
CH. D'ANGLUDET ★★ *Margaux AC, Cru Bourgeois, Haut-Médoc,
Bordeaux, France* This English-owned château makes one of
my favourite wines. Always of Classed Growth standard, it has
one of the best price-quality ratios in Bordeaux and ages
superbly for a decade or more. Best years: 1990 89 88 86 85 83 82.
PAUL ANHEUSER *Bad Kreuznach, Nahe, Germany* Very large
estate by German standards with a high (70%) percentage of
Riesling for the region. Anheuser believes in skin contact for his
white wines and it is this, perhaps, which gives the young
whites a slightly medicinal character. Best years: 1990 89 88.
ANJOU BLANC AC *Loire Valley, France* Until recently the Chenin
grape dominated Anjou's white wines, but producers have now
begun to take advantage of the law allowing them to add up to
20% Sauvignon Blanc and Chardonnay. The wines used to be

mediocre, but, from the best producers, Anjou Blanc is now a source of good straight French whites, dry or semi-sweet. Some of the better ones come from the Anjou Coteaux de la Loire sub-region. Best producers: ACKERMAN-LAURANCE, Cailleau, Daviau, Ogereau, RICHOU★. Best years: 1990 89.

ANJOU MOUSSEUX AC *Loire Valley, France* A rare AC for Anjou sparkling wines, with Chenin Blanc the principal grape. Most producers sell their wines as (more prestigious) CREMANT DE LOIRE instead. Best producer: BOUVET-LADUBAY (for their Trésor Rosé★★).

ANJOU ROUGE AC *Loire Valley, France* Like ANJOU BLANC, this is a catch-all AC covering the Maine-et-Loire department and a little bit more. Anjou is best known for ROSE D'ANJOU but the reds (from Cabernet Sauvignon, Cabernet Franc or Pineau d'Aunis) are increasingly successful. Wines made from Gamay are sold as Anjou Gamay. Anjou Rouge is usually a fruity, easy-drinking wine, with less tannin than ANJOU-VILLAGES. Best producers: Chamboureau, Clos de Coulaine★, Daviau, Lebreton, RICHOU★, Touche Noire. Best years: 1990 89 88 85.

ANJOU-VILLAGES AC *Loire Valley, France* As the Anjou AC is such a blanket term, taking in red, white, rosé and fizz of incon-sistent quality, the better Anjou red producers asked for a sepa-rate AC. Since 1985, 46 villages have been entitled to the AC Anjou-Villages for red wine only, from Cabernet Franc and Cabernet Sauvignon. Already some extremely attractive dry, fruity reds are beginning to emerge in the region with better aging potential than straight ANJOU ROUGE. Best producers: Closel, Daviau★, J Y-H Lebreton, Ogereau, Papin, RICHOU (Vieilles Vignes★★). Best years: 1990 89.

ANSELMI *Soave DOC, Veneto, Italy* Along with PIEROPAN, Roberto Anselmi has shown that SOAVE can have personality when care-fully made. Using ultra-modern methods he has honed the fruit flavours of his Soave Classico and Cru Capitel Foscarino ★ and introduced small-barrel aging for his single-vineyard Capitel Croce ★ and his luscious, SAUTERNES-like Recioto Capitelli ★★.

ANTINORI *Tuscany, Italy* World-famous Florentine family firm which has been involved in wine since at least 1385 but it is Piero Antinori, current head of the firm, who has made the Antinori name synonymous with both quality and innovation. The quality of their CHIANTI Classico wines like Pèppoli ★, Villa Antinori ★ and Tenute Marchese Riserva ★★ is generally of a high level, but it was their development of the Vino da Tavola 'Super-Tuscan' concept of superior wines outside the DOC laws that launched a quality revolution in Tuscany during the 1970s. Introducing small barrel-aging to Tuscany for the first time, TIGNANELLO ★★ (Sangiovese/Cabernet) and Solaia ★★ (Cabernet) can be great wines. Best years: 1990 88 86 85. See also Castello della Sala.

APPELLATION D'ORIGINE CONTRÔLÉE See AC.

ARAGÓN *Spain*   Most of Aragón, stretching from the Pyrenees south to Spain's central plateau, has traditionally been cheap red wine country. There have been improvements, however, especially in the cooler, hilly, northern SOMONTANO DO, which is making some top quality wines with international grape varieties. Further south on Aragón's hot, dry plains and plateaux, wine-making technology is improving in Campo de Borja DO and CARINENA DO, but results from Calatayud DO are still dull.

ARBOIS AC *Jura, France*   The largest of the specific ACs in the Jura region of eastern France. The whites are made from Chardonnay or from the local grape Savagnin which can give the wines a sherry-like flavour that is most concentrated in VIN JAUNE. There is also a very rare, sweet VIN DE PAILLE. A good Mousseux is made by the Champagne method, usually from Chardonnay. Some of the best reds and sparklers come from the commune of Pupillin. Best producers: Arlay★, Bourdy★, Désiré, Maire, Rolet; Arbois, Aubin and Pupillin★ co-ops.

L'ARDÈCHE, VIN DE PAYS DE *Rhône Valley, France*   Wines from the Ardèche department south of Lyon. The wines are similar in style to those of the larger COTEAUX DE L'ARDECHE. Best producers: ST-DESIRAT-CHAMPAGNE co-op★, Les Vignerons Ardèchois.

ARNEIS   White grape grown in the sandy soil of the Roero hills in Piedmont in north-west Italy. Arneis is DOC in ROERO, producing expensive dry, white wines which, at best, have an attractively nutty, herbal perfume and flavour of pears. Best drunk within the year. Best producers: Castello di Neive★, CERETTO, Cornarea, Deltetto★, Bruno GIACOSA, Malvira★, Vietti, VOERZIO.

CH. L'ARROSÉE ★★ *St-Émilion Grand Cru AC, Grand Cru Classé, Bordeaux, France*   This small property, just south-west of the town of St-Émilion, makes really exciting wine: rich, chewy and wonderfully luscious with a comparatively high proportion (40%) of Cabernet Sauvignon. Best years: 1990 89 88 85 83 82.

ARRUDA IPR *Oeste, Portugal*   A one-co-op region just north of Lisbon, but luckily, that co-op at Arruda dos Vinhos is among the best in the Oeste and makes a decent, inexpensive red.

ARVINE   Swiss variety from the Valais found between the communes of Vétroz and Martigny. The best grapes come from the steep slopes of Fully. Typical Arvine has a spicy, almost salty character which becomes honeyed with age. It has long aging potential. Best producers: CAVES IMESCH★, Chanton, Dom. du Mont d'Or, Maye, Raymond, Roduit, Savioz (Ch. Ravire).

41

ASCHERI *Piedmont, Italy* Winemakers in Piedmont for at least 5 centuries, Ascheri's wine style is forward and appealingly drinkable, whether it be BAROLO ★, Dolcetto ★ (especially their Cru Nirane), Nebbiolo d'Alba ★ from the San Giacomo vineyard or their wonderful MOSCATO D'ASTI ★★. Prices are also remarkably reasonable. Best years: (Barolo) 1990 89 88 86 85 82 79 78 74 71.

ASSENOVGRAD *Southern Region, Bulgaria* Lush, plummy Cabernet Sauvignon and earthy, mineral-dusted Mavrud are both good from this predominantly red wine winery. The best Assenovgrad Mavrud ages well, but doesn't gain any particular complexity with the extra years.

ASTI SPUMANTE DOC *Piedmont, Italy* Sparkling wine made from Moscato grapes grown in a large zone around the town of Asti, south-east of Turin. Much derided but at its best, it is light, scented and refreshing. Sparkling wine normally undergoes a second fermentation in order to trap the carbon dioxide gas but Asti is fermented only once and not to dryness either so that the wonderfully grapy and peachy perfumes of the Moscato grape are retained. Its light sweetness and refreshing sparkle make it wonderful with fruit and ideal at the end of the meal. Drink young. Best producers: FONTANAFREDDA, Gancia, Martini★, Viticoltori dell'Acquese★.

AU BON CLIMAT *Santa Barbara County, California, USA* Pace-setting winery in cool Santa Maria region, run by the irrepressible, irreverent, but highly talented Jim Clendenen, who spends much of his time nosing about the best cellars in Burgundy and Italy's Piedmont. The result is rich, lush Chardonnay ★, and marvellously original, intense Pinot Noir ★★, as well as Nebbiolo ★ and Bordeaux styles under the Vita Nova label. Qupé ★★, a specialist in Rhône varieties, operates from the same winery.

AUCKLAND *North Island, New Zealand* The largest city in New Zealand and one of the country's earliest wine regions. Grapes are still grown north of the city at Henderson, Kumeu/Huapai and Waimauku, and on Waiheke Island in Auckland harbour. Top wines include Cabernet Sauvignon★ blends from the Waiheke producers STONYRIDGE, Goldwater, and Peninsula; Chardonnay ★★★ and Merlot/Cabernet ★ from KUMEU RIVER; and Rothesay Chardonnay ★★ and Sauvignon Blanc ★ from COLLARDS.

L'AUDE, VIN DE PAYS DE *Languedoc, France* The largest Vin de Pays in the region, covering principally red wines, and quality varies accordingly. The best reds are soft and fruity with a bit of southern spice. Best producers: Chantovent, Domergue, de Gourgazaud, NICOLAS.

AUSBRUCH Austrian Prädikat category used for sweet wines with residual sugar levels between 27 and 30 KMW (139 and 156 Oechsle). The Germans and Austrians rely on precise measurements of sugar ripeness to place wines in their different quality categories (P.S. KMW and Oechsle do have their own entries – if you can bear to look.) Strictly speaking, this should place Ausbruch wines midway between the very sweet German Beerenauslese and Trockenbeerenauslese categories. True Ausbruch from Rust and the Neusiedler See (in Burgenland), however, is made by adding a small amount of fresh grapes to berries affected by noble rot. The result is closer to SAUTERNES than Germanic sweet styles, with less fruit flavour but more rich texture and higher alcohol. Best producers: Schandl★★, Ernst Triebaumer★★, Paul Triebaumer★★, Wenzel★★.

AUSLESE German and Austrian Prädikat category meaning that the grapes for the wine were 'selected' on the basis of having higher sugar levels. In practice they will be among the last picked. A Riesling Auslese from the Mosel can have as little as 83 Oechsle while most Baden Ausleses are sweeter and start at 105. The Austrian Auslese level is 21 KMW or 105 Oechsle. Some growers now make dry versions to go with food.

CH. AUSONE ★★ *St-Émilion Grand Cru AC, 1er Grand Cru Classé, Bordeaux, France* This elegant property, on what are perhaps the best slopes in ST-EMILION, made a dramatic return to form in the 1980s, but I'm not yet convinced these new-breed Ausones develop and improve in bottle. Best years: 1990 89 88 85 83.

AUXEY-DURESSES AC *Côte de Beaune, Burgundy, France* Auxey-Duresses is a backwater village up in the hills behind world-famous MEURSAULT. The reds should be full and round but can often seem dilute. At its best, and at 3–5 years, the white is dry, soft, nutty and hinting at the creaminess of a good Meursault, but without the loony prices. Best producers: (reds) Diconne★, Duc de Magenta★, LEROY, Roland, Thévenin; (whites) Ampeau★, Creusefond, Diconne★, Duc de Magenta★, LEROY, Prunier, Roulot. Best years: (reds) 1990 89 88 85; (whites) 1990 89 88 87 86 85.

AVA (AMERICAN VITICULTURAL AREA) System of appellations of origin established for American wines in the 1970s.

AVIGNONESI *Vino Nobile di Montepulciano DOCG, Tuscany, Italy* The Avignonesi family have been winemakers for at least 500 years, and in the late 1970s they re-established Montepulciano as one of Tuscany's best zones. Their VINO NOBILE DI MONTEPULCIANO★ is very good, but it is their range of varietals – Chardonnay (Il Marzocco ★★), Sauvignon (Il Vignola ★) and Merlot ★, – that have captured attention. Also famous is the Vino da Tavola Grifi ★★ (Sangiovese/Cabernet), and the Vin Santo ★★★ is the most sought after, and expensive, in Tuscany. Best years: 1990 88 85 83.

AYL *Saar, Germany* A top Saar village. The best known vineyard in Ayl is Kupp which produces classy, slaty wines on its steep slopes. Best producer: Heinz Wagner.

AZIENDA AGRICOLA Italian for 'estate' or 'farm'. It also indicates wine made only from grapes grown by the proprietor.

BACKSBERG *Paarl, South Africa*   One of South Africa's leading estates. Backsberg produces a wide range of wines. Used to be best at bright fruity reds, but the most impressive recent release is the 1990 Chardonnay ★: lively, limy and long.

BAD DÜRKHEIM *Rheinpfalz, Germany*   Spa town and the head-quarters of the decent Vier Jahreszeiten Kloster Limburg co-op. Best producer: Karl Schaefer.

BAD KREUZNACH *Nahe, Germany*   Spa town with 22 individual vineyard sites, but the best wines come from the steepest sites such as Brückes, Kahlenberg, Krötenpfuhl and St Martin. Not to be confused with the large Nahe district of Bereich Kreuznach. Best producer: Paul ANHEUSER.

BADEN *Germany*   Very large wine region stretching some 400km (250 miles) from Baden-Baden in the north to the Bodensee in the south. Recently Baden has taken the lead in making dry white and red wines which show off the fuller, softer flavours Germany is capable of in the warmer climate of this southern region. Many of the best non-Riesling German wines of the future will come from Baden as well as many of the best barrel-fermented and barrel-aged wines.

BAGA   Portugal's most widely planted red grape, particularly impor-tant in BAIRRADA where it can produce red wines of tremendous power and fruit. It yields well, but is late-ripening, and needs a warm autumn to give of its best.

BAILEY'S *North-East Victoria, Australia*   Old, very traditional winery at Glenrowan where Australia's most famous bush bandit, Ned Kelly, made his last stand. Bailey's makes hearty, thickly tex-tured reds from Shiraz ★ and Cabernet ★ and some of Australia's most luscious fortified liqueur Muscat and Tokay (Winemakers Selection ★★★) are heavenly, indulgent and irresistible stickies.

BAIRRADA DOC *Beira Litoral, Portugal*   Bairrada has for ages been the source of many of Portugal's best red table wines even though the region was only demarcated in 1979. These can brim over with intense raspberry and blackberry fruit, though the tannin levels in some take a few years to soften. The whites are coming on fast, too, with modern vinification methods. Best producers: CAVES ALIANCA★, CAVES SAO JOAO★, Luis PATO★, SOGRAPE★.

BALEARICS *Spain*   Visitors to Spain's Balearic Islands need hardly bother searching out the local wines. Most are made with unex-ceptional local grape varieties. Most vineyards are on Mallorca, including the new (and undeserving) DO of BINISSALEM. The Scandinavian-owned Bodega Santa Caterina isn't too bad.

CH. BALESTARD-LA-TONNELLE ★ *St-Émilion Grand Cru AC, Grand Cru Classé, Bordeaux, France*   This is a popular ST-EMILION prop-erty, making reliable wine, full of strong, chewy fruit. It is decently priced too. Best years: 1990 89 88 86 85 83 82.

BANDOL AC *Provence, France* Bandol, a lovely fishing port with vineyards perched high above the Mediterranean, produces some of the most reliable reds and rosés in the region. The Mourvèdre grape gives Bandol its character – gentle raisin and honey softness with a slight tannic, herby fragrance. The reds happily age for 10 years but can be very good at 3–4. The rosés, delicious and spicy but often too pricy, should be drunk young. There is a small amount of white wine, most of it rather neutral and sold at horrendous prices. Drink as young as possible. Best producers: Bastide Blanche, Cagueloup★, Ray Jane, Laidière, Mas de la Rouvière★, Pibarnon, Ste-Anne, TEMPIER★★, Vannières★.

BANNOCKBURN *Geelong, Victoria, Australia* The experience of several vintages spent at Burgundy's Domaine DUJAC are reflected in Gary Farr's powerful, gamy Pinot Noir ★ and MEURSAULT-like Chardonnay★★, which are among Australia's best. Best years: 1990 88 86 85.

BANYULS AC *Roussillon, France* One of the best Vins Doux Naturels. Made mainly from Grenache Noir, the strong plum and raisin flavour tastes best in a young, sweet version although older tawny styles have a certain appeal. Best producers: Cellier des Templiers★, l'Étoile, Mas Blanc, la Rectorie★.

BARBADILLO *Jerez y Manzanilla DO, Andalucía, Spain* Antonio Barbadillo, the largest sherry company in the coastal town of Sanlúcar de Barrameda, makes a wide range of good to excellent wines, in particular their salty, dry manzanilla styles and their intense, nutty, but dry amontillados and olorosos. They also make a neutral-flavoured dry white, Castillo de San Diego.

BARBERA A native of Piedmont, Barbera vies with Sangiovese as the most widely planted red grape in Italy. A vigorous, prodigious variety that gives wines of deep colour, vibrant fruit, high acidity and low tannin, it can be delicious as a tasty young quaffer or as an oak-aged marvel. The best DOC zones are Alba and Asti. Best producers: (Alba) ALTARE, CLERICO★★, Aldo CONTERNO, GAJA, Giuseppe MASCARELLO★, Prunotto, Vajra★★; (Asti) Bava, Braida, Scarpa, La Spinetta, Viticoltori dell' Acquese.

BARCA VELHA ★ *Douro DOC, Douro, Portugal* Portugal's most sought-after and expensive red table wine, made by FERREIRA, modelled on fine red Bordeaux, but using Douro grape varieties (mainly Tinta Roriz). It is made only in the very finest years – just 12 vintages since 1953.

BARDOLINO DOC *Veneto, Italy* Substantial zone centred on Lake Garda, giving, at best, light, scented red and rosé wines to be drunk very young, from the same grape mix as neighbouring VALPOLICELLA. Recently it has become too expensive. Best producers: (growers) Guerrieri-Rizzardi, Portalupi, Vigne di San Pietro; (merchants) BOLLA, Lamberti, MASI.

45

BAROLO DOCG, BARBARESCO DOCG

Piedmont, Italy

Barolo and Barbaresco, neighbouring zones either side of the town of Alba in the Langhe hills of southern Piedmont, are two of the great names of Italian wine. Both zones are hilly – Barolo has 1200ha (2970 acres) of fairly high vineyards, Barbaresco has just under 500ha (1235 acres), at lower altitudes and close to the River Tanaro, allowing the grapes to ripen earlier. Their limestone soils grow Nebbiolo grapes that give red wines of endlessly changing perfume and a sweet kernel of fruit encased by a wall of tannin that needs years to crumble.

WINE STYLES

Barbaresco's earlier ripening grapes give softer, less powerful wines and they have a minimum period in cask of one year as against two for Barolo. Differences in Barbaresco are often due more to the winemaker than to the vineyard site. However Barolo's villages give very different wine styles; La Morra and Barolo are the most perfumed, Monforte and Serralunga the densest and most structured, and Castiglione Falletto is somewhere in between. And within each village, vineyard sites are renowned for giving quite different flavours. Even so, as in Burgundy, I would buy from the producer I liked rather than choose the vineyard I had heard of.

TRADITIONAL VERSUS MODERN WINE-MAKING

Something of a style battle has been waged in the Langhe cellars over the last two decades between the 'traditional' and 'modern' approach to wine-making. The traditionalists (such as Aldo Conterno, Giacomo Conterno, Giacosa, Bartolo Mascarello, Giuseppe Mascarello) believe in making wines for aging, and are willing to countenance high levels of tannin in young wines in the belief that a protracted period in cask (anything from 3–5 years, and sometimes more) will soften the youthful austerity.

The modernists (such as Altare, Clerico, Gaja, Voerzio), however, prefer to produce wines without such searing levels of tannin that can be drunk from an earlier stage. They tend to favour less time in wood, as they wish to avoid oxidation, and prefer to use small oak barrels, to obtain wines that are suppler on the palate. The debate continues, but both sides are beginning to see the good points of the other's methods, and the improvement in the wines since the mid-1980s is nothing short of remarkable.

See also ALTARE, ASCHERI, CERETTO, CLERICO, CONTERNO, FONTANAFREDDA, GAJA, GIACOSA, MASCARELLO, PRUNOTTO, VOERZIO.

BEST YEARS

1990 89 88 86 85 82 79 78 74 71

BEST PRODUCERS

Altare, Ascheri, Borgogno, Castello di Neive, Cavallotto, Ceretto, Clerico, Aldo Conterno, Giacomo Conterno, Fontanafredda, Gaja, Bruno Giacosa, Marchesi di Barolo, Marchesi di Gresy, Bartolo Mascarello, Giuseppe Mascarello, Cordero di Montezemolo, Pio Cesare, Produttori del Barbaresco, Prunotto, Renato Ratti, Sandrone, Paolo Scavino, Sebaste, Vajra, Roberto Voerzio.

BEST VINEYARDS

Barolo Bricco Fiasco, Bricco Rocche, Brunate, Bussia Soprana, Cannubi, Cascina Francia, Falletto, Marenca-Rivette, Marcenasco, Monfalletto, Monprivato, Montanello, Rocche di La Morra, La Serra, Vigna Rionda, Villero.

Barbaresco Asili, Basarin, Bricco di Neive, Costa Russi, Marcarini, Montefico, Ovello, Rio Sordo, San Lorenzo, Santo Stefano, Sori Paytin, Sori Tildin.

47

BARÓN DE LEY★ *Rioja DOC, Navarra, Spain*   A beautifully restored 16th-century monastery making elegant, balanced red RIOJAS from grapes grown on the estate, including some 'experimental' Cabernet Sauvignon. Best years: 1986 82.

BAROSSA VALLEY *South Australia*   Headquarters to such giants as PENFOLDS, SEPPELT, ORLANDO and YALUMBA, this famous region, noted for 'port', Shiraz and Riesling, has less than 10% of the nation's vineyards but makes 60% of the wine, largely from grapes grown elsewhere in South Australia. A new lease of life for Barossa Valley grapes has come from producers such as Bethany, Grant Burge, Charles Melton, ROCKFORD and ST HALLETT.

BARRIQUE   The barrique bordelaise is the traditional Bordeaux oak barrel of 225 litres capacity. Fermenting and aging in barrels adds dramatically to the texture, spice and richness of a wine. The term barrique is also used by the Italians and Germans.

JIM BARRY *Clare Valley, South Australia*   This family-owned Clare winery recently bought the Florita vineyard, source of great Leo BURING and LINDEMANS Rieslings of yesteryear. Much-improved Cabernet Sauvignon, the Riesling ★ is always delicious and The Armagh Shiraz ★★ is a blockbuster.

BARSAC AC *Bordeaux, France*   Barsac, the largest of the 5 communes in the SAUTERNES AC, also has its own AC, which is used by most of the top properties. In general, the wines are a little less luscious than other Sauternes, but from good estates they can be marvellous. Best producers: (Classed Growths) BROUSTET★, CLIMENS★★★, COUTET★, DOISY-DAENE★★, Doisy-Dubroca★, DOISY-VEDRINES★★, NAIRAC★★; (others) Cantegril★, Gravas, Guiteronde, Liot★, de Menota, Piada. Best years: 1990 89 88 86 83 81 80 76 75.

BASEDOWS *Barossa Valley, South Australia*   Sister winery to Peter LEHMANN, Basedows makes a popular wood-aged 'Sémillon white burgundy'★; as well as soft, rich Shiraz ★ and Cabernet ★ and robust, high-alcohol Chardonnay ★.

BASSERMANN-JORDAN *Deidesheim, Rheinpfalz, Germany*   Quality estate making top Riesling★ wines with a majority in dry styles. The vineyards are mostly in the excellent villages of Deidesheim and Forst and the wines manage to show a rich and full texture, without being fat and soft. Best years: 1990 89 88 86.

CH. BASTOR-LAMONTAGNE ★★ *Sauternes AC, Bordeaux, France*   Year after year this large estate produces luscious, honeyed wine at a price which allows us to enjoy high-class SAUTERNES without taking out a second mortgage. Best years: 1990 89 88 86 85 83 82 81 80.

CH. BATAILLEY★★ *Pauillac AC, 5ème Cru Classé, Haut-Médoc, Bordeaux, France*   A byword for value-for-money and reliability among the PAUILLAC Classed Growths. Marked by a full, obvious blackcurrant fruit, not too much tannin and a luscious overlay of creamy vanilla. Lovely to drink at only 5 years old, the wine ages well for up to 15 years. Best years: 1990 89 88 86 85 83 82.

BÂTARD-MONTRACHET AC *Grand Cru, Côte de Beaune, Burgundy, France*   This Grand Cru produces some of the greatest white wines in the world – they are full, rich and balanced with a powerful, minerally intensity of fruit and fresh acidity. There are two associated Grands Crus: Bienvenues-Bâtard-Montrachet and the miniscule Criots-Bâtard-Montrachet. All are capable of aging for a decade. Best producers: J-N GAGNARD★★★, Dom. LEFLAIVE★★★, Pierre Morey,★★ RAMONET★★★, Sauzet★★★. Best years: 1990 89 88 86 85 83.

BÉARN AC *South-West France*   While the rest of South-West France has been busy producing some highly original flavours in recent years, Béarn hasn't managed to cash in. The wines (90% red and rosé) just aren't special enough, despite some decent grape varieties. Best producer: Dom. Cauhapé.

CH. DE BEAUCASTEL *Châteauneuf-du-Pape AC, Rhône Valley, France*   François Perrin makes some of the richest, most tannic reds ★★★ in CHATEAUNEUF, with an unusually high percentage of Mourvèdre and Syrah. The wines can take at least a decade to show at their best. The small production of white Beaucastel★★, made almost entirely from Roussanne, is exquisite, too. Best years: (reds) 1990 89 88 86 85 83 82 81; (whites) 1990 89 88.

BEAUJOLAIS AC *Beaujolais, Burgundy, France*   This famous red wine comes from a large area of rolling hills and valleys in southern Burgundy. Most Beaujolais nowadays appears as BEAU-JOLAIS NOUVEAU or Beaujolais Primeur but Beaujolais AC is the basic appellation. In the north, toward Mâcon, most of the reds qualify either as BEAUJOLAIS-VILLAGES or as a single Cru (10 villages which definitely do produce better but more expensive wine: BROUILLY, CHENAS, CHIROUBLES, COTE DE BROUILLY, FLEURIE, JULIENAS, MORGON, MOULIN-A-VENT, REGNIE, ST-AMOUR). In the south, toward Lyon, most of the wine is simple AC Beaujolais, a light red wine to be drunk within months of the vintage which should be lovely and fresh but is often dilute and thin. Beaujolais Supérieur simply means wine with a minimum strength of 1% more alcohol than simple Beaujolais. A tiny amount of Beaujolais Blanc is made from Chardonnay. Best producers: (reds) Carron, Charmet, Ch. de la Plume, DUBOEUF, Garlon, Jambon, Labruyère, Texier; (whites) Charmet, Dalissieux, DUBOEUF, JADOT. Best years: 1991 90.

BEAUJOLAIS NOUVEAU *Beaujolais AC, Burgundy, France*   This is the first release of bouncy, fruity Beaujolais on the third Thursday of November after the harvest. What started out as a simple celebration of the new vintage has become a much-hyped beano. Quality is generally good since much of the best BEAU-JOLAIS AC is used for Nouveau. The wine usually improves by Christmas and the New Year and the best ones are perfect for summer picnics. Best producers: Boutinot, CELLIER DES SAMSONS, La Chevalière, DROUHIN, DUBOEUF, Ferraud, JAFFELIN, Loron, Sarrau.

BEAUJOLAIS-VILLAGES AC *Beaujolais, Burgundy, France*
Beaujolais-Villages can come from 39 (supposedly superior) villages in the north of the region. Carefully made, it can represent all the gurgling excitement of the Gamay grape at its best. Best villages: Beaujeu, Lancié, Lantignié, Leynes, Quincié, St-Étienne-des-Ouillières, St-Jean-d'Ardières. Best producers: Aucoeur★, La Chevalière, Crot, Depardon, DUBOEUF, Jaffre, Large, Loron, Pivot★, Tissier, Verger. Best years: 1991 90 89.

BEAULIEU VINEYARD *Napa Valley, California, USA* Beaulieu Cabernet Sauvignon was once the pride of California. Under winemaker André Tchelistcheff, Beaulieu established the style for California Cabernet for decades. Tchelistcheff, now in his 90s, still consults but the once great Cabernets have been in a long, slow decline. Best years: 1987 86 85 84.

BEAUMES-DE-VENISE *Rhône Valley, France* Famous for its sweet wine, MUSCAT DE BEAUMES-DE-VENISE, France's best known Vin Doux Naturel; the local red wine is also very good, one of the meatier COTES DU RHONE-VILLAGES, with a ripe, plummy fruit in warm years. Best producers: (reds) Cartier, Coyeux, local co-op.

BEAUNE AC *Côte de Beaune, Burgundy, France* Beaune is the capital of the whole Côte d'Or and gives its name to the southern section, the Côte de Beaune. Almost all the wines are red, with a delicious soft red-fruits ripeness to them. There are no Grands Crus but some excellent Premiers Crus (Boucherottes, Bressandes, Clos des Mouches, Fèves, Grèves, Marconnets, Teurons, Vignes Franches). There is a small amount of white – DROUHIN make an outstandingly good creamy, nutty Clos des Mouches ★. Best producers: (growers) Besancenot-Mathouillet★★, Jacques GERMAIN★★, Lafarge★, Mussy★★, TOLLOT-BEAUT★★; (merchants) Camille-Giraud★, Chanson, DROUHIN★★, JADOT, JAFFELIN★★, LABOURE-ROI, LEROY, Moillard, Morot★. Best years: (reds) 1990 89 88 87 83 82 81; (whites) 1990 89 88 87 86 85 83 82.

BEERENAUSLESE German and Austrian Prädikat category applied to wines made from 'individually selected' grapes, which, since the grapes are always very overripe and sugar-packed, will give wines that have a rich, luscious dessert quality to them. In many instances the berries are affected by noble rot (*Edelfäule* in German). Beerenauslese wines are only produced in the best years in Germany, but in Austria they are a pretty regular occurrence. Beerenauslese wines start at 110 Oechsle in the Mosel rising to 128 Oechsle in southern Baden. Austrian Beerenauslese wines start at 25 KMW or 127 Oechsle.

CH. BELAIR ★ *St-Émilion Grand Cru AC, 1er Grand Cru Classé, Bordeaux, France* Next door to AUSONE, Belair has the same owner and winemaker and, like its neighbour, it has experienced a revival of fortunes since the 1970s. Belair's wine is lighter than Ausone but still firmly textured with restrained fruit. Best years: 1990 89 88 86 85 83 82.

BELLET AC *Provence, France* A tiny AC of usually overpriced wine, mostly white, in the hills behind Nice. Ch. de Crémat and Ch. de Bellet are the most important producers and their wines are worth seeking out if you're in the area, but I wouldn't search too hard if you aren't.

BENDIGO DISTRICT *Victoria, Australia* Warm, dry, former gold-mining region which produced some decent wines in the 19th century, then faded away completely. It was triumphantly resurrected by Stuart Anderson who planted Balgownie in 1969, and other wineries followed (including Chateau Le Amon, Heathcote, Jasper Hill, Passing Clouds and YELLOWGLEN). The best wines are full-bodied Shiraz and Cabernet.

BEREICH German for region or district within a wine region or Anbaugebiet. Bereichs tend to be large, and the use of a Bereich name, such as Bereich Bingen, without qualification is seldom an indication of quality – in most cases, quite the reverse.

BERGERAC AC *South-West France* Bergerac is the main town of the Dordogne and the overall AC for this underrated area on the eastern edge of Bordeaux. The grape varieties are mostly the same as those used in the Bordeaux ACs. The red is generally like a light, fresh claret, a bit grassy but with a good, raw blackcurrant fruit and hint of earth. In general drink young although a few estate reds can age for 3–5 years. The whites are generally lean and dry for quick drinking. Best producers: le Barradis, Belingard, Court-les-Mûts★, de Gouyat, la JAUBERTIE★, Lestignac, Panisseau, la Raye, Tour des Gendres, Treuil-de-Nailhac. Best years: 1990 89 88 85.

BERGKELDER *Stellenbosch, South Africa* In addition to producing the Fleur du Cap, Stellenryk and Kloof en Dal ranges, the Bergkelder also provides aging and marketing facilities for 19 estates, two of which it owns. Others in the fold include DE WET-SHOF, Middelvlei and Meerlust. Quality, I'm afraid, varies widely and some of the reds, in particular, suffer from a sense of wearing a stylistic straightjacket. Consequently opinion differs as to whether Bergkelder's powerful hold over these estates stifles individuality or encourages consistency.

BERINGER VINEYARDS *Napa Valley, California, USA* Beringer produces a full range of reds, whites and rosés but, in particular offers a spectacular range of top class Cabernet Sauvignons. The Private Reserve Cabernet ★★★ is one of the Napa Valley's finest yet most approachable Cabernets; the Lemmon Ranch ★★ and Chabot Vineyards ★★ when released under their own label, are only slightly less impressive. The Knight's Valley Cabernet is in a lighter but engagingly juicy style. Best years: (Cabernet Sauvignon) 1990 88 87 86 85 81.

BERNKASTEL *Mosel, Germany* Both a town in the middle Mosel and the name of a large Bereich. Top wines, however, will come only from vineyard sites within the town – the most famous of these is the fabulously priced and fabulously flavoured DOCTOR vineyard. Best producers: Lauerburg, THANISCH, WEGELER-DEINHARD.

BERRI RENMANO *Riverland, South Australia* Twin Riverland co-ops which crushed 14% of Australia's total in 1992 as well as purchasing the famous HARDY wine company. They produce largely bulk and bag-in-box wines, but top label Renmano Chairmans Selection is good for buxom Chardonnay★ and oaky Cabernet. Given the muscle this company has, I would expect its wine quality to improve considerably over the next few years.

BEST'S *Great Western, Victoria, Australia* Venerable small winery run by Viv Thomson who makes beautiful wines from estate vine-yards first planted in 1868. Delicious, clear-fruited Shiraz★★ and Cabernet★ are consistently good, and the Riesling is rapidly improving. Tropical-fruity but finely balanced Chardonnay★★ is his new star wine. Best years: (reds) 1991 90 88 87 84 80 76.

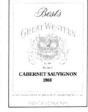

CH. BEYCHEVELLE★★ *St-Julien AC, 4ème Cru Classé, Haut-Médoc, Bordeaux, France* Although ranked as only a 4th Growth, this beautiful château usually makes wine of 2nd Growth quality. The wine has a charming softness even when young, but takes at least a decade to mature into the fragrant cedarwood and blackcurrant flavour for which ST-JULIEN is famous. Generally worth its high price. Second wine: Réserve de l'Amiral. Best years: 1990 89 87 86 85 83 82.

BIANCO Italian for 'white'.

BIANCO DI CUSTOZA DOC *Veneto, Italy* Dry white from an area overlapping the southern part of BARDOLINO. Similar in style to neighbouring SOAVE, but the addition of up to 30% of Tocai Friulano to the blend gives extra breadth and richness. Drink young. Best producers: Arvedi d'Emilei, Portalupi, Tedeschi, Vigne di San Pietro.

BIANCO VERGINE VALDICHIANA DOC *Tuscany, Italy* Pale dry white from Trebbiano and Malvasia grapes grown in southern Tuscany's Chiana valley. Best producers: AVIGNONESI, Baldetti, though neither merit a detour.

BIENVENUES-BÂTARD-MONTRACHET AC See Bâtard-Montrachet.

BIERZO DO *Castilla y León, Spain* Sandwiched between the rainy mountains of Galicia and the arid plains of the rest of Castilla y León, Bierzo makes mostly commonplace reds. But the best ones – fruity and grassy green – are a revelation and quite unlike any other Spanish efforts. Ideally the red wines are made entirely from the Mencía grape, but all must contain at least 70%. Best producer: Viñas y Bodegas del Bierzo.

BILLECART-SALMON *Champagne AC, Champagne, France* Top-notch CHAMPAGNE house and one of the few still under family control. The wines are extremely elegant – fresh and delicate – but become simply irresistible with a fair amount of aging. The non-vintage Brut ★★, non-vintage Brut Rosé★★ and the vintage Cuvée N-F Billecart ★★★ are all excellent. Best years: 1985 82.

BINGEN *Rheinhessen, Germany* Small town and also a Bereich, the vineyards of which fall in both the Nahe and Rheinhessen. The best vineyard in the town is the Scharlachberg which produces exciting wines, stinging with racy acidity and the whiff of coal smoke. Best producer: VILLA SACHSEN.

BINISSALEM DO *Mallorca, Balearic Islands, Spain* Alcoholic reds and rosés are the mainstay of this, the only Spanish DO outside the mainland. A few growers make reasonable wines but they are in short supply, even on the island. Best producers: José Ferrer, Herederos de Ribas, Jaume Mesquida.

BIONDI-SANTI *Brunello di Montalcino DOCG, Tuscany, Italy* This legendary producer claims to have created BRUNELLO DI MONTAL-CINO, and its reputation for longevity. Unfortunately, a lack of investment in the vineyards, and a tendency to believe their own press releases, robbed them of momentum, and the wines have suffered accordingly. Since 1989 they have replanted much of the estate, so with a little modesty, they could soon be producing top wines once again.

BLAGNY AC *Côte de Beaune, Burgundy, France* The red wine from this tiny hamlet above the communes of MEURSAULT and PULIGNY-MONTRACHET can be fair value, if you like a rustic Burgundy. The white is sold as Puligny-Montrachet, Meursault Premier Cru or Meursault-Blagny. Best producers: Olivier LEFLAIVE (lighter, more fragrant style), Matrot★. Best years: 1990 89 88.

BLANC French for 'white'.

BLANC DE BLANCS French term used for white wine made from one or more white grape varieties. The term is used all over France, especially for sparkling wines, but is mostly seen in CHAMPAGNE, where it denotes wine made entirely from the Chardonnay grape.

BLANC DE NOIRS French term used for white wine made from black grapes only – the juice is separated from the skins as soon as possible to avoid extracting any colour. The term is most often seen in CHAMPAGNE, where it is used to describe wine made from Pinot Noir and/or Pinot Meunier grapes.

BLANCO Spanish for 'white'.

BLANQUETTE DE LIMOUX AC *Languedoc-Roussillon, France* A hilly region south-west of Carcassonne in the Aude is a surprising place to find this sharp, refreshing sparkling wine, since most southern whites are singularly flat and dull. The secret lies in the Mauzac grape, which makes up over 80% of the wine and gives it its striking 'green apple skin' flavour – the balance is made up of Chardonnay and Chenin Blanc. The Champagne method is used to create the sparkle, although the more rustic *méthode rurale*, finishing off the original fermentation inside the bottle, is also used. Best producers: Collin, Laurens★, Limoux co-op★, Guinot, Martinolles★, Terres Blanches. Best years: 1990 89 88. See also Crémant de Limoux AC.

WOLF BLASS *Barossa Valley, South Australia*   Wolf Blass stands as one of the most important men in the modern Australian wine world because he mastered the art of creating reds and whites of high quality and consistency which were nonetheless incredibly *easy* to enjoy. His reds, blended from many regions and aged in American oak barrels, have a delicious mint and blackcurrant, easygoing charm. His Rieslings are soft and sweetish, while his other whites also possess soft, juicy fruit and sweet oak. Now owned by MILDARA. Black Label ★★, the top label for wines released at 5 years old, is expensive but good, the Yellow Label cheaper but immensely cheerful.

BLAUBURGUNDER   See Pinot Noir.

BLAUER LIMBERGER   See Blaufränkisch.

BLAUER PORTUGIESER   A big yielding vine brought to Austria in the early 19th century whence it migrated to Germany. Sometimes called just Portugieser, it produces decent red wine but generally lacks length and concentration and any really focused fruit flavours.

BLAUFRÄNKISCH   Good, ripe Blaufränkisch has a taste similar to raspberries and white pepper or even beetroot. It does particularly well in Austria where it is the principal red wine grape of Burgenland. The Hungarian vineyards (where it is called Kékfrankos) are mostly just across the border on the other side of the Neusiedler See. Called Blauer Limberger or Lemberger in Germany, almost all of it is grown in Württemberg.

BLUSH *California, USA*   Juicy-fruit, sweetish, light, pink wines made from red grapes to attract the soda-pop generation. As such they did well, and a few, like BERINGER and Bel Arbors, were lovely drinks, but the fad seems to be passing now.

BODEGA   Spanish for 'winery' or 'wine-producing company'.

BODEGAS Y BEBIDAS *Spain*   The largest wine-producing company in Spain, with wineries including CAMPO VIEJO and Marqués del Puerto in Rioja, Vinícola de Navarra, and Señorío del Condestable in Jumilla. The company also makes a *lot* of basic table wine.

BOLLA *Soave DOC and Valpolicella DOC, Veneto, Italy*   The largest producer of SOAVE and VALPOLICELLA. Founded in 1857, the firm helped create the market for these two perennial favourites. The basic wines are uninspired, but Castellero and Jago are their fine

Cru single-vineyard wines, and there are also interesting experimental wines under the Creso label.

BOLLINGER *Champagne AC, Champagne, France* One of the great CHAMPAGNE houses with good non-vintage (called Special Cuvée ★) and vintage wines (Grande Année ★★), made in a full, rich, rather old-fashioned style. (Bollinger are one of the few houses to ferment their base wine in barrels.) They also produce a range of rarer vintage Champagnes, including a Vintage RD ★★★ (RD stands for *récemment dégorgé*, or recently disgorged, showing that the wine has been lying in bottle on its yeast for longer than usual, picking up loads of flavour on the way) and Vieilles Vignes Françaises Blanc de Noirs ★★ from ancient, ungrafted Pinot Noir vines. Best years: 1985 82 79 75 70.

CH. BON PASTEUR ★★ *Pomerol AC, Bordeaux, France* This small château has established an excellent reputation under the ownership of Michel Rolland, one of Bordeaux's leading winemakers. Expensive in recent years, but they are always soft and full of lush fruit. Drink after 5–8 years. Best years: 1990 89 88 87 85.

BONNES-MARES AC *Grand Cru, Côte de Nuits, Burgundy, France* A large Grand Cru and one of the few great Burgundy vineyards to maintain consistency during the turmoil of the last few decades. Bonnes-Mares generally has a deep, ripe, smoky plum fruit, which starts rich and chewy and matures over 10–20 years. Best producers: Clair-Daü★, DROUHIN, DUJAC★★, Groffier★, Roumier★, de Vogüé. Best years: 1990 89 88 87 85 80 78.

BONNEZEAUX AC *Grand Cru, Loire Valley, France* One of the great sweet wines of France, Bonnezeaux is a 50ha (125 acre) Grand Cru inside the larger COTEAUX DU LAYON AC. The wine is made in the same way as SAUTERNES but the flavours are different, as only Chenin Blanc is used. It can age very well in vintages like 1990 and 89. Best producers: de Fesles★★★, Petite Croix★, Petit Val★, Renou★. Best years: 1990 89 88 85 83 82 78 76 70 64 59 47.

BONNY DOON *Santa Cruz Mountains AVA, California, USA* Iconoclastic operation under Randall Grahm who revels in the unexpected. He has a particular love for Rhône, Italian and Spanish varietals that no-one else in California will touch – until he does them and then there's suddenly a rush of me-too labels. He loves using fanciful brand names, Le Cigare Volant ★ is a blend of Grenache and Syrah and is Grahm's homage to CHATEAUNEUF-DU-PAPE. Old Telegram ★ (this time in homage to VIEUX TELEGRAPHE, a leading Châteauneuf estate) is 100% Mourvèdre; Le Sophiste★ is a blend of Rhône white grapes. He's planted a clutch of Italian varieties too, as well as establishing contacts in central Spain, and any orchard fruit that comes his way he distils into brilliant Eaux-de-Vie★★. Watch this space.

BORBA IPR *Alto Alentejo, Portugal* Promising IPR region in the Alto Alentejo, specializing in rich, raspberry-fruited reds. Best producers: Borba co-op★, Horta do Rocio, Quinta do Carmo★★.

BORDEAUX RED WINES

Bordeaux, France

 This large area of South-West France, centred on the historic city of Bordeaux, produces a larger volume of fine red wine than any other French region. Wonderful Bordeaux-style wines are produced in California, Australia and even Bulgaria, but the home team's top performers are still unbeatable. Around 400 million bottles of red wine a year are produced here. The best wines, known as the Classed Growths, account for a tiny percentage of this figure, but some of their lustre rubs off on the lesser names, making this one of the most popular wine styles.

GRAPE VARIETIES
Bordeaux's reds are commonly divided into 'right' and 'left' bank wines. On the left bank of the Gironde estuary, the red wines are dominated by the Cabernet Sauvignon grape, with varying proportions of Cabernet Franc, Merlot and Petit Verdot. At best they are honeyed but perfumed with blackcurrant and cedarwood. The most important left bank areas are the Haut-Médoc (especially the communes of Margaux, St-Julien, Pauillac and St-Estèphe) and, south of the city of Bordeaux, the ACs of Pessac-Léognan and Graves. On the right bank, Merlot is the predominant grape, which generally makes the resulting wines more supple and fleshy than those of the left bank. The key areas here are St-Émilion and Pomerol.

CLASSIFICATIONS
Red Bordeaux is made all over the region, from the tip of the Gironde estuary to the southern end of the Entre-Deux-Mers. At its most basic, the wine is simply labelled Bordeaux or Bordeaux Supérieur. Above this are the more specific ACs covering sub-areas (such as the Haut-Médoc) and individual communes (such as Pomerol, St-Émilion or Margaux). Single-estate Crus Bourgeois are the next rung up on the quality ladder, followed by the Classed Growths of the Médoc, Graves and St-Émilion. Many of these châteaux also make 'second wines', which are cheaper versions of their Grands Vins. Curiously Pomerol, home of Pétrus, arguably the most famous red wine in the world, has no official pecking order.

See also BORDEAUX, BORDEAUX CLAIRET, BORDEAUX SUPERIEUR, CANON-FRONSAC, COTES DE BOURG, COTES DE CASTILLON, COTES DE FRANCS, FRONSAC, GRAVES, GRAVES SUPERIEURES, HAUT-MEDOC, LALANDE-DE-POMEROL, LISTRAC, LUSSAC-ST-EMILION, MARGAUX, MEDOC, MOULIS, MONTAGNE-ST-EMILION, PAUILLAC, PESSAC-LEOGNAN, POMEROL, PREMIERES COTES DE BLAYE, PREMIERES COTES DE BORDEAUX, PUISSEGUIN-ST-EMILION, ST-EMILION, ST-ESTEPHE, ST-GEORGES-ST-EMILION, ST-JULIEN; AND INDIVIDUAL CHATEAUX.

BEST YEARS

1990 89 88 86 85 83 82 81
78 70

BEST PRODUCERS

Graves, Péssac-Léognan
Dom. de Chevalier, Haut-
Bailly, Haut-Brion.

Haut-Médoc Cantemerle, la
Lagune.

Margaux d'Angludet,
d'Issan, Ch. Margaux,
Palmer, Rausan-Ségla.

Pauillac Batailley, Grand-
Puy-Lacoste, Haut-Bages-
Libéral, Lafite-Rothschild,
Latour, Lynch-Bages,
Mouton-Rothschild, Pichon-
Lalande, Pichon-Longueville.

Pomerol Lafleur, Lafleur-
Pétrus, Petit-Village, Pétrus,
Trotanoy, Vieux-Ch.-Certan.

St-Émilion l'Angélus,
l'Arrosée, Ausone, Canon,
Cheval-Blanc, Figeac,
Magdelaine, Pavie.

St-Estèphe Calon-Ségur,
Cos d'Estournel.

St-Julien Beychevelle,
Ducru-Beaucaillou, Gruaud-
Larose, Langoa-Barton,
Léoville-Barton, Léoville-las-
Cases, Léoville-Poyferré.

BORDEAUX WHITE WINES

Bordeaux, France

 This is France's largest fine wine region but except for the sweet wines of Sauternes and Barsac, Bordeaux's international reputation is based on its reds. No one gives much thought to the area's other whites, despite the fact that they account for nearly a fifth of the 107,245ha (265,000 acres) of vines. Given the size of the region, the diversity of Bordeaux's white wines should come as no surprise. There are dry, medium and sweet styles, ranging from dreary to some of the most sublime white wines of all. Bordeaux's warm southern climate – moderated by the influence of the Atlantic and of two rivers, the Dordogne and the Garonne, is ideal for white wine production, particularly south of the city along the banks of the Garonne.

GRAPE VARIETIES
Sauvignon Blanc and Sémillon, the most important white grapes, are two varieties of considerable character and are usually blended together. They are backed up by smaller quantities of Muscadelle and Ugni Blanc.

DRY WINES
The last decade has seen enormous improvements, and the introduction of new technology and new ideas, many of them influenced by the New World, have transformed Bordeaux into one of France's most exciting white wine areas. The white wines, not only of Pessac-Léognan, an AC created for the best areas of the northern Graves in 1987, but also of basic Bordeaux Blanc and Entre-Deux-Mers, the two largest white wine ACs in Bordeaux, have improved beyond recognition.

SWEET WINES
Bordeaux's most famous whites are its sweet wines made from grapes affected by noble rot, particularly in Sauternes and Barsac. Quality improved dramatically during the 1980s as a string of fine vintages brought the wines fame and the considerable price hike enabled many properties to make long overdue improvements. On the other side of the Garonne, Cadillac, Loupiac and Ste-Croix-du-Mont also make sweet wines, but these rarely attain the richness or complexity of a top Sauternes. They are considerably cheaper, however.

See also BARSAC, BORDEAUX, BORDEAUX SUPERIEUR, CERONS, COTES DE BLAYE, COTES DE BOURG, COTES DE FRANCS, ENTRE-DEUX-MERS, GRAVES, NOBLE ROT, PESSAC-LEOGNAN, PREMIERES COTES DE BLAYE, PREMIERES COTES DE BORDEAUX, STE-CROIX-DU-MONT, SAUTERNES; AND INDIVIDUAL CHATEAUX.

BEST YEARS

(dry) 1990 89 88 87 86 85 83
(sweet) 1990 89 88 86 83 81

BEST PRODUCERS

Dry wines

(Pessac-Léognan) Dom. de Chevalier, de Fieuzal, Haut-Brion, Laville-Haut-Brion, la Louvière, Malartic-Lagravière, la Tour-Martillac; (others) Bonnet, Clos Floridène, Rahoul, Sénéjac, Thieuley, Ygrec.

Sweet wines

(Sauternes and Barsac) Bastor-Lamontagne, Broustet, Climens, Doisy-Daëne, Doisy-Védrines, de Fargues, Gilette, Guiraud, Lafaurie-Peyraguey, Nairac, Rabaud-Promis, Raymond-Lafon, Rieussec, Suduiraut, d'Yquem; (others) Clos St-Georges, la Grave, la Rame, de Ricaud.

BORDEAUX AC *Bordeaux, France* The simple Bordeaux AC is one of the most important in France. It can apply to the reds and rosés as well as the dry, medium and sweet white wines of the entire Gironde region. Most of the best wines are allowed more specific geographical ACs (such as MARGAUX or SAUTERNES) but a vast amount of unambitious, yet potentially enjoyable wine is sold as Bordeaux AC. Indeed, straight red Bordeaux – frequently labelled claret outside France – is one of the most reliable of all generic wines, with fresh grassy fruit and an attractive earthy edge. Good Bordeaux Rouge will usually benefit from a year or so of aging. Bordeaux Blanc, on the other hand, had until recently become a byword for flabby, fruitless, over-sulphured brews. However, there is now an increasing number of pleasant, clean wines, frequently under a merchant's rather than a château label, which make refreshing drinking. Drink as young as possible. Best producers: (reds) Castera, Charmail, Coste, Haut Riot, Goelane, Mau, du Moulin, de Roques, Sichel, Terrefort, Thieuley, Tour de Mirambeau; (whites) Coste, Dourthe, Eschenauer, Reynon, Sichel, Thieuley, YGREC. See also page 56.

BORDEAUX CLAIRET AC *Bordeaux, France* A very pale red wine, virtually rosé in fact, which isn't much seen around Bordeaux any more. The name 'claret', which in Britain is now applied to *any* red wine from the Bordeaux region, derives from *clairet*.

BORDEAUX SUPÉRIEUR AC *Bordeaux, France* This AC covers the same area as the basic BORDEAUX AC but the wines must have an extra $1/2$% of alcohol and a lower yield from the vines, resulting in a greater concentration of flavours. Almost all the petits châteaux, which represent the best value in Bordeaux, are labelled Bordeaux Supérieur.

BOUCHARD PÈRE ET FILS *Beaune, Burgundy, France* An important merchant and vineyard owner, with vines in some of Burgundy's most spectacular sites, including CORTON, CORTON-CHARLEMAGNE, Chevalier-Montrachet and Le MONTRACHET. The firm went through a rough patch in the 1980s but recent investment may turn things round. If so, not before time. Wines from the company's own vineyards are sold under the Domaines du Château de Beaune label.

BOUCHES-DU-RHÔNE, VIN DE PAYS DES *Provence, France* Wines from three distinct areas – the coastal area, the area around Aix-en-Provence and the Camargue. Full-bodied, spicy reds predominate, but the rosés can be good, too. Best producers: Château Bas, l'Île St-Pierre, Mas de Rey, de Ste-Césaire.

BOURGOGNE AC *Burgundy, France* Bourgogne is the French name anglicized as 'Burgundy'. As a generic appellation, it mops up all the Burgundian wine with no specific AC of its own. This means that there are massive differences in style and quality. The best wines (red and white) will usually come from a single grower who has declassified some of the wine from his top label.

In today's world of overblown prices such wines may be the only way we can afford the joys of fine Burgundy. If the wine is from a grower, the flavours should follow some sort of regional style. However, if the address on the label is of a Côte d'Or merchant, the wine could be from anywhere in Burgundy.

Pinot Noir is the main red Burgundy grape, with Gamay being used in the Mâconnais and BEAUJOLAIS. Red Bourgogne is usually light, overtly fruity in a breezy, up-front strawberry and cherry way, and should be drunk young (within 2–3 years) and just enjoyed, not fussed over. The rosé (from Pinot Noir) can be a very pleasant pink wine but sadly very little is produced.

Usually Bourgogne Blanc is a bone-dry Chardonnay wine from vineyards not considered quite good enough for a classier appellation, but vaguely in the same style. Aligoté is sometimes used and makes a sharper, more lemony style. Most straight white Burgundy should be drunk within 2 years. Best producers: (reds/growers) COCHE-DURY, GERMAIN, d'Heuilly-Huberdeau, Henri JAYER, Pierre Morey, Parent, Rion, Rossignol★; (reds/merchants) DROUHIN, JADOT, LABOURÉ-ROI, LEROY, VALLET; (reds/co-ops) BUXY★, Les Caves des Hautes-Côtes★; (whites/growers) Boisson-Morey★, Boisson-Vadot, Boyer-Martenot, Henri Clerc★, COCHE-DURY★★, Javillier★, Jobard★, René Manuel, Millau-Battault, de Villaine; (whites/merchants) DROUHIN, FAIVELEY, JADOT, JAFFELIN★, LABOURE-ROI★, Olivier LEFLAIVE; (whites/co-ops) BUXY. Best years: (reds) 1990 89 88; (whites) 1990 89 88. See also page 66.

BOURGOGNE ALIGOTÉ AC See Aligoté.

BOURGOGNE-CÔTE CHALONNAISE AC *Côte Chalonnaise, Burgundy, France* The least known of all the Burgundy regions. The Côte Chalonnaise vineyards have gained enormously in importance recently mainly because of spiralling prices on the Côte d'Or just to the north. This new AC (1990) covers vineyards in the Saône-et-Loire department around the villages of Bouzeron, RULLY, MERCUREY, GIVRY and MONTAGNY. Best producer: BUXY co-op. Best year: 1990.

BOURGOGNE GRAND ORDINAIRE AC *Burgundy, France* This is the bottom rung of the Burgundy appellation ladder and the wine is certainly not grand. You won't find the wine abroad and even in Burgundy it's mostly sold as quaffing wine for bars up and down the region.

BOURGOGNE-HAUTES CÔTES DE BEAUNE AC *Burgundy, France* As the supply of affordable Burgundy dwindled in the 1970s this backwater in the hills behind the great Côte de Beaune came into the spotlight. Now the area is reasonably prosperous and the red wines are fairly good. There is some pleasant, slightly sharp white from Chardonnay. Best producers: Les Caves des Hautes-Côtes★ (some of the best-value reds in all Burgundy), Cornu, Jacob, Joliot, Marcilly, de Mandelot, de Mercey. Best years: (reds) 1990 89 88 85; (whites) 1990 89 88.

BOURGOGNE-HAUTES CÔTES DE NUITS AC *Burgundy, France*
Attractive, lightweight wines from the hills immediately behind the Côte de Nuits. So far the best wines are the reds, with an attractive cherry and plum flavour. The white wine – apart from JAYER-GILLES – tends to be rather dry and flinty. In general drink young. Best producers: (reds) Les Caves des Hautes-Côtes★, Delauney, Dufouleur, Hudelot★, Thévenot-le-Brun; (whites) Les Caves des Hautes-Côtes★, Chaley, Cornu, Dufouleur, Hudelot, JAYER-GILLES★★ (superb oak-matured wine), Thévenot-le-Brun, Verdet★. Best years: (reds) 1990 89 88 85; (whites) 1990 89 88.

BOURGOGNE-IRANCY AC *Burgundy, France*   This northern outpost of vineyards, just south-west of Chablis, is an unlikely champion of the clear, pure flavours of Pinot Noir, but red Irancy can be delicate and lightly touched by the ripeness of plums and strawberries, and can age well. There is also a little rosé. Best producers: Bienvenu, Cantin, Colinot, Delaloge, Simmonet-Febvre. Best years: 1990 89 88.

BOURGOGNE PASSE-TOUT-GRAINS AC *Burgundy, France*
Almost always red, this is a mixture of Gamay with not less than one-third Pinot Noir. Recently the percentage of Pinot Noir has increased, yielding wines of better quality. Best producers: Chaley, Chanson, Cornu, LEROY, RION, Thomas.

BOURGUEIL AC *Loire Valley, France*   One of the Loire's best red wines comes from north of the river between the cities of Tours and Angers. Cabernet Franc is the main grape, topped up with a little Cabernet Sauvignon, and in hot years the results can be superb. If given between 5–10 years of aging they can develop a wonderful raspberry and blackcurrant fragrance. Best producers: Audebert (estate wines), Breton, Caslot-Galbrun★, Caslot-Jamet★, Demont★, DRUET★★, Lamé-Delille-Boucard★, des Raguenières★. Best years: 1990  89 88 86 85 83 82 78 76. See also St-Nicolas-de-Bourgueil.

BOUVET-LADUBAY *Saumur AC, Loire Valley, France*   Owned by the Champagne house TAITTINGER, Bouvet-Ladubay is not shy of promoting its wines, or of charging high prices. The quality of the basic range (Bouvet Brut, Bouvet Rosé) is good, but Bouvet's top wines are the vintage Saphir ★ and Trésor (Blanc ★ and Rosé ★★), the Trésor Blanc fermented in oak barrels. Bouvet-Ladubay also sells non-sparkling wine from VOUVRAY and SAUMUR.

BOUVIER Austrian grape which tends to be short on acidity and so is mainly used for sweet to ultra-sweet wines in which role it definitely achieves the richness but rarely manages to offer any other complexity as a foil. Best producers: Kracher★, Opitz★★, Weinkellerei Burgenland★.

BOUZY *Coteaux Champenois AC, Champagne, France* A leading
CHAMPAGNE village growing good Pinot Noir which is used
mainly for *white* Champagne. However, in outstanding years, a
little still red is made. It is light and high in acid. Best producers:
Bara, Georges Vesselle, Jean Vesselle. Best years: 1990 89 85.

BOWEN ESTATE *Coonawarra, South Australia* Doug Bowen makes
some of Coonawarra's best reds from estate grapes: peppery yet
profound Shiraz★★ and Cabernet★★ with beautifully balanced
flavours. Riesling and Chardonnay are presentable but less distinguished. Best years: (reds) 1990 88 87 86 84 80 79.

BRACHETTO Piedmontese grape once famous for its perfumed,
frothing and slightly sweet, light red wines. Dry versions are on
the increase (made by Scarpa and Correggia) as a number of
younger growers express a renewed interest in the grape. Given
the heavenly perfume, a revival is greatly desired by this enthusiast, for one. Best producers: VILLA BANFI, Viticoltori dell'Acquese.

CH. BRANAIRE-DUCRU★ *St-Julien AC, 4ème Cru Classé, Haut-
Médoc, Bordeaux, France* One of ST-JULIEN'S lesser lights, overshadowed by its neighbour BEYCHEVELLE, but producing some
good wines nonetheless. Branaire has one of the highest per-
centages of Cabernet Sauvignon in the Médoc, yet its wines
have a supple, chocolaty character with lots of aromatic fruit
and can be enjoyed after 4–5 years but will keep for a decade.
Second wine: Ch. Duluc. Best years: 1990 89 88 86 85 83 82 81.

BRANCO Portuguese for 'white'.

BRAND'S LAIRA *Coonawarra, South Australia* Low-profile
Coonawarra firm making big investments in new vineyards.
Lovely subtle, peachy Chardonnay★★ is the best wine. There is
also tobaccoey Cabernet★ and Cabernet-Merlot★, limy Riesling,
and peppery Original Vineyard Shiraz★.

CH. BRANE-CANTENAC *Margaux AC, 2ème Cru Classé, Haut-
Médoc, Bordeaux, France* Owned by the wealthy Lurton family, Brane-Cantenac has not lacked investment in recent years
but it doesn't show in the wines which often seem to lack the
concentration one expects from a Second Growth. Recent vintages do look more promising. Second wine: Ch. Notton. Best
years: 1990 89 88 86.

BRAUNEBERG *Mosel, Germany* Small village in the middle Mosel.
Its most famous vineyard sites are Juffer and Juffer Sonnenuhr
whose wines have a creamy gentleness rare in the Mosel. Best
producers: HAAG, LOOSEN, RICHTER.

BREAKY BOTTOM *Sussex, England* Small vineyard in the South
Downs near Lewes. Peter Hall is a wonderfully quirky, passionate grower, who makes dry, chunky Seyval Blanc★ that grows
creamy and honeyed and Burgundy-like after 3–4 years. His
crisp Müller-Thurgau★ is full of hedgerow pungency.

63

BREGANZE DOC *Veneto, Italy*   Small DOC in the hills east of
Verona and north of Vicenza. A red primarily from Merlot and a
dry white based on Tocai are supplemented by a range of varietals, including intense Cabernet and dry Vespaiolo. Best producers: Bartolomeo da Breganze co-op, Maculan★★, Villa Magna.

GEORG BREUER *Rüdesheim, Rheingau, Germany*   Firm of merchants run by Bernhard Breuer who produces some high-quality
Rheingau wines from the firm's own vineyards on the
Rüdesheimer Berg Schlossberg. In particular the 1990, 89 and
85 wines are fine. Wines like the Rivaner (Müller-Thurgau, fermented dry) and the Grauer Burgunder★ are rounded off with a
little oak.

BRIDGEHAMPTON *Long Island AVA, New York State, USA*
Outstanding Chardonnay★★ and late-harvest Rieslings★★ but
keep an eye on the Pinot Noir★ and the Merlot★ which show
promise.

BROKENWOOD *Hunter Valley, New South Wales, Australia*   High-
profile Hunter Valley winery with delicious, unfashionable
Sémillon★★, fashionable Chardonnay★; and Sauvignon Blanc-
Sémillon★. The best wines are the 100% Hunter Graveyard
Vineyard Shiraz★★ and Cabernet★★ – reds of concentration
and character for long keeping.

BROUILLY AC *Beaujolais, Burgundy, France*   Brouilly is the largest
of the 10 BEAUJOLAIS Crus and the wine is inconsistent as a
result. At its best, it's soft and fruity and gorgeously gluggable. It
can also make the best BEAUJOLAIS NOUVEAU of all. Best producers:
la Chaize, DUBOEUF (Combillaty, Garanches), Fouilloux, Hospices
de Beaujeu★ (especially Pisseveille Cuvée), Pierreux, Rolland,
Ruet, Ch. des Tours★. Best years:1990 89 88.

CH. BROUSTET★ *Barsac AC, 2ème Cru Classé, Bordeaux, France*
Good, pretty rich, sweet wine made to a high standard. Not a lot
is produced (much of the wine is sold off under the Ch. de Ségur
label). Best years: 1990 89 88 86 85 83 81 80 75 71.

BROWN BROTHERS *North-East Victoria, Australia*   Conservative
but highly successful family winery, has way outgrown its small
producer 'dad, mum and the boys' tag. There is a big emphasis
on varietal table wines. Moving into cool King Valley and
mountain-top Whitlands for its premium grapes.

WILHELM BRÜNDLMAYER *Kamptal-Donauland, Niederösterreich,*
Austria   The top estate in Langenlois, Austria's most productive
wine town, and large by Austrian standards. Willi Bründlmayer
makes wine in a variety of Austrian and international styles and
his Chardonnay★★ is the best Austrian attempt at the international idiom to date. Best years: 1990 86 83 79 77.

BRUNELLO DI MONTALCINO DOCG *Tuscany, Italy*   Famous
Tuscan zone south of Siena, traditionally noted for high wine
prices (thanks to BIONDI-SANTI) and dark, impenetrable flavours
from the Sangiovese grape grown in arid conditions. Recent

moves toward modern practices have resulted in more approachable wines from some producers, but the wines still have great depth, tannin and structure, though they may lack the finesse of the best CHIANTIS or MONTEPULCIANOS. Best producers: ALTESINO★★, Barbi★, Caparzo★, Ciacci Piccolomini, Col d'Orcia★, Cottimello, Lisini, Pertimali★★, Poggione★, Talenti, Val di Suga★, VILLA BANFI★. Best years: 1990 88 85 82.

BRUT French term for dry sparkling wines, especially CHAMPAGNE. Widely employed in other countries too. Although it is thought of as the driest style of fizz, Brut Champagne is actually allowed to have up to 15g per litre of sugar added before bottling. Brut Zéro is the driest of all but is rarely seen. Extra Dry, Sec and Demi-Sec are all sweeter than Brut Champagne.

BUÇACO PALACE HOTEL *Beira Litoral, Portugal* Go to this flamboyant 19th-century hotel to take the waters of nearby Luso, or drink the hotel's own wines ★★ which the restaurant lists in a profusion of vintages. They're some of the most interesting in Portugal, subtle and flavoursome, made from grapes from neighbouring DAO and BAIRRADA.

BUCELAS DOC *Oeste, Portugal* A tiny but historic DOC struggling in the 20th century. Bucelas wines are white, have very high acidity, and need long aging. The torch has been kept flickering by CAVES VELHAS, but the most recent arrival on the scene, Quinta da Romeira, looks likely to achieve more exciting results. Best producers: Quinta do Avelar, Quinta da Romeira.

BUENA VISTA *Carneros, California, USA* Clear, lucid wines that have instant appeal but in the reserve line are capable of extended aging. The Chardonnay Reserve ★ has rich, ripe flavours with appley fruit while the Special Selection Cabernet Sauvignon has intense cherry/currant fruit.

BUGEY See Vin du Bugey VDQS.

VON BUHL *Deidesheim, Rheinpfalz, Germany* Large, mainly Riesling estate which is currently leased to the Japanese Sanyo group. The wines are rarely subtle, but usually have a strong, confident Riesling character to them. Best years: 1990 89 88.

BULL'S BLOOD *Eger, Hungary* Bull's Blood (or Egri Bikavér as it is in Hungarian) is no longer the barrel-chested red it once was; as Kékfrankos (Blaufränkisch) grapes have replaced Kadarka in the blend, the blood has thinned, and its ability to inspire Magyar warriors is but a faint stain in the glass.

BURGENLAND *Austria* Austrian state on the eastern border with Hungary, with 4 wine regions: Neusiedlersee, including the Seewinkel with its sweet Prädikat wines and the productive commune of Gols; Neusiedlersee-Hügelland, also famous for sweet wines with its centres in Rust and Eisenstadt; Mittelburgenland, famous for its robust Blaufränkisch wines; and the more fragmented region of Südburgenland with some good reds and dry whites.

65

BURGUNDY RED WINES

Burgundy, France

 Rich in history and gastronomic tradition, the region of Burgundy covers a vast tract of eastern France, running from Auxerre, just south of Paris, to the city of Lyon. As with white Burgundy, the area's red wines are extremely diverse, sometimes frustratingly so. The explanation lies partly in the fickle nature of Pinot Noir, Burgundy's main red grape, and partly in the historic imbalance of supply and demand between growers – who grow the grapes and make and bottle much of the best wine – and merchants whose efforts have established the reputation of the wines internationally.

GRAPE VARIETIES
Pinot Noir is one of the world's most ancient varieties, prone to mutation – there arc an estimated 1000 varieties in Burgundy alone – and the range of flavours you get from the grape vividly demonstrates this. A red Épineuil from near Auxerre will be light, chalky, strawberry-flavoured, a Pinot from the Mâconnais toward Lyon will be rough and rooty and in between in the Côte d'Or – the heartland of red Burgundy – the flavours sweep through strawberry, raspberry, damson and cherry to a wild, magnificent maturity of Oriental spices, chocolate and truffles. Gamay, the grape of Beaujolais to the south, is best at producing juicy fruit flavours of strawberry and plum, demanding neither aging nor undue respect.

WINE REGIONS
The top red Burgundies come from the Côte d'Or, home to world-famous Grand Cru vineyards like Clos de Vougeot, Chambertin, Musigny, Richebourg and La Tâche. Givry and Mercurey in the Côte Chalonnaise are up-and-coming, as are the Hautes Côtes hills behind the Côte d'Or, and light but pleasant reds as well as good pink sparkling Crémant can be found near Chablis in the north. Mâconnais' reds are generally earthy and dull. Beaujolais really is best at producing bright, breezy wines full of fruit, for quaffing at a mere year old.

See also ALOXE-CORTON, AUXEY-DURESSES, BEAUJOLAIS, BEAUNE, BLAGNY, BONNES-MARES, BOURGOGNE, CHAMBERTIN, CHAMBOLLE-MUSIGNY, CHASSAGNE-MONTRACHET, CHOREY-LES-BEAUNE, CLOS DE LA ROCHE, CLOS DE TART, CLOS DE VOUGEOT, CORTON, COTE DE BEAUNE, COTE DE NUITS, COTE D'OR, CREMANT DE BOURGOGNE, ECHEZEAUX, FIXIN, GEVREY-CHAMBERTIN, GIVRY, LADOIX, MACON, MARSANNAY, MERCUREY, MEURSAULT, MONTHELIE, MOREY-ST-DENIS, MUSIGNY, NUITS-ST-GEORGES, PERNAND-VERGELESSES, PULIGNY-MONTRACHET, RICHEBOURG, LA ROMANEE-CONTI, ROMANEE-ST-VIVANT, RULLY, ST-AUBIN, ST-ROMAIN, SAVIGNY-LES-BEAUNE, LA TACHE, VOLNAY, VOSNE-ROMANEE, VOUGEOT.

BEST PRODUCERS

Côte de Nuits Bachelet, Barthod-Noëllat, Burguet, Clair, Confuron, Dujac, Grivot, A & F Gros, Jean Gros, Jayer, Jayer-Gilles, Lamarche, Leclerc, Méo-Camuzet, Mongeard-Mugneret, Pernin-Rossin, Perrot-Minot, Ponsot, Rion, Dom. de la Romanée-Conti, Rossignol-Trapet.

Côte de Beaune d'Angerville, Boillot, Gagnard, Lafarge, Lafon, Matrot, de Montille, Jean-Marc Morey, Morot, Mussy, Pousse d'Or, Tollot-Beaut.

Côte Chalonnaise Jacquesson, Joblot, Juillot, Rodet, Suremain, Thénard, de Villaine.

Beaujolais Descombes, des Jacques, Ch. du Moulin-à-Vent, Pelletier, Thivin, des Tours.

Merchants Duboeuf, Drouhin, Faiveley, Jadot, Labouré-Roi, Olivier Leflaive, Leroy, Rodet, Vallet Frères.

Co-ops Buxy, Cave des Hautes Côtes, Fleurie.

BURGUNDY WHITE WINES

Burgundy, France

 White Burgundy has for generations been thought of as the world's leading dry white wine. The top wines have a remarkable succulent richness of honey and hazelnut, melted butter and sprinkled spice, yet are totally dry. Such wines are all from the Chardonnay grape and are generally grown in the communes of Aloxe-Corton, Meursault, Puligny-Montrachet and Chassagne-Montrachet, where limestone soils and aspect of the vineyard provide perfect conditions for slow, ripening of the grapes.

WINE STYLES

However Burgundy encompasses far more wine styles than this, even if none of them quite attain the peaks of quality of those 4 villages on the Côte de Beaune.

Chablis in the north traditionally produces very good steely wines, aggressive and tart when young, but nutty and rounded – though still very dry – after a few years. Modern Chablis is generally a softer, milder wine, easy to drink young, and sometimes nowadays enriched with aging in new oak barrels.

There is no doubt that Meursault and the other Côte d'Or villages can produce stupendous wine, but it is in such demand that unscrupulous producers are often tempted to maximize yields and cut corners on quality. Consequently white Burgundy from these famous villages must be approached with caution. Lesser-known villages like Pernand-Vergelesses and St-Aubin often provide good wine at lower prices.

The Côte Chalonnaise is becoming very important for quality white wine now that oak barrels are being used more often for aging. Rully and Montagny are the most important regions, though Givry and Mercurey can produce nice white too.

The minor Aligoté grape makes some reasonable acidic wine, especially in Bouzeron. Further south the Mâconnais is a large region, two thirds planted with Chardonnay. Most of the wine is dull and flat and not all that cheap, but there is some fair sparkling Crémant de Bourgogne, and some good vineyard sites, in particular in St-Véran and in Pouilly-Fuissé, where an occasional stunning wine can be found.

See also ALOXE-CORTON, AUXEY-DURESSES, BATARD-MONTRACHET, BEAUJOLAIS, BEAUNE, BOURGOGNE, CHABLIS, CHASSAGNE-MONTRACHET, CORTON, CORTON-CHARLEMAGNE, COTE DE BEAUNE, COTE DE NUITS, COTE D'OR, CREMANT DE BOURGOGNE, FIXIN, GIVRY, LADOIX, MACON, MARSANNAY, MERCUREY, MEURSAULT, MONTAGNY, MONTHELIE, MONTRACHET, MOREY-ST-DENIS, MUSIGNY, NUITS-ST-GEORGES, PERNAND-VERGELESSES, PETIT CHABLIS, POUILLY-FUISSE, POUILLY-LOCHE, POUILLY-VINZELLES, PULIGNY-MONTRACHET, RULLY, ST-AUBIN, ST-ROMAIN, ST-VERAN, SAVIGNY-LES-BEAUNE, VOUGEOT, YONNE.

BEST YEARS

1990 89 88 86 85 82

BEST PRODUCERS

Chablis Dauvissat, Droin, Durup, Fèvre, Laroche, Michel, Raveneau.

Côte d'Or Ampeau, Blain-Gagnard, Bonneau du Martray, Carillon, Coche-Dury, Marc Colin, Fontaine-Gagnard, Gagnard, Jobard, Lafon, Dom. Leflaive, Matrot, Jean-Marc Morey, Pierre Morey, Michelot, Ramonet, Sauzet.

Côte Chalonnaise Derain, Jacquesson, la Folie, Rodet, Steinmaier, de Villaine.

Mâconnais Ch. Fuissé, Goyard, Leger-Plumet, Luquet, Noblet, Thevenet.

Merchants Chartron & Trébuchet, Drouhin, Duboeuf, Faiveley, Jadot, Jaffelin, Labouré-Roi, Louis Latour, Olivier Leflaive, Leroy.

Co-ops Buxy, La Chablisienne, Prissé, Viré.

LEO BURING *Barossa Valley, South Australia* Once the great name in Australian Riesling but now slightly left behind. As part of the SA Brewing conglomerate, there are many corporate-blend labels: respectable Padthaway Chardonnay★ and Sauvignon Blanc, fruity Barossa/Coonawarra Cabernet★ and serviceable Riesling, but the Special Bin Eden Valley and Watervale Rieslings★★★ of the 1970s are manna from heaven. Best years (Riesling) : 1979 75 73 72.

BÜRKLIN-WOLF *Wachenheim, Rheinpfalz, Germany* One of a small handful of great traditional winemakers in the Rheinpfalz, this is one of Germany's biggest estates, making about 50 different wines. Although the Rieslings★ are good, other grapes also contribute successfully to the mix, in particular Scheurebe★ and the red Dornfelder★. Best years: 1990 89 88 86 85 81 79.

BUXY, CAVE DES VIGNERONS DE *Côte Chalonnaise, Burgundy, France* Based in the Côte Chalonnaise, this is among Burgundy's top co-ops, producing affordable, well-made Chardonnay and Pinot Noir. The light, oak-aged BOURGOGNE Pinot Noir★ and the red and white Clos de Chenôves★, as well as the nutty, white MONTAGNY★ are all good and, hallelujah, reasonably priced.

BUZET AC *South-West France* Good BORDEAUX-style red wines from the same mix of grapes and at a lower price. There is very little rosé and the whites are rarely exciting. Best producer: Buzet-sur-Baïse co-op (especially Cuvée Napoléon).

CA' DEL BOSCO *Franciacorta, Lombardy, Italy* This model estate, owned by Maurizio Zanella, makes some of Italy's finest – and most expensive – wines, including outstanding Spumante★★ and Crémant★★, good Franciacorta Rosso★, startlingly good Chardonnay★ and a Bordeaux blend, Maurizio Zanella★ that puts many a Classed Growth to shame.

CABERNET D'ANJOU AC *Loire Valley, France* Higher in alcohol than ROSE D'ANJOU and generally slightly sweeter. Drink young. Best producers: Bertrand, Poupard, de Tigné, Verdier.

CABERNET FRANC Often unfairly dismissed as an inferior Cabernet Sauvignon, Cabernet Franc comes into its own in cooler areas or areas where the soil is damper and heavier. It can have a strong, grassy freshness linked to a raw but tasty blackcurrant and raspberry fruit. In France it thrives in the Loire Valley (particularly in Anjou, Saumur and Touraine). In Bordeaux, especially in ST-EMILION and POMEROL, Cabernet Franc is an important part of the blend for red wine. Italy has used the variety with considerable success for generations in the North-East.

CABERNET SAUVIGNON See page 72.

CAHORS AC *South-West France* Cahors, the leading red wine of the South-West after BORDEAUX, has been famous since Roman times. The dark, tannic wine is made from at least 70%

Auxerrois (Bordeaux's Malbec) and has an unforgettable flavour of plum and raisin richness. With age it takes on a deep tobaccoey spicy hue. Best producers: la Caminade, Cayrou★, la Coutale★, de Gamot★, Gaudou★, Haute-Serre★, Quattre et Treilles★, Triguedina★. Best years: 1990 89 88 86 85.

CALABRIA *Italy*   The 'toe' of Italy is one of its poorest regions. CIRO, Donnici and Savuto are hearty reds from the native Gaglioppo grape, the whites from the Greco grape are less interesting, except in sweeter versions. Though renowned for its wines in Greek times, Calabria produces little more than tourist thirst-quenchers today.

CÁLEM *Port DOC, Douro, Portugal*   The largest family-owned Portuguese port shipper. Their best wines are aged tawnies★ and Colheitas★★, complex and delicious, with creamy texture and endless layers of flavour. Best years: (Colheitas) 1962 57; (vintage ports) 1985 75 70.

CALERA *San Benito, California, USA*   Calera has come to set the standard for California Pinot Noir. The owner-winemaker Josh Jensen makes three Pinots, Reed Vineyard★★, Selleck Vineyard★★★ and Jensen Vineyard★★★. They are complex, balanced wines with great power and originality and capable of extended aging. Mt Harlem Chardonnay★★ looks set to be as excitingly original as the Pinot Noir. Small amounts of Viognier★★★ are succulent with sensuous fruit and perfume. Best years: 1991 90 88 87 86 85 79.

CALIFORNIA *USA*   California's importance is not simply in being the leading wine producer in the USA, the state's influence on the world of wine is far wider than that. Most of the great revolutions in technology and style that have transformed the expectations and achievements of winemakers in every country of the world – including France – were born in the ambitions, and fashioned by the commitment and determination, of a band of great Californian winemakers during the 1960s and 1970s. It is they who challenged the old order with its tightly regulated, self-serving élitism, democratizing the world of fine wine in the process, to the great benefit of every wine drinker on the planet. This revolutionary fervour is less evident now, as California justifiably basks in its achievements as one of the world's great wine regions, but it would do well not to forget the principles and passions that first lit the flame.

A few figures: there are 131,530ha (325,000 acres) of wine grapes, producing over 400 million gallons of wine annually, about 90% of all wine made in the USA. A large proportion comes from the hot, inland Central Valley but most of California's 700-plus wineries are in the cool coastal strip north of Los Angeles. See also Carneros, Central Coast, Central Valley, Mendocino County, Monterey County, Napa County, Napa Valley, Rutherford, San Luis Obispo County, Santa Barbara County, Sonoma County.

CABERNET SAUVIGNON

Cabernet Sauvignon from places like Bulgaria, Chile, Australia, California, even parts of southern France, has become so popular that many people may not realize where it all started – and how Cabernet has managed to become the great, all-purpose, omnipresent red wine grape of the world.

WINE STYLES

Bordeaux Cabernet It all began in Bordeaux. With the exception of a clutch of Merlot-based beauties in St-Émilion and Pomerol, all the greatest red Bordeaux wines are based on Cabernet Sauvignon, with varying amounts of Merlot, Cabernet Franc, and possibly Petit Verdot and Malbec also blended in. The blending is necessary because by itself, Cabernet makes such a strong, powerful, aggressive and assertive wine. Dark and tannic when young, often to an impenetrable degree, the great Bordeaux wines need 10–20 years for the aggression to fade, the fruit becoming sweet and perfumed as fresh blackcurrants, with a dry fragrance of cedarwood, of cigar boxes mingling magically among the fruit. It is this character which has made red Bordeaux famous for at least two centuries.

Cabernet Worldwide When winemakers in other parts of the world sought role models to try to improve their wines, most of them automatically chose Cabernet Sauvignon. It was lucky that they did, because not only is this variety easy to grow in almost all conditions – cool or warm, dry or damp – but that unstoppable personality always powers through. The cheaper wines are generally made to accentuate the blackcurrant fruit and the slightly earthy tannins They are drinkable young, but able to age surprisingly well. The more ambitious wines are aged in oak barrels, often new, to enhance the tannin yet also to add spice and richness capable of developing over a decade or more. Sometimes the Cabernet is blended – usually with Merlot, but occasionally, as in Australia, with Shiraz.

European Cabernets Many vineyards in southern France now produce excellent, affordable Cabernet. Some of the best wines from Spain have been Cabernet, and Portugal has also had success. Italy's whole red wine industry was turned on its head by the success of Cabernet in Tuscany; while Eastern Europe, in particular Bulgaria, already provides us with some of the most affordable high quality reds in the world.

New World Cabernets California's wine reputation was created by its strong, weighty Cabernets, while both Australia and New Zealand place more emphasis on easy fruit. Chile has made the juicy, blackcurranty style very much her own, and Argentina, Mexico and South Africa are showing they want to join in too.

BEST PRODUCERS

France
Bordeaux Cos d'Estournel, Dom. de Chevalier, Ducru-Beaucaillou, Gruaud-Larose, d'Issan, Latour, Léoville-Las-Cases, Margaux, Mouton-Rothschild, Pichon-Longueville, Rausan-Ségla; *Languedoc* Mas de Daumas Gassac.
Provence Richeaume, Trévallon.

Other European Cabernets
Italy Ghiaie della Furba, Ornellaia, Sassicaia.

Portugal Quinta da Bacalhôa.

Spain Jean León, Marqués de Griñon, Torres.

New World Cabernets
Australia Cape Mentelle, De Bortoli Yarra Valley, Dromana Estate, Henschke, Moss Wood, Penfolds (Bin 707), Petaluma, Yarra Yering.

New Zealand Te Mata Coleraine, Vavasour.

USA (California) Beringer (Reserve), Caymus, Diamond Creek, Dunn, Groth, The Hess Collection, Laurel Glen, Mayacamas, Mondavi (Reserve), Newton, Ridge Montebello, Silver Oak.

73

CALITERRA *Curicó, Chile*   A joint venture, terminated in 1991, between ERRAZURIZ and the Napa winery, FRANCISCAN VINEYARDS, whose president, Agustin Huneeus, was born in Chile. A lush, toasty Reserva Chardonnay★ shows a commendable ability to tailor wines to export tastes. The Reserva Cabernet Sauvignons ★, Chilean from head to toe, impress with their soft, fresh, pure, blackcurranty fruit but early promise is being marred by inconsistency at the moment.

CH. CALON-SÉGUR ★ *St-Estèphe AC, 3ème Cru Classé, Haut-Médoc, Bordeaux, France*   For a long time this was ST-ESTEPHE's leading château. In the mid-1980s the wines were not as good as they should have been, given their high price. Recent vintages have been more impressive. Second wine: Marquis de Ségur. Best years: 1990 89 88 82.

CAMERON *Willamette Valley AVA, Oregon, USA*   A fairly new producer of Pinot Noir ★ and Chardonnay ★, made in both a regular and a reserve version. Thrillingly whacky wines, and the passion of the owner, John Paul, persuades me to give his remarkable flavours the benefit of the doubt. Best years: 1990 88 87.

CAMPANIA *Italy*   The region of Naples and Vesuvius, but a virtual desert for the wine lover. It has the lowest percentage of DOC wines of any Italian region, but this is due more to inertia on the part of Campanians than to any intrinsic defect in soil, climate or grape varieties. The best wines come from the red Aglianico (Taurasi) and Piedirosso grapes, and the white Greco, Falanghina and Fiano grapes. Best producer: MASTROBERARDINO.

CAMPILLO *Rioja DOC, País Vasco, Spain*   The relaunch of Campillo (formerly a subsidiary label of FAUSTINO MARTINEZ) has produced some of the most exciting new red RIOJAS ★★ seen for several years. The wines are pure Tempranillo, with masses of ripe, velvety fruit. Best years: 1985 82 81.

CAMPO VIEJO *Rioja DOC, Rioja, Spain*   The largest producer of RIOJA. The Reservas ★ and Gran Reservas ★ are reliably good as is the elegant, all-Tempranillo Reserva Viña Alcorta ★. The excellent Marqués de Villamagna Gran Reservas ★★ have a delicious blackcurrant fruit and soft oak all too rare in Rioja. Best years: (reds) 1985 83 82 80 78.

CANARY ISLANDS *Spain*   Most wine-making here takes place on Tenerife, especially in a north-coast region called Tacoronte-Acentejo, which may be promoted to DO status soon. So far, the rosés and whites are not worth drinking, but the young reds, made mostly from the Listán Negro grape, can be nice gluggers. Best producers: Bodegas Monje, Viña Norte.

CANBERRA DISTRICT *New South Wales, Australia*   Cool, high altitude (800m/2600 ft) may sound good but here presents many difficulties which few winemakers have yet overcome. Most offerings so far have had a distinct tinge of the home winemaker. Best producers: Brindabella Hills, Clonakilla, Doonkuna, Lark Hill.

CANNONAU Sardinian grape variety related to Spain's Garnacha and France's Grenache Noir. In Sardinia it produces deep, tannic reds but the modern, dry red table wines are gaining in popularity. Traditional sweet and fortified styles can still be found (see ANGHELU RUJU). Best producers: (lighter, modern styles) Dolianova, Dorgali, Ogliastra and Oliena co-ops.

CH. CANON ★★ *St-Émilion Grand Cru AC, 1er Grand Cru Classé, Bordeaux, France* Canon makes some of the richest, most concentrated ST-EMILIONS. In good vintages the wine is impressively tannic to start with and will keep well for a dozen years or more. Best years: 1990 89 88 86 85 83 82 79.

CANON-FRONSAC AC *Bordeaux, France* This AC is the heart of the FRONSAC region. The wines are quite strong when young but can age for 10 years or more. Best producers: Canon, Canon-de-Brem, Haut-Mazeris, Moulin-Pey-Labrie, Vrai-Canon-Bouché, Vrai-Canon-Boyer. Best years: 1990 89 88 85 83 82 79 78.

CH. CANTEMERLE ★★ *Haut-Médoc AC, 5ème Cru Classé, Bordeaux, France* Since its takeover by the large merchant house of CORDIER in 1980, Cantemerle has improved beyond recognition. In general the wine is relatively delicate, needing only 7–10 years aging. Second wine: Villeneuve de Cantemerle. Best years: 1990 89 88 87 86 85 83 82.

CANTERBURY *South Island, New Zealand* In the arid, cool-climate centre of the South Island, the region's long, cool, ripening season favours white varieties, particularly Chardonnay, Pinot Gris, Sauvignon Blanc and Riesling, as well as Pinot Noir. The flavours the area's small wineries bring into being are potentially some of the most exciting in New Zealand. Best producers: French Farm, GIESEN, ST HELENA, WAIPARA SPRINGS.

CANTINA SOCIALE Italian for a co-op, an important force in Italian viniculture, controlling about 60% of the country's production.

CAPE MENTELLE *Margaret River, Western Australia* Leading Margaret River winery, with buzzy New Zealand offshoot CLOUDY BAY, is co-owned by VEUVE CLICQUOT and visionary founder David Hohnen. Superb full-throttle Cabernet ★★ and Shiraz ★★, impressive Chardonnay ★★, tangy Sémillon-Sauvignon Blanc ★★ and, expressing Hohnen's California training, chewy Zinfandel ★. Best years: 1991 90 88 86 83 82 78.

CAPEL VALE *South-West Coastal Plain, Western Australia* Radiologist Peter Pratten's winery makes fine Riesling ★, Gewürztraminer, Chardonnay ★★ and Sémillon-Sauvignon Blanc ★. The reds are big and rather stolid.

CARBONIC MACERATION See Macération carbonique.

CH. CARBONNIEUX *Pessac-Léognan AC, Cru Classé de Graves, Bordeaux, France* The largest of the GRAVES Classed Growth properties, now part of the PESSAC-LEOGNAN AC. The white wine ★★ has improved considerably since 1988, profiting from the introduction of 50% new oak. The red★ sometimes seems to lack stuffing, but has also gained in complexity over the last few years. Second wine: La Tour-Léognan. Best years: (whites) 1990 89 88 85; (reds) 1990 89 88 86.

CARCAVELOS DOC *Oeste, Portugal*   Carcavelos is a tiny, moribund DOC for an undistinguished brown fortified wine made from a mixture of red and white grapes in prime tourist development country between Lisbon and Cascais. The wine from Quinta dos Peses, the only remaining estate in the DOC, is ludicrously expensive.

CAREMA DOC *Piedmont, Italy*   Tiny quantities of wine trickle from the Nebbiolo vines grown on the steep, rocky slopes of this small zone in northern Piedmont. Lighter than most other Nebbiolos, these wines can have great elegance and perfume. Production is confined to two producers, the co-op, and Luigi Ferrando whose Black Label★ wines, made only in the best vintage, can be outstanding, and will age for up to 25 years. Best years: 1985 83 82.

CARIGNAN   The dominant red grape in the south of France and responsible for much, boring cheap, harsh wine. But when made by carbonic maceration, the wine can have delicious spicy fruit. Old vines are capable of thick, rich, impressive reds. Common in California and Chile for everyday reds. Although initially a Spanish grape (as Cariñena or Mazuelo) it is not that widespread there, though useful for adding colour in RIOJA and Catalonia.

LOUIS CARILLON & FILS *Puligny-Montrachet, Côte de Beaune, Burgundy, France*   An excellent, but often underrated family-owned estate in PULIGNY-MONTRACHET. The emphasis here is on traditional, slightly savage white wines of great concentration, rather than new oak. Look out for the three Premiers Crus – Les Referts ★★, Champ Canet ★★ and Les Perrières ★★ – and the tiny, but exquisite production of Bienvenues-Bâtard-Montrachet ★★★. The red wines – from CHASSAGNE-MONTRACHET ★, ST-AUBIN ★ and MERCUREY ★ – are extremely good, too. Best years: 1990 89 88 86 85.

CARIÑENA DO *Aragón, Spain*   The largest DO of Aragón, baking under the merciless sun in inland eastern Spain, Cariñena has traditionally been a land of cheap, deep red, alcoholic wines from Garnacha. However, a switch to Tempranillo grapes has begun, and some growers now pick early. Even so most Cariñena, red, white or rosé, is still cheap and cheerless. Best producer: Bodegas San Valero (Monte Ducay, Don Mendo).

CARMENET VINEYARD *Sonoma Valley AVA, California, USA*   Carmenet sets out to make BORDEAUX-style reds and whites and is probably California's most successful exponent, producing deep, complex reds ★★ and long-lived, barrel-fermented whites ★★. Best years: 1991 90 88 87 86.

CARMIGNANO DOCG *Tuscany, Italy* Red wine from the Montalbano hills west of Florence, largely created by the Medici in the 16th and 17th centuries, and revived in the 1960s by Ugo Contini Bonacossi of Capezzana, the area's dominant producer. Arguing that the Medici had experimented with Cabernet, he brought back cuttings from LAFITE in Bordeaux for his own vineyards. The blend (85% Sangiovese/15% Cabernet) gives one of Tuscany's finest and most distinctive wines. Never deep in colour, they have great intensity and display remarkable longevity. DOCG since 1988 for Riserva★★ and 1990 for Normale★. Look to Capezzana also for good rosé, Vinruspo, a lighter red, Barco Reale (soon to be DOC), and a fine Vin Santo★. Best producers: Ambra, Artimino, Bacheretto, Capezzana, Il Poggiolo, Treffiano. Best years: 1990 88 85.

CARNEROS AVA *California, USA* Hugging the northern edge of San Francisco Bay, Carneros includes parts of both Napa and Sonoma Counties. The area is windswept and chilly with heavy morning fog off the Bay and is one of California's top, cool-climate areas, making it highly suitable for Chardonnay and Pinot Noir, both as table wine and as a base for sparkling wine production. Best producers: ACACIA, Bouchaine, BUENA VISTA, Carneros Creek, CLOS DU VAL, Gloria Ferrer, Mont St John Cellars, DOMAINE MUMM (Winery Lake), RASMUSSEN, SAINTSBURY.

CARR TAYLOR *Sussex, England* David Carr Taylor's long-established vineyard and winery north of Hastings has consistently produced good whites from Reichensteiner, Gutenborner and Schönburger while the Non-Vintage Sparkling wine has blazed a promising trail for the vineyards of England's south-facing chalk slopes.

CASA VINICOLA Italian for 'wine house'. It means a producer who buys in wines or grapes and sells it under his name, similar to a French merchant or *négociant*. It covers a multitude of sins, but some of the best, like Bruno GIACOSA, PUIATTI and ANTINORI, also come under this heading.

CASSIS AC *Provence, France* Cassis is a picturesque fishing port near Marseille and because of its situation, its white wine is the most overpriced on the French Riviera. Based on Ugni Blanc and Clairette, the wine isn't that special, but can be good if fresh. The red wine is dull at best but the rosé can be pleasant (especially from a single estate). Best producers: Clos Ste-Magdelaine, Ferme Blanche, Mas Calendal, du Paternel.

CASTEL DEL MONTE DOC *Puglia, Italy* An arid, hilly zone inland from Bari, provides the ideal habitat for the Uva di Troia grape which, in the hands of a top producer, can be transformed into long-lived red wine of astonishing character. The white wine is merely decent. Best producer: RIVERA★.

CASTELLBLANCH *Cava DO, Catalonia, Spain* One of the world's largest Champagne-method sparkling wine companies, owned by another giant CAVA company, FREIXENET. Brut Zéro and Crystal are fresh, simple fizzes.

CASTELL'IN VILLA *Chianti Classico DOCG, Tuscany, Italy* One of CHIANTI Classico's finest estates, producing notable Chianti Classico ★★★ and a Vino da Tavola, Balsastrada★★, which combine power, elegance and longevity in a way that few Tuscan wines ever manage. Best years: 1990 88 86 85 83.

CASTELLO DEI RAMPOLLA *Chianti Classico DOCG, Tuscany, Italy* Located in the 'golden shell' of Panzano, this is one of the outstanding CHIANTI Classico★★ estates. Sammarco ★★★ (70% Cabernet/30% Sangiovese) is one of Tuscany's best Vino da Tavolas. Best years: 1990 88 86 85 82.

CASTELLO DELLA SALA *Orvieto DOC, Umbria, Italy* Beautiful property, just north of Orvieto, belonging to the ANTINORI family. As well as unexciting ORVIETO it produces Cervaro della Sala★, an oak-aged blend of 80% Chardonnay and 20% Grechetto that gets better with each vintage. The sweet wines, particularly Muffato della Sala★, are good. Best years: 1990 89 88.

CASTELLO DI VOLPAIA *Chianti Classico DOCG, Tuscany, Italy* Volpaia, a beautiful property in CHIANTI Classico, was one of the first to begin selling wines under the estate label. Their Chianti Classico ★ is light and perfumed, but perhaps the best wine is the Vino da Tavola Coltassala ★★, made predominantly from Sangiovese. Their Sangiovese/Cabernet blend, Balifico ★, is also successful in top vintages. Though once a pacesetter, Volpaia has a great deal of work to do to re-establish its position in the top flight. Best years: 1988 85 82.

CASTELL'SCHES DOMÄNENAMT *Castell, Franken, Germany* The former Castell principality is now part of Bavaria, but the prince still has his vines to console him. Attractive Müller-Thurgau wines with fresh, summery fruit come from the Casteller Herrenberg and a classic Franconian Silvaner from the Casteller Hohnart ★. Also rich Ausleses★ from Rivaner. Best years: 1990 89 88 83 81.

CASTILLA-LA MANCHA *Spain* The biggest wine region in Spain – the biggest, indeed, in the world at over 700,000ha (1.73 million acres) – making nearly half of all Spanish wine. It is hot, dry country with poor soil. The DOs of the central plateau, La MANCHA and VALDEPEÑAS, make mostly whites from the Airén grape, and some good reds from the Cencibel (Tempranillo). Méntrida DO and Almansa DO make mostly rustic though sometimes pleasant reds.

VIGNERONS CATALANS *Roussillon, France* This substantial Perpignan-based association of growers and co-ops sells a wide range of wines. Founded in 1964, it has encouraged members to invest in modern technology and to experiment with new grape varieties. Its COTES DU ROUSSILLON and COTES DU ROUSSILLON-VILLAGES blends are relentlessly consistent. There are now more exciting wines in Roussillon but none more reliable.

CATALONIA *Spain*   Wine standards vary considerably among the 8 DOs of this Spanish yet very independent-minded region. The PENEDES, between Barcelona and Tarragona, has the greatest concentration of technically equipped wineries in Spain, as well as a tasty smattering of international vine varieties. ALELLA, up the coast, makes adequate whites, and inland Costers del Segre makes excellent reds and whites at the RAIMAT estate. In the south, mountainous PRIORATO and the hills of Tarragona and Terra Alta are still behind the times. Ampurdán-Costa Brava up by the French border has sadly been left in the quality trough of an easy local tourist market lapping up whatever is made. Catalonia also makes most of Spain's CAVA sparkling wines in an industry centred in the Penedés.

CAVA DO *Spain*   Cava, the Catalan and hence Spanish name for Champagne-method sparkling wine, is made in 159 towns and villages scattered over northern Spain, but more than 95% are in Catalonia. Here the grapes used are the local trio of Parellada, Macabeo and Xarel-lo. The best value, fruitiest Cavas are generally the youngest, with no more than the minimum 9 months' aging. Some good Catalan Cavas are made with the Chardonnay grape but, frankly, Cava is still a somewhat dull drink in all but the best examples. Best producers: Castell de Villarnau, Cavas Hill, CODORNIU, JUVE Y CAMPS★, MARQUES DE MONISTROL★, Mont Marçal, Parxet, RAIMAT, Raventós i Blanc, Rovellats★.

CAVE CO-OPÉRATIVE   French for a co-operative cellar, where members bring their grapes for vinification and bottling under a collective label. In terms of quantity alone, the French wine industry is dominated by its co-ops. Quality is another story altogether – the best are excellent, but many lack both investment and a director of sufficient passion and vision to persuade the members the effort is worthwhile. Nevertheless, the basic quality of co-op wines has improved enormously in the last decade. Co-ops often use less workaday titles, such as Caves des Vignerons, Producteurs Réunies, Union des Propriétaires, Union des Producteurs or Cellier des Vignerons. See Buxy, Catalans, Celliers des Samsons, la Chablisienne, Mont Tauch, Oisly-et-Thésée, Plaimont.

CAVES ALIANÇA *Beira Litoral, Portugal*   Based in BAIRRADA, Caves Aliança is one of Portugal's largest wine companies. Definitely among Bairrada's modernists, Aliança makes crisp, fresh, white and soft, approachable red Bairradas ★, as well as buying in wine to blend good red Dão ★ and Douro ★. Best years: (reds) 1990 89 85 83.

CAVES IMESCH *Valais, Switzerland* Company making a full range of Valais wines from a rooty dry Amigne ★ to a spicy Arvine ★; from an earthy, Pinot Noir-dominated DOLE ★ to a thirstquenching Fendant. Their Pinot Noir du Valais ★ can be very deep and characterful for a Swiss Pinot Noir.

CAVES SÃO JOÃO *Beira Litoral, Portugal* A traditional-seeming but discreetly modernist company. They were pioneers of cool-fermented, white BAIRRADA, and have made some tremendous Cabernet Sauvignons from their own vines. They are best known, though, for their rich, complex reds including Frei João ★ from Bairrada and Porta dos Cavalheiros ★★ from DAO – they demand at least a decade of aging to show their quality. Best years: (reds) 1991 88 85 83.

CAVES VELHAS *Oeste, Portugal* Caves Velhas buys, blends, matures and sells wines from all over Portugal. Its non-DOC brands (Romeira, Caves Velhas Clarete and Caves Velhas Garrafeira) are largely made of Ribatejo wine. For many years, it was the only commercial producer of the historic BUCELAS denomination, though the wine was hardly memorable.

CAYMUS VINEYARDS *Napa Valley AVA, California, USA* Caymus Cabernet Sauvignon is a deep, ripe, intense, and generally tannic style, that is never less than good in its regular bottling ★ and can be outstanding as a Special Selection ★★★. There is also excellent Zinfandel ★. Best years: 1990 88 87 86 85 84 80 79.

DOMAINE CAZES *Rivesaltes, Roussillon, France* The Cazes brothers make outstanding MUSCAT DE RIVESALTES ★★, but also produce a wide range of red and white table wines from the Roussillon area, mainly as COTES DU ROUSSILLON and Vin de Pays des Côtes Catalanes. Look out for the soft, fruity Le Canon du Maréchal ★ and the small production of barrel-fermented Chardonnay ★. Best years: 1991 90 89 88.

CELLIER DES SAMSONS *Beaujolais, Burgundy, France* A group of 10 quality-minded co-ops, producing consistently good wines from the Beaujolais and Mâconnais regions. The best are sold under the Cuvée Authentique label. Look out for the MOULIN-A-VENT, BEAUJOLAIS-VILLAGES, ST-VERAN, and MACON-VILLAGES.

CENCIBEL See Tempranillo.

CENTRAL COAST AVA *California, USA* A huge and rather meaningless AVA covering virtually every vineyard between San Francisco and Los Angeles with a number of sub-AVAs, such as Santa Cruz, Santa Ynez, Santa Maria and Monterey bouncing around inside. However, these are some of the best of California's new, cool-climate areas and will soon become well-known in their own right.

CENTRAL OTAGO *South Island, New Zealand* The only wine region in New Zealand with a continental rather than maritime climate. The long, cool ripening season may prove to be ideal for flavour development in early-ripening varieties such as Pinot

Noir, Gewürztraminer and Chardonnay, even if it's risky for later varieties such as Riesling. I still find many of the wines encouraging rather than convincing. Best producers: Black Ridge, Chard Farm, Gibbston Valley, Rippon Vineyards.

CENTRAL VALLEY *Chile*   The heart of Chile's wine industry, stretching from Aconcagua in the north to Maule in the south. The climate is Chile's most temperate, and all the major producers are sited here. Best producers: CALITERRA, CONCHA Y TORO, COUSINO MACUL, ERRAZURIZ, LOS VASCOS, Montes, SANTA RITA, MIGUEL TORRES, VILLARD, VINA CANEPA, Viña Linderos.

CENTRAL VALLEY AVA *California, USA*   This vast area grows nearly 80% of California's grapes, mostly used for cheap wines. The quality of wine has improved over the past few years, but it is still an overheated area where irrigated vineyards produce excess tonnage, often siphoned off into production of brandies and grape concentrate. It is said that you cannot produce exciting wine in the Central Valley, but the conditions are not that different to Australia's Riverland or many parts of Spain and southern France or the hinterland of Washington State. What seems to be lacking is the will to improve quality. The only areas with any claim to quality are the Sacramento Valley and the Sacramento Delta area. Best producers: Guild, Las Viñas, MONDAVI Woodbridge, R H Phillips, Quady.

CÉPAGE   French for grape variety. Often followed on labels by the name of a single variety, such as Merlot or Chardonnay.

CERETTO *Piedmont, Italy*   This merchant house, under the direction of brothers Bruno and Marcello Ceretto, has gained quite a reputation for itself as one of the great modern producers in BAROLO. Their style is soft and fragrant, with low levels of tannin, but this has resulted in wines from the late 1970s and early 1980s failing to live up to their earlier hype. With the help of consultant oenologist Donato Lanati, it is to be hoped that their wines, Barolo (from Bricco Roccha★), Barbaresco (Bricco Asili★) and white Arneis Blange will regain levels of quality previously claimed, but seldom attained.

CÉRONS AC *Bordeaux, France*   An AC for sweet wine in the GRAVES region of Bordeaux. The rather soft, mildly honeyed wine is not quite so sweet as SAUTERNES except in years like 1990, and for that reason not so well known, nor so highly priced. Most producers now make dry wine under the Graves label. Best producers: de Cérons★, Grand Enclos du Château de Cérons★, Haura, Mayne-Binet. Best years: 1990 89 86 83.

CHABLAIS *Vaud, Switzerland*   A sub-region of the Vaud south-east of Lake Geneva. Most of the vineyards lie on the alluvial plains but two villages, Yvorne and Aigle benefit from much steeper slopes and produce really tangy whites and good reds. Most of the thirstquenchingly dry whites are made from the Chasselas or Dorin as it is called locally. The reds are made from Pinot Noir.

A rosé speciality is the Oeil de Perdrix (partridge eye), also made from Pinot Noir; it is an enjoyable summer wine. Drink the whites and rosés young. Best producers: Badoux★, Delarze★, Grognuz★.

CHABLIS AC *Burgundy, France*   Chablis, in the Serein valley halfway between Paris and Dijon, is Burgundy's northernmost outpost. Chardonnay ripens here with difficulty and there is a dreadful record of frost. The price of the wine is high, often too high, given that some Chablis can be not much better than decent MUSCADET. Chablis' other problem is that its name has become synonymous in many parts of the world with cheap, dry-to-medium, white-to-off-white wine from any available grape. Real Chablis is always white and dry, but with a light, unassertive fruit which can make for delicious drinking. An increasing number of producers are experimenting with oak barrel aging, resulting in some full, toasty, positively rich dry whites. In general straight Chablis AC should be drunk at 1–2 years old, but the better producers often make wine which can improve for 3–5 years. Best producers: Brocard★, La CHABLISIENNE co-op★★, Defaix★★, DROIN★, DROUHIN★★, DURUP★, Laroche★, Long-Depaquit★, MICHEL, Pinson★, RAVENEAU, Régnard★, Simmonet-Febvre★, Vocoret★. Best years: 1990 89 88 86 85 83.

CHABLIS GRAND CRU AC *Burgundy, France*   The 7 Grands Crus vineyards (Bougros, Les Preuses, Vaudésir, Grenouilles, Valmur, Les Clos and Les Blanchots) that face south-west across the small town of Chablis are the heart of the AC. Grand Cru producers, in general, have been making some exceptional wines in the 1980s, especially those who have used oak to mature their wines, adding a rich warmth to the otherwise taut flavours. DROIN and Fèvre are the most enthusiastic users of new oak. Never drink the wine too young, 5–10 years is the normal timescale before you begin to see why you spent your money. Best producers: DAUVISSAT, Defaix★★, DROIN★★★, Fèvre★★, Long-Depaquit★, MICHEL, Pinson★, RAVENEAU★★★, Régnard★, Robin★★, Servin★, Simmonet-Febvre★★, Vocoret★★. Best years: 1990 89 88 86 85 83 82 81.

CHABLIS PREMIER CRU AC *Burgundy, France*   Just over a quarter of CHABLIS' vineyards are designated Premier Cru, below Grand Cru in the pecking order. Some of these are on splendid slopes (the best are Montée de Tonnerre, Vaillons and Monts de Milieu) but many of the newer ones are on slopes of questionable quality. As such Premiers Crus vary widely in quality, but are always relatively expensive. The wines should taste bigger and more intense than basic Chablis and may take as long as 5 years to show full potential. Best producers: La CHABLISIENNE co-op★, DAUVISSAT★★, Defaix★★, DROIN★★, Fèvre★, MICHEL★★, RAVENEAU★★, Régnard★, Simmonet-Febvre★, Testut★, Tremblay★, Vocoret★. Best years: 1990 89 88 86 85 83 82 81.

LA CHABLISIENNE *Chablis, Burgundy, France*   A substantial co-op producing nearly one third of all CHABLIS. The wines are always reliable and can sometimes aspire to greatness. The best are the oaky Grands Crus – especially Les Preuses ★★ and Grenouilles (sold as Ch. Grenouille ★★) – but the basic unoaked Chablis ★, the Cuvée Vieilles Vignes ★★ and the numerous Premiers Crus★ are excellent, as is the red BOURGOGNE Épineuil made from Pinot Noir. Best years: (whites) 1990 89 88 86 85; (reds) 1990 89 88.

CHALONE *Monterey, California, USA*   Producers of very concentrated Pinot Noir ★★ and huge, full-blown but slow-developing Chardonnay ★ from vineyards on the arid eastern slope of the coastal range in mid-Monterey County. Also produces very good Pinot Blanc ★ and Chenin Blanc★ – as well as Reserve bottlings of Pinot Noir ★★ and Chardonnay ★★. These are strongly individualistic wines. Best years: (Chardonnay) 1990 89 84; (Pinot Noir) 1990 86 83 82 81 80.

CHAMBERS *Rutherglen, Victoria, Australia*   Timeless family winery making sheer nectar in the form of liqueur Muscat and Tokay. The secret is Bill Chambers' ability to draw on ancient stocks put down in wood by earlier generations. His 'Special' ★★ and 'Old' ★★★ blends are national treasures. The Cabernet is inexpensive and good; but the whites are pedestrian.

CHAMBERTIN AC *Grand Cru, Côte de Nuits, Burgundy, France*
The village of GEVREY-CHAMBERTIN, the largest Côte de Nuits commune, has no fewer than 8 Grands Crus (Chambertin, Chambertin-Clos-de-Bèze, Chapelle-Chambertin, Charmes-Chambertin, Griotte-Chambertin, Latricières-Chambertin, Mazis-Chambertin and Ruchottes-Chambertin) which can produce some of Burgundy's greatest and most intense red wine. Its rough hewn fruit, seeming to war with fragrant perfumes for its first few years, creates remarkable flavours as the wine ages. Chambertin and Chambertin-Clos-de-Bèze are the greatest vineyard sites, but overproduction is a recurrent problem. Even so, the best examples are wonderful and they can age for decades. Best producers: Bachelet★★, Damoy★, DROUHIN, FAIVELEY★★★, Mugneret★, Pernot-Fourrier★★, Perrin-Rossin★★, Perrot-Minot★★★, Ponsot★, Rebourseau★, Rémy★, Rossignol-Trapet★★★, Roty★, Roumier★, Rousseau★★, Taupenot★, Tortochot★. Best years: 1990 89 88 87 85 83 80 78 76.

CHAMBERTIN-CLOS-DE-BÈZE AC   See Chambertin AC.
CHAMBOLLE-MUSIGNY AC *Côte de Nuits, Burgundy, France*   AC with the potential to produce the most fragrant, perfumed red Burgundy, but many of the wines suffer from over-cropping and over-sugaring. Recent signs that more young producers are now bottling their own wines are very encouraging. Best producers: Amiot★, Barthod-Noëllat★★, DROUHIN, DUJAC, GRIVOT, Hudelot-Noëllat★★, JADOT, LEROY, Marchand★★, Mugnier★, Roumier★, Serveau★, de Vogüé★. Best years: 1990 89 88 85 83.

CHAMPAGNE AC

Champagne, France

The Champagne region produces the most celebrated sparkling wines in the world. East of Paris, it is the most northerly AC in France – a place where grapes struggle to ripen fully. Champagne is divided into five distinct areas – the best are the Montagne de Reims where Pinot Noir performs brilliantly, and the Chardonnay-dominated Côte des Blancs south of Épernay. If you buy a bottle of Coteaux Champenois, still wine from the area, you can see why they decided to make bubbly instead; it tastes mean and tart, but is transformed by the Champagne method to some of the most complex wines of all.

That's the theory anyway, and for 150 years or so the Champenois have suavely persuaded us that their product is second to none. It can be too, except when it is released too young or sweetened to make up for a lack of richness. A combination of high prices and competition from other sparkling wines has produced a glut of Champagne. But as Champagne expertise begins to turn out exciting sparklers in California, Australia and New Zealand, the Champagne producers must re-focus on quality or lose much of their market for good.

The Champagne trade is dominated by large companies or houses, called *négociants-manipulants*, recognized by the letters NM on the label. The *récoltants-manipulants* (recognized by the letters RM) are growers who make their own wine.

STYLES OF CHAMPAGNE

Non-vintage Most Champagne is a blend of two or more vintages. Quality varies enormously, depending on who has made the wine and how long it has been aged. Most Champagne is sold as Brut, which is a dry, but not bone-dry style.

Vintage Champagne made with grapes from a single vintage. As a rule, it is only made in the best years.

Blanc de Blancs Champagne made solely from Chardonnay.

Blanc de Noirs Champagne made entirely from black grapes, either Pinor Noir, Pinot Meunier, or a combination of the two.

Rosé Pink Champagne, made either from black grapes or (more usually) by mixing a little still red wine into white Champagne.

Crémant Champagne at a lower pressure than normal.

De luxe cuvée In theory the finest Champagne and certainly always the most expensive, residing in the fanciest bottles.

See also BILLECART-SALMON, BOLLINGER, BRUT, CHAMPAGNE ROSE, DEUTZ, GRANDE MARQUE, ALFRED GRATIEN, CHARLES HEIDSIECK, KRUG, LANSON, LAURENT-PERRIER, METHODE CHAMPENOISE, MOET & CHANDON, POL ROGER, LOUIS ROEDERER, RUINART, TAITTINGER, VEUVE CLICQUOT.

BEST YEARS

1990 89 88 85 85 83 82 79

BEST PRODUCERS

Houses Billecart-Salmon, Bollinger, Charbaut, Deutz, Alfred Gratien, Charles Heidsieck, Henriot, Jacquesson, Krug, Lanson, Laurent-Perrier, Moët & Chandon, Joseph Perrier, Louis Roederer, Pol Roger, Pommery, Ruinart, Salon, Taittinger, Veuve Clicquot.

Growers Arnould, Bauser, Beerens, Billiot, Cattier, Clouet, Dufour, Gimmonet, Gremillet, Launois, Mandois.

De luxe cuvées Clos de Mesnil (Krug), Comtes de Champagne (Taittinger), Cristal (Louis Roederer), Cuvée Sir Winston Churchill (Pol Roger), Dom Pérignon (Möet & Chandon), Dom Ruinart (Ruinart), Grand Siècle (Laurent- Perrier), RD (Bollinger).

CHAMPAGNE METHOD See Méthode champenoise.

CHAMPAGNE ROSÉ AC *Champagne, France* Good pink CHAM-
PAGNE has a delicious fragrance of cherries and raspberries to go
with the fizz. The top wines can age well, but most pink
Champagne should be drunk on release. The present vogue is for
very dry styles with little difference in flavour from ordinary
white Champagne. Best producers: BILLECART-SALMON★★,
Charbaut, KRUG★, LANSON★, LAURENT-PERRIER★★, MOET &
CHANDON★★, Pommery, ROEDERER★, TAITTINGER (Comtes de
Champagne★). Best years: 1986 85 83 82. See also page 84.

CHAPELLE-CHAMBERTIN AC See Chambertin AC.

M CHAPOUTIER *Rhône Valley, France* There have been enormous
improvements at this traditional company since Michel
Chapoutier took over the wine-making in 1988. They make
wines from all over the Rhône Valley, but specialize in the
northern Rhône. Their HERMITAGE La Sizeranne ★★, CROZES-
HERMITAGE★ and COTE-ROTIE ★★ are all on top form these days.
Best years: 1990 89 88.

CHARDONNAY See page 88.

CHARENTAIS, VIN DE PAYS DES *France* Wines from the Cognac
area in western France. Ugni Blanc-based whites predominate
and can be good if consumed young. There are also increasing
amounts of Chardonnay and Sauvignon Blanc. The reds (from
Bordeaux varieties) are good value too if you like a grassy tang
to your wine. Best producer: Mellinger.

CHARMES-CHAMBERTIN AC See Chambertin AC.

CHARTA A German organization with a distinctive symbol (repre-
senting a twin light Romanesque window) founded in 1984 in
order to protect the image of the best Rheingau Rieslings. The
accent is on dry Trocken wines which are thought to go well
with food but the problem often is that so much time is spent
worrying about how the food will be affected everyone has forgotten about putting enough flavour in the wine.

CHARTRON & TRÉBUCHET *Puligny-Montrachet, Côte de Beaune,
Burgundy, France* Small, quality merchant specializing in
white wines from the Côte de Beaune and the Côte Chalonnaise.
The wines tend to be light and elegant, with the exception of
the rich, unctuous CORTON-CHARLEMAGNE ★★, and BATARD-
MONTRACHET ★★, and good ST-AUBIN Premier Cru★.

CHASSAGNE-MONTRACHET AC *Côte de Beaune, Burgundy,
France* More than half the wine produced in Chassagne-
Montrachet is red, but its reputation has always been for whites.
Some of Burgundy's greatest white wine vineyards (part of Le
MONTRACHET and BATARD-MONTRACHET and all of Criots-Bâtard-
Montrachet) are within the village boundary. The white
Chassagne Premiers Crus are not as well-known, but can offer
big, nutty, toasty wines, especially if aged for 4–8 years.
Ordinary white Chassagne-Montrachet is usually a thoroughly

enjoyable high-quality Burgundy. Red Chassagne is always a little earthy, peppery and plummy and can be a bit of an acquired taste, even though the price is not too frightening. The top wines can age for up to a decade. Look out for the following Premiers Crus: Clos de la Boudriotte, Clos St-Jean and Clos de la Chapelle. Best producers: (whites) Bachelet-Ramonet★, Blain-Gagnard★★, COLIN★, Duc de Magenta★, Fontaine-Gagnard★, J-N GAGNARD★★, Lamy★, Albert Morey★★, RAMONET★★★; (reds) Bachelet, CARILLON★, Clerget★, Gagnard-Delagrange★, Albert Morey★, RAMONET. Best years: (whites) 1990 89 88 87 86 85 83 82; (reds) 1990 89 88 85 83 82.

CH. CHASSE-SPLEEN ★★ *Moulis AC, Cru Bourgeois, Haut-Médoc, Bordeaux, France*   Chasse-Spleen is not a Classed Growth – but you'd never know it, either from the marvellously ripe, contrated taste of the wines, or from the tremendous reputation the property built during the 1980s by the quality obsession of the proprietor, Bernadette Villars. Second wine: L'Ermitage de Chasse-Spleen. Best years: 1990 89 88 87 86 83 82.

CHASSELAS   In most of the world, Chasselas is considered a table grape. Only in Alsace, Baden (where it is called Gutedel) and Switzerland (called Dorin, Perlan or Fendant) is it thought to make a decent wine. The best Swiss Chasselas has a slight prickle and is a perfect, refreshing, light-hearted drink.

CHÂTEAU   French for a castle, used all over the world to describe a wide variety of wine estates. Some, such as Château MARGAUX, are truly palatial. In the A–Z all French châteaux are listed under their individual names.

CHÂTEAU CARRAS *Macedonia, Greece*   The reds from this no-expense-spared winery are better than the whites, but even so the Greek sun makes itself felt in dryish flavours of coffee and prunes. After a bright start with help from Bordeaux's Professor Peynaud, quality became very erratic, but seems to be on the up again.

CHÂTEAU-CHALON AC *Jura, France*   This is the most prized – and pricy – VIN JAUNE, Jura's great speciality. It is difficult to find, even in the region itself, but is worth tracking down. Best producers: Bourdy★, Courbet★, Macle, Perron.

CHÂTEAU-GRILLET AC ★★★ *Rhône Valley, France*   A single estate south of Vienne renowned as one of the smallest ACs in France. This rare, exciting Rhône white is made from the Viognier grape and has a magic reek of orchard fruit and harvest bloom when young, although it will age very well. It is *very* expensive – but then there's very little of it. Best years: 1990 88 86 85 83.

CHATEAU MONTELENA *Napa Valley, California, USA*   Two very successful Chardonnays, a taut but well-balanced Napa wine and a lusher, more exotic Alexander Valley★ example. The Cabernet Sauvignon ★★ is a consistently outstanding wine.

CHARDONNAY

I'm always getting asked, 'When will the world tire of Chardonnay?' And I reply 'Not in my lifetime'. Wine critics may pine for something else to write about, wine experts may decide they want to explore the flavours available from other grapes, but for the vast majority of wine drinkers the Chardonnay revolution has only just begun, and to many people good dry white wine simply equals Chardonnay. And that's that. Chardonnay is still in very short supply round the world – less than half of a percent of the total vineyard acreage is so far growing the variety – yet it is without question the world's most popular white grape.

WINE STYLES

France Although a relatively neutral variety if left alone (this is what makes it so suitable as a base wine for top-quality Champagne-method sparkling wine), it can ripen in almost any conditions, with a subtle gradation of flavours going from the sharp apple core greenness of Chardonnay grown in Champagne or the Loire, through the exciting, bone-dry yet succulent flavours of white Burgundy, to a round, perfumed flavour in Languedoc-Roussillon.

Other regions Italy produces Chardonnay bone dry and lean as well as fat, spicy and lush. Spain does much the same. South Africa is only just getting to grips with the variety, but California and Australia virtually created their reputations on great viscous, almost syrupy, tropical fruits and spice-flavoured Chardonnays. They've both toned down the flavours now, though New Zealand is now producing some wonderfully exotic wine, and Chile and Argentina have found it easy to grow and are rapidly learning how to make fine wine from it too. Add Germany, Canada and New York State and you'll see it can perform almost anywhere.

Using oak The reason for all these different flavours lies in Chardonnay's wonderful susceptibility to the winemaker's aspirations and skills. And the most important manipulation is the use of the oak barrel for fermenting and aging the wine. Chardonnay is the grape of the great white Burgundies and these are fermented and matured in oak (not necessarily new oak) but the effect is to give a marvellous round, nutty richness to a wine that is yet savoury and dry.

The New World winemakers sought to emulate the great Burgundies, thus planting Chardonnay and employing thousands of oak barrels – mostly new – and their success, and the enthusiasm with which wine drinkers embraced the wine have caused winemakers everywhere else to see Chardonnay as the perfect variety – easy to grow, easy to turn into wine and easy to sell to an adoring public.

BEST PRODUCERS

France
Chablis la Chablisienne, Dauvissat, Defaix, Droin, Fèvre, Michel, Raveneau; *Côte d'Or* Carillon, Clerc, Coche-Dury, Colin, Dubreuil-Fontaine, Lafon, Laguiche, Dom. Leflaive, Matrot, Pierre Morey, Ramonet, Sauzet; *Pouilly-Fuissé* Guffens-Heynens, Ferret, Ch. Fuissé, Noblet.

Other European Chardonnays
Italy Caparzo, Gaja, Lageder (Portico dei Leoni).

Portugal Cova da Ursa.

Spain Torres (Milmanda).

New World Chardonnays
Australia Dalwhinnie, Lakes Folly, Leeuwin Estate, Lindemans Padthaway, Mountadam, Nicholson River, Petaluma, Pipers Brook, Rosemount, Yarra Yering.

New Zealand Kumeu River, Martinborough, Te Mata Elston, Waipara Springs.

USA Calera, Chalone, Edna Valley, Flora Springs, Franciscan (Cuvée Sauvage), Kistler, Matanzas Creek, Mondavi (Reserve), Newton.

CHÂTEAU MUSAR *Ghazir, Lebanon* Founded by Gaston Hochar in the 1930s and now run by his Bordeaux-trained son Serge. Musar is famous for having made wine every year bar two (1976 and 84) throughout the chaos of Lebanon's civil war. From an unlikely blend of Cabernet Sauvignon, Cinsaut and Syrah, comes a wine of real if wildly exotic class – full, with lush, sweet, spicy fruit and deceptively good aging potential. Hochar himself says that red Musar★★ 'should be drunk at 15 years'. Also Musar Blanc, a new blend of 90% Chardonnay and 10% Sauvignon Blanc. Best years: (reds) 1983 81 77 72 70 69 64.

CHATEAU ST JEAN *Sonoma, California, USA* The winery lives on the reputation of its rich, thickly-textured Chardonnays, including the well-known Robert Young Vineyards Chardonnay★. But there are changes underway with the release early in 1992 of a Reserve Cabernet Sauvignon 1988★ and a lighter-style Sonoma Valley Chardonnay. Best years: 1991 90 88.

CHATEAU STE MICHELLE *Washington State, USA* A pioneering winery with an enormous range of wines, including several vineyard-designated Chardonnays and Cabernet Sauvignons of good quality, especially the Cold Creek Vineyard★ wines. Makes good Riesling, both dry and sweet, and increasingly interesting wines from Sémillon, Sauvignon or a blend of both. Columbia Crest is a budget operation producing mostly good-value wines, and a particularly fine Merlot ★.

CHATEAU TAHBILK *Goulburn Valley, Victoria, Australia* Wonderfully old-fashioned family company making traditionally big, gumleafy/minty reds, matured only in old wood. Regional speciality Marsanne ★ is perfumed and attractive. Other whites tend to lack finesse, but Shiraz ★ and Cabernet ★★ are full of character, even if they need years of cellaring. Best years: (reds) 1988 86 81 79 78 76 71 64 62.

CHÂTEAUMEILLANT VDQS *Loire Valley, France* An obscure VDQS in central France miles away from any decent vineyards. BEAUJOLAIS' Gamay is the chief grape but the drab, rooty flavours of the reds and rosés leaves me pining for a glass of real Beaujolais.

CHÂTEAUNEUF-DU-PAPE AC *Rhône Valley, France* A large vineyard area between Orange and Avignon that used to be one of the most abused of all wine names. Now, much Châteauneuf comes from single estates, the wine is no longer cheap and it deservedly ranks as one of France's top wines. There are two styles of red: a light, deliciously, juicy style ready to drink young but which can age 5 years or more; and the more traditional style, dark and rich, which may need aging for 5 years or more and can last for 20. Always get an estate wine, and these are distinguished by the papal coat of arms embossed on the neck of the bottle. Only 3% of Châteauneuf is white. Made mainly from Grenache Blanc and Clairette, these wines can be surprisingly good. They are best drunk young, at 1–2 years, although the top wines will age for 5 years or more. Best producers: (traditional reds) BEAUCASTEL★★★, Bosquet des Papes★, Caboche, Chante-Cigale★, Chante-Perdrix★, CLOS DES PAPES★★★, FONT DE MICHELLE★★, Fortia★, GRAND TINEL★★, RAYAS★★★, VIEUX TELEGRAPHE★★; (modern, fruitier reds) Brunel★, Clos du Mont Olivet★, Font du Loup★★, Nalys★, Quiot★, Sabon; (whites) BEAUCASTEL★★, FONT DE MICHELLE★★, Mont Redon, la Nerthe★, VIEUX TELEGRAPHE★. Best years (reds): 1990 89 88 86 85 83 81 78.

GÉRARD CHAVE *Rhône Valley, France* Gérard Chave has deservedly achieved superstar status in recent years. His red HERMITAGE★★★ is one of the world's great wines, a thick, complex expression of the Syrah grape at its best, requiring 10 years in bottle to open out. His wonderful white Hermitage★★★ sometimes even outlasts the reds as it quietly moves towards its creamy, nutty zenith. Also a small amount of excellent red ST-JOSEPH★★. Very expensive, but worth the money. Best years: (reds) 1990 89 88 86 85 83 82 81 79 78; (whites) 1990 89 88 82.

CHÉNAS AC *Beaujolais, Burgundy, France* This is the smallest of the Beaujolais Crus and its wines, usually quite tough when young, benefit enormously from 2 or more years' aging and can often last a decade. Best producers: Champagnon★, de Chénas, Lapierre, Perrachon, Robin★. Best years: 1991 90 89 85.

CHENIN BLANC One of the most underrated great white wine grapes in the world. Found mainly in the Loire Valley where it is also called Pineau de la Loire, it is responsible for the great sweet wines of QUARTS DE CHAUME and BONNEZEAUX as well as being the grape for VOUVRAY, sweet or dry, and much other Anjou white, including being the main grape for the Loire sparkling wines. South Africa has long used Chenin (also known as Steen) for easy-drinking, dryish whites, but while California and Australia employ it as a useful blender, New Zealand has produced the best single-varietal examples.

CH. CHEVAL BLANC ★★★ *St-Émilion Grand Cru AC, 1er Grand Cru Classé, Bordeaux, France* The leading ST-EMILION estate and likely to remain so for the foreseeable future. Right on the border with POMEROL, it seems to share some of Pomerol's sturdy richness, but with an extra spice and fruit that is impressively, recognizably unique. Best years: 1990 89 88 86 85 83 82 81.

CHEVALIER-MONTRACHET AC See Montrachet AC.

CHEVERNY VDQS *Loire Valley, France* A little-known area south of Blois with a mixed bag of mainly fairly acidic wines. The local speciality is the white Romorantin grape which is used to make a harsh, bone-dry wine, but the best whites are from Chardonnay. There are pleasant Sauvignon, Pinot Noir and Gamay wines too and a bracing Champagne-method fizz. Best producers: Cazin, Cheverny co-op, Gendrier, Gueritte, Tessier.

91

CHIANTI DOCG

Tuscany, Italy

Chianti is the most famous of all Italian wines, but there are many Chianti styles, depending on what grapes are used, where they are grown, and by which producer. Chianti can be a light, fresh, easy-drinking red wine, but with a characteristic hint of bitterness, like a slightly aggressive Beaujolais in style, or it can be an intense, structured yet sleek and refined wine in the same league as the best Bordeaux properties – but again with a twist of bitterness and austerity at its core.

Sangiovese is the main Chianti grape, but regulations require blending with other grapes of which the soft Canaiolo is the most common, but Merlot, Syrah and Cabernet are also used. Theoretically some white grapes should also be included but many leading producers refuse to comply.

CHIANTI WINE ZONES

The Chianti vineyards are scattered over much of central Tuscany. The name Chianti derives from the hilly, wooded zone north of Siena, in the communes of Radda, Gaiole and Castellina in what is today Chianti Classico. During the Middle Ages the name became so popular that in 1716 the Grand Duke of Tuscany issued an edict defining the area in which Chianti could be produced – one of the first examples of legal delimitation of a wine-producing area. In 1932 a law was promulgated defining 7 different zones for Chianti, and the modern DOC and DOCG regulations have reinforced these definitions.

Classico The original (if slightly enlarged) zone from the hills between Florence and Siena. Styles vary, though the wines equal those from Rufina as the best of Chianti.

Colli Aretini The hills of Arezzo produce soft, medium-bodied wines for easy drinking.

Colli Fiorentini A large zone, curving around the western, northern and eastern borders of Classico. Styles range from light and quaffable to some of the best Riservas produced.

Colli Senesi Covers a broad tract of hills south of Siena, generally giving a fairly chunky style of wine.

Colline Pisane Soft light wines from the hills of Pisa.

Montalbano Lighter, easy-drinking wines from the hills west of Florence. Best wines tend to claim DOC Carmignano.

Rufina The smallest zone, situated north-east of Florence. Produces some of the best and longest-lived of all Chiantis.

See also ANTINORI, CASTELL'IN VILLA, CASTELLO DEI RAMPOLLA, CASTELLO DI VOLPAIA, FELSINA BERARDENGA, FRESCOBALDI, ISOLE E OLENA, MONTE VERTINE, RIECINE, RUFFINO.

BEST PRODUCERS

Chianti Classico Antinori, Castellare, Castell'in Villa, Castello dei Rampolla, Castello di Ama, Castello di Cacchiano, Castello di Fonterutoli, Castello della Paneretta, Castello di Volpaia, Felsina Berardenga, Fontodi, Isole e Olena, Le Masse di San Leolino, Monsanto, Monte Vertine, Peppoli, Podere Il Palazzino, Riecine, Ruffino (Riserva Ducale), San Felice, Vecchie Terre di Montefili, Vignamaggio.

Colli Fiorentini Castello di Poppiano, Fattoria la Querce, Fattoria di Sammontana, Fattoria Lugignano, Fattoria Montellori, Pasolini dall'Onda, San Vito in Flor di Selva.

Colli Senesi Amorosa, Castello di Farnetella, Castello di Monteriggioni, Pacina, Pietraserena.

Montalbano Artimino, Capezzana.

Rufina Bossi, Castello di Nipozzano, Grignano, Selva-piana, Travignoli, Villa di Vetrice.

CHIARETTO Italian for a rosé wine, usually lighter than rosato. Used mainly in BARDOLINO and RIVIERA DEL GARDA BRESCIANO.

CHINON AC *Loire Valley, France*   The best red wine of the Loire valley, made mainly from Cabernet Franc. The wine is full of raspberry fruit and fresh summer earth when young, yet can improve for 20 years and more to a fragrant, ethereal shadow of the great châteaux of the MEDOC. It's always worth buying a single-estate wine. Best producers: Baudry★, COULY-DUTHEIL★★, Gouron★, JOGUET★★, Jean-Maurice Raffault★★, Olga Raffault★, Dom.de la Roncée★. Best years: 1990 89 88 85 83 82 78 76 64.

CHIROUBLES AC *Beaujolais, Burgundy, France*   The lightest, most delicately fragrant of the BEAUJOLAIS Crus but expensive for what is often only a marginally superior BEAUJOLAIS-VILLAGES. Best producers: Charvet, de la Grosse Pierre, DUBOEUF, Javernand, Passot. Best years: 1991 90 89.

CHIVITE *Navarra DO, Navarra, Spain*   Longtime leader in wine exports from NAVARRA, owned and run by the Chivite family. The wine is reliable to very good. They make some of Spain's best rosés, plus the red 125 Aniversario 1985 ★ .

CHOREY-LÈS-BEAUNE AC *Côte de Beaune, Burgundy, France*   One of those tiny, forgotten villages that make good if not great Burgundy at prices most of us can still afford and with some committed producers too. The wines can age for 5–8 years. Best producers: DROUHIN, GERMAIN★, Goud de Beaupuis, TOLLOT-BEAUT★. Best years: 1990 89 88 85 83 82.

CHURCHILL GRAHAM *Port DOC, Douro, Portugal*   When Johnny and Caroline Graham started Churchill (her maiden name) Graham in 1981, it was the first new port shipper for 50 years. The wines are good, particularly the Churchill Vintage Character ★ and Crusted ★ ports.

CINQUETERRE DOC *Liguria, Italy*   From beautiful hills that rise precipitously above the sea at La Spezia this wine sells to the tourists, no matter what the quality. At its best, it is dry and crisp, and provides a decent glass to go with local fish. The sweet white, called Sciacchetrà and made from Passito grapes, can be excellent. Best producers: Cappellini, Cinqueterre co-op.

CINSAUT Found mainly in the southern Rhône, Provence and the Midi of France. It gives a light-coloured wine even at the best of times, with a fresh, but rather fleeting, neutral fruit. It is popular as a blender in South Africa and in Lebanon's Château MUSAR.

CIRÒ DOC *Calabria, Italy*   The fact that this was the wine offered to champions in the ancient Olympics still seems a more potent reason to buy it than the current quality of much Cirò. The DOC covers a dry white from the Greco grape, a rare dry rosé and an occasionally decent, full-bodied red from the Gaglioppo grape. Best producers: Caparra, Ippolito, Librandi.

CH. CISSAC ★ *Haut-Médoc AC, Cru Bourgeois, Bordeaux, France*
High-quality wines made by proudly traditional methods: old
vines, lots of wood and meticulous selection for the final blend.
The wines are deeply coloured and very slow to mature. Best
years: 1990 89 88 86 85 83 82 78.

BRUNO CLAIR *Marsannay, Côte de Nuits, Burgundy, France*
A young, up-and-coming winemaker based in the comparatively
unfashionable village of MARSANNAY, Bruno Clair produces a large
range of excellent wines from a broad span of vineyards there as
well as in FIXIN, GEVREY-CHAMBERTIN, GIVRY, SAVIGNY and VOSNE-
ROMANEE. Most of his wine is red, but there is a small amount of
white ★ and a delicious Marsannay rosé ★. Top wines are his
CHAMBERTIN Clos de Bèze ★★ and vineyard-designated Marsannay
reds ★. Best years: 1990 89 88 87 85.

CLAIRETTE DE DIE TRADITION AC *Rhône Valley, France*   One of
the undeservedly forgotten sparkling wines of France. Sometimes
the wine is made wholly from Clairette grapes and can be a little
dull, but the 'Tradition'★ style is 50% Muscat and the result is
a dry or off-dry wine with a lovely creamy bubble and an
orchard-fresh fragrance of ripe grapes and springtime flowers.
The Champagne method may be used, but the *méthode Dioise*
preserves the Muscat scent far better. By this method the bottle
re-fermentation is stopped before all the sugar is converted to
carbon dioxide and alcohol and the wine is filtered and re-
bottled under pressure. Drink young. Best producers: Clairette de
Die co-op★; also Achard-Vincent★, Andrieux, Magord, Raspail★.

A CLAPE *Cornas, Rhône Valley, France*   The leading estate in
CORNAS. Clape's wines ★★★ are consistently among the best in
the Rhône – dense, tannic and full of rich, roasted fruit. Clape
also makes brilliant COTES DU RHONE, both red ★★ and white ★.
Best years: 1990 89 88 86 85 82.

LA CLAPE *Coteaux du Languedoc AC, Languedoc, France*   The
mountain of La Clape rears unexpectedly from the flat coastal
fields south-east of Narbonne. The vineyards here are a Cru
within the COTEAUX DU LANGUEDOC AC and produce some of the
best Aude wines. There are excellent whites from Bourboulenc
and Clairette plus good reds and rosés, mainly from the
Carignan. Best drunk young although the whites can age. Best
producers: Boscary, Hue, Pech-Redon★, de St-Exupéry, Ségura.

CLARE VALLEY *South Australia*   Upland valley north of Adelaide
with a deceptively moderate climate, able to grow fine, aromatic
Riesling, marvellously textured Sémillon and rich, robust Shiraz
and Cabernet-based reds. Best producers: (whites) ADAMS, BARRY,
BLASS (Gold Label), Grosset, KNAPPSTEIN, Mitchell, PETALUMA, Pike;
(reds) ADAMS, BARRY, Mitchell.

CLARET English term for red Bordeaux wines, taken from the
French word *clairet*, which was traditionally used to describe a
lighter style of red Bordeaux.

CH. CLARKE ★ *Listrac, Cru Bourgeois, Haut-Médoc, Bordeaux,* *France* Part of the Rothschild empire, this property had millions spent on it during the late 1970s and the wines are now reaping the benefit. They have an attractive blackcurrant fruit and a warm oaky richness. Saddled with a name like Clarke, how could they fail to be seductive? Second wine: Ch. Malmaison. Best years: 1990 89 88 86 85 83.

CLERICO *Piedmont, Italy* Domenico Clerico is one of the best of the younger generation of BAROLO producers. He produces an impressive Barolo★★ and one of the best Barberas★★, both of which have a wonderful balance of fresh fruit, acidity and tannin. Best years: 1990 88 85.

CLIMAT French term used, mainly in Burgundy, to describe an individual vineyard which is not a Grand or Premier Cru.

CH. CLIMENS ★★★ *Barsac AC, 1er Cru Classé, Bordeaux, France* The leading estate in BARSAC with a deserved reputation for rich, elegant wines with a light, lemony acidity that keeps them fresh. Easy to drink at 5 years, a good vintage will be richer and more satisfying after 10–15 years. Second wine: Les Cèdres (and delicious too). Best years: 1990 89 88 86 83 81 80 76 75.

CLOS French for a walled vineyard – as in Burgundy's CLOS DE VOUGEOT. Also commonly incorporated into the names of estates (CLOS DES PAPES), regardless of whether they are walled or not.

CLOS DU BOIS *Sonoma, California, USA* Winery that generally shows off the gentle, fruit-dominated flavours of Sonoma Chardonnay, Merlot and Cabernet. Top vineyard selections can be exciting, especially Calcaire Chardonnay★, rich, strong Briarcrest Cabernet Sauvignon★, and Marlstone★, a red Bordeaux blend. Best years: 1990 88 87 86.

CLOS DES PAPES *Châteauneuf-du-Pape AC, Rhône Valley, France* Paul Avril is one of the outstanding CHATEAUNEUF-DU-PAPE producers. His reds★★★ have an unusually high proportion of Mourvèdre, which explains their longevity but enough Grenache to be approachable in their youth and provide the thrilling initial blast of fruit. The whites★★ take on the nutty character of aged Burgundy after a decade in bottle. Best years: 1990 89 88 86 85 82 79 66.

CLOS RENÉ ★ *Pomerol AC, Bordeaux, France* This is wonderfully plummy, juicy, fleshy wine from the less fashionable western side of the POMEROL AC. You can drink Clos René young, but it also ages well for at least 10 years. Sometimes sold under the label Moulinet-Lasserre. Best years: 1990 89 88 85 83 82 81.

CLOS DE LA ROCHE AC *Grand Cru, Côte de Nuits, Burgundy,* *France* The best and biggest of the five MOREY ST-DENIS Grands Crus. It has a lovely, bright, red-fruits flavour when young, which should get richly chocolaty or gamy as it ages. Best producers: Castagnier-Vadey★★★, DUJAC★★, Perrot-Minot★★★, Ponsot★★, Rousseau★★. Best years: 1990 89 88 85 83 82 78.

CLOS DE TART AC ★★ *Grand Cru, Côte de Nuits, Burgundy, France*
Grand Cru in the village of MOREY ST-DENIS, and entirely owned
by one firm – the Burgundy merchant Mommessin. The wine,
light and dry at first, can develop a delicious savoury richness as
it ages. Best years: 1990 89 88 85 83 82.

CLOS DU VAL *Napa Valley, California, USA* A sometimes overlooked
Napa producer of elegant, focused Cabernet Sauvignon★★,
Chardonnay★, Merlot, Pinot Noir and Zinfandel★. The wines are
beautifully balanced and can age more interestingly than many
other Napa wines. Best years: 1990 88 87 86 85 84.

CLOS DE VOUGEOT AC *Grand Cru, Côte de Nuits, Burgundy, France*
Founded by Cistercian monks in the 14th century this large
vineyard is now divided among 80 owners as a result of the
French laws of inheritance. This multiplicity of ownership has
turned Clos de Vougeot into one of the most unreliable Grand
Cru Burgundies. However, when it is good it is wonderfully
fleshy wine turning dark and exotic with age. Best producers:
Arnoux★, Confuron★, DROUHIN, GRIVOT★★, Jean Gros★★, JAYER,
Lamarche★★, LEROY★★, MEO-CAMUZET★★★, Rebourseau★. Best
years: 1990 89 88 85 83 80 78.

CLOUDY BAY *Marlborough, South Island, New Zealand* New
Zealand's most successful winery, Cloudy Bay achieved instant
cult status with the first release of the zesty, herbaceous
Sauvignon Blanc ★★★ in 1985. Now controlled by the
Champagne house VEUVE CLICQUOT, Cloudy Bay also makes stylish
Chardonnay ★★, Cabernet-Merlot ★, and a high-quality
Champagne-method sparkling wine★. Best years: 1991 90 89.

J F COCHE-DURY *Meursault, Côte de Beaune, Burgundy, France*
Jean-François Coche-Dury is a modest superstar, quietly turning
out some of the finest wines on the Côte de Beaune. His best
wines are his CORTON-CHARLEMAGNE ★★★ and MEURSAULT
Perrières ★★★, but everything he makes is excellent, even his
BOURGOGNE Blanc ★★. His red wines ★★, from VOLNAY and AUXEY-
DURESSES, tend to be slightly cheaper than the whites and should
be drunk younger, too. Best years: 1990 89 88 86 85.

COCKBURN *Port DOC, Douro, Portugal* Best known for its Special
Reserve ruby, Cockburns has much more than that to offer.
Cockburns vintage ★★ is stylishly cedary and now very much
back on form, and the aged tawnies ★★ are creamy and nutty.
Best years: (vintage ports) 1985 83 70 67 63.

CODORNÍU *Cava DO, Catalonia, Spain* The biggest Champagne-
method sparkling wine company in the world. Codorníu's
Chardonnay fizz★ is especially good but all their sparklers are
better than the CAVA average. The spectacular Art Nouveau
buildings of the winery and 30km (19 miles) of underground
cellars in San Sadurní de Noya are really worth a visit. Codorníu
also own the top-quality wine estate of RAIMAT in Costers del
Segre and the still wine company of Masía Bach in the PENEDES.

COLARES DOC *Oeste, Portugal*   Ramisco vines are planted on sand-dunes and made into tooth-curdlingly tannic wines. They're *said* to soften with age, but in fact generally just wither away. A new vineyard project by Carvalho, Ribeiro & Ferreira may be the last hope for this archaic DOC.

COLDSTREAM HILLS *Yarra Valley, Victoria, Australia*   Lawyer/wine writer James Halliday's high profile project, set in one of the loveliest corners of the Yarra Valley, is expanding quickly as more vineyards come into full production. Pinot Noir ★★ is one of Australia's best: sappy and smoky with a fragrant cherry fruit. Chardonnay ★★ has subtlety and delicacy but real depth as well. Reserve★★ labels of both are outstanding as are the Steel's Range second wines. Best years: 1991 90 88.

COLHEITA See Port.

MARC COLIN *St-Aubin, Côte de Beaune, Burgundy, France*   An excellent, but often underrated domaine specializing in reds and whites from CHASSAGNE-MONTRACHET★ and ST-AUBIN★. The St-Aubin Premiers Crus ★★ are fine value, but Colin's most exquisite wine is his tiny production of Le MONTRACHET ★★★. Best years: 1990 89 88 86 85 83.

COLLARDS *Henderson, Auckland, New Zealand*   A small family winery that produces some of the country's finest white wines including Hawkes Bay Chardonnay ★★, Rothesay Chardonnay ★★ and Marlborough Chardonnay ★. Sauvignon ★ is also delicious. Collards Dry Chenin Blanc ★ is the best example of its type in the country. Best years: 1991 90 89.

COLLI ALBANI DOC *Lazio, Italy*   Wine zone around Lake Albano south of Rome offering a cheaper, usually decent alternative to neighbouring FRASCATI. Best producer: Colli Albani co-op.

COLLI BERICI DOC *Veneto, Italy*   Based in the hills south of Vicenza, this DOC covers 7 varietals, best of which are dry whites from Garganega and Tocai, and reds from Cabernet. Best producers: Ca' Bruzzo, Costozza, Villa dal Ferro.

COLLI BOLOGNESI DOC *Emilia, Italy*   Wine zone in the Apennine foothills near Bologna. Traditionally slightly sweet and frothing, today, some concessions have been made to international taste and the best wine is now the Cabernet from Terre Rosse. Riesling Italico and Pignoletto, two dry whites, can be decent thirst quenchers. Best producer: Terre Rosse★.

COLLI ORIENTALI DEL FRIULI DOC *Friuli-Venezia Giulia, Italy*   North-east Italian DOC, covering 20 different types of wine. Best known for its sweet whites from the Ramandolo sub-zone and the overrated Picolit, but it is the reds, from the indigenous Refosco as well as imports like Cabernet and dry whites, from Tocai, Ribolla, Pinot Bianco and Malvasia Istriana, that show how exciting the wines can be. Prices are high. Best producers: Abbazia di Rosazzo★, Dorigo★, Dri★★, Livio Felluga★, Ronco del Gnemiz★, Volpe Pasini★. Collavini is cheaper and reliable.

COLLI PIACENTINI DOC *Emilia, Italy*   The hills south of Piacenza are home to some of Emilia's best wines. The DOC covers 11 different types of wine, the best of which are the red Gutturnio (an appealing blend of Barbera and Bonarda) and the medium-sweet white Malvasia. Best producers: Fugazza★, La Stoppa, Vigevani.

COLLINES RHODANIENNES, VIN DE PAYS DES *Rhône Valley, France*   A Vin de Pays for wines from between Vienne and Valence. The best wines are varietal Gamay and Syrah, although there are some good juicy Merlots, too. Best producers: ST-DESIRAT-CHAMPAGNE CO-op★, Les Vignerons Ardèchois.

COLLIO DOC *Friuli-Venezia Giulia, Italy*   80% of the Collio Goriziano DOC is situated in Yugoslavia, but the best part, the growers will tell you, is the 20% that remains in Italy. These hills are the home of some of Italy's best and most expensive dry white wines. This zone has often been at the crossroads of history and the Cabernet, Pinot Grigio, Sauvignon and Pinot Bianco attest to Napoleon's influence, while the Riesling and Traminer are reminders of the days when this area was part of the Austro-Hungarian Empire. Best producers: Borgo del Tiglio★, Ca' Ronesca★, Enofriulia★, Marco Felluga★, Gradnik★, Gravner★★, JERMANN★, PUIATTI★★, SCHIOPETTO★★, Venica★, Villa Russiz★.

COLLIOURE AC *Roussillon, France*   This tiny fishing port tucked away in the Pyrenean foothills only a few miles from the Spanish border is also an AC and makes throat-warming red wine which is capable of aging for a decade but marvellously aggressive when young. Best producers: Dom. de Baillaury★, Celliers des Comtes, Cellier des Templiers, Mas Blanc, la Rectorie★, Dom. la Tour Vieille. Best years: 1990 89 88 86 85.

COLOMBARD   In France, Colombard has traditionally been distilled to make Armagnac and Cognac, but is now emerging as a table wine grape in its own right, notably as a Vin de Pays des COTES DE GASCOGNE. At its best, it has a lovely, crisp acidity and fresh, aromatic fruit. The largest plantings of the grape are in California, where it generally produces rather less distinguished wines, but South Africa can produce fair examples.

COMMANDARIA *Cyprus*   The Crusaders went batty about this dark brown, challengingly treacly wine made from red Mavro and white Xynisteri grapes, sun-dried for two weeks before vinification and solera aging. Still pretty decent stuff but only potentially one of the world's great rich wines.

COMTÉ TOLOSAN, VIN DE PAYS DU *South-West France*   A large Vin de Pays covering most of the area to the south and east of Bordeaux. The robust reds, using local varieties such as Duras, Tannat and Fer Servadou blended with Cabernet Sauvignon, Cabernet Franc and Merlot, are your best bet, but don't overlook the rosés. Best producer: Labastide-de-Levis co-op.

COMTÉS RHODANIENS, VIN DE PAYS DES *Rhône Valley and Savoie, France*   A catch-all Vin de Pays covering a large area. Most of the wines are red, produced from Syrah, Gamay, Cinsaut and Grenache, but the whites, particularly those containing Viognier, Sauvignon and Chardonnay are good too. Best producer: ST-DESIRAT-CHAMPAGNE co-op★, Les Vignerons Ardèchois.

CONCA DE BARBERÁ DO *Catalonia, Spain*   This is one of the tip-top quality wine areas of Spain, but you rarely see the region's name as most of the wine is sold to CAVA producers in the Penedés. The cool climate here is ideal for quality grapes and for fine table wine, not just fizz. TORRES and CODORNIU grow excellent Chardonnay, Cabernet Sauvignon, Pinot Noir, Merlot and Tempranillo here, but they sell the wine under the better-known names of neighbouring PENEDES and Costers del Segre. Best producers: Torres (Milmanda)★★, CODORNIU (for RAIMAT).

CONCHA Y TORO *Maipo, Chile*   Despite the presence of a German winemaker, Goetz von Gersdorff, Chile's biggest wine producer and exporter turns out more impressive reds than whites, which tend to be lean and over-processed. The unoaked Cabernet Sauvignon, Merlot and Cabernet/Merlot blend are good, as is the Casillero del Diablo Cabernet Sauvignon, with richer, more concentrated fruit. The 1991 Marqués de Casa Concha Chardonnay ★ however, suggests the white tide may be turning: it's soft, creamy and concentrated, with an intimation of the pure, bright fruit I'm fond of in the reds.

CONDADO DE HUELVA DO *Andalucía, Spain*   This very hot region between Cadiz and the Portuguese Algarve has always made sherry-like (but not sherry quality) wines from the local Zalema grape. But the modern trend is to pale, neutral table wines. Best producers: (table wines) Bollullos co-op, Sovicosa (Viña Odiel).

CONDRIEU AC *Rhône Valley, France*   The unattractive village of Condrieu, on the precipitous right bank of the Rhône, is the unlikely birthplace of one of the world's great white wines. In recent years because of the great demand for this wonderful fragrant wine, made entirely from Viognier, there have been a lot of new plantings, which will increase, though not necessarily improve, production. Condrieu fades with age and is remarkably expensive, but at 1–3 years old the wine is a sensation everyone should try at least once. Best producers: DELAS★★, Dezormeaux★★, Dumazet★★, GUIGAL★★, Jurie des Camiers★, Pinchon★★, de Rozay★★, Vernay★★★. Best years: 1990 89 88.

CONTERNO *Piedmont, Italy*   One of the great names of BAROLO. Brothers Aldo and Giovanni went their separate ways in 1969, with the latter starting out on his own and the former retaining the family winery of Giacomo Conterno. This means we can now derive double the pleasure from Barolos like Granbussia ★★★ (Aldo) and Monfortino ★★★ (Giovanni). Best years: 1990 89 88 86 85 82 78.

CONTINO *Rioja DOC, Rioja, Spain* A gem of an estate on some of the finest RIOJA land, half-owned by CVNE, which has given a much-needed boost to Rioja's quality image. The wine is made by CVNE and always sold as a Riserva ★★, bursting with concentrated, blackberry fruit. Best years: 1987 85 82.

COONAWARRA *South Australia* On a limestone belt thinly veneered with hallowed terra rossa soil, this small cigar-shaped and mercilessly flat, parchy land can produce sublime Cabernets with blackcurrant leafy flavours, and spicy Shirazes that age for many years. Some disappointingly light wines have been made in recent years and there is no doubt that if Coonawarra wishes to uphold its great reputation, some of its producers are going to have to re-think their attitude to quality. Chardonnay and Riesling can be good. Best producers: BOWEN, HOLLICK, KATNOOK, Leconfield, LINDEMANS, MILDARA, ORLANDO, PARKER, PENFOLDS, PENLEY, PETALUMA, ROSEMOUNT, WYNNS.

CORBANS *Auckland, Gisborne and Marlborough, New Zealand* New Zealand's second largest wine company behind MONTANA and brand names include Cooks, Stoneleigh and Robard & Butler. Stoneleigh Sauvignon Blanc ★ and Rhine Riesling ★★, both made with Marlborough fruit, perfectly capture the best of each variety and show well their regional styles. Private Bin Chardonnay ★ and Noble Rhine Riesling ★★ are two fine small production wines. Best years: 1991 90 89 86.

CORBIÈRES AC *Languedoc, France* This remote, windswept region was only granted its AC in 1985 but good reds, are appearing thick and fast. These beefy red wines with lots of juicy fruit and more than a hint of the wild hillside herbs are excellent young – and will happily age for years from the best estates. White Corbières is rarely more than adequate. Drink as young as possible. Best producers: Caraguilhes★, Fontsainte, Étang des Colombes, LASTOURS★★, Ollieux, de Reverend, Voulte-Gasparets★, also Cascastel, Embres-et-Castelmaure and MONT TAUCH★ co-ops.

Château de Lastours
Corbières
Appellation Corbières Contrôlée

CORDIER *Bordeaux, France* A large Bordeaux merchant, which also owns several important châteaux, including Clos des Jacobins, GRUAUD-LAROSE, CANTEMERLE, LAFAURIE-PEYRAGUEY and MEYNEY. Jean Cordier owns TALBOT in his own right.

CORNAS AC *Rhône Valley, France* The northern Rhône's up-and-coming star, especially as the wines of neighbouring HERMITAGE and COTE-ROTIE have spiralled upwards in price in recent years. When young, the wine is a thick, impenetrable red, almost black in the ripest years. Most need 10 years aging. Best producers: de Barjac★, CLAPE★★★, DELAS, JABOULET, Juge★, Michel★, VERSET★★, Voge★. Best years: 1990 89 88 85 83 80 78.

101

CORSICA *France*   This Mediterranean island has made some pretty undistinguished wines in the past. The last decade has seen a welcome trend towards quality, with co-ops and local growers investing in better equipment and planting noble grape varieties – such as Syrah, Merlot, Cabernet Sauvignon and Mourvèdre for reds, and Chardonnay and Sauvignon Blanc for whites – to complement the local Nielluccio, Vermentino and Sciacarello. Whites and rosés are pleasant for drinking young; reds are more exciting and can age for 3–4 years. See also Ajaccio, l'Île de Beauté, Patrimonio, Vin de Corse.

CORTESE   White grape variety planted primarily in south-eastern Piedmont in Italy. It is also used in the Colli Tortonesi and Alto Monferrato DOCs as well as for GAVI, and can also be labelled simply as Cortese del Piemonte. Though Gavi is overrated, the grape can produce decent, fairly acidic, dry whites.

CORTON AC *Grand Cru, Côte de Beaune, Burgundy, France*   The Corton AC covers both red and white wine. It is the only red Grand Cru in the Côte de Beaune and ideally the wines should have the burliness and savoury power of the top Côte de Nuits wines, combined with the more seductive perfumed fruit of Côte de Beaune. Red Corton should take 10 years to mature, but too many modern examples never make it. Very little white Corton is made. **Best producers:** Chandon de Briailles★★, Chevalier★★, Dubreuil-Fontaine★★, Rapet★★, Senard★, TOLLOT-BEAUT, Voarick★. **Best years:** 1990 89 88 87 85 83 78.

CORTON-CHARLEMAGNE AC *Grand Cru, Côte de Beaune, Burgundy, France*   Corton-Charlemagne, at the top of the famous Corton hill, is the largest of Burgundy's white Grands Crus. It can produce some of the most impressive white Burgundies – rich, buttery and nutty. The best wines only show their real worth at 10 years or more. **Best producers:** Bonneau du Martray★★★, Dubreuil-Fontaine★★, JADOT★★, Laleure-Piot★, LATOUR★★, Rapet★★. **Best years:** 1990 89 88 86 85 83 82.

CORVO *Sicily, Italy*   The brand name used for the Sicilian wines made by the Duca di Salaparuta firm. Basic red and white Corvo are pretty basic, but there is now a superior white called Colomba Platino and an excellent red, Duca Enrico ★.

CH. COS D'ESTOURNEL ★★★ *St-Estèphe AC, 2ème Cru Classé, Haut-Médoc, Bordeaux, France*   Now the top name in ST-ESTEPHE, and one of the leading châteaux in all Bordeaux. Despite a high proportion of Merlot (just under 40%) the wine is classically made for aging and usually needs 10 years to show really well. Recent vintages have been dark, brooding, and packed with long-term potential. Second wine: Ch. de Marbuzet. **Best years:** 1990 89 88 86 85 83 82 81 79 76.

COSECHA Spanish for 'vintage'.

COSTIÈRES DE NÎMES AC *Languedoc, France*   A large AC between Nîmes and Arles in the Gard. I prefer the rosés, especially when really young, to the reds which can be rather earthy. Only a little white is produced but at its best can be light and appley. Best producers: l'Amarine, Roubaud, de la Tuilerie.

CÔTE   French word for a slope or hillside, which is where many, but not all, of the country's best vineyards are to be found. The names of specific slopes have been adopted as appellations (COTE-ROTIE, COTE DE BROUILLY) and even whole regions (Côte d'Or).

CÔTE DE BEAUNE *Côte d'Or, Burgundy, France*   The southern part of the Côte d'Or centred on the town of Beaune. Beginning at the hill of Corton north of Beaune, the Côte de Beaune progresses south as far as Les Maranges with white wines gradually taking over from red. The Côte de Beaune AC itself covers red wine but is very rare. Best producers: Chantal Lescure, Joliette, LABOURE-ROI.

CÔTE DE BEAUNE-VILLAGES AC *Côte de Beaune, Burgundy, France*   The general AC covering 16 villages. Most producers use their own village name nowadays but if the wine is a blend from several villages it is sold as Côte de Beaune-Villages and most merchants produce a relatively undistinguished version.

CÔTE DE BROUILLY AC *Beaujolais, Burgundy, France*   The Côte de Brouilly is a steep hill in the middle of the BROUILLY AC producing extra-ripe grapes. The wine, a 'super-Brouilly', is good young but can age well for several years. Best producers: Conroy★, DUBOEUF, Ravier★, Thivin★, Verger. Best years: 1991 89 88.

CÔTE CHALONNAISE   See Bourgogne-Côte Chalonnaise.

CÔTE DE NUITS *Côte d'Or, Burgundy, France*   This is the northern part of the great Côte d'Or and is *not* an AC. Almost entirely red wine country, the vineyards start in the southern suburbs of Dijon and continue in a narrow swathe often only a few hundred yards wide to below the town of Nuits-St-Georges. The villages are some of the greatest wine names in the world – GEVREY-CHAMBERTIN, VOUGEOT, CHAMBOLLE-MUSIGNY, VOSNE-ROMANEE and NUITS-ST-GEORGES.

CÔTE DE NUITS-VILLAGES AC *Côte de Nuits, Burgundy, France*   An AC specific to the villages of Corgoloin, Comblanchien and Prissey in the south of the Côte de Nuits and Brochon and FIXIN in the north. Although not much seen, the wines are often good, not very deep in colour but with a nice cherry fruit. There is a tiny amount of white produced. Best producers: (reds) Durand★, Julien, RION, Rossignol★, Tollot-Voarick.

CÔTE D'OR *Burgundy, France*   Europe's most northern great red wine area and also the home of some of the world's best dry white wines. The name, meaning 'golden slope', refers to a 48km (30 mile) stretch between Dijon and Chagny which divides into the Côte de Nuits in the north and the Côte de Beaune in the south.

CÔTE-RÔTIE AC *Rhône Valley, France*

The Côte-Rôtie or 'roasted slope' produces one of France's greatest red wines. The Syrah grape bakes to super-ripeness on these steep slopes and the small amount of white Viognier sometimes included in the blend gives Côte-Rôtie an exotic, heavenly fragrance quite unexpected in a red wine. Lovely young, it is much better aged for 10 years. Best producers: Burgaud★, Champet★★, CHAPOUTIER★★ (since 1988), DELAS★★ (single vineyard), Dervieux-Thaize, GUIGAL★★★, JABOULET (since 1988), JAMET★★, JASMIN★★★, Rostaing★, Vernay★. Best years: 1991 90 89 88 85 83 82 80 78.

COTEAU French for a slope or hillside.

COTEAUX D'AIX-EN-PROVENCE AC *Provence, France*

This AC, mainly reds and rosés, was the first in the south to acknowledge that Cabernet Sauvignon can enormously enhance the local varieties of Grenache, Cinsaut, Mourvèdre and Carignan. The reds can age, but it is best to catch them young. Some quite good fresh rosé is made while the whites, mostly still traditionally made, are pleasant but hardly rivetting. Best producers: (reds) Château Bas, de Beaupré, Fonscolombe, Salen, du Seuil, Vignelaure; (whites) de Beaupré, Fonscolombe, du Seuil.

COTEAUX DE L'ARDÈCHE, VIN DE PAYS DES *Rhône Valley, France*

Wines from the southern part of the Ardèche department. Look out for the increasingly good varietal reds made from Cabernet Sauvignon, Syrah, Merlot or Gamay and whites from Chardonnay or Sauvignon Blanc. Best producer: Louis LATOUR, ST-DESIRAT-CHAMPAGNE co-op★, Les Vignerons Ardèchois.

COTEAUX DE L'AUBANCE AC *Loire Valley, France*

Smallish AC parallel to the COTEAUX DU LAYON AC. Now enjoying a renaissance for sweet or semi-sweet whites from Chenin Blanc. Most producers, however, prefer to make red, rosé or dry white ANJOU AC which is easier to sell. Best producers: Bablut★, Chauvin★, Papin★, RICHOU (Cuvée Les Trois Demoiselles★★). Best years: 1990 89 88 86 85 83.

COTEAUX DES BAUX-EN-PROVENCE AC *Provence, France*

An exciting new AC, in particular because it shows that organic farming can produce spectacular results. Good-quality fruit and inspirational wine-making mean that the reds and rosés can be some of the best in the south of France. There is very little white so far. Best producers: Mas de la Dame★, Mas de Gourgonnier★, Terres Blanches★, de TREVALLON★★★.

COTEAUX CHAMPENOIS AC *Champagne, France*

The AC for still wines from Champagne. The wines are fairly acid with a few exceptions, notably from the villages of BOUZY and Ay. Best producers: Bara, BOLLINGER, Ch. de Saran★ (MOET & CHANDON), Joseph Perrier, LAURENT-PERRIER, G Vesselle. Best years: 1990 89 88 85 82.

COTEAUX DU LANGUEDOC AC *Languedoc, France* Large and increasingly successful AC between Montpellier and Narbonne in the Languedoc, producing over 40 million bottles of beefy red and tasty rosé. Eleven of the best villages can now add their own names to the AC, including Cabrières, La CLAPE, Montpeyroux, Pic St-Loup, St-Drézery and St-Georges-d'Orques.

COTEAUX DU LAYON AC *Loire Valley, France* Sweet wine from the Layon Valley south of Angers. The wine is made from Chenin Blanc grapes that have been attacked by noble rot. There have been great improvements recently, and in great years like 90 and 89 and from a talented grower, this can be one of the world's great sweet wines. Seven villages can use the Coteaux du Layon-Villages AC (one of the best is Chaume) and put their own name on the label, and these wines, in particular, are definitely underpriced for the quality. Two small sub-areas, BONNEZEAUX and QUARTS DE CHAUME, have their own ACs. Best producers: Bidet★, de Breuil★★, Clos de Ste-Catherine★★, Delesvaux★★, Fresne★, Guimonière★, Jolivet★, la Motte★, Ogereau★, Joseph Renon★★, Sauveroy★★, Soucherie★. Best years: 1990 89 88 85 83 82 76 75.

COTEAUX DU LYONNAIS AC *Rhône Valley, France* Good, light, Beaujolais-style reds and a few whites and rosés from scattered vineyards between Villefranche and Lyon. Drink young. Best producers: Descottes, DUBOEUF, Fayolle.

COTEAUX DU TRICASTIN AC *Rhône Valley, France* From the southern Drôme these are light, fresh reds and rosés with attractive juicy fruit. Only a little white is made but is worth looking out for as a fairly good, nutty drink to consume within the year. Best producers: de Grangeneuve, Lônes, Tour d'Elyssas.

COTEAUX VAROIS VDQS *Provence, France* An area to watch in the Var with new plantings of classic grapes. Best producers: Clos de la Truffière, Deffends, St-Estève, St-Jean.

CÔTES DE BERGERAC AC *South-West France* The AC covers good quality reds made from the same grapes as BERGERAC AC but with a higher minimum alcohol level. Côtes de Bergerac Moelleux AC is the name for sweet wines. Best producers: La Mayne, Tour des Gendres.

CÔTES DE BLAYE AC *Bordeaux, France* The AC for white wines from the right bank of the Gironde. Almost all of the best whites of the area are now dry. Drink young. Best producer: Marinier.

CÔTES DE BOURG AC *Bordeaux, France* Mainly a red wine area inside the larger COTES DE BLAYE, where the best producers and the local co-op at Tauriac are making great efforts. The reds are quite full, with a pleasant blackcurrant fruit and can age successfully for 6–10 years. A little white is made, most of which is bone dry and rather lifeless. Best producers: de Barbe, Bousquet, Brulescaille, la Croix-Millorit, Falfas, Guerry, Haut-Guiraud, Rousset, Tauriac co-op, Tayac. Best years: 1990 89 88 85 83 82.

105

CÔTES DE CASTILLON AC *Bordeaux, France* As the price of decent red Bordeaux climbs ever upward, Côtes de Castillon wines have remained an excellent, reasonably priced alternative – a little earthy but full and round. Depending on the vintage the wine is delicious between 3 and 10 years. Best producers: de Belcier★, les Hauts de Granges, Manoir du Gravoux, Moulin-Rouge, Parenchère, de Pitray. Best years: 1990 89 88 86 85 83 82.

CÔTES DE DURAS AC *South-West France* AC, between ENTRE-DEUX-MERS and BERGERAC in the Lot-et-Garonne, with two very active co-ops which offer extremely good, fresh, grassy reds and whites from traditional Bordeaux grapes but at distinctly lower prices. Drink the wines young. Best producers: Conti, Cours, Ferrant, Laulan, co-ops at Duras and Landerrouat.

CÔTES DE FRANCS AC *Bordeaux, France* Mainly red wine from a tiny but up-and-coming area east of ST-EMILION. The quality is helped by the investment in the area by several leading POMEROL and St-Émilion producers. Already delicious, expect great wines from here in the future – and remember – you saw it here first. Best producers: La Claverie★, de Francs★, Puyguéraud★★. Best years: 1990 89 88 86 85 83.

CÔTES DU FRONTONNAIS AC *South-West France* From north of Toulouse these are some of the most original reds in South-West France. Négrette is the chief grape and the wine can be superb and positively silky in texture. It can age well but I prefer it young. There is a little fairly good rosé. Best producers: de Baudare, Bellevue-la-Forêt★, la Colombière, Flotis★, Laurou, Montauriol★, la Palme★.

CÔTES DE GASCOGNE, VIN DE PAYS DES *South-West France* Mainly white wines from the Gers department. This is Armagnac country, but the tangy-fresh, fruity table wines are tremendously good – especially when you consider that they were condemned as unfit for anything but distillation only a decade ago. Best producers: Aurin, GRASSA★, Union des Producteurs PLAIMONT★, Hugh RYMAN★, Dom. de Joy, Dom. St Lannes.

CÔTES DU JURA AC *Jura, France* The regional AC for Jura covers a wide variety of wines including local specialities, VIN JAUNE and VIN DE PAILLE. The local white Savagnin grape makes strong-tasting whites and Chardonnay is used for some good dry whites and Champagne-method sparklers. The reds and rosés can be rather good when made from Pinot Noir but when from the local Poulsard and Trousseau grapes can be a bit weird. Drink young. Best producers: Arlay, Bourdy, Gréa, Pupillin co-op.

CÔTES DU LUBÉRON AC *Rhône Valley and Provence, France* East of Avignon in the Durance Valley, the landscape is dominated by the Montagne du Lubéron and wine production by the co-ops. The light, easy wines are for drinking within the year when they are refreshing and enjoyable. Best producers: des Blancs Canorgue, de l'Isolette, Val Joanis, Mille, la Tour-d'Aigues co-op.

106

CÔTES DU MARMANDAIS VDQS *South-West France* The Marmandais producers in the Lot-et-Garonne have always set out to make Bordeaux look-alikes and the red wines achieve a fair amount of success. Best producer: Cocumont co-op.

CÔTES DE MONTRAVEL AC *South-West France* Small area within the BERGERAC AC for sweet and medium-sweet whites from Sémillon, Sauvignon Blanc and Muscadelle. Drink young. Dry wines are sold as Bergerac Sec. Best producer: Gourgueil.

CÔTES DE PROVENCE AC *Provence, France* Large AC for mainly reds and rosés and showing signs of improvement in recent years. The reds and rosés are generally much fruitier now but should still be drunk young. The whites are not very memorable. Best producers: (reds) Barbeyrolles, Commanderie de Peyrassol, Féraud★, Gavoty★, les Maîtres Vignerons de St-Tropez, Minuty, Pampelonne, Richeaume★, Rimauresq, St-Maur; (whites) Commanderie de Peyrassol, l'Estandon, Féraud, Gavoty★, Hauts de St-Jean.

CÔTES DU RHÔNE AC *Rhône Valley, France* The general AC for the whole Rhône Valley. Over 90% is red and rosé mainly from Grenache with some Cinsaut, Syrah, Carignan and Mourvèdre to add lots of warm, spicy southern personality. Modern wine-making has revolutionized the style and today's wines are generally juicy and spicy and easy to drink, ideally within 2 years. Most white is made by the co-ops and sold under merchants' labels. Drink as young as possible. Best producers: (reds) Aussellons, Cantharide, Cru de Coudoulet, DUBOEUF, de Fonsalette★, les Gouberts, GRAND MOULAS★, GUIGAL★, JABOULET, Mont-Redon, Mousset, Pascal, de Ruth, St-Estève; (whites) Chambovet, DUBOEUF, Pelaquié, Rabasse-Charavin, STE-ANNE★★; co-ops at Chusclan and Laudun. Best years: (reds) 1991 90 89 88 86 85.

CÔTES DU RHÔNE-VILLAGES AC *Rhône Valley, France* AC for wines with a higher minimum alcohol content than COTES DU RHONE, covering 16 villages in the southern Rhône that have traditionally made superior wine (especially Cairanne, Séguret, Valréas, Sablet, Visan for reds; Chusclan, Laudun, Visan for rosés; Chusclan, Laudun for whites). Almost all the best wines are red – they have a marvellous spicy flavour and tannin and can age for up to 10 years. Best producers: Ameillaud★, Beaumes-de-Venise co-op, Boisson, Brusset, Cartier, Combe★, Grangeneuve, l'Oratoire St-Martin, Pelaquié★, Présidente, Rabasse-Charavin★, St-Antoine, STE-ANNE★★, Trignon★, Vacquéyras co-op, Verquière. Best years: 1990 89 88 85.

CÔTES ROANNAISES VDQS *Loire Valley, France* In the upper Loire the nearest large town is Lyon, the capital of BEAUJOLAIS, and so it is quite logical that the chief grape here is Gamay. Almost all the wine is red and in general should be drunk very young. Best producers: Chargros, Chaucesse, Lapandéry, Lutz, Serol, Villeneuve.

CÔTES DU ROUSSILLON AC *Roussillon, France* Large AC south of Perpignan for mainly red wines. So long as the wine is young, both red and rosé provide some of southern France's best-value drinking. The small amount of white wine is mainly unmemorable. Production is dominated by the co-ops, some of them with enlightened winemakers. Best producers: Vignerons CATALANS, CAZES★, Charmette, Corneilla, de Jau, Jaubert-Noury, Joliette, Mas Rous, Piquemal, Rey, Rivesaltes co-op, Salvat, Sarda-Mallet.

CÔTES DU ROUSSILLON-VILLAGES AC *Roussillon, France* AC covering red wines from the best sites in the northern part of CÔTES DU ROUSSILLON. The wine, from villages like Caramany and Latour-de-France, is wonderfully juicy when young but can age for several years. Best producers: CAZES★, Cap de Fouste, Dom. Gauby★, Ch. Montner, de Jau, Sarda-Mallet, St-Martin; also Agly, Bélesta, Vignerons CATALANS, Latour-de-France co-ops.

CÔTES DE ST-MONT VDQS *South-West France* A good VDQS for quite sharp but fruity reds and some fair rosés and dry whites. Best producer: Union des Producteurs PLAIMONT★.

CÔTES DU TARN, VIN DE PAYS DES *South-West France* Wines from the Tarn department around Toulouse-Lautrec's home town of Albi. The whites should be sharp but fruity and the young reds are enjoyable too. Best producer: Labastide-de-Levis co-op.

CÔTES DE THAU, VIN DE PAYS DES *Languedoc, France* Red, white and rosé from the shores of Lake Thau, west of the Mediterranean town of Sète. The whites are often surprisingly good for the Midi. Best producers: de Gaujal, Genson, UCA Vignerons Garrigues and the co-ops at Pinet and Pomerols.

CÔTES DE THONGUE, VIN DE PAYS DES *Languedoc, France* Mainly red wines from 14 villages north-east of Béziers. Most are dull quaffers made from Carignan, but recent plantings of classic grapes by dynamic estates are more than promising. Best producer: Dom. de l'Arjolle, Dom. de Bellevue.

CÔTES DU VENTOUX AC *Rhône Valley, France* An increasingly successful AC with vineyards on the slopes of the magnificent Mt Ventoux on the eastern side of the Rhône Valley near Carpentras, especially when the wine is well-made from a single estate or blended by a serious merchant. The reds can have a lovely juicy fruit, or in the case of JABOULET and la

VIEILLE FERME, some real stuffing. There is only a little white wine. Best producers: Anges, Crillon, JABOULET, Pascal, la VIEILLE FERME.

CÔTES DU VIVARAIS VDQS *Rhône Valley, France* In the Ardèche and northern Gard typical southern Rhône grapes produce light, fresh reds and rosés, for drinking young, but plantings of classic varieties (Cabernet Sauvignon and Syrah) are producing deep-flavoured, rich wines of surprising quality and irresistible price. Best producers: Orgnac l'Aven co-op, Dom. de Vigier.

EL COTO *Rioja DOC, Rioja, Spain* El Coto Crianza ★ is one of the few utterly reliable, widely available reds to drink in restaurants right across Spain. Coto de Imaz ★ is the name for the savoury, fragrant Reservas and Gran Reservas. Best years: (reds) 1988 87 85 82 81 78 75 70.

COULY-DUTHEIL *Chinon, Loire Valley, France* Large merchant house responsible for 10% of the CHINON AC. Couly-Dutheil have their own vineyards for their best wines, particularly Clos de l'Écho ★★ and Clos de l'Olive ★. The firm's top Chinon, selected from the best vats each year, is sold as La Baronnie Madeleine ★★ and combines delicious raspberry fruit with a considerable capacity to age. Couly-Dutheil also sell a range of other Touraine wines. Best years: 1990 89 88 86 85 83 82 81.

PIERRE COURSODON *St-Joseph AC, Rhône Valley, France* A good family-owned domaine producing rich ST-JOSEPH from very old vines. The red wines ★★ need as much as a decade to show all the magnificent cassis and truffle and violety richness of the best Rhône reds, especially the top wine, called Le Paradis St-Pierre★★. Pierre Coursodon also produces tiny quantities of white St-Joseph ★, which should be drunk young. Best years: (reds) 1990 89 88 86 85 83.

COUSIÑO MACUL *Maipo, Chile* Chile's most traditional and respected winery does things the Chilean way: fermentation for the reds in beechwood tuns, then aging in large American oak casks for up to a decade. But usually it works: lush, mellow, smoky fruit sings out of wines like the 1988 Merlot Limited Release ★ or the 1985 Antiguas Reservas Cabernet Sauvignon ★ .

CH. COUTET★ *Barsac AC, 1er Cru Classé, Bordeaux, France* BARSAC'S largest Classed Growth property but outstripped by the AC's other First Growth, CLIMENS. Coutet wine has the potential to be as sweet and exquisite as CLIMENS, but nowadays rarely achieves it, though recent vintages do at last exhibit welcome richness. Best years: 1990 89 88 86 83 76 75.

COWRA *New South Wales, Australia* New and very promising district with a reliable warm climate and good water supplies for irrigation. It produces soft, peachy Chardonnay and spicy, cool-tasting Shiraz. Best producers: MCWILLIAMS (Barwang vineyard), MOUNTARROW (Arrowfield), ROTHBURY.

CRÉMANT French term for up-market sparkling wine from Alsace, Bordeaux, Burgundy, Limoux and the Loire, imposing stricter regulations than those for ordinary fizz. The term has been used in Champagne for wines with less pressure (3 atmospheres instead of 6) but will be banned there from 1994 onwards.

CRÉMANT D'ALSACE AC *Alsace, France* Good, Champagne-method sparkling wine from Alsace, usually made from Pinot Blanc. Riesling, Pinot Gris and Pinot Noir are also permitted.

Reasonable quality, if not great value for money. Best producers: Cattin, Dopff au Moulin, Dopff & Irion, Ginglinger, Willy
Gisselbrecht, KUENTZ-BAS, Muré, Ostertag, Willm, Wolfberger.

CRÉMANT DE BOURGOGNE AC *Burgundy, France* Most
Burgundian Crémant is white and is made either from
Chardonnay alone or blended with Pinot Noir. The result, especially in ripe years, is full, soft, almost honey-flavoured – if you
give the wine the 2-3 years aging needed for mellowness to
develop. The best rosé comes from the Chablis and Auxerre
regions in northern Burgundy. Best producers: Delorme, Lucius-
Grégoire, Simmonet-Febvre; co-ops at Bailly (the best for rosé),
Lugny, St-Gengoux-de-Scissé and Viré.

CRÉMANT DE LIMOUX AC *South-West France* Sparkling wine AC
introduced in Limoux from 1990. The wines must have a minimum of 30% Chardonnay and/or Chenin Blanc, but no more
than 20% of each. The rest of the blend is made from the local
Mauzac grape. The wines are aged on lees for a year and generally have more complexity than straight BLANQUETTE DE LIMOUX,
but should be drunk young. They are among the leading French
sparkling wines produced outside Champagne. Best producers:
Antech, Guinot, Laurens★, Limoux co-op★, Martinolles★, Vadent.

CRÉMANT DE LOIRE AC *Loire Valley, France* The AC for
Champagne-method sparkling wine in Anjou and Touraine, created in 1975 in an effort to improve Loire fizzes. With stricter
regulations than those for VOUVRAY and SAUMUR, the result is a
more attractive wine, with more fruit, more yeast character and
a more caressing mousse. It is usually good to drink as soon as
it is released and can be excellent value. Best producers: Berger,
Gabillière, Girault, Michaud★, OISLY-ET-THESEE co-op★,
Passavent★.

CRÉPY AC *Savoie, France* Light, relatively acidic white wines
made with Chasselas from vineyards south of Lake Geneva.
Drink as young as possible. Best producers: Goy, Mercier.

CRIANZA Spanish term for the youngest official category of
matured wine. A Crianza wine, white, rosé or red, must have
had at least two years' aging before sale.

CRIMEA *Ukraine* This Black Sea peninsula has been an important
centre of wine production since the early 19th century. Its
greatest wines are the historical treasures of the Massandra collection: superb dessert and fortified wines, originally destined for
the Tsar's summer palace at Livadia. Present-day wine-making
seems understandably but regrettably aimless.

CRIOTS-BÂTARD-MONTRACHET AC See Montrachet AC.

CROFT *Port DOC, Douro, Portugal* Croft's vintage ports ★★ are
often deceptively light in their youth, but they develop into subtle,
elegant wines. The 10-year-old tawny★ is the best of the rest
from this 300-year-old port shipper. Best years: (vintage ports)
1977 75 70 66 63.

CROZES-HERMITAGE AC *Rhône Valley, France* The largest of the northern Rhône ACs. Ideally the red should have a full colour with a strong, meaty but rich flavour. You can drink it young but in ripe years from a hillside site it improves greatly for 3–6 years. The quality has improved dramatically in the last 5 years. The best whites are extremely fresh, clean and racy. In general drink white Crozes young before the floral perfume disappears. Best producers: (reds) Bégot, Caves des Clairmonts, DELAS★, Desmeure★, Fayolle★, GRAILLOT, JABOULET (Thalabert★★), Michelas, Pochon, Tardy & Ange; (whites) Desmeure★, Fayolle★, JABOULET, Pradelle. Best years: (reds) 1991 90 89 88 85 83 82; (whites) 1991 90 89 88.

CRU French for a specific plot of land, or a particular estate and its title. Bordeaux, Burgundy and Champagne use the term to distinguish between individual vineyard sites, or the estates which own them. In Burgundy the growths are divided into Grands (great) and Premiers (first) Crus, and apply solely to the actual land. In Champagne the same terms are used for whole villages. In Bordeaux there are various hierarchical levels of Cru referring to estates rather than their actual vineyards.

CRU BOURGEOIS French term for wines from the MEDOC which are ranked immediately below Crus Classés. The best of these, such as d'ANGLUDET in MARGAUX, and de PEZ in St-Estèphe make very fine wines and are a match for many a Classed Growth.

CRU CLASSÉ The Classed Growths are the aristocracy of Bordeaux, enobled by the classifications of 1855 (for the MEDOC, BARSAC and SAUTERNES), 1954, 1969 and 1985 (for ST-EMILION) and 1947, 1953 and 1959 (for GRAVES). Curiously, POMEROL has never been classified. The modern classifications are more reliable than the 1855 version, which was based solely on the price of the wines at the time of the Great Exhibition in Paris, but in terms of prestige, the 1855 classification remains the most important. With the exception of a single alteration in 1973, when Ch. MOUTON-ROTHSCHILD was elevated to First Growth status, the list has not changed since 1855. It is certainly in need of revision.

HANS CRUSIUS *Traisen, Nahe, Germany* Probably the best estate in the Nahe, Hans and Peter Crusius, father and son, produce legendary wines on their Traiser Bastei★★ vineyard. Equally good are their wines from the Schloss Böckelheimer Felsenberg★★ which manage to be both rich and flinty with superb complexity. Best years: 1990 89 88 86 85 81.

CULLENS *Margaret River, Western Australia* One of the original and best Margaret River vineyards, run by the Cullen women (winemakers are Vanya and her mother Diana). The Chardonnay★★ is one of the region's richest and most complex; Sémillon ★ and Sauvignon Blanc ★ are made deliberately non-herbaceous; Cabernet Merlot ★ is soft and deep, and Reserve Cabernet Sauvignon ★★ can be simply magnificent.

CUVAISON *Napa Valley, California, USA* Cuvaison built a great reputation for brooding, dark but unapproachable reds in the 1970s but has taken quite a while to get into a more up to date stride. Now they produce excellent Merlot ★★, and good, but not thrilling Chardonnay. Best years: 1990 88 87.

CUVE CLOSE A bulk process used to produce inexpensive sparkling wines. The second fermentation, which produces the bubbles, takes place in tank rather than in the bottle (as in the superior, but more costly Champagne method). Also known as the Charmat method, after its inventor Eugène Charmat. Having been derided for years, it is now clear that if the grapes are good, the results can be excellent, and often, as with ASTI SPUMANTE, it is the best method for preserving freshness.

CUVÉE French for literally the contents of a single vat or tank, but more commonly used to describe a wine selected by an individual producer for reasons of style or quality. Cuvée Spéciale or Cuvée de Reserve on the label may or may not mean something better than the usual offering.

CVNE *Rioja DOC, Rioja, Spain* Compañía Vinícola del Norte de España is the full name of this long-established firm, but it's usually known as 'coonay'. CVNE's brilliant new, ultra-modern winery, would even be the envy of many state-of-the-art Australian wineries. Monopole ★ is one of RIOJA'S only remaining well-oaked whites; the red Viña Real ★ is rich and meaty, and the top Gran Reserva, Imperial ★★, is long-lived and impressive. Best years: (reds) 1985 82 81 78 76.

DIDIER DAGUENEAU *Pouilly-Fumé AC, Loire Valley, France* The wild man of POUILLY-FUME, a much-needed innovator and quality fanatic in a complacent region. Best-known for his barrel-fermented Sauvignon Blanc called Silex ★★. Best years: 1990 89 88.

DÃO DOC *Beira Alta, Portugal* Dão has steep slopes ideal for vineyards, a great grape-growing climate and characterful local grape varieties. Yet most wines are fruitless and flat and mean. At last things are changing, led by the thrusting SOGRAPE and FONSECA SUCCESSORES. Whites are being freshened up, and reds are beginning to realize their long-promised potential. Best producers: CAVES ALIANCA★, CAVES SAO JOAO★★, Conde de Santar, FONSECA SUCCESSORES★, SOGRAPE★.

RENÉ DAUVISSAT *Chablis AC, Burgundy, France* One of the top three domaines in CHABLIS, specializing in concentrated, oak-aged wines from two Grand Cru and three Premier Cru sites. This is Chablis at its most complex – refreshing, seductive and beautifully structured with the fruit balancing the subtle influence of oak. Look out in particular for La Forest ★★ and the more aromatic Vaillons ★★. Best years: 1990 89 88 86 83.

DE BORTOLI *Riverina, New South Wales, Australia* Large family-owned winery with sublime botrytis Sémillon ★★★, head and shoulders above a vast range of inexpensive Riverina quaffers. They're also crafting some of Yarra Valley's best Chardonnay ★★, Cabernet ★ and Shiraz ★.

DANIE DE WET *Robertson, South Africa* White-wine specialist producing De Wetshof sold via the BERGKELDER, and Danie de Wet sold from the estate. Chardonnay, Sauvignon Blanc and Riesling are taken most seriously here, with the Danie de Wet 1990 Bateleur Chardonnay ★ and 1990 Clos de Roche Chardonnay ★ both achieving creamy, mineral complexity.

DEHLINGER *Russian River AVA, California, USA* Outstanding Pinot Noir ★★ from estate vineyards in the cool Russian River region a few miles from the Pacific. The wines should be best at 5–10 years old. Best years: 1990 88 87.

DEINHARD See Wegeler-Deinhard.

DELAS FRÈRES *Rhône Valley, France* An underrated merchant based near Tournon selling wines from the entire Rhône Valley. The wines from its own northern Rhône vineyards have improved enormously in recent vintages and are now on a par with the best merchant or *négociant* bottlings in the area. Look out for the explosively aromatic CONDRIEU ★★, best drunk young, as well as its single-vineyard, dense, powerful HERMITAGE ★★, which needs as much as a decade to reach its peak and the perfumed single-vineyard COTE-ROTIE ★★. In a lighter style, the CROZES-HERMITAGE ★ is a good bet. Best years: (reds) 1990 89 88 86 85 83 78; (whites) 1990 89 88.

DELATITE *Mansfield, Victoria, Australia* The Ritchies were graziers who got involved in wine when diversifying their farm. Their high-altitude vineyard in sight of Victoria's snowfields grows delicate, aromatic Riesling ★★ and Traminer ★★; also subtle Chardonnay ★ and extravagantly fruity reds. The Pinot Noir ★★ is hauntingly perfumed and Devil's River ★★ is a very smart Bordeaux blend. Best years: 1990 88 87 86 82.

DELEGATS *Henderson, Auckland, North Island, New Zealand* Medium-sized family winery specializing in Chardonnay, Cabernet Sauvignon/Merlot, and Sauvignon Blanc from the Hawkes Bay and Marlborough (Shingle Peak brand) regions. A reliable producer rather than a memorable one, but prices are keen. Best years: 1991 90 89 87.

DEMI-SEC French for medium-dry.

DENBIES *Surrey, England* The giant among English vineyards, with 100ha (247 acres) planted since 1986 on chalky soils outside Dorking. Twenty different varieties have produced, so far, a range of wines from the adequate to the truly exciting. The Dornfelder red ★ is memorable for an English effort, the Pinot Noir and sparklers are good, and the whites show a perfume that almost makes you forgive them their rather exalted prices.

DEUTZ *Champagne AC, Champagne, France*   A Champagne house which is probably better known for its Californian and New Zealand fizz than for its Champagne. Unfairly so, perhaps, because this small, family-owned company produces excellent, medium-priced Champagne. The non-vintage ★ is always reliable, but the top wine is the weightier Cuvée William Deutz ★★. Best years: 1986 85 82.

DÉZALEY *Vaud, Switzerland*   One of the top wine communes in the Vaud, making surprisingly powerful wines from the white Chasselas grape. Best producers: J D Fonjallaz (l'Arbalète)★, Massy, Conne, Pinget★, Testuz.

DI MAJO NORANTE *Molise, Italy*   The most important wine name in the small region of Molise, located on Italy's Adriatic coast. For years, their Ramitello red★ (from Aglianico and Montepulciano) and white★ (from Falanghina) have been standard bearers for the region, but their recent range of wines made from traditional southern varieties like Greco, Fiano, Aglianico and Moscato have transformed them into one of the best and most influential of southern Italy's producers.

DIAMOND CREEK *Napa Valley AVA, California, USA*   Small estate specializing in Cabernet, from three vineyards – Red Rock Terrace★★★, Gravelly Meadows★★★, Volcanic Hill★★★. These are huge, tannic wines that when I taste them young I swear won't ever come round. Yet there's always a sweet, perfumed inner core of fruit that gradually spreads out to envelop the tannin over 5–10 years, producing one of California's great Cabernet experiences. Best years: 1988 87 86 85 84 80 75.

DO (DENOMINACÍON DE ORIGEN)   Spain's equivalent of the French quality wine category, AC, regulating origin and production methods. Some Spanish DOs frankly don't deserve the title.

DOC (DENOMINAÇÃO DE ORIGEM CONTROLADA)   The top regional classification for Portuguese wines since 1990. Formerly called *Região Demarcada* or RD.

DOC (DENOMINACÍON DE ORIGEN CALIFICADA)   New Spanish quality wine category, one step up from DO, with stricter controls. So far only RIOJA qualifies.

DOC (DENOMINAZIONE DI ORIGINE CONTROLLATA)   Italian quality wine category, regulating origin, grape varieties and production methods. To be honest, there are far too many of them, frequently enshrining dull flavours and outmoded vineyard and winery practices. The surge in expensive, quality-inspired Vino da Tavolas is in direct response to the DOC system.

DOCG (DENOMINAZIONE DI ORIGINE CONTROLLATA E GARANTITA)   The highest tier of the Italian wine laws, so far only attained by 8 wines. The Garantita means that quality is supposed to be guaranteed by strict regulations and a tasting panel. It seems to have been helpful in raising quality for wines such as CHIANTI, BAROLO and VINO NOBILE DE MONTEPULCIANO.

114

DOCTOR *Bernkastel, Mosel, Germany* Famous vineyard behind the town of Bernkastel (and not to be confused with the Doktor vineyard at Dexheim in the Rheinhessen). The wines are very beautiful, slow-maturing, 100% Rieslings. Best producers: Lauerburg, THANISCH, WEGELER-DEINHARD.

CH. DOISY-DAËNE ★★ *Barsac, 2ème Cru Classé, Bordeaux, France* A consistently good BARSAC property and unusual in that the sweet wine is made exclusively from Sémillon, giving it an extra richness. It ages well for 10 years or more. Doisy-Daëne Sec, sold under the GRAVES AC, is a particularly good, perfumed, dry, white wine. Drink young. Best years: (sweet) 1990 89 88 86 83 82 80 79; (dry) 1990 89 88.

CH. DOISY-VÉDRINES ★★ *Barsac AC, 2ème Cru Classé, Bordeaux, France* Next door to DOISY-DAENE, Doisy-Védrines's sweet wine is quite different in style as it is fermented and aged in barrel. This makes it fatter and more syrupy than most BARSAC wines. Best years: (sweet) 1990 89 88 86 85 83 82 80 76 75.

DOLCE Italian for sweet.

DOLCETTO One of Italy's most charming native grape varieties, producing purple wines bursting at the seams with fruit. Grown almost exclusively in Piedmont, it is DOC in 7 zones, with styles ranging from the intense and rich in Alba, Ovada and Dogliani to the lighter, more perfumed versions in Acqui and Asti. Usually best drunk within a year or two of the vintage.

DÔLE *Valais, Switzerland* Red wine from the Swiss Valais which must be made from at least 51% Pinot Noir, the rest being Gamay. Dôle is generally a light wine – the deeper, richer (100% Pinot Noir) styles have the right to call themselves Pinot Noir. Best wines: CAVES IMESCH★, G Clavier, M Clavier★, J Germanier★, Gilliard, Mathier★, Mathier-Kuchler, Maye, Orsat, Raymond, Roduit, A Schmid, Zufferey.

DOMAINE French word for a wine estate, used to describe anything from a few vines in the back garden to the heights of Domaine de la ROMANÉE-CONTI.

DOMAINE CHANDON *Yarra Valley, Victoria, Australia* Moët's Aussie offshoot is the Yarra Valley's showpiece winery. Makes leading Pinot Noir/Chardonnay Champagne-method fizz ★★ and occasional Blanc de Blancs and Blanc de Noirs. Green Point Vineyards label is used in export markets.

DOMAINE CHANDON *Napa Valley, California, USA* The first French-owned sparkling wine house in California, Chandon has maintained fairly good quality, particularly the Reserve ★, despite having to use a lot of grapes from unsuitably warm vineyards. Étoile is a new super-reserve which is playing to mixed reviews. Chandon also makes Shadow Creek sparkling wines from grapes purchased outside Napa.

115

DOMAINE DE CHEVALIER *Pessac-Léognan AC, Cru Classé de Graves, Bordeaux, France* This small estate for mainly red wine can produce some of Bordeaux's finest wines. The reds★★★ always start out dry and tannic but over 10–20 years gain that fragrant cedar, tobacco and blackcurrant flavour which can leave you breathless with pleasure. The brilliant white★★★ is both fermented and aged in oak barrels and in the best vintages will still be improving at 15–20 years. Best years: (reds)1990 89 88 85 83 82 81 78; (whites) 1990 89 88 86 85 83 82 81 79 78 75.

DOMAINE MUMM *Napa Valley AVA, California, USA* Subsidiary of MUMM Champagne house makes Cuvée Napa Brut Prestige ★★, one of California's classiest sparklers, although the more expensive Vintage Reserve ★ runs a close second. A Blanc de Noirs ★ is of far better quality than most pink Champagnes. Also a new single-vineyard sparkling wine, Winery Lake Cuvée.

DOMECQ *Jerez y Manzanilla DO, Andalucía and Rioja DOC, País Vasco, Spain* Domecq, the largest of the sherry companies, is best known for its reliable fino, La Ina ★. The top-of-the range wines, dry Amontillado 51-1A★★★, Sibarita Palo Cortado ★★★ and Venerable Pedro Ximénez★★, are spectacular. Domecq are also the world's biggest brandy producers, and make light, elegant red RIOJA ★ from their own extensive vineyards.

DOMINUS *Napa Valley AVA, California, USA* Red wine only from this partnership between California vineyard owners and Christian Moueix, director of Bordeaux's PETRUS. Wines are based on Cabernet Sauvignon with leavenings of Merlot and Cabernet Franc. The dense, rich 1987★★ is the finest yet, but a merciless tannic assault has been a problem in some vintages.

DONAULAND-CARNUNTUM *Niederösterreich, Austria* Amorphous wine region either side of Vienna and on both banks of the Danube, from St Pölten in the west to the Czech border at Bratislava (Pressburg) in the east. Klosterneuburg with its famous Augustinian monastery is at the centre. The best villages are Inzersdorf, Klosterneuburg, Wagram and Göttlesbrunn.

LA DORDOGNE, VIN DE PAYS DE *South-West France* A modest Vin de Pays covering the entire Dordogne department. The Sémillon-based whites are best drunk young, but the fruity BERGERAC-style reds can age for a year or two.

DOURO DOC *Douro, Portugal* As well as a flood of port and basic table wine, some of Portugal's top, soft-textured reds come from here. There are good whites, made from the more aromatic white port varieties, such as SOGRAPE Planalto ★. Best producers: FERREIRA (for BARCA VELHA★), FONSECA SUCCESSORES, QUINTA DO COTTO★ ★ , Quinta da Pacheca, SOGRAPE.

DOUX French for sweet.

DOW *Port DOC, Douro, Portugal* Grapes for Dow's vintage ports ★★ come mostly from the Quinta do Bomfim, near Pinhão. Quinta do Bomfim ★ also makes single Quinta vintage ports in 'off-vintages'. Dow ports are all relatively dry, and the 30-year-old tawny ★★ is excellent. Best years: (vintage ports) 1985 83 80 77 70 66 63.

DRAUTZ-ABLE *Heilbronn, Württemberg, Germany* Promising red winemaker from Württemberg making wines with intense colour and taste. Best years: 1990 89 88.

JEAN-PAUL DROIN *Chablis AC, Burgundy, France* One of the Yonne's most energetic young producers, Jean-Paul Droin sells half his production to LABOURE-ROI, but bottles no fewer than 14 different wines under his own label. Apart from his CHABLIS ★ and PETIT CHABLIS ★, all of Droin's wines are fermented and/ or aged in oak barrels. The best wines are the big, buttery Chablis Grands Crus – Montmains ★★, Bougros★★, Vaudésir★★ and Grenouilles ★★. Best years: 1990 89 88 86 83.

DROMANA ESTATE *Mornington Peninsula, Victoria, Australia* Garry Crittenden started the peninsula's model vineyard in 1982, using latest techniques for Pinot ★, Chardonnay ★★ and Cabernet/Merlot ★★ wines which are squeaky clean and modern but with well-focused fruit flavours. Schinus Molle is a popular second label, particularly successful for Chardonnay ★, Sauvignon Blanc ★ and Sparkling Wine ★.

JOSEPH DROUHIN *Beaune, Burgundy, France* One of the best Burgundian merchants, with substantial vineyard holdings in CHABLIS and the Côte d'Or and an impressive domaine in Oregon, USA. Drouhin makes a consistently good, if expensive, range of wines from all over Burgundy. The names that attract the most attention are the BEAUNE Clos des Mouches, red★★ and white★★, and Le MONTRACHET ★★★ from the Domaine du Marquis de Laguiche. Drouhin offers better value in Chablis ★★ and less glamorous Burgundian ACs, such as RULLY ★ and ST-AUBIN ★★. The BEAUJOLAIS is always good, but overall Drouhin's whites are (just) better than the reds. Best years: (reds) 1990 89 88 85 83; (whites) 1990 89 88 86 85 82.

PIERRE-JACQUES DRUET *Bourgueil, Loire Valley, France* A passionate young producer of top-notch BOURGUEIL and small quantities of CHINON. Druet makes three Bourgueils, Les Cent Boisselées ★, Cuvée Reservée ★★ and ·Cuvée Grand Mont ★★, each a commendably intense expression of the Cabernet Franc grape, bursting with dark cherry and blackcurrant fruit. The wines need 3–5 years to show at their best. Best years: 1990 89 88 87 85 83.

DRY CREEK AVA *Sonoma County, California, USA* Best known for Zinfandel and Cabernet Sauvignon, this valley runs just west of the ALEXANDER VALLEY AVA. Best producers: Domaine Michel, Dry Creek Vineyards, Meeker, Preston, Rafanelli.

GEORGES DUBOEUF *Beaujolais, Burgundy, France*   Known, with some justification, as the King of BEAUJOLAIS, Georges Duboeuf is responsible for more than 10% of the wine produced in the region. Given the size of his operation, the quality of the wines is high. Duboeuf also makes and blends wine from the Mâconnais and the Rhône Valley. His BEAUJOLAIS NOUVEAU is always among the best, but his top wines are those he bottles for small growers, particularly Jean Descombes ★ in MORGON, Domaine des Quatre Vents ★, La Madone★ in FLEURIE and Domaine de la Tour de Bief ★★ in MOULIN-A-VENT. Duboeuf also makes and blends wine from the Mâconnais and the Rhône Valley. His crisp ST-VERAN ★ is worth looking out for.

DUCKHORN *Napa Valley AVA, California, USA*   This winery has earned a well-deserved reputation for its Merlot ★ ★ if you like a chunky, tannic style, however the Cabernet Sauvignon ★ and Sauvignon Blanc ★ may provide easier drinking. Best years: (Merlot) 1990 88 85 84 81 78; (Cabernet Sauvignon) 1990 88 87 86.

CH. DUCRU-BEAUCAILLOU ★★★ *St-Julien AC, 2ème Cru Classé, Haut-Médoc, Bordeaux, France*   The epitome of ST-JULIEN, mixing charm and austerity, fruit and firmness. During the 1970s it was effortlessly ahead of the other Second Growths. Several now equal Ducru but none surpass it. Second wine: La Croix-Beaucaillou. Best years: 1990 89 88 86 85 83 82 81 78.

DUJAC *Morey St-Denis, Côte de Nuits, Burgundy, France*   One of Burgundy's leading winemakers, based in MOREY ST-DENIS, but with some choice vineyards also in VOSNE-ROMANEE and GEVREY-CHAMBERTIN. The wines are all good, including the small quantity of Morey St-Denis blanc, but the outstanding Dujac bottlings are the three Morey St-Denis Grands Crus – Clos de la Roche ★★, Bonnes Mares ★★ and Clos St-Denis★★ – all of which will age for a decade or more. Owner Jacques Seysses has also had a very positive influence on many young Burgundian winemakers. Best years: 1990 89 88 87 85 83 78.

DUNN VINEYARDS *Napa Valley, California, USA*   Massive, concentrated, hauntingly perfumed, long-lived Cabernet Sauvignon ★ ★ ★ is the trademark of Randy Dunn's wines from Howell Mountain. His Napa Valley Cabernets ★★ are more elegant but less memorable. Best years: 1990 88 87 86 85 84 82.

DURBACH *Baden, Germany*   Unusually for Baden, in Durbach Riesling (called here Klingelberger) is something of a speciality. Another speciality is Traminer, called here Klevner (normally a synonym for Pinot Blanc!). Best producers: Franckenstein, Heinrich Männle, Wolff Metternich, von Neveu.

DURIF   See Petite Sirah.

JEAN DURUP *Chablis, Burgundy, France*   The largest vineyard owner in CHABLIS, Jean Durup is a great believer in unoaked Chablis, and his wines tend to be clean and well-made without any great complexity. His top Chablis is the Premier Cru

Fourchaume ★. Durup wines appear under a variety of labels, including l'Eglantière, Ch. de Maligny and Valéry.

ÉCHÉZEAUX AC *Grand Cru, Côte de Nuits, Burgundy, France* The village of Flagey-Échézeaux, hidden down in the plain away from the vineyards, is best known for its two Grands Crus, Échézeaux and smaller and more prestigious Grands-Échézeaux which are sandwiched between the world-famous CLOS DE VOUGEOT and VOSNE-ROMANÉE. Few of the growers have made a name for themselves but there are some fine wines with a lovely, smoky, plum richness, and a soft texture that age well over 10–15 years to a gamy chocolaty depth. Best producers: DROUHIN, Engel★, GRIVOT, JAYER, Lamarche★★, Mongeard-Mugneret★★, Dom. de la ROMANEE-CONTI★★★, Sirugue★. Best years: 1990 89 88 86 85 83 80 78 76.

EDELZWICKER See Alsace AC.

EINZELLAGE German for an individual vineyard site or slope which is generally farmed by several growers. The name is preceded on the label by that of the village; e.g. the Wehlener Sonnenuhr is the Sonnenuhr vineyard in Wehlen. Naturally the mention of a particular site should signify a superior wine.

EISWEIN Rare, chiefly German and Austrian, late-harvested wine made by waiting until the arrival of the winter frosts and picking the grapes and pressing them while they are frozen. The effect is to concentrate the sweetness of the grape as most of the liquid is removed as ice. Must weights vary in Germany from 110 Oechsle in the Mosel to 128 Oechsle in Baden. In Austria the figure is 25 KMW or 127 Oechsle. Any grape varieties may be used. Canada is now showing some potential as a producer of Eiswein too.

NEIL ELLIS *Stellenbosch, South Africa* One of the Cape's leading wine-making consultants produces his own wines from vineyards in different parts of the province. The 1991 Whitehall Sauvignon Blanc ★, from the cool-climate Elgin area, is a bracingly leafy wine; while the lemony 1991 Chardonnay★★ and the taut, minty, chewy 1990 Cabernet Sauvignon ★★ come from Stellenbosch and show the potential of the area when grape-growing and wine-making techniques improve.

ELTVILLE *Rheingau, Germany* This town makes some of the Rheingau's most racy Riesling wines. Best producers: Fischer, Hans Hulbert, Staatsweingüt Eltville, von Simmern.

EMILIA-ROMAGNA *Italy* Central eastern province divided into Emilia and Romagna districts, chiefly infamous for LAMBRUSCO in Emilia. See also Romagna.

ENGLISH VINEYARD *Kent, England* One of England's leading contract winemakers, Kit Lindlar, produces a crisp, severe, Loire Valley Sauvignon lookalike called, simply, English Vineyard Dry. For consistency of style it's produced from a mix of grapes and, sometimes, a mix of vintages.

ENTRE-DEUX-MERS AC *Bordeaux, France*   This AC increasingly represents some of the freshest, brightest, snappiest dry white wine in France and the techniques of cold fermentation and of leaving skins in contact with juice for a few hours before fermentation, are behind the revival. In general, drink the wine of the latest vintage, though the better wines will last a year or two. The sweet wines are sold as PREMIERES COTES DE BORDEAUX, St-Macaire, LOUPIAC and STE-CROIX-DU-MONT. Best producers: Bonnet★, Canet, les Gauthiers, Launay, Laurétan, Moulin-de-Launay, la Rose du Pin, Thieuley★ , Tour de Mirambeau, Toutigeac.

ERBALUCE DI CALUSO DOC *Piedmont, Italy*   Usually a pleasant waxy, dry white, occasionally sparkling, from the Erbaluce grape. However, as Caluso Passito, when the grapes are semi-dried before fermenting, this can be one of Italy's great sweet wines, dark, luscious and nutty. Best producers: (Caluso Passito) Boratto★ ★ , Ferrando★ ★ .

ERDEN *Mosel, Germany*   Small village in the middle Mosel whose vineyards face it across the river. Erden's most famous vineyards are Prälat and Treppchen. The wines are marked by a slight mineral character. Best producers: LOOSEN, Mönchhof.

ERMITAGE   Swiss name for the Marsanne grape of the northern Rhône Valley. It is mostly found in the central Valais where the wines stop short of fermenting out dry, leaving a touch of sweetness and they can develop a lovely round, honeyed character. Best producer: Orsat (Marsanne Blanche)★ .

ERRÁZURIZ *Aconcagua Valley, Chile*   Careful producer of Chardonnay, Merlot and Cabernet Sauvignon and gradually achieving consistency. Top wines include a silky yet sinewy Barrel-Fermented Chardonnay Reserva ★, a juicily pure Merlot ★ and the intense, mint-and-blackcurrant Don Maximiano Cabernet Sauvignon ★, made from 100-year-old vines. Sauvignon Blanc at last began to show a good grassy style from the 1992 vintage.

ERZEUGERABFÜLLUNG   German for 'bottled by the producer', as opposed to Abfüllung, which could mean that just about anyone might have bottled it.

ESCHENAUER *Bordeaux, France*   Medium-quality Bordeaux merchant which sells a range of wines under its own label. It also markets the much more impressive wines of RAUSAN-SEGLA and SMITH-HAUT-LAFITTE on an exclusive basis.

EST! EST!! EST!!! DI MONTEFIASCONE DOC *Lazio, Italy*   Modest white from the shores of Lake Bolsena accorded its undeserved reputation because of an apocryphal story of a bishop's servant sent ahead to scout out good wines. Getting so excited about this one, he re-iterated the thumbs-up code three times. Perhaps it had been a long day. Best producers: Bigi, Falesco, Mazziottio.

120

ETCHART *Salta, Argentina*   Go-ahead winery benefitting from the consultancy of Bordeaux whizz-kid Michel Rolland, with high-sited vineyards in the Andes foothills at Cafayate, producing an irresistible Torrontés ★, fragrant, flowery and delicate, as well as good Cabernet Sauvignon and some, rich, powerful Malbec★ .

L'ÉTOILE AC *Jura, France*   A tiny area within the COTES DU JURA which has its own AC for whites, mainly from Chardonnay and Savagnin, and for VIN JAUNE. There is some good Champagne-method too. Best producers: Ch. de l'Étoile★ , l'Étoile co-op, Domaine de Montbourgeau.

CH. L'ÉVANGILE ★★ *Pomerol AC, Bordeaux, France*   Made by one of Bordeaux's most talented winemakers, Michel Rolland, the wine can be rich and exciting. But I still remain unconvinced it's worth the high asking price. Now owned by the Rothschilds of LAFITE-ROTHSCHILD. Best years: 1990 89 88 85 83 82 79 75.

EVANS FAMILY *Hunter Valley, New South Wales, Australia*   Len Evans' tiny Hunter vineyard grows majestic Chardonnay ★★ (made at ROTHBURY), highly regarded sparkling wine (PETALUMA-made), as well as Gamay and Pinot Noir. Nearly all the wine is sold privately or ex-winery – or drunk by Len with his friends.

EVANS & TATE *Margaret River, Western Australia*   Important Western Australian winery and a classy producer of complex Margaret River Chardonnay ★, well structured Merlot ★ and cur-ranty Cabernet ★. The grassy Sémillon and Sémillon blends are less interesting. Gnangara Shiraz is a leading Swan Valley brand made by the winery.

ÉVENTAIL DE VIGNERONS PRODUCTEURS *Beaujolais, Burgundy, France*   The most successful and powerful of the BEAUJOLAIS growers' associations formed to improve quality and marketing of their wines. The standard is consistently high. Look out for Louis Desvignes ★ in MORGON, Georges Passot ★ in CHIROUBLES and André Pelletier ★ in JULIENAS.

EYRIE VINEYARDS *Willamette Valley AVA, Oregon, USA*   One of the leading Pinot Noir ★ producers in Oregon but in poor years the wines can be withdrawn and thin. The Chardonnay ★ shows nice varietal fruit while the popular Pinot Gris flies off the shelves.

JOSEPH FAIVELEY *Nuits-St-Georges, Côtes de Nuits, Burgundy, France*   Faiveley is rarely mentioned in the same sentence as the best-known Burgundian *négociants*, such as JADOT and DROUHIN, but this merchant makes excellent red wines (especially CHAMBERTIN Clos de Bèze ★★★ and Mazis-Chambertin ★★), princi-pally from its substantial vineyard holdings. The much cheaper MERCUREY reds ★ are also very attractive. The Côte Chalonnaise whites from RULLY ★★ and Mercurey ★, and the oak-agcd BOUR-GOGNE Blanc represent outstanding value. Best years: (reds) 1990 89 88 85 83 78; (whites) 1990 89 88 85.

FALERNO DEL MASSICO *Campania, Italy* Falernian, from north of Naples, was one of the ancient Romans' superstar wines. The revived DOC, with a white Falanghina and reds from Aglianico and Primitivo at least looks promising. Best producers: Michele Moio, Villa Matilde.

CH. DE FARGUES ★★ *Sauternes AC, Bordeaux, France* Owned by the Lur-Saluces family who also own d'YQUEM, the quality of this fine, rich wine is more a tribute to their commitment than to the inherent quality of the vineyard.

FAUGÈRES AC *Languedoc, France* Faugères, with its hilly vineyards stretching up into the mountains north of Béziers in the Hérault, was the first of the Languedoc communes to make a reputation of its own. What marks it out from other Languedoc reds is its ripe, soft, rather plummy flavour, and though it is a little more expensive than neighbouring wines, the extra money is well worth it. There is very little white made. Best producers: Faugères co-op, du Fraisse, Grézan★ , Haut-Fabrègues★ , la Liguière, St-Aimé. Best years: 1991 90 89 88 86 85.

FAUSTINO MARTÍNEZ *Rioja DOC, País Vasco and Rioja, and Cava DO, Spain* Family-owned and technically very well equipped, this RIOJA company makes good Reserva ★ and Gran Reserva ★★ red Riojas in distinctive dark, frosty bottles, as well as a fruity, BEAUJOLAIS-style Vino Joven or Viña Faustina ★ , and pleasant whites and rosés. Best years: (reds) 1987 85 82 81.

FELSINA BERARDENGA *Chianti Classico DOCG, Tuscany, Italy* Leading CHIANTI estate making full, chunky wines usually in need of several years' aging in bottle, but quality is generally outstanding. Most notable are the single-vineyard Chianti Classico Riserva 'Rancia' ★★★ and Fontalloro ★★, a Sangiovese Vino da Tavola. Best years: 1990 88 85.

FENDANT *Valais, Switzerland* Chasselas wine from the steep slopes of the Swiss Valais. Good Fendant should be ever so slightly *spritzig* with a spicy character which makes it refreshing and light-hearted. It is best drunk *very* young, but a good example can age for years, becoming more like Chardonnay in time. The best is said to come from the slopes above Molignon and Montibeux, or from around Sion or Uvrier. Best producers: CAVES IMESCH, Jacques Germanier, Orsat.

FERREIRA *Port DOC, Douro DOC, Douro, Portugal* This old established port house has now been bought by SOGRAPE, producers of Mateus Rosé. However Sogrape have shown great talent in modernizing and improving much of Portugal's table wine industry, so the new arrangement should prove good for quality. Ferreira already produce the famous BARCA VELHA★ table wine, but are best known for excellent tawny ports, either the creamy, nutty Quinta do Porto 10 year-old ★ or the Duque de Braganza 20 year-old ★★. Their vintage port★ is improving too. Best years: (vintage ports) 1987 85 83 78 77 70 66 63.

FETZER VINEYARDS *Redwood Valley, California, USA* Mendocino winery making consistently drinkable, low-priced wines, both under the Fetzer label and the Bel Arbors second label. The Reserve wines, Barrel select Cabernet Sauvignon and Chardonnay are a step up but I feel they could be better. The Zinfandel Special Reserves★ are concentrated, fruity wines with a lot of staying power.

FIANO Distinctive, low yielding southern Italian white grape variety. Best producers: DI MAJO NORANTE (Molise), MASTROBERARDINO★ (Fiano di Avellino DOC in Campania).

CH. DE FIEUZAL *Pessac-Léognan AC, Cru Classé de Graves, Bordeaux, France* One of the most up-to-date properties in the region and the delicious, ripe, oaky wine sells at a high price. The rich, complex red ★★★ is drinkable almost immediately because of its gorgeous, succulent fruit but it will easily age for a decade or more. Less than 10% of the wine is white ★★★ but it is stupendous stuff and a leader among Bordeaux's new wave whites. Second wine: (red) l'Abeille de Fieuzal. Best years: (reds) 1990 89 88 87 86 85 83 82 81 78; (whites) 1990 89 88 87 86 85.

CH. FIGEAC ★★ *St-Émilion Grand Cru AC, 1er Grand Cru Classé, Bordeaux, France* Topnotch ST-ÉMILION property whose wine has a delightful fragrance and gentleness of texture. The wine is lovely young yet ideally should age for 10–12 years. Second wine: la Grangeneuve de Figeac. Best years: 1990 89 88 87 86 85 83 82 78 76 75.

FILLIATREAU *Saumur-Champigny, Loire Valley, France* The leading grower in SAUMUR-CHAMPIGNY, producing four different, richly-flavoured Cabernet Francs – Jeunes Vignes ★, Lena Filliatreau ★★, La Grande Vignolle ★★, and Vieilles Vignes ★★ – as well as SAUMUR Rouge ★. In a good vintage, Filliatreau's top reds can age for up to 15 years. He also makes a small amount of SAUMUR Blanc. Best years: 1990 89 88 85.

FINO See Jerez y Manzanilla DO.

FITOU AC *Languedoc-Roussillon, France* Dark red Fitou was one of the 1980s success stories – its burly flavour comes from Carignan and the wine will age well for at least 5–6 years. Best producers: Castex, Colomer, MONT TAUCH CO-op★, des Nouvelles, Vignerons du VAL D'ORBIEU. Best years: 1991 90 89 88.

FITZ-RITTER *Bad Dürkheim, Rheinpfalz, Germany* Good estate making fresh Riesling★ in stainless steel. The reds are made in a rather sweet style. Best years: 1990 89 88.

FIXIN AC *Côte de Nuits, Burgundy, France* Despite being next door to the great village of GEVREY-CHAMBERTIN, Fixin has never been able to produce anything really magical. The wines are worthy enough and tannic enough to last, but they rarely taste exciting and are often sold off under the COTE-DE-NUITS-VILLAGES label.

Recent vintages have shown improvements. Best producers: Berthaut, Bordet, Durand-Roblot★, Gelin et Molin, Joliet. Best years: (reds) 1990 89 88 87 85 83 80 78.

FLAGEY-ÉCHÉZEAUX AC See Échézeaux AC.

FLEURIE AC *Beaujolais, Burgundy, France* The third largest, but best-known BEAUJOLAIS Cru. Good Fleurie reveals the happy, carefree flavours of the Gamay grape at its best, plus heady perfumes and a juicy sweetness which can leave you gasping with delight. Not surprisingly, demand has meant that many of the wines are now woefully over-priced. Best producers: Bernard, Charret, Chignard, DUBOEUF★ (named vineyards), FLEURIE co-op, la Grande Cour, Montgénas, Paul. Best years: 1991 90 89 88 85.

FLEURIE-EN-BEAUJOLAIS, CAVE CO-OPÉRATIVE DE *Fleurie AC, Beaujolais, Burgundy, France* This excellent co-op, right in the heart of the attractive village of FLEURIE, produces some of the most aromatic, gluggably fruity wines in BEAUJOLAIS. Prices are high but that, sadly, is the case with most Fleurie.

FLORA SPRINGS *Napa Valley AVA, California, USA* A white wine specialist still feeling its way with the reds. Several Chardonnays are released with barrel-fermented Reserves ★★ some of Napa's best. Merlot ★ and Cabernet ★ can be good when the fruit is given its head. The red Bordeaux-blend Trilogy is still showing the signs of too much intellect and not enough passion.

ÉMILE FLORENTIN *St-Joseph AC, Rhône Valley, France* Traditional, organically-produced ST-JOSEPH, both red ★ and white ★, from very old vines. The wines are rather rustic, and can seem to lack fruit when young, but they age superbly well. Best years: (reds) 1990 89 88 85 83; (whites) 1990 89 85 84.

FONSECA *Port DOC, Douro, Portugal* Owned by the same group as TAYLOR'S, Fonseca makes ports in a rich, densely plummy style. Fonseca vintage ★★★ is magnificent, the aged tawnies ★★ uniformly superb – even their LBV★ is way better than most. Fonseca Guimaraens ★★ is the name of the 'off-vintage vintage'. Best years: (vintage ports) 1985 83 77 70 66 63.

FONSECA INTERNACIONAL *Terras do Sado VR, Oeste, Portugal* Best known for Lancers, the slightly sparkling pink (and white) wines bottled in crocks massively popular in the USA. Fonseca Internacional also make a pleasant but bland Lancers fizz by a method known as the 'Russian continuous'.

J M DA FONSECA SUCCESSORES *Setúbal Peninsula, Portugal* One of Portugal's most go-ahead wineries, with so many projects, it's difficult to keep up. Their most exciting reds are from the Alentejo, in particular the J S Rosado Fernandes Tinto Velho ★★, from REGUENGOS and the fleshy, oaky Morgado de

Reguengos ★, from Portalegre. In DAO the figgy, minty Casa da Insua ★ red is much better than most. From the Setúbal Peninsula south of Lisbon, they produce the tough, long-lived Periquita ★, the blackcurranty Quinta da Camarate ★ and the famous Moscatel de Setúbal ★ (now simply known as 'Setúbal').

FONT DE MICHELLE *Châteauneuf-du-Pape AC, Rhône Valley, France*   Owned by the endearing Gonnet brothers, this much-improved estate is currently among the top performers in CHATEAUNEUF-DU-PAPE. The reds ★★ and whites ★★ are stylish, but still heady with richness and southern herb fragrance – and they're not too expensive. Best years: 1990 89 88.

FONTANAFREDDA *Barolo, Piedmont, Italy*   One of the most impor-tant Piedmont estates, based in the old BAROLO hunting lodge of the King of Italy. In addition to a commercial Barolo, they also produce a range of Piedmontese varietals, several single-vine-yard Barolos★ and a good Spumante, Contessa Rosa. Best years: 1990 88 85.

FORST *Rheinpfalz, Germany*   Small village with 6 individual vine-yard sites, including the Ungeheuer or 'Monster'; wines from the Monster can indeed be quite savage with a wonderful mineral intensity and richness in the best years. Other famous vineyards are the Jesuitengarten and the Mariengarten. Best producers: BURKLIN-WOLF, WEGELER-DEINHARD, Werlé.

FRANCIACORTA DOC *Lombardy, Italy*   DOC east of Milan famous for high-quality, Champagne-method fizz from Pinot Bianco, Chardonnay and Pinot Nero. Also decent dry whites from Pinot Bianco and Chardonnay, and good reds from Cabernet Franc, Barbera, Nebbiolo and Merlot. Best producers: (fizz) Bellavista★★, Berlucchi★, CA' DEL BOSCO★, Cavalleri★. Best years: (reds) 1990 88.

FRANCISCAN VINEYARD *Napa Valley, California, USA*   Consist-ently good wines at fair prices centred on vineyards in the heart of the Napa Valley. The Cuvée Sauvage Chardonnay ★★★ is an absolutely blockbusting, courageous mouthful, but the Cabernet Sauvignon-based Meritage Red ★ is developing a very attractive style. Estancia is a second label with remarkably good-value Chardonnay from Central Coast and Cabernet Sauvignon ★ from Alexander Valley and its own Meritage★ as well. Franciscan also owns Mt Veeder Winery where lean but intense Cabernet Sauvignon ★★ of great minerally depth and complexity is made.

FRANKEN *Germany*   Wine region incorporated into the kingdom of Bavaria at the beginning of the 19th century producing wines recognizable by their squat, green Bocksbeutel bottles (now more familiar because of the Portuguese wine, Mateus Rosé). Müller-Thurgau has now replaced Silvaner as the dominant grape. The most famous vineyards are on the hillsides around the city of Würzburg. Although dry or Trocken wines are now a vogue in all Germany's wine regions, Franken has always spe-cialized in dry wines.

FRASCATI DOC *Lazio, Italy* Rome's quaffing wine made from
Trebbiano/Malvasia (the more Malvasia the better). Best producers: Colli di Catone, Fontana Candida, Pallavicini, Villa Simone.

FREIE WEINGÄRTNER WACHAU *Wachau, Niederösterreich, Austria*
A large co-op at Dürnstein. Despite its size, it regularly produces
some of Wachau's top white wines (especially the Grüner
Veltliners and Rieslings). The Achleiten vineyard in
Weissenkirchen is probably their best site for Riesling ★. Avoid
the reds. Best years: 1990 88 86 83 77.

FREISA Italian Piedmont grape making sweet, foaming, 'happy-
juice' reds, now rather out of fashion. Some producers are now
making a modern dry style which is very tasty. Best producers:
(sweet) Aldo CONTERNO, GAJA; (dry) Giacomo CONTERNO, Bartolo
Mascarello★, Aldo Vajra★.

FREIXENET *Cava DO, Catalonia, Spain* The second biggest Spanish
sparkling wine company (after CODORNIU) makes fizzes of generally unexciting quality in a vast network of cellars – which can
be visited by a small train – in San Sadurní de Noya. Cordon
Negro Brut is world famous for its black bottle.

FRESCOBALDI *Tuscany, Italy* Important Florentine company
selling large quantities of inexpensive blended CHIANTIS, but from
their own vineyards they produce good to excellent wines at
Nippozzano ★ (especially the Montesodi ★★ label) and Remole ★
in Chianti Rufina, Tenuta di Pomino ★ in POMINO and
Castelgiocondo in BRUNELLO DI MONTALCINO. Best years: 1990 88 85.

FRIULI-VENEZIA GIULIA *Italy* Located in north-east Italy, bordering Slovenia and Austria, this region is particularly noted for its
white wines from Pinot Grigio, Pinot Bianco, Sauvignon and Tocai
grown in the hill zones of COLLIO and COLLI ORIENTALI. These grapes
also thrive in the flatland DOCs of Aquileia, ISONZO, Latisana and
GRAVE DEL FRIULI, though red Merlot and Refosco grown to provide
Venice with its pasta wine, are more successful.

FRIZZANTE Italian for semi-sparkling wine, often sweetish.

FROG'S LEAP *Napa Valley AVA, California, USA* They take
Sauvignon Blanc ★ very seriously here. Also a better than average Chardonnay ★, plus a Cabernet Sauvignon ★ with more
grassy blackcurrant flavour than usual, and Zinfandel ★ with a
delicious black cherry fruit.

FRONSAC AC *Bordeaux, France* A small area west of POMEROL
making wines of reasonable quality and value. With a bit more
effort by producers to upgrade wine-making techniques, they
would be more widely known. Best producers: la Dauphine★,
Mayne-Vieil, la Rivière★, la Grave, la Valade, la Vieille Cure, Villars.
Best years: 1990 89 88 86 85 83 82 79 78.

CH. FUISSÉ *Pouilly-Fuissé, Mâconnais, Burgundy, France* Jean-Jacques Vincent is the leading grower in POUILLY-FUISSE, producing rich, ripe, concentrated Chardonnays. Top wines are the three Pouilly-Fuissés – Jeunes Vignes Cuvée Première★, the oak-fermented Ch. de Fuissé★★ and the memorably, richly textured Ch. de Fuissé Vieilles Vignes★★★. He also makes a fine ST-VERAN★, a BEAUJOLAIS and has a substantial *négoçiant* business specializing in wines of the Mâconnais. Best years: 1991 90 89 88 86 85 78.

FUMÉ BLANC See Sauvignon Blanc.

JEAN-NOËL GAGNARD *Chassagne-Montrachet AC, Côte de Beaune, Burgundy, France* One of a bewildering number of Gagnards in CHASSAGNE-MONTRACHET, Jean-Noël consistently makes the best wines. His top wine is rich, toasty BATARD-MONTRACHET★★★, but his other whites are first rate, too, particularly Morgeot Premier Cru★★. Gagnard's elegant reds★ are not quite as good as his whites, but are still among the most enjoyable in Chassagne. Best years: 1990 89 88 86 85 83 82.

GAILLAC AC *South-West France* The whites, mainly from Mauzac with its sharp, but attractive, green apple bite, are rather stern, but from a decent grower or the revitalized co-ops can be extremely refreshing. Little of the red and rosé has any great character, but from Jean Cros can have a startling dry pepperiness. The star of Gaillac at the moment is the outstanding sparkling wine, made by either the Champagne method or the *méthode rurale*, and ideally not quite dry and packed with fruit. Tecou co-op makes oak-aged Cuvée Passion and Cuvée Séduction. The labels don't say in which order they should be drunk. Drink all Gaillac as young as possible. Best producers: Albert, Boissel-Rhodes, Bosc Long, Cros, Labarthe, Labastide de Lévis co-op (since 1988), Larroze, Mas Dignon, Plageoles, Tecou co-op.

GAJA *Barbaresco DOCG, Piedmont, Italy* Angelo Gaja brought about the transformation of Piedmont from being a sleepy, old-fashioned region that Italians swore made the finest red wine in the world, yet the rest of the world disdained, to being an area buzzing with excitement. Gaja is to be thanked for introducing international wine-making standards into what was a parochial, backward area; and for charging such staggeringly high prices that the wine world took notice – thus giving other Piedmont growers the chance at last to get a decent return for their labours. Into this fiercely conservative area, full of fascinating grape varieties but proudest of the native Nebbiolo, he also introduced the great French grape varieties like Cabernet Sauvignon★, Sauvignon Blanc★ and Chardonnay★★★. Gaja's traditional strength has always been in single-vineyard BAR-BARESCO (his Sori San Lorenzo★★, Sori Tildin★★★ and Costa Russii★★, are often cited as Barbaresco's best). His first BAROLO released in 1992 should show whether he can make great traditional Piedmontese wine. Best years: 1990 89 88 85 82 79 78.

GALESTRO *Tuscany, Italy*   Bone-dry, neutral white from Trebbiano
and Malvasia grown in CHIANTI, but the whole idea smacks more
of a marketing exercise to soak up excess white grapes rather
than a new departure in white wine pleasures. Best producers:
ANTINORI, FRESCOBALDI, Ruffino, Teruzzi e Puthod.

GALICIA *Spain*   Up in Spain's hilly, verdant north-west, Galicia is
renowned for its fine but expensive Albariño whites. There are
three DOs: RIAS BAIXAS can make excellent, fragrant Albariño
whites, with modern equipment and serious wine-making.
Ribeiro has also invested heavily in new equipment, and better
local white grapes are now being used. Impoverished, mountainous Valdeorras makes predominantly red (and usually rough)
wines from Garnacha and Mencía.

E&J GALLO *Central Valley, California, USA*   The world's biggest
winery (over 25% of the total US market) has been trying to go
up-market in recent years, directing a lot of attention toward its
vineyards in Sonoma County where in the near future estate-
bottled wines will be produced. Unofficial preview wines generally look promising, but the up-market range released so far
always looks out of its depth against the competition. Gallo operates under a myriad of labels, many of them in the jug wine category which Gallo handles pretty well.

GAMAY   The only grape allowed for red BEAUJOLAIS. In general
Gamay wine is rather rough-edged and quite high in raspy acidity, but in Beaujolais, so long as the yield is not too high, it can
achieve a wonderful, juicy-fruit gluggability, almost unmatched
in the world of wine. Elsewhere in France, it is highly successful
in the Ardèche, increasingly so in the Loire and less so in the
Mâconnais, where it is used for rather dry, occasionally pleasant, light reds and rosés. It is grown elsewhere around the world
but so far without any distinction.

GARD, VIN DE PAYS DU *Languedoc, France*   Mainly reds and
rosés from the western side of the Rhône delta. Most Gard red is
light and spicy but the rosé is better, and when drunk young,
can be fresh and attractive. With modern wine-making the
whites can be good. Best producer: St-Gilles co-op.

GARNACHA BLANCA   See Grenache Blanc.

GARNACHA TINTA   See Grenache Noir.

GARRAFEIRA   Portuguese term for wine from an outstanding vintage, with ½% more alcohol than the minimum required, and
two years' aging in vat or barrel, followed by one in bottle for
reds, and six months of each for whites. Term also used by merchants for some of their best blended and aged wines.

GATTINARA DOCG *Piedmont, Italy*   One of the most capricious of
Italy's top red wine areas, capable of both great things and
dross. Situated in northern Piedmont and recently elevated to

DOCG, the Nebbiolo wines should be softer and lighter than BAROLO but possessing a delicious, black plums, tar and roses flavour – if you're lucky, but few producers have shown much consistency yet. Vintages follow those for Barolo, but the wines should be drunk within 10 years. Best producers: Antoniolo, Le Colline, Fiore, Nervi, Traviglini. Best years: 1990 88 85.

GAVI DOC *Piedmont, Italy*   Overpriced, faddish Piedmont white wine. Luckily they drink most of it in Turin, because this Cortese-based, lemony white certainly isn't worth the price. If you must drink it young. Best producers: Nicola Bergaglio (La Minaia in particular), Castello di Tassarolo, La Chiara, La Giustiniana, La Raia, La Scolca.

CH. GAZIN ★★ *Pomerol AC, Bordeaux, France*   One of the largest châteaux in POMEROL, situated next to the legendary PETRUS. The wine, traditionally a succulent, sweet-textured Pomerol, wonderful to drink young, but capable of long aging, has been an inconsistent performer over the years, but has hit top form since 1988, as Christian Moueix of PETRUS has taken an interest in the estate. I look forward to seeing if it's regained the knack. Best years: 1990 89 88.

GEELONG *Victoria, Australia*   Another region revived in the 1960s after being destroyed by phylloxera in the 19th century, but expansion has been erratic so far. Climate and wine potential are as good as the Yarra, with the same grapes excelling. Pinot Noir is exciting, but  Chardonnay, Riesling, Sauvignon Blanc and Cabernet also impress. Best producers: BANNOCKBURN, Idyll, Scotchmans Hill.

GEISENHEIM *Rheingau, Germany*   Village famous for its wine school, founded in 1870. It was here that the Müller-Thurgau grape, now one of Germany's most widely planted grapes, was bred in 1882. Geisenheim's most famous vineyard is the Rothenberg, the name indicating the vineyard's red soils which produce strong, earthy wines. Best producers: von Francken-Seirstorpff, Schumann-Nägler, von Zweierlein.

GELTZ ZILLIKEN *Saarburg, Saar, Germany*   Estate specializing in Rieslings★ from the Saarburger Rausch vineyard. In 1990 their wines were among the best in the Saar. Best years: 1990 89 88.

JACQUES GERMAIN *Chorey-Lès-Beaune, Côte de Beaune, Burgundy, France*   The sleepy village of CHOREY-LES-BEAUNE is the source of some of the Côte d'Or's best value reds and, along with TOLLOT-BEAUT, François Germain is the AC's best-known producer. As well as an elegant red, called Ch. de Chorey★, he makes a series of richer BEAUNE Premiers Crus (his Teurons ★★ and Vignes Franches ★★ are both superb) and reasonably-priced PERNAND-VERGELESSES Blanc★. The reds are best drunk after 2–6 years in bottle. Best years: 1990 89 88 86 85.

GEVREY-CHAMBERTIN AC *Côte de Nuits, Burgundy, France*
Gevrey-Chambertin is an infuriating village – with its world
famous CHAMBERTIN Grands Crus it is capable of making some of
the most delicious red Burgundies, but too often it produces a
succession of pale, lifeless semi-reds which don't really deserve
the AC at all. There was a welcome renewal of will among producers in the late 1980s. Good examples of straightforward
Gevrey-Chambertin village wine are proud, big-tasting Burgundy at its best, aging well for 6–10 years. The Premiers Crus and
Grands Crus, in the right hands, combine power and perfume in
a magical yet impressive way after 7–15 years aging. Best producers: Bachelet★, Burguet★★, Camus★, CLAIR, Damoy★, DROUHIN,
FAIVELEY, JADOT, Leclerc★, Magnien★, RODET, Rossignol★★, Roty★,
Rousseau★★, Trapet★, Varoilles★. Best years: 1990 89 88 87 85
83 80 78.

GEWÜRZTRAMINER A popular grape all over the world, but it
reaches its peak in France's Alsace. It is also grown, with mixed
results, in Australia, New Zealand, Oregon, California,
Czechoslovakia, Austria, Germany and Italy's Alto Adige where
it is generally called Traminer. As Heida it is grown in
Switzerland. *Gewürz* means spice and Gewürztraminer wine certainly can be spicy and exotically perfumed but remarkably in
Alsace, while they exude sensuality, the wines generally show
delightful balance. Styles vary enormously, from the fresh, light,
florally perfumed wines produced in Italy to the rich, luscious,
late-harvest ALSACE VENDANGE TARDIVE.

GHEMME DOC *Piedmont, Italy*   A red, Nebbiolo-based wine produced on the opposite bank of the Sesia river to GATTINARA. Best
producers: Antichi Vigneti di Cantalupo, Le Colline.

BRUNO GIACOSA *Piedmont, Italy*   One of the great intuitive winemakers of the Langhe hills south of Alba. He is an unashamed
traditionalist, leaving his BAROLOS and BARBARESCOS in cask for up
to 6 years. His Barbaresco Santo Stefano ★★ and Barolo Rio
Sordo ★★ are particularly good. Best years: 1990 88 85 82.

GIESEN *Canterbury, South Island, New Zealand*   Canterbury's
largest winery makes fine botrytized Riesling ★★★ and botrytized
Müller-Thurgau ★, as well as outstanding dry Riesling ★★, complex, oaky Chardonnay ★, an attractive Sauvignon Blanc ★ and
even a little Pinot Gris ★. Best years: 1991 89.

GIGONDAS AC *Rhône Valley, France*   Formerly a COTES DU RHONE-
VILLAGES, Gigondas deservedly gained its own AC in 1971
because the wines, mostly red with a little rosé and made
mainly from Grenache, have fists full of chunky personality.
Best producers: Beaumet-Bonfils, Faraud, les Gouberts, GUIGAL,
JABOULET, Longue-Toque, de Montmirail, les Pallières, Pascal, de
Piaugier, Raspail, St-Gayan. Best years: 1990 89 88 86 85 83 81.

CH. GILETTE ★★ *Sauternes AC, Bordeaux, France*   This astonishing property makes one of the most original SAUTERNES. The wine is stored in concrete vats as opposed to the more normal wooden barrels. This virtually precludes any oxygen contact, and it is oxygen that ages a wine. Consequently, when released at 20–30 years old, they are busting with life and lusciousness. Best years: 1967 59 55 53 49.

GIPPSLAND *Victoria, Australia*   Scattered, diverse wineries, all tiny but with massive potential, along the southern Victorian coast, led by Nicholson River with its fantastic, MONTRACHET-like Chardonnay ★★★. Pinot Noir from Nicholson River★ and Bass Phillip★ is very good but I think Briagolong ★★ is even better, one of Australia's most original Pinot Noirs. The McAlister ★, a Bordeaux blend, has also produced some tasty flavours.

GISBORNE *North Island, New Zealand*   Gisborne, with its hot, dry climate and fertile soils, has shown that it is capable of producing quality as well as quantity. Local growers have christened their region 'The Chardonnay Capital of New Zealand' and Gewürztraminer is another success. Good reds, however, are hard to find. All large Auckland companies use Gisborne fruit. Best producers: MILLTON, MATAWHERO.

CH. GISCOURS ★★ *Margaux AC, 3ème Cru Classé, Haut-Médoc, Bordeaux, France*   A large MARGAUX property with enormous potential that is not always realized. Giscours' magic is that it can produce wines of delectable scent yet pretty solid structure. After a dull patch recent vintages look to be picking up again. Best years: 1990 89 86 85 83 82 81 80 79 78 75.

GIVRY AC *Côte Chalonnaise, Burgundy, France*   An important Côte Chalonnaise village. The reds have an intensity of fruit and ability to age that is not common in the region. In recent years the whites have improved considerably and there are now some attractive fairly full, nutty examples. Best producers: Chofflet (reds only), Derain, Joblot, Ragot, THENARD★. Best years: (reds) 1990 89 88 85 83 82; (whites) 1990 89 88 86 85.

GLEN ELLEN *Sonoma Valley, California, USA*   Producers of very consumer-friendly wines which have gained a large following due to careful pricing, very aggressive promotion and never underestimating the American sweet tooth.

CH. GLORIA ★★ *St-Julien AC, Cru Bourgeois, Haut-Médoc, Bordeaux, France*   A fascinating property, created by one of Bordeaux's grand old men, the late Henri Martin, out of tiny plots of Classed Growth land scattered all round ST-JULIEN. His obsession raised Gloria's wine during the 1960s and 1970s to both Classed Growth quality and price. Generally very soft and sweet-centred, the wine nonetheless ages well. But he desperately wanted to own a Classed Growth and he finally succeeded when he bought ST-PIERRE in 1982. Second wine: Peymartin. Best years: 1990 89 88 86 85 83 82.

GOLAN HEIGHTS WINERY *Golan Heights, Israel*   Israel's leading quality wine producer. Cool summers, well-drained high altitude vineyards and wine-making that combines the latest Californian techniques with kosher strictures have resulted in good Sauvignon Blanc ★ and Cabernet Sauvignon ★ and excellent, oaky Chardonnay ★★. Yarden is the label used for top-of-the-range wines, while Golan and Gamla are mid-range labels.

GOLD SEAL *Finger Lakes, New York State, USA*   Historically impor-tant because of experiments with vinifera grapes. Now owned by Vintners International which produce a line of standard wine under several labels, including Charles Fournier.

GOLDENMUSKATELLER   The Moscato Giallo grape, is known as Goldenmuskateller in northern Italy's Alto Adige. Here it is made in both highly scented and dry, and slightly sweet ver-sions. Best producer: Tiefenbrunner★ (dry style).

GONZÁLEZ BYASS *Jerez y Manzanilla DO, Andalucía, Spain*   Tío Pepe ★, the high quality fino brand of this huge, top quality sherry firm, is the world's biggest selling sherry. Their top range of old sherries is superb: intense, dry Amontillado del Duque ★★★, and two rich, complex olorosos, sweet Matusalem ★★★ and medium Apostoles ★★. One step down is the Alfonso Dry Oloroso ★.

GOULBURN VALLEY *Victoria, Australia*   The Goulburn river is a serene, beautiful thread of contentment running through Victoria's parched grazing lands. Surprisingly few vineyards have been established here but these do produce very individual wines. The region is best known for Marsanne white. Best pro-ducers: CHATEAU TAHBILK, MITCHELTON, Tisdall (Mount Helen).

GRAACH *Mosel, Germany*   Village in the middle Mosel with 4 vineyard sites, the most famous being Domprobst and Himmelreich. A third, the Josephshöfer, is wholly owned by the von KESSELSTATT estate in Trier. The wines have an attractive roundness to balance their steely acidity. Best producers: von KESSELSTATT, LOOSEN, J J PRUM, WEGELER-DEINHARD, Weins-Prüm.

GRACIANO   A rare but excellent Spanish grape, traditional in Rioja and Navarra, but low-yielding. It makes lovely, plummy, fra-grant reds and its high acidity adds life when blended with the good quality, but low-acid Tempranillo.

GRAHAM *Port DOC, Douro, Portugal*   Another port shipper in the Symington empire, making rich, florally scented vintage port ★★, sweeter than DOW's and WARRE's, the two other main Symington brands, but with a pretty firm backbone if you want to age it. In years when a 'vintage' is not declared, they make a rich, gutsy wine called Malvedos ★. Best years: (vintage ports) 1985 83 80 77 70 66 63.

ALAIN GRAILLOT *Crozes-Hermitage AC, Rhône Valley, France* This excellent estate, only established in 1985, stands out as a producer of powerfully concentrated rich, fruity reds. The top wine is called La Guirande ★★, but his basic Crozes ★★ is wonderful, too. Best years: 1990 89 88.

GRAN RESERVA Top category of Spanish wines from a top vintage, with at least 5 years' aging for reds and 4 years' for whites.

GRAND CRU French for literally, a 'great growth' or vineyard. These are supposedly the best sites in Alsace, Burgundy, Champagne and parts of Bordeaux and should produce the most exciting wines. However the term only applies to the vineyard site. What the grower decides to do there, and what the winemaker then does with the grapes is up to them.

CH. GRAND MOULAS *Côtes du Rhône, Rhône Valley, France* Marc Ryckwaert makes first-rate COTES DU RHONE ★ from Grenache and a lick of Syrah that is absolutely delicious young but will age for 3–5 years if you must. He also makes very good COTES DU RHONE-VILLAGES ★ (red and white) and a rich, Syrah-based Grande Reserve called Cuvée de l'Écu ★★ which really is worth aging. Best years: 1991 90 89 88.

CH. GRAND-PUY-DUCASSE ★ *Pauillac AC, 5ème Cru Classé, Haut-Médoc, Bordeaux, France* This used to be one of the duller PAUILLAC Classed Growths, but the wines have improved enormously since the mid-1980s. Recent vintages have been particularly impressive, with lots of supple, blackcurrant fruit. Second wine: Artigues-Arnaud. Best years: 1990 89 88 86 85 82.

CH. GRAND-PUY-LACOSTE ★★ *Pauillac AC, 5ème Cru Classé, Haut-Médoc, Bordeaux, France* This wine is classic PAUILLAC, with lots of blackcurrant and cigar-box perfume. As the years pass the flavours mingle with the soft sweetness of new oak into one of Pauillac's most memorable taste sensations. Owned by the Borie family of DUCRU-BEAUCAILLOU. Second wine: Lacoste-Borie. Best years: 1990 89 88 86 85 83 82 81 79 78.

GRAND TINEL *Châteauneuf-du-Pape AC, Rhône Valley, France* One of the Rhône's most under-valued producers, Elie Jeune makes big, rich, Grenache-dominated reds ★★ with a piercing aroma of cassis that age superbly. The vines are very old here and it shows in the concentration of the wine. Best years: 1990 89 88 86 85 83 81 79 78.

GRANDE MARQUE Champagne's self-appointed élite – a grouping of the larger, better-known houses – is known as the Syndicat des Grandes Marques. Their products, which vary from the sublime to the virtually undrinkable, are known as Grandes Marques, or great brands.

133

GRANDS-ÉCHÉZEAUX AC See Échézeaux AC.

YVES GRASSA *Vin de Pays des Côtes de Gascogne, South-West France* The most innovative producer of COTES DE GASCOGNE, who transformed Gascony's thin raw whites into some of the snappiest, fruitiest, bone-dry wine in France. Grassa has also been experimenting with oak-aged ★ and late-harvest ★ styles.

ALFRED GRATIEN *Champagne AC, Champagne, France* This small company makes some of my favourite Champagne. In the modern world of Champagne, where many companies are obsessed with brand image, Gratien declares that its image is the quality of the wine and nothing else. Its wines are made in wooden casks, which is very rare nowadays. The non-vintage ★★ blend is usually 4 years old when sold, rather than the more normal 2 years. The vintage ★★ wine is deliciously ripe and toasty when released but can age for another 10 years. Best years: 1985 82 79 75.

GRATIEN ET MEYER *Loire Valley, France* Also owners of the quality-minded Champagne house Alfred GRATIEN, Gratien & Meyer is an important Loire producer in its own right. Its reputation rests on its SAUMUR MOUSSEUX, particularly its rich, biscuity Cuvée Flamme ★★ and Rosé Brut ★. They make a little CREMANT DE LOIRE★ – and their sparkling red Cuvée Cardinal★ is unusual and fun – a rare combination in France.

GRAVE DEL FRIULI DOC *Friuli-Venezia Giulia, Italy* DOC covering 15 wine styles in western Friuli. Good affordable Merlot, Refosco, Chardonnay, Pinot Grigio, Traminer and Tocai. Best producers: Ca' Bolani★, Vescovo, Pighin, Pittaro, Plozner★.

GRAVES AC *Bordeaux, France* The Graves region covers the area south of Bordeaux to Langon, but the generally superior villages in the northern half broke away in 1987 to form the PESSAC-LEOGNAN AC. However, all is not lost, as a new wave of wine-making is sweeping through the southern Graves. Nowadays, there are plenty of bone-dry whites, with lots of snappy freshness, as well as soft, nutty barrel-aged whites, and some juicy, quick-drinking reds. Best producers: Cabannieux, Clos Floridène★, Domaine la Grave★, Magence, RAHOUL, Respide-Médeville, Roquetaillade-La-Grange, St-Pierre. Best years: (reds) 1990 89 88 86 85 83 82; (whites) 1990 89 88 87 86.

GRAVES SUPÉRIEURES AC *Bordeaux, France* White Graves, dry, medium or sweet, with a minimum alcohol level of 12% as opposed to 11% for Graves. The AC has never really caught on because of the confusion between dry and sweet wines, but the sweet wines can, in good years, make decent substitutes for the more expensive SAUTERNES. Best producer: (sweet) Clos St-Georges★. Best years: 1990 89 88 86.

GREAT WESTERN *Victoria, Australia* Distinguished old region in central-western Victoria, mainly known for sparkling wine. It is now much reduced in importance but still produces some of

Australia's greatest Shiraz – as table wine, sparkling red and even port! Best producers: BEST's, Cathcart Ridge, Montara★, MOUNT LANGI GHIRAN, SEPPELT.

GRECHETTO Very attractive Italian white variety centred on Umbria, making tasty, anise-tinged dry whites for quick consumption and also contributes to Vin Santo in Tuscany. Best producers: ADANTI, Antonello, Caprai, Rocca di Fabbri.

GRENACHE BLANC A common white grape in the South of France, but without many admirers. Except me, that is, because I love the pale, wispy, pear-scented wine just flecked with anise that a careful producer can achieve. Best at 6–12 months old. Also grown as Garnacha Blanca in Spain.

GRENACHE NOIR Among the world's most widely-planted red grapes – the bulk of it in Spain where it is called Garnacha Tinta. It is a hot climate grape and in France it reaches its peak in the southern Rhône, especially in CHATEAUNEUF-DU-PAPE where it combines great alcoholic strength with rich raspberry fruit and a wild windswept perfume hot from the herb-strewn hills. It is generally given more tannin and acid by blending with Syrah, Cinsaut or other southern French grapes. It can make wonderful heady rosé in TAVEL, LIRAC and COTES DE PROVENCE, as well as in NAVARRA in Spain. In RIOJA it adds weight to the frequently light Tempranillo. Also widely grown in California and Australia, but not respected except by original thinkers like Randall Grahm of BONNY DOON in California who makes lovely rosés and reds from old vines, and Charles Melton in Australia who makes gutsy Nine Popes Red★. See also Cannonau.

GRGICH HILLS CELLAR *Napa Valley AVA, California, USA*   Mike Grgich was the winemaker at CHATEAU MONTELENA when that winery's Chardonnay shocked the Paris judges by finishing ahead of French Chardonnays in the famous 1976 tasting. At his own winery he makes ripe, tannic Cabernet Sauvigon ★ and a huge, old-style Zinfandel ★★ that is one of the best in California, but the winery's reputation has been made by a big, ripe, oaky Chardonnay ★★ that year by year proves to be one of the Napa's best-selling, high-priced wines. Best years: 1991 90 88 87.

GRIGNOLINO An Italian red grape native to Piedmont that can produce light-coloured but intensely flavoured wines. DOC in the Monferrato Casalese and Asti hills, and also made in Alba. HEITZ makes a rare version in California. Best producers: Aldo CONTERNO, Rivetti, Scarpa, Vietti.

GRIOTTE-CHAMBERTIN AC See Chambertin AC.

JEAN GRIVOT *Vosne-Romanée, Côte de Nuits, Burgundy, France*
Étienne Grivot is among the most respected young growers in Burgundy but, since he took over from his father in the mid-1980s, the wines have been somewhat inconsistent. The top wines can be spectacularly good – dense, full of fruit and capable of aging for 15 years or more. I have certainly had brilliant bottles of CLOS DE VOUGEOT ★★, RICHEBOURG ★★ and VOSNE-ROMANEE Les Beaumonts ★★, but recent vintages have been slightly disappointing, given the reputation and high prices of the wines. Best years: 1990 89 88 87 85 83 82 78.

GROOT CONSTANTIA *Constantia, South Africa* This 300-year-old estate, owned by the government, has had difficulties in the past deciding whether it's simply a tourist attraction (it has 300,000 visitors a year to cope with) or a serious wine producer. Recent vintages still make me think the tourism has the upper hand, though Sauvignon Blanc and Chardonnay aren't bad. The reds desperately need more fruit.

GROS PLANT DU PAYS NANTAIS VDQS *Loire Valley, France* From the damp, marshy salt-flats around Nantes, Gros Plant can be searing stuff but this acidic wine is surprisingly well-suited to the great platefuls of seafood guzzled in the region. Best producers: Bois-Bruley, Clos des Rosiers, Cuvée du Marquisat, Guindon, Hallereau, Métaireau, Sauvion. Best years: 1991 90 89.

GROSSLAGE German term for a grouping of a number of villages and communes, therefore somewhere between a village and a Bereich. Some Grosslages are not too big, and have the advantage of allowing small amounts of higher Prädikat wines to be made from the production of several individual vineyards. In other cases, however, the use of vast Grosslage names such as Niersteiner Gutes Domtal serves only to make the consumer believe he's buying something special when he isn't.

CH. GRUAUD-LAROSE ★★★ *St-Julien AC, 2ème Cru Classé, Haut-Médoc, Bordeaux, France* This is one of the largest ST-JULIEN estates and makes brilliant wines that are only now getting the acclaim they deserve. The leading château of the CORDIER group. The vintages of the 1980s have been made darker and deeper, sweetened with wood and toughened with tannin. Less easy to drink young, they should be even more exciting when they're mature at up to 20 years or so. Second wine: Sarget de Gruaud-Larose. Best years: 1990 89 88 86 85 84 83 82 81 79 78.

GRÜNER VELTLINER Grown extensively in every Austrian wine region with the exception of Styria. The grape is at its best, however, in Kamptal-Donauland, the Wachau and the large, amorphous Weinviertel region, where the soil and slightly damp climate, especially in the east, bring out all the characteristic lentilly, white-peppery aromas in the fruit. Czechoslovakia also has some success with it.

GUIGAL *Côte-Rôtie AC, Rhône Valley, France*   Marcel Guigal is among the most famous names in the Rhône, producing wines from his company's own vineyards in CÔTE-RÔTIE as well as from purchased grapes. Guigal's top wines – La Mouline ★★★, La Turque ★★★ and La Landonne ★★★ – are unbelievably expensive, but also spectacularly good if you don't mind a dark, oaky sweetness masking the wines' fruit for the first few years of its life. CONDRIEU ★★ is also very fine, if oaky,  but HERMITAGE ★ is merely good, while the much cheaper CÔTES DU RHÔNE ★ is a delicious wine outperforming its humble AC with ease. Best years: 1990 89 88 85 83 82 81.

CH. GUIRAUD ★★ *Sauternes AC, 1er Cru Classé, Bordeaux, France*   A property that was hauled up from near extinction by the Canadian Narby family, convinced Guiraud could be one of SAUTERNES' greatest wines. Selecting only the best grapes and using 50% new oak each year they have returned Guiraud to the top quality fold. Best years: 1990 89 88 86 83 82 81.

GUNDERLOCH-USINGER *Nackenheim, Rheinhessen, Germany*   Up-and-coming estate on the Rhine terrace. Their best vineyard is the Nackenheimer Rothenberg★. Best years: 1989 88 87.

LOUIS GUNTRUM *Nierstein, Rheinhessen, Germany*   A very large estate by German standards producing a range of wines from very dry to sweet using both traditional varieties and new crossings. The classiest are the single-vineyard wines from Oppenheim and Nierstein. Best years: 1990 89 88 86 85 81.

FRITZ HAAG *Brauneberg, Mosel, Germany*   Top Mosel grower with sites on the Brauneberger Juffer and Brauneberger Juffer Sonnenuhr. It was just his luck to be involved in a major re-organization of his Juffer site and so make almost no wine in the great 1990 vintage. He partially made up for this with brilliant 1990 ★★★ from Juffer Sonnenuhr. Best years: 1990 89 88 85 83 79.

HALBTROCKEN German for medium dry. In Germany medium dry wine has less than 18g per litre of residual sugar though sparkling wine is allowed up to 50g per litre. In Austria medium dry has only 9g per litre. But the high acid levels in German wines often make them seem drier and harsher.

HALLAU *Schaffhausen, Switzerland*   Important wine commune in German-speaking eastern Switzerland, best known for fair Blauburgunder (Pinot Noir). Best producer: Hans Schlatter.

HAMILTON RUSSELL VINEYARDS *Hermanus, South Africa*   Tim Hamilton-Russell has been a persistent critic of South Africa's all-powerful wine establishment, and it has meant that his 'small operation obsessed with quality' has not found the going easy. Yet the 1988 Pinot Noir ★★, with its spare, pure, lingering fruit and graceful structure, and the 1991 Chardonnay ★ and

137

1990 Chardonnay Reserve ★★, supple, svelte and full, are some of South Africa's few world class wines, rewarding his dogged – but undoubtedly sophisticated – determination.

THOMAS HARDY & SONS *Southern Vales, South Australia* Fine quality across the board. Siegersdorf Riesling and several varietals under the Leasingham and Nottage Hill labels are tasty and affordable; Hardy Collection Chardonnay ★★, Fumé Blanc and Cabernet are better – and still affordable. Lush Chateau Reynella Cabernet ★★ caps the McLaren Vale reds. The Eileen Hardy range has dense Shiraz ★ and rich, heady, oak-perfumed Chardonnay ★★. Now owned by Berri Renmano.

HARVEYS *Jerez y Manzanilla DO, Andalucía, Spain* Harveys is the biggest of the sherry firms, thanks to Bristol Cream. The standard range is unexciting, but the up-market 1796 wines are much better. Fino Tio Mateo ★ is an authentically light, dry fino.

HATTENHEIM *Rheingau, Germany* Fine Rheingau village with 13 individual vineyard sites, including a share of the famous Marcobrunn vineyard. Best producers: von Simmern, Georg Müller Stiftung, SCHLOSS REINHARTSHAUSEN, SCHLOSS SCHONBORN.

CH. HAUT-BAGES-LIBÉRAL ★★ *Pauillac AC, 5ème Cru Classé, Haut-Médoc, Bordeaux, France* This obscure property is fast becoming one of my favourite PAUILLAC wines – loads of unbridled delicious fruit, positively hedonistic style – and I can afford it! The wines will age well but are ready to drink at 5 years. Best years: 1990 89 88 86 85 83 82.

CH. HAUT-BAILLY ★★ *Pessac-Léognan AC, Cru Classé de Graves, Bordeaux, France* Haut-Bailly makes the softest and most charming wines among the GRAVES Classed Growths and has shown welcome improvement in the late 1980s. Agreeably drinkable very early, but they also age fairly well. Second wine: la Parde-de-Haut-Bailly. Best years: 1990 89 88 86 85 82 81 79.

CH. HAUT-BATAILLEY ★ *Pauillac AC, 5ème Cru Classé, Haut-Médoc, Bordeaux, France* Despite being owned by the Bories of DUCRU-BEAUCAILLOU, this small estate has made too many wines that are light and pleasant, attractively spicy, but lacking any real class and concentration. Recent vintages have improved and it is at last becoming more substantial. Best years: 1990 89 88 85 83 82.

CH. HAUT-BRION *Pessac-Léognan AC, 1er Cru Classé, Graves, Bordeaux, France* Haut-Brion was the only Bordeaux property outside the Médoc to be included in the great 1855 Classification, when it was accorded First Growth status. The excellent gravel-based vineyard is now part of Bordeaux's suburbs and the red wine ★★★ frequently does, but by no means always, deserves its exalted status. There is also a small amount of white Haut-Brion ★★★. At its best it is fabulous wine, magically rich yet marvellously dry, blossoming out over 5–10 years. Second wine: (red) Bahans-Haut-Brion. Best years: (reds) 1990 89 88 86 85 83 81 79 78; (whites) 1990 89 88 87 86 85 83 82 81 79 76.

CH. HAUT-MARBUZET ★★ *St-Estèphe AC, Cru Bourgeois, Haut-Médoc, Bordeaux, France* Impressive ST-ESTEPHE wine with great, rich, mouthfilling blasts of flavour and lots of new oak. Best years: 1990 89 88 86 85 83 82 81 78.

HAUT-MÉDOC AC *Bordeaux, France* AC for the southern half of the Médoc peninsula. All the finest gravelly soil is in this section and the Haut-Médoc AC covers all the decent vineyard land not included in the 6 separate village ACs (MARGAUX, MOULIS, LISTRAC, ST-JULIEN, PAUILLAC and ST-ESTEPHE). The wines vary widely in quality and style. Best producers: d'Agassac, Barreyres, Belgrave★, Camensac★, CANTEMERLE★, Castillon★, CISSAC, Coufran, Hanteillan★, la LAGUNE★★, Lamarque★, LANESSAN★, LAROSE-TRINTAUDON★, Liversan, Malescasse, Ramage-la-Batisse, Sénéjac★, la Tour-Carnet, la Tour-du-Haut-Moulin.

HAUT-MONTRAVEL AC *South-West France* Fairly pleasant, sweet white wines produced from hillside vineyards at the western limit of the BERGERAC region. The wines are sweeter than straight MONTRAVEL and COTES DE MONTRAVEL. Best producer: Gourgueil.

HAUT-POITOU AC *Loire Valley, France* Wines from south of the Loire Valley on the way to Poitiers, which are very similar in style to the Loire. Crisp, zingy Sauvignons and Chardonnays, slightly green Cabernet and Gamay reds and good fresh rosés. In general drink the wines young. The Haut-Poitou co-op at Neuville dominates production.

HAUTE VALLÉE DE L'AUDE, VIN DE PAYS DE LA *Languedoc-Roussillon, France* The best still wines from the Limoux sparkling wine district. Most of the wine produced is white, with particular emphasis on Chardonnay. Best producers: Astruc, Buoro, Vialade.

HAUTES-CÔTES DE BEAUNE AC See Bourgogne-Hautes Côtes de Beaune AC.

HAUTES-CÔTES DE NUITS AC See Bourgogne-Hautes Côtes de Nuits AC.

HAWKES BAY *North Island, New Zealand* One of New Zealand's oldest and most prestigious wine regions. High sunshine hours, moderately predictable weather during ripening and a complex array of soil patterns makes it ideal for a wide range of wine-making styles. Chardonnay, Cabernet Sauvignon and Merlot are the area's greatest strengths. Sauvignon Blanc is generally a bit flat. Best producers: Brookfields, Esk Valley, NGATARAWA, C J Pask, Montana MacDonald Winery, TE MATA, Vidal.

HEEMSKERK *Northern Tasmania, Australia* Major Tasmanian winery operating in a severe and marginal climate. Wines from Chardonnay, Pinot Noir and Riesling are erratic but brilliant at best. Champagne-method fizz ★ is made in partnership with Louis ROEDERER.

139

DR HEGER *Ihringen, Baden, Germany* Dr Heger specializes in Rieslings and Spätburgunders in Germany's warmest wine village. The wines are left on their lees producing exciting, complex fruit, the whites ★ in particular gaining wonderful sensuous apricot and honey flavours. Best years: 1990 89 88.

HEIDA Swiss name for grape thought to be either the Savagnin of the French Jura or the Gewürztraminer which don't taste remarkably similar to me, but there you go. And, just to be difficult, in the Swiss Valais it is known as the Paien. In Switzerland above the town of Visp at Visperterminen, Heida is grown at heights of around 1000m (3280ft), the highest altitude vineyards in Europe and the wine is correspondingly pungent and mountain mad. Best producers: Chanton, St Jodern.

CHARLES HEIDSIECK *Champagne AC, Champagne, France* Under new owners Rémy Martin, a lot of effort has gone into improving the quality in recent years. The non-vintage blend ★ is richer than it used to be, even if the price has crept up to a ridiculous level, and the Blanc de Blancs ★★ is now one of the best on the market. Also look out for the rosé ★ and the prestige cuvée, called Champagne Charlie ★. Best years: 1986 85.

HEITZ CELLARS *Napa Valley AVA, California, USA* The star attraction here is the Martha's Vineyard Cabernet Sauvignon ★★. Heitz also makes a Bella Oaks Vineyard Cabernet Sauvignon ★ which has its fans and a straight Cabernet ★ that takes time to understand, but can be good. I would sound more enthusiastic if I felt that recent problems in the cellar had been admitted and addressed with a bit more enthusiasm. Grignolino Rosé is attractive picnic wine. Best years: (Martha's Vineyard) 1986 85 75 74; (Bella Oaks) 1986 80 77.

HENSCHKE *Adelaide Hills, South Australia* Fifth-generation winemaker Stephen Henschke and viticulturist wife Prue make some of Australia's grandest reds from old vines in Eden Valley. Hill of Grace ★★★, a stunning wine with dark exotic flavours comes from a single, century-old plot of Shiraz. Mount Edelstone Shiraz ★★ and Cyril Henschke Cabernet ★★ are also brilliant wines. The whites ★ are full and intensely flavoured too, despite often coming from unfashionable varieties. Best years: (reds) 1991 90 88 86 84 82 80 78 72.

HÉRAULT, VIN DE PAYS DE L' *Languedoc, France* A huge Vin de Pays, covering the entire Hérault department. Red wines predominate, based on Carignan, Grenache and Cinsaut, and most of wine is sold in bulk. But things are changing. There are lots of hilly vineyards with great potential, and MAS DE DAUMAS GASSAC is merely the first of what I hope will be many exciting reds from the region. The whites are improving too. Best producers: du Bosc, Jany, MAS DE DAUMAS GASSAC★★, de la Masette.

HERMITAGE AC *Rhône Valley, France* Great Hermitage, from steep vineyards above the town of Tain l'Hermitage in the northern Rhône, is revered throughout the world as a rare, rich, red wine – expensive, memorable and classic. Not all Hermitage achieves such an exciting blend of flavours because the vineyard area is not large and some merchants will take any grapes just to list Hermitage. But the best growers, with mature red Syrah vines, can create superbly original wine, needing 5–10 years' aging even in a light year and a minimum of 15 years in a ripe vintage. White Hermitage, from Marsanne and Roussanne, is rather less famous but the best wines, made by traditionalists,  can outlive the reds, sometimes lasting as long as 40 years. Some winemakers, like JABOULET, are making modern, fruity, fragrant whites that are lovely at 1–2 years old. Best producers: Belle★★, CHAPOUTIER★★ (since 1988), CHAVE★★, DELAS★★ (single vineyard), Desmeure★, Fayolle★★, Ferraton★★, Gray (whites only★), Grippat★, GUIGAL★, JABOULET★★★ (since 1988), Sorrel★★. Best years:1990 89 88 85 83 82 80 78 76 71 70.

THE HESS COLLECTION *Napa Valley AVA, California, USA* A recent arrival in Napa Valley but already earning rave reviews for the Cabernet Sauvignon ★★ which is showing all the intense lime and black cherry originality of its Mt Veeder fruit, without coating it with impenetrable tannins.

HESSISCHE BERGSTRASSE *Germany* Small, warm wine region near Darmstadt. Much of the wine-making is in the hands of the local co-op, although the Staatsweindomäne also makes good wine. There has been less flirtation with new grape varieties here than elsewhere in Germany, and Riesling is still the most prized creation. Eisweins are a speciality.

HEURIGE *Austria* Fresh, young wine drunk in the many taverns in the Viennese hills. Once the wine is a year old it is called *Altwein* or 'old wine'. It goes without saying that no really good wine is sold as Heurige, yet a few swift jugs of it quaffed in the hills can make for a great evening, but keep the aspirin handy.

HEYL ZU HERRNSHEIM *Nierstein, Rheinhessen, Germany* Top estate on the Rhine terrace practising organic farming. They always produce some ★★ wines especially from the Brudersberg, Pettenthal, Hipping and Ölberg sites but are inconsistent lower down the scale. Best years: 1990 89 88.

HIDALGO *Jerez y Manzanilla DO, Andalucía, Spain* Hidalgo's Manzanilla La Gitana ★★ is deservedly the best-selling man-zanilla in Spain. Hidalgo is still family owned, and only uses grapes from its own vineyards. Brands include Mariscal ★, Fino Especial and Miraflores, Amontillado Napoleon ★★, Oloroso Viejo ★★ and Jerez Cortado ★★.

141

FRANZ HIRTZBERGER *Wachau, Niederösterreich, Austria* One of
the Wachau's top growers. His best wines are the Rieslings from
Singerriedel★★ and Hochrain ★★. The best Grüner Veltliner
comes from the Honifogl site ★. Best years: 1990 86 83.

HOCHHEIM *Rheingau, Germany* Village best known for having
given the English the word 'Hock' for Rhine wine, but with good
individual vineyard sites especially Domdechaney and
Kirchenstück. On the Königin Victoria Berg there is even a statue
of the 19th-century British queen who swore by the therapeutic
qualities of Hock after she'd stopped off there for a picnic. Best
producers: Aschrott, SCHLOSS SCHONBORN, Staatsweingut Eltville.

HOLLICK *Coonawarra, South Australia* Winery making a broader
range of good wines than normally found in Coonawarra: limy
Riesling ★, subtle Chardonnay ★, competent Champagne-method
Pinot/Chardonnay ★, silky, tobaccoey Cabernet Merlot ★ and
somewhat richer Ravenswood Cabernet Sauvignon ★★. Best
years: 1991 90 88.

HOSPICES DE BEAUNE *Côte de Beaune, Burgundy, France* Scene
of a highly theatrical auction on the third Sunday in November
each year, the Hospices de Beaune is an historic foundation
which sells wine from its substantial holdings in the COTE D'OR
to finance its charitable works. The prices obtained at auction
often bear no relation to the quality of the wines, which can be
extremely mixed. Best wines: Docteur Peste ★★ (CORTON), Clos
des Avaux ★★ (BEAUNE), Dames de la Charité ★★ (POMMARD),
François de Salins ★★ (CORTON-CHARLEMAGNE) but these ratings
are for the potential of the site and on the understanding they've
been vinified and bottled properly. I honestly cannot recommend
any of the most recent vintages. Best years: (reds) 1985 83 80 78.

HOUGHTON *Swan Valley, Western Australia* Western Australia's
biggest winery, with massive output of 'White Burgundy' (called
Houghton's 'Supreme' in the EC). Also good Sémillon, Verdelho,
Chardonnay and Cabernet rosé.

VON HÖVEL *Konz-Oberemmel, Saar, Germany* Von Hövel owns
some prestigious sites in the Saar valley including the whole of
the Oberemmeler Hütte★ and a chunk of the Scharzhofberg★★
Vineyard. 1990 was a spectacular year for the estate. Best years:
1990 89 88 85.

GASTON HUET *Vouvray AC, Loire Valley, France* Gaston Huet is
the grand old man of VOUVRAY. He may have passed on the day-
to-day running of this famous family estate to his son-in-law,
Noël Pinguet, but Huet still takes a keen interest in the wines.
Huet's wines are complex, traditional Vouvrays which will happily age for up to 50 years in a great vintage. As well as a very
good Vouvray Mousseux ★★, the estate produces three marvellous still wines – Le Haut Lieu ★★★, Clos du Bourg ★★ and Le
Mont ★★, which can be dry, medium-dry or sweet, depending
on the vintage. Best years: 1990 89 85 76 64 47.

HUGEL ET FILS *Alsace AC, Alsace, France*   Arguably the most famous name in Alsace, thanks to assiduous marketing and (sometimes) the quality of its wines. As well as wines from their own vineyards, Hugel also buys in grapes for basic range wines. Best wines are the sweet ALSACE VENDANGE TARDIVE ★★ and SELEC- TION DES GRAINS NOBLES ★★★, but Hugel's everyday stuff is quite frankly, pretty ordinary. Best years: 1990 89 85 83.

HUNTER VALLEY *New South Wales, Australia*   The Hunter's fame belies the fact that it grows only 3% of the nation's grapes. NSW's oldest wine region overcomes a tricky climate to make fascinating, ageworthy Sémillon and, rich buttery Chardonnay. The reds are soft, earthy and meet less universal approval. Shiraz is the mainstay, aging well but often developing a leath- ery overtone. There is also some Cabernet and Pinot Noir. Premium region is the Lower Hunter Valley around Pokolbin, while the Upper has the largest plantings but few wineries. Best producers: Allanmere, BROKENWOOD, LAKE'S FOLLY, LINDEMANS, MCWILLIAMS, Peterson, ROSEMOUNT, ROTHBURY, TYRRELL'S, WYNDHAM.

HUNTERS *Marlborough, South Island, New Zealand*   One of Marlborough's star winemakers. They boast super-stylish Sauvignon ★★★, lean and elegant Chardonnay ★★, vibrant Riesling ★, and even a reputedly luscious botrytized Chardonnay that is New Zealand's most expensive wine – which is probably why I haven't tried it yet! Best years: 1992 91 89.

HANS IGLER *Mittelburgenland, Austria*   The top grower for Blaufränkisch wines in Mittelburgenland and a skilful wine- maker who rarely overstates a nuance of flavour. Some of his Blaufränkisch wines are aged in (mostly new) oak ★. More recently he has turned his attention to Cabernet Sauvignon. Best years: 1990 89 86 83.

ÎLE DE BEAUTÉ, VIN DE PAYS DE L' *Corsica, France*   The only Corsican Vin de Pays. There are some increasingly good wines being made from Syrah, Cabernet Sauvignon, Nielluccio, Sciaccarello and Merlot (for reds), Grenache and Barbarossa (for rosés) and Chardonnay and Vermentino (for whites). Best pro- ducers: Aleria co-op, Casinca co-op, Uval.

IPR (INDICAÇÃO DE PROVENIÊNCIA REGULAMENTADA) Portuguese classification for wine regions hoping to qualify for DOC status one day.

IRANCY AC   See Bourgogne-Irancy AC.

IRON HORSE VINEYARDS *Sonoma, California, USA*   Outstanding sparkling wines with the Brut ★★ and the Blanc de Blancs ★★★ tasting delicious on release but, showing great ability to age. A Blanc de Noirs ★ called 'Wedding Cuvée', and a deeply coloured Brut Rosé ★ complete the line-up. Often overlooked are the Iron Horse table wines including a Cabernets ★ (Cabernet Sauvignon/Cabernet Franc blend), a good Pinot Noir ★ and a barrel-fermented Chardonnay ★.

143

ISOLE E OLENA *Tuscany, Italy*   One of the pacesetters in CHIANTI Classico, this fine estate is run by Paolo de Marchi. His Chianti Classico ★★, characterized by a clean, elegant and spicily perfumed fruit, excels in every vintage. His Cepparello ★★★, a 100% Sangiovese Vino da Tavola, is one of the best of this new breed. There is also excellent Syrah★★, Cabernet Sauvignon ★★ and Chardonnay ★, as well as great Vin Santo ★★★. Best years: 1990 89 88 86 83.

ISONZO DOC *Friuli-Venezia Giulia, Italy*   Less expensive but classy southern neighbour of COLLIO. The DOC covers 20 styles, including Merlot, Chardonnay, Pinot Grigio and Sauvignon. Best producers: Attems★, Stelio Gallo, Vescovo, Zampar.

CH. D'ISSAN ★★ *Margaux AC, 3ème Cru Classé, Haut-Médoc, Bordeaux, France*   In the late 1980s this lovely moated property produced some of the most scented and delicious wines in the whole of MARGAUX. It is one of the few properties which does manage to display the violet perfume and cassis fruit for which Margaux is famous. Best years: 1990 89 88 86 85 83 82 81 78.

PAUL JABOULET AÎNÉ *Rhône Valley, France*   During the 1970s Jaboulet led the way in both quality of wine and in raising the world's awareness of the great quality of Rhône Valley wines, yet during the 1980s, though the company prospered, the quality of wine faltered badly. But recent vintages, far fuller of fruit, less manipulated, and proud of their origins once more, make it look as though Jaboulet is back on the quality bandwagon. If so, welcome back. When on form their best wines are top red HERMITAGE La Chapelle ★★★ and white Chevalier de Stérimberg ★★. Also good COTE-ROTIE ★, excellent CROZES-HERMITAGE Thalabert ★★, fine juicy ST-JOSEPH Le Grand Pompée ★★ and sweet, perfumed MUSCAT DE BEAUMES-DE-VENISE ★. Best years: 1990 89 88 83 78.

LOUIS JADOT *Beaune, Burgundy, France*   A leading Burgundian merchant based in Beaune with a breadth of range only matched by DROUHIN, and with exclusive rights to the estate wines of the Duc de Magenta ★★. Jadot have particularly extensive vineyard holdings for red wines, but it is the firm's whites which have earned its reputation. Jadot are good in Grands Crus like BATARD-MONTRACHET ★★ and CORTON-CHARLEMAGNE ★★ but it is in lesser ACs like ST-AUBIN ★★ and RULLY ★★ that they really show what they can do. With their top wines, after leading white Burgundy in quality during the 1970s, the 80s have been heavier and flatter, impressive, but not thrilling. Best years: 1990 89 88 85.

JAFFELIN *Beaune, Burgundy, France*   Owned by Joseph DROUHIN, but run separately. Jaffelin sells a large range of wine from the Côte d'Or, the Côte Chalonnaise and the Beaujolais. The lesser ACs – RULLY ★, ST-ROMAIN ★, BOURGOGNE Blanc ★ and BEAUJOLAIS – are the best value but don't overlook the CLOS DE VOUGEOT ★★ and BEAUNE Les Avaux ★★. Best years: 1990 89 88 85.

JOSEPH JAMET *Côte-Rôtie AC, Rhône Valley, France*   Jean-Paul and Jean-Luc Jamet are two of the most talented young growers of COTE-ROTIE. If anything, the wines ★★ from this excellent estate have improved even further since they took over from their father, Joseph, and they age well for a decade or more. Best years: 1991 90 89 88 87 85 83 82.

JARDIN DE LA FRANCE, VIN DE PAYS DU *Loire Valley, France* This country wine covers most of the Loire Valley. Production is large and often exceeds 50 million bottles – mostly white, from Chenin and Sauvignon, and very cheap. There is an increasing amount of good Chardonnay too. The few reds and rosés are generally light and sharp. Best producer: Bablut, des Forges, Hauts de Sanziers..

ROBERT JASMIN *Côte-Rôtie AC, Rhône Valley, France*   The COTE-ROTIES★★★ made by Robert Jasmin and his son Patrick are some of the most intensely aromatic red wines in the Rhône Valley, with a delicious exuberance of gluggable young fruit and a heavenly scent which somehow manage to settle gracefully into middle age. The wines are at their best after 4–5 years, but will keep for much longer. Best years: 1991 90 89 88 87 85 83 82.

JASNIÈRES AC *Loire Valley, France*   A tiny AC on the Loir river north of Tours which makes bone-dry white from Chenin Blanc. Best producers: la Chanière, Fresneau, Pinon. Best years: 1990 89 88.

CH. LA JAUBERTIE *Bergerac, South-West France*   The most innovative domaine in BERGERAC, run since 1973 by the Englishman Nick Ryman, producing fresh, aromatic wines with lots of fruit. The rosé ★ and dry white ★ should be drunk young, but the red★ can age for up to 5 years. Best years: 1990 89 88.

HENRI JAYER *Vosne-Romanée, Burgundy, France*   In 1988 the vineyards of this famous Burgundian estate were divided between MEO-CAMUZET, Jayer himself and Jayer's nephew Emmanuel Rouget. Henri Jayer has kept vineyards in VOSNE-ROMANEE ★★★ and NUITS-ST-GEORGES ★★★. Jayer's wines are some of the greatest in Burgundy, showing all the heady perfume and exhilarating fruit, enriched by oak that top Burgundy is supposed to be all about. Best years: 1990 89 88 85 80 78.

ROBERT JAYER-GILLES *Côtes de Nuits, Burgundy, France*   A cousin of Henri JAYER, Robert Jayer-Gilles produces expensive but extremely high-quality wines. He makes good ALIGOTE★ and wonderful Hautes Côtes de Nuits Blanc ★★, as well as a range of new-oak dominated but superbly structured red, including ECHEZEAUX ★★★ and NUITS-ST-GEORGES Les Damodes ★★. Best years: 1990 89 88 87 86 85.

JEKEL *Arroyo Seco, California, USA*   A pioneer in Monterey in the early 1970s, Bill Jekel has recently been through the mill financially – through no fault of his own – but he appears to be back on track with Riesling ★ in a semi-sweet, sweet and late-harvest style as well as a rich but herbaceous Cabernet Sauvignon.

JEREZ Y MANZANILLA DO/SHERRY

Andalucía, Spain

Sherry is a much-abused name, adopted by bulk wine-makers in various parts of the world – including Britain and Cyprus – to describe cheap, inferior wines. Real sherry comes only from the triangle of vineyard land between the Andalucian towns of inland Jerez, and Sanlúcar de Barrameda and Puerto de Santa María by the sea. The best sherries can be spectacular, and remarkably inexpensive.

Three main factors contribute to the high potential quality of wines from this region: the chalky-spongy albariza soil where the best vines grow, the Palomino Fino grape – unexciting for table wines but potentially great once transformed by the sherry-making processes – and a natural yeast called flor, which is found in very few other parts of the world. All sherry must be a minimum of 3 years old, but fine sherries age in barrel for much longer. Sherries must be blended through a solera system, whereby older barrels of sherry are refreshed with wine from younger ones, thus maintaining the mature style of the oldest wine in the solera.

MAIN SHERRY STYLES

Finos, manzanillas and amontillados These sherries derive their extraordinary, tangy, pungent flavours from flor. Young, newly-fermented wines destined for these styles of sherry are deliberately fortified very sparingly to just 15–15.5% alcohol before being put in barrels for their minimum of 3 years' maturation. The thin, soft, oatmeal-coloured mush of flor grows on the surface of the wines, protecting them from the air (and therefore keeping them pale) and giving them a characteristic sharp, pungent tang. Manzanillas are fino-style wines that have matured in the cooler seaside conditions of Sanlúcar de Barrameda, where the flor grows thickest and the fine tang is most accentuated. True amontillados are simply fino sherries that have continued to age after the flor has died (after about 5 years) and so finish their aging period in contact with air. These should all be bone dry. Medium-sweet amontillados are merely concoctions for the export market.

Oloroso This type of sherry is strongly fortified after fermentation to deter the growth of flor. Olorosos therefore mature in barrel in contact with the air, which gradually darkens them while they develop rich, intense, nutty and raisiny flavours.

Other styles Palo cortado is an unusual, deliciously nutty, dry style somewhere in between amontillado and oloroso. Sweet oloroso creams and pale creams are almost without exception enriched solely for the export market.

See also BARBADILLO, DOMECQ, GONZALEZ BYASS, HARVEYS, HIDALGO, LUSTAU, OSBORNE, VALDESPINO.

BEST PRODUCERS AND WINES

Barbadillo (Manzanilla Fina, Principe Manzanilla Pasada, Oloroso Seco).

Caballero (Puerto Fino).

Díez Mérito (Don Zoilo Fino, Victoria Regina Oloroso).

Domecq (La Ina Fino, Sibarita Palo Cortado, Venerable Pedro Ximénez).

Garvey (San Patricio Fino, Palo Cortado, Amontillado Tio Guillermo, Pedro Ximénez).

González Byass (Tio Pepe Fino, Matusalem Oloroso Muy Viejo, Apostoles Oloroso Viejo, Amontillado del Duque Seco y Muy Viejo, Noé Pedro Ximénez).

Hidalgo (Manzanilla Pasada, Jerez Cortado).

Lustau (Almacenista single-producer wines).

La Riva (Tres Palmas Fino).

Valdespino (Inocente Fino, Tio Diego Amontillado, Don Tomás Amontillado, Pedro Ximénez Solera Superior).

147

JERMANN *Friuli-Venezia Giulia, Italy* Silvio Jermann, though situated in Friuli's COLLIO zone in north-east Italy, produces only Vino da Tavolas from Chardonnay, Pinot Grigio and Riesling, a blend called Vintage Tunina★, mainly based on Sauvignon and Chardonnay, and a barrel-fermented Chardonnay★ called 'Where the Dreams have no End', in homage to his favourite pop group, U2. The wines are plump and generous (and pricy), but often lack the length of the best in Collio.

CHARLES JOGUET *Chinon AC, Loire Valley, France* A talented artist, sculptor and poet, Charles Joguet is also the leading winemaker in CHINON. His wines demonstrate an impressive richness of flavour which owes more to Bordeaux than to the Loire. There are four different reds – Cuvée du Clos de la Curé★★, Clos du Chêne Vert★★, Les Varennes du Grand Clos★★ and Clos de la Dioterie★★ – all of which require aging for 5–10 years or more for the full beauty to show. There is also a little rosé. Best years: 1990 89 88 85 82 81 76.

JOHANNISBERG *Rheingau, Germany* Just about the most famous of all the Rhine villages with 10 individual vineyard sites, including the very famous Schloss Johannisberg.

KARL-HEINZ JOHNER *Bischoffingen, Baden, Germany* New wave, barrique-aging producer who spent some time making the wines at LAMBERHURST in England. A passionate enthusiast for new oak, the delightful perfumed fruit of his Pinot Noir★ and Pinot Blanc★ nonetheless shines through. Best years: 1990 89 88.

JORDAN *Alexander Valley, Sonoma, California, USA* Ripe, fruity Cabernet Sauvignon★★ with a distinct cedary character that is rare in California. The Chardonnays are nothing special and a new sparkling wine released in 1991 under the J label leaves a lot to be desired.

TONI JOST *Bacharach, Mittelrhein, Germany* The man who gives the Mittelrhein an international dimension. From his Bacharacher Hahn vineyard he makes delicious racy Rieslings★ including well structured Halbtrockens★ with balmy, pine-scented fruit. His Auslese★★ can add a creaminess without losing the scent of fresh pine needles. Best years: 1990 89 88.

JULIÉNAS AC *Beaujolais, Burgundy, France* One of the most northerly BEAUJOLAIS Crus, Juliénas makes delicious, 'serious' Beaujolais which can be big and tannic enough to develop in bottle. Best producers: Descombes★, DUBOEUF★, Ch. de Juliénas, Juliénas co-op, Pelletier★. Best years: 1991 90 89 88 85.

JULIUSSPITAL WEINGUT *Würzburg, Franken, Germany* A 16th-century charitable foundation which makes dry wines – very good Silvaners (the local speciality) and the occasional Riesling that's pretty special as well. Look out for the wines from the estate's holdings in the famous Würzburger Stein vineyard, grapefruity Silvaners★★ and petrolly Rieslings★★. Best years: 1990 89 88 85 81.

JUMILLA DO *Murcia and Castilla-La Mancha, Spain*   Jumilla's reputation in Spain is for big, rough, alcoholic reds but there are
now some fruitier, fresher, lighter reds too. There are also some
fruity rosés made, like the reds, from Monastrell, and a very few
boring whites. Best producers: Altos de Pio, Castillo, Cerillares,
Domino de Alba, Taja, Umbría Novel.

JURA   See Arbois, Château-Chalon, Côtes du Jura, L'Étoile.

JURANÇON AC *South-West France*   The historic, sweet white
wine of the western Pyrenees. Made from late-harvested and
occasionally botrytized grapes, it can be heavenly. The rapidly
improving dry wine, Jurançon Sec can be crisp, dry and refreshing. Best producers: Cauhapé★★, Clos Cancaillau★★, Clos
Uroulat★★, Cru Lamouroux★★, Guirouilh★★.

JUVÉ Y CAMPS *Cava DO and Penedés DO, Catalonia, Spain*   Juvé y
Camps is well-respected, ultra-traditional – and expensive.
Unusually among the Catalan companies, most of the grapes
come from their own vineyards. Fruitiest Cava is Reserva de la
Familia Extra Brut ★, but the rosé and the top brand white Cava
Gran Juvé are also good.

KABINETT   Lowest level of Prädikat wines in Germany, with Oechsle
levels ranging from 67 in the Mosel, where, with alcohol naturally as low as 7%, this is one of Europe's lightest wines, to 85
Oechsle for a Baden Ruländer, where the wine will have higher
alcohol and much more body. In Austria a Kabinett wine must
be 17 KMW or 84 Oechsle.

KALTERESEE   See Lago di Caldaro.

KAMPTAL-DONAULAND *Niederösterreich, Austria*   New wine
region either side of the Danube below Krems producing some of
Austria's best dry whites.

KANONKOP *Stellenbosch, South Africa*   Winemaker Beyers Truter
is South Africa's leading Pinotage exponent. His Pinotage
Auction Reserve★★ gets lavish new-oak treatment.

KARTHÄUSERHOF *Trier, Ruwer, Germany*   Top Ruwer estate run
by the Tyrell family. Their great vineyard is the Eitelsbacher
Karthäuserhofberg, from which they made 14 Riesling wines in
1990, ranging from QbA ★ to Eiswein ★★★. Even ordinary QbA
wines can be exciting. Best years: 1990 89 88 86 75.

KATNOOK ESTATE *Coonawarra, South Australia*   Katnook make
often-exceptional Chardonnay★★, Sauvignon Blanc ★ and
Cabernet Sauvignon ★★, very expensive but usually up to the
mark. Second label: Riddoch Estate. Best years: 1991 90 88.

KÉKFRANKOS   See Blaufränkisch.

KENDALL-JACKSON *Clear Lake, California, USA*   Producers in
Lake County of modest but wildly successful Chardonnay and
Cabernet Sauvignon under the Vintner's Reserve label, which
seem to have grown steadily sweeter, presumably to please the
great American public's taste buds. A series of vineyard-
designated Zinfandels ★★ are the best wines so far.

KENWOOD VINEYARDS *Sonoma Valley, California, USA* Reliable producer especially for a very drinkable Zinfandel ★ with good varietal character, outstanding Sauvignon Blanc ★★ and serviceable Cabernet Sauvignon. Under a reserve Jack London label an intense, complex Cabernet Sauvignon ★★ and dense, concentrated Zinfandel ★.

VON KESSELSTATT *Trier, Mosel, Germany* Estate making good but rarely thrilling Riesling wines from some top sites at Graach (Josephshöfer) in the Mosel, Scharzhofberg in the Saar and at Kasel in the Ruwer. Best years: 1990 89 88.

KHAN KRUM *Eastern Region, Bulgaria* Winery producing some of Bulgaria's best whites, like the oaky Reserve Chardonnay and the delicate, apricotty Riesling/Dimiat Country Wine.

KIEDRICH *Rheingau, Germany* Small village whose most famous vineyard site is the Sandgrub which can give superbly rich concentrated wines of the sort which appealed greatly to the last German Kaiser. Best producer: WEIL.

KIONA *Yakima Valley AVA, Washington State, USA* A tiny operation in sagebrush country, Kiona has a young but growing reputation for its barrel-fermented Chardonnay ★, its big, rich Cabernet Sauvignon ★★ and its excellent sweet Riesling ★★.

KISTLER *Sonoma, California, USA* This mountain top winery in the Mayacamas range is one of California's hottest Chardonnay producers. Wines are made from four different vineyards (Kistler Estate and Dutton Ranch can be ★★★, the others ★★)and although there are quite considerable differences, they all possess great complexity with good aging potential. Best years: 1991 90 89 88 87.

KLEIN CONSTANTIA *Constantia, South Africa* Meticulously run vineyard behind Cape Town's Table Mountain. Crisp, vivid 1990 Sauvignon Blanc ★, cleanly nutty 1990 Chardonnay ★, fresh 1987 Cabernet Sauvignon ★ and smoky 1987 Shiraz ★ stand out, plus the beautifully packaged 1987 Vin de Constance ★★, an apricotty dessert Muscat.

KMW The Austrians use KMW or Klosterneuburger Mostwaage as a scale to determine the must weight or original sugar in freshly-picked grapes. Like Oechsle degrees in Germany, each quality category sets a minimum number of KMW (eg 19 KMW for Spätlese). 1 KMW is the equivalent of about 5 Oechsle.

TIM KNAPPSTEIN *Clare Valley, South Australia* Leading Clare winery part-owned by Wolf BLASS but with its namesake very much in control. Fine Riesling ★★ and Traminer ★, subtly oaked Fumé Blanc ★, solid Cabernet ★, Cabernet Merlot ★ and Chardonnay ★.

KNUDSEN-ERATH *Willamette Valley AVA, Oregon, USA* Oregon's second largest producer makes stylish Pinot Noirs that have been gaining greater concentration of fruit in recent vintages. Knudsen-Erath's Chardonnay can also be good. Best years: (Pinot Noir) 1986 85 83.

KNYPHAUSEN *Erbach, Rheingau, Germany*   Leading Rheingau producer. The wines can be a little austere in their youth but they fill out massively with time. The Erbacher Marcobrunn 1990 merits ★★. Best years: 1990 89 88 85 83.

KRONDORF *Barossa Valley, South Australia*   Important Barossa producer that rather lost its way after being taken over by MILDARA. Things are now looking up: rich, oaky Show Chardonnay ★★ is better than ever, Coonawarra 'Hermitage' is good drinking and Sémillon ★ is oaky but with enough fruit to cope.

KRUG *Champagne AC, Champagne, France*   Krug is a serious (and seriously expensive) Champagne house. The non-vintage is called Grande Cuvée ★★★ and knocks spots off most other de luxe brands. Splendid on release, it gets much more exciting with 1–2 years' extra aging. There is also an excellent vintage wine ★★, a rosé ★ and a single-vineyard Clos du Mesnil Blanc de Blancs ★★★. Best years: 1985 82 81 79.

KUENTZ-BAS *Alsace AC, Alsace, France*   A small Alsace *négociant*, with high-quality wines from its own vineyards (labelled Réserve Personnelle) and from purchased grapes (called Cuvée Tradition). Look out for the Eichberg Grand Cru ★★ and the excellent Vendange Tardive ★★ wines. Best years: 1990 89 88 86 85.

KUMEU/HUAPAI *Auckland, North Island, New Zealand*   A small but significant viticultural area north west of Auckland. The 8 wineries profit from their proximity to New Zealand's capital. Best producers: Coopers Creek, KUMEU RIVER, NOBILO, SELAKS.

KUMEU RIVER *Kumeu, Auckland, North Island, New Zealand* This family winery has been transformed by New Zealand's first Master of Wine, Michael Brajkovich, who has created a range of adventurous, high-quality wines. Remarkably intense Chardonnay ★★★, unconventional oak-aged Sauvignon Blanc ★ and softly stylish Merlot/Cabernet Sauvignon ★ are Kumeu River's most obvious successes. Best years: 1991 90 89 87.

KWV *South Africa*   Officially a co-op that unites the grape growers of South Africa (few of whom make wine), the KWV also has legislative authority over the South African wine industry. As a bureaucracy, it has certainly provided stability and security for its members, but it has also stifled innovation and creativity. Wines like the plummy red blend Roodeberg, the easy-drinking Chenin Blanc or the apple-and-lemon KWV Sauvignon Blanc offer good value and it would be a damning indictment of South Africa's quality potential if they didn't. Best of all their many wines are the neglected Muscat and port-style fortified wines, including superb-value dated Vintage ★★ and Colheita-style Late Bottled Vintage ★★ wines.

151

LA CREMA *Sonoma, California, USA*　After some early struggles, La Crema has blossomed into a producer of well-balanced, rich Chardonnay, especially the Reserve Chardonnay★ and an attractively fruity Pinot Noir. Crème de Tête★ is a delightful blend of Chenin Blanc, Sémillon and Chardonnay.

LABOURÉ-ROI *Nuits-St-Georges, Burgundy, France*　Probably the most reliable and price conscious of all the Burgundian merchants, specializing in white wines. The reds have improved out of all recognition during the 1980s.　The CHABLIS ★★, BOUR-GOGNE Blanc ★ and MEURSAULT ★★ are all benchmark wines and the NUITS-ST-GEORGES ★★, CHAMBOLLE-MUSIGNY ★, BEAUNE★ and MARSANNAY★ are excellent too. Best years: 1990 89 88 85.

LACRYMA CHRISTI DOC *Campania, Italy*　Since DOC was introduced in 1983, things have improved for the red from Piedirosso and the white from Verdeca, but the name is always more evocative than the wine. Best producer: MASTROBERARDINO.

LADOIX AC *Côte de Beaune, Burgundy, France*　The most northerly village in the Côte de Beaune and one of the least known. The wines are usually sold as CORTON, ALOXE-CORTON or Aloxe-Corton Premier Cru and the less good ones as Ladoix-Côte de Beaune or COTE DE BEAUNE-VILLAGES. There are several good growers in the village and Ladoix wine, mainly red, quite light in colour and a little lean in style, is reasonably priced. Best producers: (reds) Capitain, Chevalier★, Cornu, Nudant; (whites) Cornu. Best years: (reds) 1990 89 88 85 83.

CH. LAFAURIE-PEYRAGUEY ★★ *Sauternes AC, 1er Cru Classé, Bordeaux, France*　Owned by the large Bordeaux merchants CORDIER, Lafaurie-Peyraguey was one of the most improved SAUTERNES properties of the 1980s and is frequently nowadays one of the best Sauternes of all. The wines can age well too. Best years: 1990 89 88 86 85 83 82 81 80 79.

CH. LAFITE-ROTHSCHILD ★★★ *Pauillac AC, 1er Cru Classé, Haut-Médoc, Bordeaux, France*　This PAUILLAC First Growth is frequently cited as the epitome of elegance, indulgence and expense – but the wine can be wretchedly inconsistent. There have been great improvements of late but as the wine often needs 15 years and can take 30 years or more to achieve the magical and unlikely marriage of cedar fragrance and lean but lovely blackcurrant fruit, we won't know for quite a while yet quite how good these 'new' Lafites are going to be. So it gets its ★★★ rating but not without reservations. Second wine: Moulin des Carruades. Best years: 1990 89 88 86 85 82 81 79 76.

CH. LAFLEUR ★★★ *Pomerol AC, Bordeaux, France*　Using some of POMEROL'S most traditional wine-making, this tiny estate makes Pomerols that seriously rival those from the great PETRUS for sheer power and flavour and indeed in recent years has begun to pull ahead of PETRUS for hedonistic richness and concentration. Best years: 1990 89 88 86 85.

CH. LAFLEUR-PÉTRUS ★★ *Pomerol AC, Bordeaux, France* Like the better-known PETRUS and TROTANOY, this is owned by the dynamic MOUEIX family. But, unlike its stablemates, Lafleur-Pétrus is situated entirely on gravel soil and tends to produce tighter wines with less immediate fruit but considerable elegance and cellar potential. Among POMEROL'S top dozen properties.

LAFON *Meursault, Côte de Beaune, Burgundy, France* The leading producer in MEURSAULT and one of Burgundy's current superstars, with a reputation and high prices to match. Dominique Lafon produces rich, powerful Meursaults that spend as long as two years in barrel and age superbly in bottle. As well as excellent Meursault, especially Clos de la Barre ★★, Les Charmes ★★★ and Les Perrières ★★★, Lafon makes a tiny amount of Le MONTRACHET ★ ★ ★ and most individual and exciting reds from VOLNAY ★★. Best years: 1990 89 88 86 85 83 82 79.

CH. LAFON-ROCHET ★★ *St-Estèphe AC, 4ème Cru Classé, Haut-Médoc, Bordeaux, France* Good-value affordable Classed Growth claret, usually showing a very attractive, deep, dry, blackcurrant fruit that ages well. Best years: 1990 89 88 86 85 83 82 79.

LAGEDER *Alto Adige DOC, Trentino-Alto Adige, Italy* Leading producer in northern Italy's ALTO ADIGE, making medium-priced but unmemorable varietals under the Lageder label, and expensive single-vineyard wines that really steal the show. The heavily oaked Cabernet★ and Chardonnay★★ under the Löwengang or Portico dei Leoni labels, and the Pinot Grigio Benefizium Porer ★★ are the stars. Best years: 1990 88 87 85.

LAGO DI CALDARO DOC *Trentino-Alto Adige, Italy* At its best a lovely, delicate, barely red, youthful glugger from Italy's mountainous north, tasting of strawberries and cream and bacon smoke. However, some overproduced Lago di Caldaro scarcely passes muster as red wine at all. Also known as Kalterersee. Kalterersee Auslese is not sweet, but has $1/2$% more alcohol. Best producers: Hofstätter, LAGEDER, K Martini, Prima & Nuova co-op, St Michael Eppan co-op, Tiefenbrunner, Walch.

CH. LAGRANGE ★★ *St-Julien AC, 3ème Cru Classé, Haut-Médoc, Bordeaux, France* Since the Japanese company Suntory purchased this estate in 1983, the leap in quality has been astonishing. No longer an amiable, shambling ST-JULIEN, this has become a single-minded wine of good fruit, meticulous winemaking and fine quality. Second wine: Les Fiefs de Lagrange. Best years: 1990 89 88 86 85 83 82.

LAGREIN This highly individual, black grape variety is only planted in Italy's Trentino-Alto Adige region, where it produces deep coloured, brambly, chocolaty reds of considerable distinction called Lagrein Dunkel (or *scuro* in Italian). It also makes a full-bodied yet attractively scented rosé (known as Kretzer). Best producers: Anton Gojer, Grai★, LAGEDER, Tiefenbrunner.

153

CH. LA LAGUNE ★★ *Haut-Médoc AC, 3ème Cru Classé, Haut-Médoc,*
Bordeaux, France   The wine from this Classed Growth, the clos-
est to Bordeaux city, is consistently excellent – full of the charry,
chestnut warmth of good oak and a deep, cherry-blackcurrant-
and-plums sweetness which, after 10 years or so, becomes outstanding claret. Best years: 1990 89 88 86 85 84 83 82 78 76 75.

LAKE'S FOLLY *Hunter Valley, New South Wales, Australia*   Esoteric
wines with an eager following, thanks to the charismatic Dr
Max Lake. Austere Chardonnay ★★★ ages slowly but intrigu-
ingly to a masterly antipodean yet Burgundy-like peak,
Cabernet ★★ is supple and beautifully balanced at best but
doesn't always live up to its reputation. Best years: 1991 90 89
87 85 83 81.

LALANDE-DE-POMEROL AC *Bordeaux, France*   North of its more
famous neighbour POMEROL, Lalande-de-Pomerol produces full,
ripe wines with an unmistakeable mineral edge that are very
attractive to drink at only 3–4 years old, but age reasonably
well too. Even though they lack the concentration of top
Pomerols the wines are not particularly cheap. Best producers:
Annereaux★, Bel-Air, Belles-Graves, Bertineau, Clos des Templiers,
Grand-Ormeau, Hautes-Tuileries, Lavaud-la-Maréchaude★, St-
Vincent, Siaurac★, Tournefeuille. Best years: 1990 89 88 85 83 82.

LAMBERHURST *Kent, England*   One of England's steadiest and
most reliable producers, and the only triple winner of the Gore-
Browne Trophy (England's leading wine award) – twice for a
Schönburger and once for a Huxelrebe.

LAMBRUSCO *Emilia-Romagna, Italy*   Lambrusco is actually a black
grape variety, grown in four DOC zones on the plains of Emilia,
and one around Mantova in Lombardy, but it is the red and
white screwcap bottles labelled as non-DOC Lambrusco that
have made the name famous, even though some of them may
contain no wine from the Lambrusco grape at all. Originally a
dry or semi-sweet, sparkling red or white wine whose high acidity naturally partnered the rich local food, technology has led to
huge quantities of anonymous, sweetened Frizzante wines from
just about anywhere in Italy being let loose on the unsuspecting
public. Best producers: (traditional style) Bellei, Cavicchioli;
(screwtop style) Chiarli, Giacobazzi, Oreste Lini, Riunite.

LANDWEIN German or Austrian country wine and the equivalent
of French Vin de Pays. The wine must have a territorial definition and may be chaptalized to give it more body.

CH. LANESSAN ★ *Haut-Médoc AC, Cru Bourgeois, Haut-Médoc,*
Bordeaux, France   Attractive but austere Cru Bourgeois from
the commune of Cussac-Fort-Médoc that hardly ever uses new
oak barrels, yet often achieves Fifth Growth standard and is
never over-priced. Lanessan tends to be at its best in top vintages and can easily age for 8–10 years. Second wine: Dom. de
Ste Gemme. Best years: 1990 89 88 85 83 82.

CH. LANGOA-BARTON ★★ *St-Julien AC, 3ème Cru Classé, Haut-Médoc, Bordeaux, France* Owned by the Barton family since the 1820s, Langoa is usually lighter in style than its stablemate LEOVILLE-BARTON, but is still an extremely impressive, and reasonably-priced wine. Best years: 1990 89 88 86 85 83 82.

LANGUEDOC-ROUSSILLON *Midi, France* Traditionally a source of some very undistinguished cheap wine, this large area of southern France, running from Nîmes to the Spanish border and covering the departments of the Gard, Hérault, Aude and Pyrénées-Orientales, is now turning out some very exciting red wines. Temperature-controlled vinification and a growing sense of regional pride have wrought the transformation, hand in hand with better grape varieties and an increasing number of ambitious producers, from the heights of MAS DE DAUMAS GASSAC to some very good local co-ops. The best wines are the reds, particularly those from CORBIERES and MINERVOIS and some new wave Cabernets, Merlots and Syrahs, as well as the more traditional Vins Doux Naturels, such as BANYULS, MAURY and MUSCAT DE RIVESALTES; but we're going to see a lot of exciting whites in the next few years as well. See also Aude, Bouches-du-Rhône, Collioure, Costières de Nîmes, Coteaux du Languedoc, Côtes du Roussillon, Côtes du Roussillon-Villages, Côtes de Thau, Côtes de Thongue, Faugères, Fitou, Gard, Haute Vallée de l'Aude, Hérault, Mont Bouquet, Muscat de Frontignan, Muscat de Mireval, Muscat de St-Jean-de-Minervois, Oc, Pyrénées-Orientales, St-Chinian, Vallée du Paradis.

LANSON *Champagne AC, Champagne, France* A mass-market fizz whose brilliant 'why not?' advertising campaign has done much to democratize the image of Champagne. The non-vintage Black Label ★ is good, reliable stuff, while the rosé ★ and vintage★★ wines, especially the de luxe blend, called Noble Cuvée ★★, aspire to greater things. Recent changes of ownership place a question mark over Lanson's future style and quality. Best years: 1986 85 83 82 79.

CH. LAROSE-TRINTAUDON ★ *Haut-Médoc AC, Cru Bourgeois, Haut-Médoc, Bordeaux, France* Since it was planted from scratch in 1966, this estate, the largest in the Médoc, has produced substantial amounts of good-quality, affordable red Bordeaux. The wines are made to drink at about 5 years but can age for 10. Best years: 1990 89 88 86 85 83 82.

CH. LASCOMBES ★ *Margaux AC, 2ème Cru Classé, Haut-Médoc, Bordeaux, France* This large and important MARGAUX Second Growth has been very inconsistent during the 1970s and 1980s to put it mildly, but I hope the 1990 and 89 vintages – promising some of the tantalizing fresh flowers and blackcurrant perfume of which Lascombes is capable – will mark a permanent improvement. The Chevalier de Lascombes rosé is rather good, too. Second wine: Segonnes. Best years: 1990 89 86 85.

155

CH. DE LASTOURS *Corbières AC, Languedoc, France*   A large estate in CORBIERES, producing some of the most exciting wines in the Midi. The top white is Dry de Corbières ★, an interesting blend of Muscat, Malvoisie and Grenache Blanc. But the out-standing wines are the reds – particularly the Cuvée Simon Descamps ★★ and the oaky Cuvée Boisée ★★. Best years:1990 89 88 86 85.

CH. LATOUR ★★★ *Pauillac AC, 1er Cru Classé, Haut-Médoc, Bordeaux, France*   Latour's great reputation is based on power-ful, long-lasting classic wines. Throughout the 1950s, 60s and 70s the property stood for consistency and a refusal to compro-mise in the face of considerable financial pressure. Strangely, however, in the early 1980s there was an attempt to make lighter, more fashionable wines with mixed results. The late 1980s saw a return to classic Latour, much to my relief. Its rep-utation for making fine wine in less successful vintages is well-deserved. Second wine: Les Forts de Latour. Best years: 1990 89 88 86 82 81 79 78 75 70.

LOUIS LATOUR *Beaune, Burgundy, France*   Controversial mer-chant almost as well-known for his COTEAUX DE L'ARDECHE Chardonnays, as for his Burgundies. Latour's white Burgundies are much better than the reds, although the red CORTON-Grancey ★ can be good. Latour's oaky CORTON-CHARLEMAGNE ★★, from his own vineyard, is his top wine, but there is also good CHEVALIER-MONTRACHET ★★, BATARD-MONTRACHET ★★ and Le MONTRACHET ★★. Even so, as these are the greatest white vine-yards in Burgundy, there really should be a higher rating in there somewhere. Best years: 1990 89 88 86 85 83 82.

CH. LATOUR-À-POMEROL ★★ *Pomerol AC, Bordeaux, France*   Now directed by Christian Moueix of PETRUS fame, this property makes luscious wines, with loads of gorgeous fruit, and enough tannin to age well. Best years: 1990 89 88 85 83 82 81 79.

LATRICIÈRES-CHAMBERTIN AC   See Chambertin AC.

LAUREL GLEN *Sonoma Mountain AVA, California, USA*   Owner-winemaker Patrick Campbell makes only Cabernet Sauvignon ★★★ at his mountaintop winery, with some Merlot and Cabernet Franc grown for blending. This is rich wine with deep fruit flavours and it ages to a perfumed, complex Bordeaux style after 6–10 years that is rare in California. Second label: Counterpoint. Best years: 1990 88 87 86 85.

LAURENT-PERRIER *Champagne AC, Champagne, France*   A large, family-owned Champagne house whose wines consistently offer flavour and quality at (fairly) reasonable prices. The full-flavoured, biscuity non-vintage ★★ is one of the best, the vin-tage ★★ is delicious while the top wine, Cuvée Grand Siècle ★★★ is among the finest Champagnes of all. Also very good rosé, as non-vintage ★★ and vintage Alexandra Grand Siècle ★★. Best years: 1985 82 79.

CH. LAVILLE-HAUT-BRION ★★★ *Pessac-Léognan AC, Cru Classé de Graves, Bordeaux, France* This is the white wine of la MIS-SION-HAUT-BRION and is one of the finest white GRAVES, with a price tag to match. The wine is fermented in barrel and needs 10 years aging or more to reach its savoury but luscious peak. Best years: 1990 89 88 86 85 83 82 81 79 78.

LAZIO *Italy* This central Italian region is best known for FRASCATI – Rome's white glugger. There are various other similarly bland whites from Trebbiano and Malvasia and an unlimited supply of unmemorable red from the Cesanese, but ideally when in Rome, drink wines from somewhere else.

LEEUWIN ESTATE *Margaret River, Western Australia* Margaret River high-flier, with pricy Chardonnay ★★★ that could be Australia's nearest thing to Le MONTRACHET. The Cabernets have been patchy but at best are ★★, blackcurranty yet with a cool lean edge.

DOM. LEFLAIVE *Puligny-Montrachet, Côte de Beaune, Burgundy, France* The most famous white Burgundy producer of all, with extensive holdings in some of the world's greatest vineyards (BATARD-MONTRACHET, Chevalier-Montrachet and, since 1990, Le MONTRACHET itself). The price of the wines is correspondingly high and in recent vintages, notably 1987 and 88, there have been a number of disappointing wines. The basic PULIGNY-MONTRACHET, in particular, has suffered from over-generous yields. The arrival of the talented Pierre Morey as winemaker in 1989 seems to have been a change for the better. These criticisms aside, the top wines here – Pucelles ★★, Chevalier-Montrachet ★★ and Bâtard-Montrachet ★★★ – are consistently delicious. They are capable of aging for up to 20 years in bottle, developing a rich, toasty elegance that almost lives up to the hype. Best years: 1990 89 86 85.

OLIVIER LEFLAIVE FRÈRES *Puligny-Montrachet, Côte de Beaune, Burgundy, France* As well as co-managing Domaine LEFLAIVE with his cousin Anne-Claude, Olivier Leflaive runs his own extremely successful *négociant* business, also based in PULIGNY-MONTRACHET. The company specializes in crisp, modern white wines from the Côte d'Or and the Côte Chalonnaise that may lack a little local magic but are good examples of international-standard Chardonnay. The best-value wines are those from lesser ACs – ST-ROMAIN ★, MONTAGNY ★, MERCUREY Blanc ★ and RULLY ★★ – but the rich, oaky BATARD-MONTRACHET ★★★ is the star turn. Best years: 1990 89 88 86.

PETER LEHMANN *Barossa Valley, South Australia* A popular, father figure in the Barossa, Lehmann has no vineyards, buying from hundreds of Barossa smallholders. Quality is on the up and in 1991 releases will be the best ever, with finely tuned Chardonnay ★★, lemony Sémillon★★, stylish Cabernet blend ★ and splendidly rich, old-fashioned and trophy-winning Shiraz from 1989 ★★, showing old-style Barossa fruit at its best.

157

JEAN LEÓN *Penedés DO, Catalonia, Spain*   Jean León emigrated to California and worked as a taxi driver and waiter before starting a Hollywood restaurant. In the late 1960s he established his own vineyards back in Spain to supply the restaurant's house wine. The style is Californian, the reds ★★ rich and blackcurranty, made from Cabernet Sauvignon with Cabernet Franc and Merlot, the Chardonnay ★★ rich, biscuity and pineappley, fermented in oak. Best years: (reds) 1987 85 83 81 78.

CH. LÉOVILLE-BARTON ★★★   *St-Julien AC, 2ème Cru Classé, Haut-Médoc, Bordeaux, France*   Made by Anthony Barton, whose family has run this ST-JULIEN property since 1821, this excellent claret is a traditionalist's delight. Dark, dry and tannic, the wines are difficult to taste young and therefore often underestimated, but over 10–15 years they achieve a lean yet sensitively proportioned classical beauty rarely equalled in Bordeaux. Moreover, they are extremely fairly priced. Praise be. Best years: 1990 89 88 86 85 83 82 81 78 75.

CH. LÉOVILLE-LAS-CASES ★★★   *St-Julien AC, 2ème Cru Classé, Haut-Médoc, Bordeaux, France*   This is the largest of the three Léoville properties and probably now the most exciting of all the ST-JULIEN wines. A direct neighbour of the great LATOUR, there are certain similarities in the wines. Since 1975 Las-Cases has been making wines of startlingly deep, dark concentration. From a good year the wine really needs 15 years of aging and should last happily for 30. Second wine: Clos du Marquis. Best years: 1990 89 88 86 85 83 82 81 79 78 75.

CH. LÉOVILLE-POYFERRÉ ★★   *St-Julien AC, 2ème Cru Classé, Haut-Médoc, Bordeaux, France*   Until comparatively recently, this was the least good of the three Léoville properties. The 1980s saw a marked improvement with a string of excellent wines produced under Didier Cuvelier, who has gradually increased the richness of the wine without wavering from its austere style. Since the 1986 vintage these are approaching the top level and need 8–10 years aging to blossom. Second wine: Moulin-Riche. Best years: 1990 89 88 87 86 85 83 82.

LEROY *Auxey-Duresses, Burgundy, France*   This medium-sized merchant tucked away in the back streets of AUXEY-DURESSES, is run by the inimitable Lalou Bize-Leroy who, until a recent palace coup, was co-proprietor of the Domaine de la ROMANEE-CONTI. The best wines here are the long-lived reds, especially those from the former Domaine Noellat, which Leroy purchased in 1988 – CLOS VOUGEOT ★★, RICHEBOURG ★★ and ROMANEE ST-VIVANT ★★, but Bize-Leroy's selections from other growers are consistently top-notch as, I'm afraid, are her prices. Best years: 1990 89 88 87 86 85 83 78.

LIEBFRAUMILCH *Rheinpfalz, Rheinhessen, Nahe and Rheingau,*
♀ *Germany* A branded wine from the Rheinpfalz, Rheinhessen,
Nahe or the Rheingau which must be made of 70% Riesling,
Silvaner, Müller-Thurgau or Kerner grapes. Liebfraumilch is
sweetish, low in acidity and well-suited to drinking on its own
without food. At best it is a well-constructed commercial wine
which appeals to the uninitiated wine drinker. Liebfraumilch
was a crucially important factor in introducing millions to wine
during the 1980s, but since it has a relentlessly down-market
image, its very success has tarnished the reputation of
Germany's finer wines. Best producers: Sichel (Blue Nun),
Valckenberg (Madonna).

LIGURIA *Italy* Thin coastal strip of north-west Italy, running from
the French border at Ventimiglia to the Tuscan border. Best
known wines are the RIVIERA LIGURE DI PONENTE, CINQUETERRE and
ROSSESE DI DOLCEACQUA DOCs.

LINDEMANS *Murray River, Victoria, Australia* Large, historic com-
pany now part of SA Brewing and based increasingly at
Karadoc-on-Murray, Australia's largest wine-making complex.
Best wines are old-fashioned Hunter Valley Shiraz★★ ('bur-
gundy' and Steven Vineyard), Chardonnay★★ and
Sémillons★★★ (labelled 'chablis', 'white burgundy' and
Sémillon!). There is a trio of good red Coonawarra wines: ele-
gant St George Cabernet★, spicy Limestone Ridge Shiraz
Cabernet★ and multi-variety Pyrus★. Padthaway
Chardonnay★★ is tremendous stuff, and can be amazingly
cheap given the quality. The mass-market Bin 65 Chardonnay★
is a flagship wine for Australian Chardonnay abroad. Best years:
(Hunter Shiraz) 1991 87 86 83 82 80 79 73 70 65; (Sémillon) 1991
90 89 88 87 86 80 79 78 75 72 70 68; (Coonawarra) 1991 90 88 86.

LINGENFELDER *Grosskarlbach, Rheinpfalz, Germany* One of the
most highly regarded winemakers in Germany. Rainer
Lingenfelder's talent is indisputable: a simple Scheurebe becomes
superb in his hands, as is clear from the Grosskarlbacher
Burgweg Spätlese Trocken ★★ with its aromas of grapefruit, pine
and apricots; his Spätburgunder ★★ is one of Germany's best red
wines (the 1989 was rich in cocoa and raspberry flavours), and
he also makes excellent Dornfelder★. To top it all he makes
heavenly Riesling★★ on his Freinsheimer Goldberg site. Best
years: 1990 89 88 83.

JEAN LIONNET *Cornas, Rhône Valley, France* Jean Lionnet produces dense, tannic CORNAS★★ in a fairly modern style. The
emphasis here is on new oak aging, and the wines can seem
charmless and lacking in fruit when young. It's worth waiting
for 6–7 years, as they do age extremely well. Lionnet also produces COTES DU RHONE★ from his younger Cornas vines, and a little white ST-PERAY. Best years: 1990 89 88 85 83.

LIQUOROSO Italian term for fortified wine.

LIRAC AC *Rhône Valley, France*   An excellent, but underrated AC between TAVEL and CHATEAUNEUF-DU-PAPE, making wines which resemble its more famous neighbours. The reds have the dusty, spicy fruit of Châteauneuf without quite achieving the intensity of the best examples. They can age well but are delicious young. The rosé is more refreshing than Tavel with a lovely strawberry fruit and the white can be good – but drink them both young before the perfume goes.   Best producers: Assémat, Devoy, Fermade, Maby★, St-Roch, Ségries, la Tour. Best years: 1990 89 88 86 85.

LISTEL *Golfe de Lion, Languedoc, France*   Listel is the largest vineyard owner in France, with over 1620ha (4000 acres) mainly on the sand-flats of the Camargue. Listel is best known for its Gris de Gris (a rather dull rosé), Brut de Listel, an equally dull sparkling wine, and a sweet, grapy concoction called Pétillant de Listel. Their varietal wines, particularly Sauvignon and Cabernet Sauvignon, are more interesting.

LISTRAC AC *Haut-Médoc, Bordeaux, France*   Set several miles back from the Gironde and away from the best gravel ridges, Listrac is one of the six specific ACs within the HAUT-MEDOC. The wines can be good without ever being thrilling, and are marked by solid fruit, a lightly coarse tannin and an earthy flavour. Best producers: la Bécade, Cap de Léon-Veyrin, CLARKE, Fonréaud, Fourcas-Dupré, Fourcas-Hosten, Grand Listrac co-op, Lestage. Best years: 1990 89 88 86 85 83 82.

LOCOROTONDO DOC *Puglia, Italy*   Nutty, crisp, dry white from the south to drink young. Best producers: Candido, De Castris, Locorotondo co-op.

LOIRE *France*   The Loire river cuts right through the heart of France from only 50km (30 miles) west of the Rhône Valley to the Atlantic Ocean way to the north-west. The upper reaches of the Loire are the home of world-famous Sancerre and POUILLY-FUME. The region of Touraine makes good Sauvignon Blanc while at VOUVRAY and MONTLOUIS the Chenin Blanc grape makes some pretty good fizz and still whites, ranging from sweet to very dry. The Loire's best reds are made at CHINON and BOURGUEIL mainly from Cabernet Franc. Anjou is famous for ROSE D'ANJOU but the best wines are white, either sweet from the Layon valley or very dry Chenin from SAVENNIERES. Finally, near the mouth of the river around the city of Nantes is MUSCADET. See also Anjou Blanc, Anjou Mousseux, Anjou Rouge, Anjou-Villages, Bonnezeaux, Cabernet d'Anjou, Châteaumeillant, Cheverny, Coteaux de l'Aubance, Coteaux du Layon, Côtes Roannaises, Crémant de Loire, Gros Plant du Pays Nantais, Haut-Poitou, Jardin de la France, Ménétou-Salon, Muscadet des Coteaux de la Loire, Muscadet de Sèvre-et-Maine, Pouilly-sur-Loire, Quarts de Chaume, Quincy, Rosé de Loire, St-Nicolas-de-Bourgueil, Saumur, Saumur-Champigny, Saumur Mousseux, Touraine, Touraine-Mousseux.

LOMBARDY *Italy* Lombardy, the richest and most populous of all Italian regions, is a larger consumer than producer of wine, with its capital, Milan, drinking vast quantities of wines from the OLTREPO PAVESE and FRANCIACORTA DOC zones, as well as a number of imported wines, not only from the rest of Italy, but also from France. This greater interest in consumption than production means that few of Lombardy's wines match those of Piedmont, Veneto or Tuscany for either quality or interest. Many of its best grapes go to provide base wine for Italy's thriving Spumante Seco industry.

DR LOOSEN *Bernkastel, Mosel, Germany* Loosen's St Johannishof estate has portions of some of the Mosel's most famous vineyards: Treppchen and Prälat in Erden, Würzgarten in Urzig, Sonnenuhr in Wehlen, Himmelreich in Graach and Lay in Bernkastel. Young Ernst Loosen took over in 1988 and since then the wines have gone from strength to strength with most wines achieving ★★, and some, especially from Wehlen, reaching ★★★. One of Germany's foremost protagonists of organic methods. Best years: 1990 89 88 85 83 76.

LÓPEZ DE HEREDIA *Rioja DOC, Rioja, Spain* A charmingly old-fashioned, family-owned RIOJA company, who still age wines for a long time in old oak casks. Reds and traditional, oaky whites are excellent – the younger wines are called Viña Cubillo ★ or Viña Bosconia ★, and the mature wines Viña Tondonia ★★. Best years: (reds) 1985 76.

LOS LLANOS *Valdepeñas DO, Castilla-La Mancha, Spain* A huge, scrupulously clean and well-equipped winery in central Spain renowned for its excellent value, mature, oak-aged red Señorío de Los Llanos ★ in both Reserva and Gran Reserva qualities. Best years: (reds) 1984 82 81.

LOS VASCOS *Colchagua Valley, Chile* Co-owned by Bordeaux's LAFITE-ROTHSCHILD since 1988, this estate, midway down Chile's Central Valley, is best at Cabernet Sauvignon ★, which is splendidly deep, its mint-and-blackcurrant fruit lent seriousness by prominent though pliant tannins. The whites from Los Vascos are merely on par for Chile, but that's not really good enough from a winery boasting the involvement of a top flight operator like LAFITE.

CH. LOUDENNE *Médoc AC, Cru Bourgeois, Bordeaux, France* This lovely pink château on the banks of the Gironde has been owned by the English firm Gilbeys since 1875. The wines, both red and white, are gentle in style, but tend to lack excitement. Best years: 1990 89 88 86.

LOUPIAC AC *Bordeaux, France* A sweet wine area across the Garonne from BARSAC. The wines are attractively sweet without being gooey. Drink young, though they can age. Best producers: du Cros, Loupiac-Gaudiet, Mazarin, de Ricaud. Best years: 1990 89 88 86 85 83.

161

CH. LA LOUVIÈRE *Pessac-Léognan AC, Bordeaux, France* One of the GRAVES' rising stars and its growing reputation is almost entirely due to André Lurton who has revitalized the property over the last 30 years. The well-structured reds ★★ and fresh, Sauvignon-based whites ★★ are excellent value for money. Best years: (reds) 1990 89 88 86 85 82; (whites) 1990 89 88.

LUGANA DOC *Lombardy, Italy* Full-bodied, occasionally perfumed Trebbiano dry white from south of Lake Garda. Best drunk young, though Ca' dei Frati wines can develop excitingly over several years. Best producers: Ca' dei Frati, Provenza, Visconti.

LUNGAROTTI *Torgiano DOC, Umbria, Italy* Leading producer of TORGIANO. Lungarotti also makes good whites from local grapes and Chardonnays, Miralduolo and Vigna I Palazzi★, as well as a very good sherry style – as far as I know, unique in Italy.

LUSSAC-ST-ÉMILION AC *Bordeaux, France* One of the ST-EMILION satellite ACs. Much of the wine, which tastes like a lighter St-Émilion, is made by the local co-op and should be drunk within 4 years of the vintage. However, certain properties are worth seeking out. Best producers: Barbe-Blanche, Bel-Air, Courlat, Haut-Milon, Lyonnat, Villadière. Best years: 1990 89 88 85.

EMILIO LUSTAU *Jerez y Manzanilla DO, Andalucía, Spain* Emilio Lustau specializes in supplying 'own label' wines to supermarkets. Quality is generally good, and there are some real stars at the top of their range, especially the Almacenista range ★★, very individual dry sherries from small, private producers.

CH. LYNCH-BAGES★★★ *Pauillac AC, 5ème Cru Classé, Haut-Médoc, Bordeaux, France* I am a great fan of Lynch-Bages – with its almost succulent richness, its gentle texture and its starburst of flavours, all butter, blackcurrants and mint and it is now one of PAUILLAC'S most popular wines. Because of its Fifth Growth status, it was inclined to be underpriced; I couldn't say that now, but it's still excellent value. It is impressive at 5 years, beautiful at 10 years and irresistible at 20. Second wine: Haut-Bages-Avérous. Best years: 1990 89 88 87 86 85 83 82 81 79.

MACÉRATION CARBONIQUE Vinification method used mainly in the BEAUJOLAIS region, but increasingly in the South of France and the Loire, to produce fresh fruity reds for drinking young. Rather than having their stems ripped off and being crushed, bunches of grapes are fermented whole in closed containers – a process which extracts lots of fruit and colour, but little tannin.

MÂCON AC *Mâconnais, Burgundy, France* The basic Mâconnais AC, but most whites in the region are labelled under the superior AC, MACON-VILLAGES. The wines are rarely exciting. Mâcon-Blanc, especially, is a rather expensive basic quaffer, since the use of the magic variety Chardonnay has permitted prices to boom without justification. Drink as young as possible. Mâcon Supérieur has a slightly higher minimum alcohol level. Best producer: DUBOEUF. Best years: 1991 90 89.

MÂCON-VILLAGES AC *Mâconnais, Burgundy, France* Mâcon-
Villages should be an enjoyable, fruity, fresh Chardonnay wine
for everyday drinking at a fair price, but because it comes from
Chardonnay, the world's most popular grape, the wines are
often overpriced. Forty-three villages in the region can call their
wine Mâcon-Villages or add their own name, as in Mâcon-Viré.
Best villages: Chardonnay, Charnay, Clessé, Igé, Lugny, Prissé,
St-Gengoux-de-Scissé, Uchizy, Viré. Best producers: Bonhomme,
de Chervin, de la Condemine, Guichard, Manciat-Poncet, de
Roally, Thévenet, Tissier, co-ops at Chardonnay, Clessé, Lugny,
Prissé, St-Gengoux-de-Scissé, Viré. Best years: 1991 90 89.

MADEIRA DOC *Madeira, Portugal* Is Madeira a glorious, sub-
tropical holiday resort, with soupy, fortified wines fit only for
sauce-making, or a serious wine region? Internationally famous
by the 17th century, modern Madeira was shaped by the phylloxera epidemic 100 years ago,
which wiped out the vine-
yards. Replantation was with
hybrid vines resistant to
phylloxera, but vastly inferior
to the 'noble' and traditional
Malvasia (or Malmsey), Boal (or Bual), Verdelho and Sercial
varieties. Now there are incentives to replant the vineyards with
the noble grapes, but progress is slow.

The typically burnt, tangy Madeira taste comes from the
process of heating the young wine, either directly in huge vats
or more gently in wooden casks. Most Madeira is then fortified
and sweetened with grape juice before bottling. Basic Madeira is
mostly made from Tinta Negra Mole (whatever it says on the
label), and only in the Reserves (5 years old), Special Reserves
(10 years old), Exceptional Reserves (15 years old) and Vintage
wines (from a single year, aged in cask for 20 years, then in bottle for 2 years) will you find wines actually made from Malmsey,
Bual, Verdelho and Sercial. The best Madeira can survive to a
great age but it's a rare beast in modern times. Best producers:
Artur Barros e Sousa, Blandy's, Cossart Gordon, d'Oliveira.

MADEIRA WINE COMPANY *Madeira DOC, Madeira, Portugal* The
Madeira Wine Company ships more than half of all Madeira
exported in bottle. Brand names are Blandy's, Cossart Gordon,
Leacock, Lomelino, Rutherford & Miles.

MADIRAN AC *South-West France* In the gentle Vic Bilh hills north
of Pau there has been a steady revival of the Madiran AC as viti-
culturalists have discovered ways to propagate the difficult
Tannat vine successfully. Several of the best producers are now
using new oak and this certainly helps soften the rather aggressive wine. Best producers: Arricau-Bordes, d'Aydie, Barréjat,
Boucassé, Cru du Paradis, Montus, Peyros, Union des
Producteurs PLAIMONT. Best years: 1990 89 88 85.

163

CH. MAGDELAINE ★★ *St-Émilion Grand Cru AC, 1er Grand Cru Classé, Bordeaux, France* Owned by the quality-conscious company of MOUEIX, these are dark, rich, aggressive wines, yet with a load of luscious fruit and oaky spice. In lighter years the wine has a gushing, easy, tender fruit and can be enjoyed at 5–10 years. Best years: 1990 89 88 86 85 83 82 75.

MÁLAGA DO *Andalucía, Spain* Málaga is a curious blend of sweet wine, alcohol and juices (some boiled up and concentrated, some fortified, some made from dried grapes) and production is dwindling. The label generally states colour and sweetness. The best Málagas are intensely nutty, raisiny and caramelly. Best producer: Scholz Hermanos.

CH. MALARTIC-LAGRAVIÈRE ★ *Pessac-Léognan AC, Cru Classé de Graves, Bordeaux, France* This is one of the few GRAVES Classed Growths whose reputation has been upheld by its white wine rather than its red (though the red is good too and ages beautifully). The tiny amount of white is made from 100% Sauvignon Blanc and softens after 3–4 years into a really lovely nutty wine. Best years: (reds) 1989 88 85 83 82 81 78; (whites) 1989 88 87 86 85.

MALVASIA This grape, widely planted in Italy, is found in many guises, both white and red. In Friuli, it is known as the Malvasia Istriana, and produces tight, fragrant wines of great charm, while in Tuscany, Umbria and the rest of central Italy, it is used to improve the blend for wines like ORVIETO and FRASCATI. On the islands, Malvasia is used in the production of rich, sweet wines in Bosa and Cagliari (in Sardinia) and in Lipari off the coast of Sicily to make really tasty, apricotty sweet wines. As a black grape, Malvasia Nera is blended with Negroamaro in southern Puglia, while in Piedmont, a paler skinned relation produces frothing light reds in Castelnuovo Don Bosco, just outside Turin.

LA MANCHA DO *Castilla-La Mancha, Spain* Spain's vast, flat central plateau, surrounded by mountains which ward off the rain, is Europe's biggest delimited wine area. Whites are the mainstay, never exciting (since the dominant Airén grape has little character) but nowadays often fresh, fruity and attractive. Modern reds, using the Cencibel (Tempranillo) grape, and without the traditional addition of white grapes, can be light and fruity, or richer, sometimes with a dash of Cabernet Sauvignon. There is still much old-style, rough La Mancha wine, but progress is fast. Best producers: Fermin Ayuso Roig (Viña Q, Estola), Nuestra Señora de Manjavacas co-op, Rodriguez y Berger (Viña Santa Elena ★), Julian Santos Aguado (Don Fadrique), Torres Filoso (Arboles de Castillejo ★), Vinícola de Castilla (Castillo de Alhambra, Señorío de Guadianeja ★).

MANZANILLA See Jerez y Manzanilla DO.

MARANGES AC *Côte de Beaune, Burgundy, France* New AC created in 1989 to cover the southern Côte de Beaune. Quite attractive wines in a light way, though many growers continue to sell them as COTE DE BEAUNE-VILLAGES. Best years: 1990 89.

MARCHE *Italy* Large region stretching from the Apennines to the coastal resorts of the Adriatic. Occasional good white Verdicchio and reds from Montepulciano (especially ROSSO CONERO), plus delightful sparkling, red Vernaccia di Serrapetrona.

MARCILLAC AC *South-West France* Strong, dry red wines (there is a little rosé), largely made from the local grape Fer. The reds are rustic but full of fruit and should be drunk between 2 and 5 years. Best producer: Marcillac-Vallon co-op.

MARGARET RIVER *Western Australia* The first Australian region planted on scientific advice, in the late 1960s. It quickly established its name as a leading quality area for Cabernet Sauvignon, with marvellously deep, structured wines sometimes recalling Classed Growth Bordeaux. Later, Chardonnay started to shine, as did grassy, appley Sémillon, tropical Sauvignon Blanc and spicy Verdelho. Best producers: CAPE MENTELLE, CULLENS, EVANS & TATE, LEEUWIN ESTATE, MOSS WOOD, VASSE FELIX.

MARGARIDE *Almeirim IPR, Ribatejo, Portugal* Best producer so far in the vast Ribatejo area. The Casal do Monteiro★ and Convento da Serra★ wines are good. Best years: 1990 89 86 85 84 83.

MARGAUX AC *Haut-Médoc, Bordeaux, France* Centred on the village of Margaux but including Soussans in the north and Cantenac, Labarde and Arsac in the south. The pale gravel banks dotted through the vineyards mean that the wines are rarely heavy and should have a divine perfume when mature at 7–12 years. Best producers: (Classed Growths) d'ISSAN★★, MARGAUX★★★, PALMER★★, RAUSAN-SEGLA★★★; (others) d'ANGLUDET★★, Monbrison★★, SIRAN★★. Best years: 1990 89 88 86 85 83 82.

CH. MARGAUX ★★★ *Margaux AC, 1er Cru Classé, Haut-Médoc, Bordeaux, France* The greatest wine in the Médoc. Between 1978 and 1990 the Mentzelopoulos family have produced flawless wines as great as any MARGAUX ever made. Recent ownership changes should not affect the wine as inspired winemaker Paul Pontallier remains in charge. There is also some delicious white, Pavillon Blanc, made from Sauvignon Blanc, but it must be the most expensive wine sold under the  BORDEAUX AC label by a mile. Second wine: (red) Pavillon Rouge. Best years: (reds) 1991 90 89 88 87 86 85 83 82 81 80 79 78; (whites) 1990 89 88 86 85.

MARINO DOC *Lazio, Italy* Dry white FRASCATI lookalike from south of Rome, similar both in grape mix (Malvasia and Trebbiano) and style (soft and neutral). Best producer: Colle Picchioni.

MARLBOROUGH *South Island, New Zealand* Marlborough has
enjoyed such spectacular success as a quality wine-producing
region it is now difficult to imagine that the first vines were
planted as recently as 1973. Long cool, relatively dry ripening
and free-draining stony soils are the major viticultural assets. Its
snappy, aromatic Sauvignon Blanc first brought the region fame
worldwide. Fine-flavoured Chardonnay, steely Riesling, elegant
Champagne-method fizz and luscious botrytized wines are the
region's other great successes. Best producers: CLOUDY BAY,
HUNTERS, Le Brun, MONTANA, Stoneleigh, VAVASOUR, Wairau River.

MARNE ET CHAMPAGNE *Champagne AC, Champagne, France*
The largest co-op in Champagne, producing in excess of 10 million bottles under dozens of different labels, mainly for supermarkets. A less publicized fact is that Marne et Champagne also
sells wine to some of the Champagne houses.

MARQUÉS DE CÁCERES *Rioja DOC, Rioja, Spain* Go-ahead RIOJA
winery making crisp, aromatic, modern whites★ and rosés★,
and fleshy, fruity reds★ with the emphasis on aging in bottle,
not barrel. Best years: 1986 85 82 78 76 75 70.

MARQUÉS DE GRIÑON *Rueda, Castilla-La Mancha, Spain* Carlos
Falco studied wine-making in California and then planted vines
on his family estate. The white is an all-Verdejo RUEDA★, crisp
and grassy, and the red is a full-flavoured, minty, long-lived
Cabernet Sauvignon★★ (with a little Merlot). Falco's next creations were the Durius wines, a red★★ blended from RIBERA DEL
DUERO Tinto Fino and Toro Garnacha, a rosé made from Toro
Garnacha and a white from Toro Malvasía. Best years: (reds)
1990 89 86 85.

MARQUÉS DE MONISTROL *Cava DO and Penedés DO, Catalonia,
Spain* Martini & Rossi own this beautiful winery. The young
Brut Selección★ is the freshest and fruitiest CAVA. The still
whites, Blanc de Blancs★ and Blanc en Noirs★, are good, the
reds unexceptional. Drink the youngest available.

MARQUÉS DE MURRIETA *Rioja DOC, Rioja, Spain* The RIOJA
bodega to which all others aspire. Ultra-traditional yet recently
re-equipped with glistening new fermentation vats for reds and a
Californian bottling line. The white Etiqueta Blanca Crianza
wine has been replaced by the honeyed, oaky El Dorado★. The
reds are at least Reservas★, notable for their depth of mulberry
fruit, and occasionally Gran Reserva★★ or even Castillo
Ygay★★, wine from the very best vintages, released only after at
least 20 years. Best years: 1986 85 70 68 59 42.

MARQUÉS DE RISCAL *Rioja DOC, País Vasco, and Rueda DO,
Castilla y León, Spain* A near total clear-out of old barrels from
the historic bodega should eliminate the musty character that
has bedevilled the Riscal reds since the 1970s. Reds will
improve from 1987 onwards. Watch out for Barón de Chirél★★,
the brilliant new (expensive) blend of RIOJA grapes with Cabernet

Sauvignon. Whites come from RUEDA: the basic Rueda is clean if unexciting, the fresh, grassy Sauvignon Blanc and soft, oaky Reserva Limousin are better. Best years: (reds) 1987 onwards.

MARSALA DOC *Sicily, Italy* Fortified wines, more sought after these days for filling confectionery or for use in sauces, but once as highly esteemed as sherry or Madeira. A taste of an old Vergine (unsweetened) Marsala, intense yet fine and complex, will show why. Today most Marsala is sweetened. Purists would say that sweetening mars the delicate nuances displayed by the base wine, but the provision remains, under DOC law, for sweetening the Fine and Superiore versions. Best producers: (Vergine) Florio, Pellegrino, Rallo; also De Bartoli (VECCHIO SAMPERI★★, and Il Marsala Superiore★).

MARSANNAY AC *Côte de Nuits, Burgundy, France* Village almost in the Dijon suburbs which is best known for its rosé, which can be quite pleasant but a little too austere and dry. The red is rapidly proving itself to be one of Burgundy's most fragrant wines, if never very full in texture. There is very little white but it is dry and nutty and good. Best producers: Chenu, Clair-Daü, Fougeray★, Huguenot, JADOT, LABOURE-ROI★, Quillardet★. Best years: 1990 89 88 86 85.

MARSANNE An undervalued grape which produces rich, nutty wines in the northern Rhône (HERMITAGE, CROZES-HERMITAGE, ST-JOSEPH and ST-PERAY), often in partnership with the more lively Roussanne. It is also planted in Switzerland, and performs brilliantly in Australia at CHATEAU TAHBILK★ and MITCHELTON★.

MARTINBOROUGH *Wairarapa, North Island, New Zealand* Moderately cool, dry climate, free-draining infertile soils and an uncompromising attitude toward quality are this tiny region's greatest assets. Martinborough makes some of the country's top Pinot Noirs but it is also capable of turning out big, complex Chardonnay, intense, ripe Cabernet Sauvignon blends, full-flavoured yet elegant Sauvignon Blanc and honeyed, botrytized Riesling. Best producers: Ata Rangi, Dry River, MARTINBOROUGH VINEYARD, Palliser.

MARTINBOROUGH VINEYARD *Martinborough, North Island, New Zealand* Since 1986 many of the country's best Pinot Noirs come from this winery, although their efforts have now attracted a bevy of challengers. Winemaker Larry McKenna's heart may be in Pinot Noir ★★★ but he also makes impressive Chardonnay★★, and strong spicy Riesling ★. Best years: 1991 90 89 88 87 86.

MARTÍNEZ BUJANDA *Rioja DOC, País Vasco, Spain* Family-owned firm that makes some of the best 'modern' RIOJAS. Whites and rosés are young and crisp, reds ★★ are full of fruit *and* age very well. Best years: (reds) 1990 87 85 81.

167

LOUIS M MARTINI *Napa Valley, California, USA* During the 1980s the wines from this well-respected Napa winery changed from being deep and rich to a relatively light, though pleasant, and cheap style. Recently the winery has turned to a more concentrated style of wine based on single vineyards and a range of reserve wines, so far with mixed results. The Monte Rosso Cabernet Sauvignon ★★ is stunning.

MARZEMINO Beloved of Mozart's Don Giovanni, the fame of this red grape today is confined largely to northern Italy's Trentino region, where it makes deep-coloured, plummy and zesty reds that are best drunk within 3–5 years. Best producers: Letrari, Spagnolli, De Tarczal.

MAS DE DAUMAS GASSAC *Vin de Pays de l'Hérault, Languedoc, France* Ebullient Aimé Guibert is the best-known producer in the Languedoc as he has proved that the Hérault, normally associated with cheap table wine, is capable of producing great red wines that can age in bottle. The Daumas Gassac rosé is a little dull, but the tannic yet rich Cabernet Sauvignon-based red ★★ and the fabulously scented white ★★★ (Viognier, Muscat, Chardonnay and Petit Manseng) are brilliant. Best years: (reds) 1990 89 88 87 85 83 82 81.

MASCARELLO *Piedmont, Italy* Two first-rate producers sport this famous BAROLO name. The old house of Giuseppe Mascarello (now run by grandson Mauro) is renowned for dense, chunky Dolcettos (Bricco Ravera★★ and the relatively lighter Corsini★) and intense BARBERA (particularly Ginestra★), but the pride of the house is their Barolo from the Monprivato★★★ vineyard, consistently one of the best wines in Barolo. Bartolo Mascarello is one of the great old-fashioned producers of Barolo★★★, yet his wines have an exquisite perfume and balance as well. Both his Dolcetto★★ and Freisa★ are excellent. Best years: 1990 89 88 85 82 78.

MASI *Veneto, Italy* This family firm, headed by Sandro Boscaini, is one of the driving forces in VALPOLICELLA and SOAVE. Their Campo Fiorin ★, a Ripasso Valpolicella, is worth looking out for, as is their AMARONE ★ from the Mazzano vineyard.

MASTROBERARDINO *Campania, Italy* This famous family firm has long flown the flag for southern Italy. They are best known for their red TAURASI and white Greco and Fiano.

MATANZAS CREEK *Sonoma, California, USA* Sauvignon Blanc ★ is taken very seriously here and the results show in a complex, pleasing wine; Chardonnay ★★ is excitingly rich and toasty but not overblown. The Merlot ★★ can have a succulence and creaminess that is simply irresistible. Best years: 1991 90 88 87.

168

MATARO See Mourvèdre.

MATAWHERO *Gisborne, North Island, New Zealand* Highly individual wines, using natural yeasts, long maceration periods and malolactic fermentation for varieties such as Gewürztraminer★★. It's lovely spicy stuff, and the Chardonnay★, Pinot Noir★ and an intense Cabernet Sauvignon/Merlot ★ are pretty special too.

MATUA VALLEY *Waimauku, Auckland, North Island, New Zealand* Ross and Bill Spence have explored many wine-making and viticultural options to produce their present range of stylish, high-quality wines. Best wines include the charming, full-bodied Judd Estate Chardonnay★★, luscious and strongly varietal Gewürztraminer★★, Merlot★★, Cabernet Sauvignon ★, a creamy oak-aged Sauvignon Blanc★★, and marvellously tangy Marlborough Sauvignon Blanc★★★. Best years: 1992 91 90 89 86.

CH. DE MAUCAILLOU ★ *Moulis AC, Cru Bourgeois, Haut-Médoc, Bordeaux, France* Maucaillou shows that you don't have to be a Classed Growth to make high quality claret. The Dourthe family are dedicated owners and the wine is expertly made – soft but classically flavoured. It matures quickly but ages well for 10–12 years. Best years: 1990 89 88 86 85 83 82 81.

MAURY AC *Roussillon, France* A Vin Doux Naturel made mainly from Grenache Noir grapes on the borders of Languedoc and Roussillon. This strong, sweetish wine can be made in either a young, fresh style or the locally revered old rancio style. Best producers: Cave des Vignerons, Mas Amiel.

MAXIMIN GRÜNHAUS *Grünhaus, Ruwer, Germany* The best estate in the small Ruwer area. Carl von Schubert vinifies separately the wines of his 3 vineyards (Abtsberg, Bruderberg and Herrenberg), making chiefly dry wines of great subtlety and distinction. In 1990 Schubert made 10 different wines apiece on the Herrenberg and Abtsberg, the best of which were easily ★★★. Best years: 1990 89 88 85 83 81 79 78.

MAZIS-CHAMBERTIN AC See Chambertin AC.

MAZOYÈRES-CHAMBERTIN AC See Chambertin AC.

McWILLIAMS *Riverina, New South Wales* Large family winery whose best wines are the Mount Pleasant range from the Lower Hunter Valley: classic bottle-aged Sémillons including Elizabeth★★★, buttery Chardonnays★★ and special-vineyard Shirazes ★ – Old Paddock, Old Hill and Rose Hill. Also classy liqueur Muscat★★ and 'sherries'★ from Riverina, and exciting table wines from new Barwang★ vineyard in the Young region. Best years: (Hunter Sémillon) 1991 90 88 87 86 85 82 80 79.

MÉDOC AC *Bordeaux, France* The Médoc peninsula north of Bordeaux on the left bank of the Gironde produces a good fistful of the world's most famous reds. These are all situated in the southern, more gravelly half of the area or HAUT-MÉDOC AC. The Médoc AC, for reds only, covers the northern part of the peninsula. Here, in these flat clay vineyards, the Merlot grape

169

dominates. The wines can be very attractive, dry but juicy and most are best to drink at 3–5 years old. **Best producers:** La Cardonne, Lacombe-Noaillac, Les Ormes-Sorbet, Patache d'Aux, Plagnac, POTENSAC, La Tour-de-By★, La Tour-St-Bonnet, Vieux Ch. Landon. **Best years:** 1990 89 88 85 83 82.

MEERLUST *Stellenbosch, South Africa* A Meerlust Cabernet Sauvignon was the first wine to turn me on to South Africa's great potential at the end of the 1970s. I was doing a photo session and the photographer opened the bottle to try to get me to sit still, I suspect. The wine was fragrant, cedary, with ripe blackcurrant fruit – a ST-JULIEN claret in all but name. I wish I could say I've been able to repeat the experience, but I have not found any recent Meerlust Cabernets or Rubicons (a Bordeaux-blend) of the same style. The potential is obviously there, but I find modern Meerlust reds dry and tight and I long for one of South Africa's great wines to sing again.

MENDOCINO COUNTY *California, USA* The northernmost county of the North Coast AVA. The best growing areas are Anderson Valley AVA, a cool east-west valley opening up to the Pacific Ocean and a good area for sparkling wines and the occasional Pinot Noir; and Redwood Valley AVA, a warmer area with good results from Zinfandel and Cabernet Sauvignon. **Best producers:** Handley Cellars, Jepson, Lazy Creek, Lolonis, McDowell Valley, Navarro, Obester, Olson, Parducci, ROEDERER, Scharffenberger.

MÉNÉTOU-SALON AC *Loire Valley, France* Extremely attractive, Sauvignon whites and cherry-fresh Pinot Noir reds and rosés from just west of SANCERRE. **Best producers:** de Chatenoy, Chavet, Denis, Mellot, Pellé★, Teiller. **Best years:** 1990 89 88.

MÉO-CAMUZET *Vosne-Romanée, Côte de Nuits, Burgundy, France* Super-quality Côte de Nuits estate, thanks in no small measure to the advice of Henri JAYER, a third of whose estate passed to Méo-Camuzet in 1988. The style is heavily influenced by Jayer – new oak barrels and luscious, rich fruit combining to produce superb wines, which also age well. The CORTON ★★★ and CLOS VOUGEOT ★★★ are the top wines here, but don't miss the two VOSNE-ROMANEE Premiers Crus, Aux Brulées ★★ and Les Chaumes ★★. **Best years:** 1990 89 88 87.

MERCUREY AC *Côte Chalonnaise, Burgundy, France* Most important of the four main Côte Chalonnaise villages. The red is usually pleasant and strawberry flavoured, and can take some aging. There is not much white but I like its buttery, even spicy taste. It is best drunk at 3–4 years old. **Best producers:** (reds) Chanzy, FAIVELEY★, Juillot★, RODET★★, Saier, de Suremain, Voarick; (whites) CHARTRON & TREBUCHET, Faiveley (Clos Rochette), Genot-Boulanger★, Juillot, RODET (Chamirey★). **Best years:** 1990 89 88 85.

MERITAGE An unnecessary and confusing piece of marketing nomenclature for red or white wines made in California from Bordeaux grape varieties.

MERLOT A classic grape and the backbone of Bordeaux's ST-EMILION and POMEROL wines, as well as other Bordeaux reds. Throughout the world there is a demand for red wines which have the Bordeaux flavours yet which can be drunk young, and Merlot fits the bill superbly. It is rich, juicy, often blackcurrant and minty. As well as in Bordeaux, it is found all over South-West France and the Midi where the soft, juicy fruit can make a dramatic difference to simple Vin de Pays. California has had great success producing beautifully fruity but well-structured Merlot, and New Zealand is beginning to produce exciting examples. Good Merlot is also made in Washington State, Chile, Hungary and Bulgaria. Merlot produces largely light quaffers in Switzerland and Italy, but good stuff comes out of Friuli. Australia and South Africa are still working out how to grow it.

GEOFF MERRILL *Southern Vales, South Australia* High-profile winemaker who combines the rare talents of instinctive feel for wine and marketing ability. His restored stone winery Mount Hurtle produces soft, friendly Cabernet★, Chardonnay-Sémillon★ and quaffable Grenache rosé, but the best is yet to come.

MÉTHODE CHAMPENOISE The Champagne method was developed, if not necessarily invented, in the Champagne region, and it is now used for all the world's finest sparkling wines. The key to the process is that a second fermentation takes place in bottle, producing carbon dioxide which, kept in solution under pressure gives the wine its fizz. From 1995 the term (but not, of course, the process) will be restricted to CHAMPAGNE. See also Cuve Close.

MEURSAULT AC *Côte de Beaune, Burgundy, France* The biggest and most popular white wine village in the Côte d'Or. There are no Grands Crus, but a whole cluster of Premiers Crus. The general standard of wine is variable due to the worldwide demand. The deep-golden wine is lovely to drink young but better aged for 5–8 years. Only a little Meursault red is made. Best producers: Ampeau★, Boisson-Vadot★, COCHE-DURY★★★, DROUHIN, JADOT, Jobard★★, LAFON★★★, Matrot★★, Michelot-Buisson★★, Pierre Morey★★, Potinet-Ampeau★, Ropiteau-Mignon★, Roulot★. Best years: 1990 89 88 86 85.

JOS MEYER ET FILS *Alsace AC, Alsace, France* Traditional company, making excellent wine, whether as a merchant or as a producer in its own right. The top wines are Gewürztraminer (particularly Les Archenets★★) and Pinot Blanc (Les Lutins★). Best years: 1990 89 86 85 83.

CH. MEYNEY★ *St-Estèphe AC, Cru Bourgeois, Haut-Médoc, Bordeaux, France* One of the most reliable ST-ESTEPHEs with a real effort being made by the owners CORDIER in recent years. The result is big, broad-flavoured wine with lovely, dark, plummy fruit. Second wine: Prieur de Meyney. Best years: 1990 89 88 86 85 83 82 81 78 75.

LOUIS MICHEL & FILS *Chablis AC, Burgundy, France* The prime exponents of unoaked CHABLIS. The top Crus – Les Clos ★★, Montmains ★★ and Montée de Tonnerre ★★ – are fresh-flavoured and long-lived. Best years: 1990 89 88 86 83.

MIDI *France* A loose geographical term, virtually synonymous with Languedoc-Roussillon, covering the vast, sunbaked area of southern France between the Pyrenees and the Rhône Valley.

MILDARA *Murray River, Victoria, Australia* Based at Mildura on the Murray River, but the best wines are from large Coonawarra vineyards and include the hugely popular and fairly priced Jamieson's Run ★ (Shiraz-based red and Chardonnay white). Also owns Balgownie, Wolf BLASS, KRONDORF, YELLOWGLEN.

MILLTON *Gisborne, North Island, New Zealand* Organic vineyard whose top wines include the sophisticated and individual Clos St Anne Chardonnay ★, botrytized Opou Vineyard Riesling ★★ and ambitiously complex Barrel-Fermented Chardonnay ★. Best years: 1992 91 90 89.

MINERVOIS AC *Languedoc, France* Attractive wines from north-east of Carcassonne. The area's great strength is organization, and big companies like NICOLAS have worked hard with local co-ops to produce good-quality, juicy, quaffing wine at reasonable prices. Mostly red wine full of ripe, red fruit and pine-dust perfume, for drinking young. It can age, especially if a little new oak has been used. Best producers: de Blomac, Chantovent, Domergue, Fabas, Festiano, de Gourgazaud, Meyzonnier, NICOLAS, Paraza, Ste-Eulalie, Vassière, Villerambert-Julien.

CH. LA MISSION-HAUT-BRION ★★ *Pessac-Léognan AC, Cru Classé de Graves, Bordeaux, France* I always find la Mission wines powerful but, unlike its neighbour HAUT-BRION, never charming. Their strength is in massive, dark fruit and oak flavours and they often need 20 years or so before they are ready. Best years: 1990 89 88 85 82 81 79 78 75.

MITCHELTON *Goulburn Valley, Victoria, Australia* Important winery with Victoria's most consistently fine Riesling ★★. Oaked and un-oaked Marsanne ★ is a speciality; sparkling Nattier Brut is a Marsanne Chardonnay blend. Reds from Shiraz ★ and Cabernet ★ are ultra-fruity modern styles.

MITTELRHEIN *Germany* Small, unsung (as far as great wine is concerned, that is) and northerly wine region which falls in the scenically stunning Rhine Valley either side of Koblenz. About 75% of the wine here is Riesling but unlike other German regions, the Mittelrhein has been in decline over the last few decades. The vineyard sites are steep and difficult to work – although breathtaking for tourists to gawp at. Some wines are successfully turned into Sekt and most of DEINHARD's Lila Imperial comes from the region. The best growers (like Toni JOST) cluster around Bacharach in the south, and produce wines of a striking mineral tang and dry, fruity intensity.

MOELLEUX French for soft or mellow, used to describe sweet or medium sweet wines.

MOËT & CHANDON *Champagne AC, Champagne, France* Moët & Chandon's enormous production of more than 25 million bottles a year dominates the Champagne market. A good bottle of non-vintage Moët ★ can be absolutely delightful – soft, creamy and a little spicy. The vintage wine ★ is more consistent, and usually has a good strong style to it while latest releases of rosé ★★ show a Pinot Noir floral fragrance depressingly rare in modern Champagne. Dom Pérignon ★★★ is their de luxe cuvée and it can be one of the greatest Champagnes of all, but you've got to age it for a number of years or else you're simply wasting your money on the fancy bottle. Best years: 1986 85 83 82.

MONBAZILLAC AC *South-West France* Bergerac's leading sweet wine. Most of it is light, vaguely sweet and entirely forgettable, usually from the efficient but unadventurous co-op. This style won't age, but a real, truly rich, late-harvested Monbazillac can happily last 10 years. Best producers: la Borderie, le Fagé, Hébras★★, la JAUBERTIE, Ch. de Monbazillac (made by the local co-op), Treuil-de-Nailhac★. Best years: 1990 89 88 86 85 83.

ROBERT MONDAVI *Napa Valley, California, USA* Robert Mondavi is a Californian institution, spreading the gospel of Californian wine from his Napa home base. Mondavi is best known for the regular bottling Cabernet Sauvignon ★ and the Reserve Cabernet Sauvignon ★★★. The regular bottlings are more open and fruity with the emphasis on early drinkability, while the Reserve wines possess enormous depth and power. Winemaker Tim Mondavi has put a great deal of energy into Pinot Noir over the past few years and the results are beginning to pay off. Again, there is a regular bottling of Pinot Noir ★ and a Reserve Pinot Noir ★★★ which are improving with every vintage. The Pinots are vel-vety smooth and supple wines with great style, perfume and balance. For many years the Mondavi trade-mark wine was Fumé (Sauvignon)  Blanc but in recent years Chardonnay has become the winery leader (the Reserve ★★ can be superb), but the quality is inconsistent. The Mondavis also own Byron Winery in Santa Barbara County, Vichon Winery in Napa, OPUS ONE in Napa in partnership with the Rothschilds, and in partnership with the Franzia family own Montpellier, a bud-get line of varietal wines, as well as the Mondavi Woodbridge winery where inexpensive varietal wines are produced. Best years: (Cabernet Sauvignon Reserve) 1990 88 87 86 85 84 82 81 79; (Pinot Noir Reserve) 1991 90 88 87. (Chardonnay Reserve) 1991 90 88 87.

MONICA DI SARDEGNA DOC *Sardinia, Italy* Monica, a red grape of Spanish origin, produces soft, easy-drinking red wines in Sardinia. This DOC covers all Monica grown on the island, much of which is in the southern part, though there is another DOC, Monica di Cagliari, for a sweet red wine.

MONT BOUQUET, VIN DE PAYS DU *Languedoc, France* Situated to the north-west of Nîmes, this is red wine country, focusing on the main southern French varieties – Grenache, Cinsaut and Carignan – with increasing amounts of Syrah. These are good basic wines. Best producer: Garrigue.

MONT TAUCH, LES PRODUCTEURS DU *Fitou, Languedoc-Roussillon, France* A big, quality-conscious co-op based in the Fitou region, but producing a large range of Midi wines, from good gutsy FITOU ★ and CORBIERES ★ to rich MUSCAI DE RIVESALTES ★ and light but gluggable Vin de Pays du Torgan. Best years: (whites and rosés) 1991 90; (reds) 1991 90 89 88.

MONTAGNE-ST-ÉMILION AC *Bordeaux, France* A ST-EMILION satellite which can produce rather good red wines. The wines are normally ready to drink in 4 years but age quite well in their slightly earthy way. Best producers: Calon, Corbin, Plaisance, Roudier, des Tours, Vieux-Ch.-St-André. Best years: 1990 89 88 85 83 82.

MONTAGNY AC *Côte Chalonnaise, Burgundy, France* The most southerly of the four Côte Chalonnaise village ACs. In general the wines are dry and rather lean, but now that some producers are aging their wines for a few months in new oak, there has been a great improvement. Drink within 3 years. Best producers: Arnoux, BUXY co-op★, Louis LATOUR, Martial de Laboulaye, B Michel, Roy, Steinmaier, Vachet★. Best years: 1991 90 89 88.

MONTANA *Auckland, Gisborne, Hawkes Bay and Marlborough, New Zealand* Montana crushes around 45% of New Zealand's grape crop, making it easily the country's largest winemaker, and it has consistently made some of New Zealand's best value wines. The Sauvignon Blanc ★★ and Chardonnay ★★ are in a considerable way to thank for putting New Zealand on the international map. The company now wants to prove that big can also be best. To achieve that goal they have established The McDonald Winery, a small (by Montana standards) winery in Hawkes Bay from which they plan to produce top Chardonnay and Cabernet Sauvignon/Merlot. The first release of a creamy, stylish Church Road Chardonnay★★ (1990) looks very promising. Their Special 'Reserve' bottlings, particularly of Chardonnay, in Marlborough, also bode well. Montana make good Lindauer fizz★ and with the help of the Champagne house DEUTZ they have released the rich, full-bodied Deutz Marlborough Cuvée NV

Brut ★★, which is now rated as one of New Zealand's and the world's, finest sparkling wines.

MONTE VERTINE *Tuscany, Italy*   Though based in the heart of CHIANTI CLASSICO, Monte Vertine is most famous for its Vino da Tavolas, particularly Le Pergole Torte ★★. This was the first of the new style 'Super Tuscans' made solely with Sangiovese (in 1977), and remains one of the best. Owner Sergio Manetti, fed up with battling against the authorities, does not now make a Chianti Classico, bottling his Sangiovese/Canaiolo blend as Il Sodaccio ★★ instead. Best years: 1990 88 85.

MONTECARLO DOC *Tuscany, Italy*   Small zone east of Lucca. The whites (from Trebbiano beefed up with grapes like Sémillon and Pinot Grigio) show potential and have more flavour than other Tuscan whites. The red, a Sangiovese/Syrah blend, shows equal promise. Best producers: Buonamico, Carmignani, Michio.

MONTECILLO *Rioja DOC, Rioja, Spain*   High quality RIOJAS, red, white and rosé, in both young and mature styles. Viña Cumbrero ★ (both red and white) is young and fruity. The rich, fruity, subtly oaky Viña Monty ★★ red Gran Reservas are, unusually for Rioja, aged in French oak barrels and combine delicacy with real flavour. Best years: (reds) 1987 85 82 81 78.

MONTEFALCO DOC *Umbria, Italy*   Though the Sangiovese/ Sagrantino blend, Montefalco Rosso, is one of Umbria's most impressive red wines, it is the Sagrantino grape (a powerful, deep-coloured, tannic variety) on its own that makes this zone the home of Umbria's finest red wines. The dry red Sagrantino di Montefalco can be excellent, but Sagrantino Passito, a sweet red made from dried grapes, is glorious. Best producers: ADANTI★★, Antonelli, Caprai★. Best years: 1990 88 85.

MONTEPULCIANO   This grape, grown mostly in eastern Italy, has no discernible link with the Tuscan town of Montepulciano and its Sangiovese-based wine VINO NOBILE. The grape produces deep-coloured, fleshy, spicy wines with moderate tannin and acidity. It is DOC in Abruzzo, and is blended with Sangiovese to produce ROSSO CONERO and ROSSO PICENO in the Marche. It is used for blending in Umbria, and the Tuscans are now showing increased interest in it. Best producers: (Montepulciano d'Abruzzo) Cornacchia, Illuminati★, Nicodemis, Tollo, Valentini★.

MONTEREY COUNTY *California, USA*   A large Central Coast county south of the San Francisco bay area. The most important AVAs are Arroyo Seco, Chalone, Carmel Valley and Salinas Valley. The best grapes are Chardonnay, Riesling and Pinot Blanc with some good Cabernet Sauvignon and Merlot on hillside vineyards in Carmel Valley. Best producers: CHALONE, Durney, JEKEL, la Reina, Monterey Peninsula Winery, The Monterey Vineyard, Morgan, Smith & Hook, Ventana.

MONTHÉLIE AC *Côte de Beaune, Burgundy, France*   An attractive, mainly red wine village lying halfway along the Côte de Beaune between the more famous communes of MEURSAULT and VOLNAY. The wines generally have a lovely, cherry fruit and make pleasant drinking at a good price. Best producers: Olivier LEFLAIVE, LEROY, Monthélie-Douhairet★, Parent, Potinet-Ampeau, Ropiteau-Mignon, Roulot★, Suremain, Thévenin-Monthélie★. Best years: (reds) 1990 89 88 85 83 82; (whites) 1990 89 88 86 85.

MONTICELLO CELLARS *Napa Valley, California, USA*   In the early 1980s owner Jay Corley focused on white wines producing some very good, full-fruited Chardonnays★, but in the mid-1980s he began buying in Cabernet Sauvignon and Merlot for a range of reds which has now overtaken the whites. There are two Cabernet Sauvignons, the Corley Reserve★ in a big, classic California style and the Jefferson Cuvée, a softer more approachable wine. Also some fairly impressive yeasty sparkling wine under the Montreaux★ label.

MONTILLA-MORILES DO *Andalucía, Spain*   Sherry-style wines that are sold almost entirely as lower-priced sherry substitutes. However, the wines *can* be superb – particularly the top dry amontillado, oloroso and rich Pedro Ximénez styles – and if you think top sherry is underpriced they're almost giving this stuff away. There are also light, fruity but uncharacterful dry whites. Best producers: Alvear (top labels only), Gracia Hermanos.

HUBERT DE MONTILLE *Volnay, Burgundy, France*   Estate producing some of the most concentrated, ageworthy red wines on the Côte de Beaune. If you're willing to wait for 10 years or more, de Montille's VOLNAYS and POMMARDS are very rewarding wines. The Volnay Champans★★, Pommard Les Épenots★★★ and Pommard Les Pezerolles★★ are all well worth their high prices. Best years: 1990 89 88 85 83 80 78.

MONTLOUIS AC *Loire Valley, France*   On the opposite bank of the Loire to the VOUVRAY AC, Montlouis wines are made from the same Chenin grape and in similar styles (dry, medium and sweet and Champagne-method fizz) but tend to be a touch more rustic since the grapes rarely ripen quite as well. Two-thirds of the production is Mousseux, a green, appley fizz. The still wines need aging for 5–10 years, particularly the sweet or Moelleux version, but the fizz might as well be drunk young. Best producers: Berger, Delétang, Levasseur, Moyer. Best years: 1990 89 88 86 85 83 82 78 76 70.

MONTRACHET AC *Côte de Beaune, Burgundy, France*   Those of us who love white Burgundy dream of Montrachet. This world-famous Grand Cru straddles the boundary between the villages of CHASSAGNE-MONTRACHET and PULIGNY-MONTRACHET, with another Grand Cru, Chevalier-Montrachet immediately above it on the slope. Le Montrachet produces wines with a unique combination of concentration, finesse and perfume – white Burgundy at its most sublime. Chevalier's higher elevation yields a slightly leaner wine that is less explosive in its youth, but good examples will become ever more fascinating over 20 years or more. Best producers: COLIN★★★, LAFON★★★, Laguiche★★, Dom. LEFLAIVE★★, RAMONET★★★, Dom. de la ROMANEE-CONTI★★★, THENARD★★. Best years: 1990 89 88 86 85 83 82 78 71 70.

MONTRAVEL AC *South-West France* Dry, medium-dry and sweet white wines from the western end of the Bergerac region. Not much in fashion and production is declining. Reds are labelled as BERGERAC AC. Best producers: de Gouyat, de Roque Peyre.

CH. MONTROSE ★★ *St-Estèphe AC, 2ème Cru Classé, Haut-Médoc, Bordeaux, France* Montrose used to be thought of as the leading ST-ESTEPHE property, famous for its dark, brooding wine that would take around 30 years of aging before it was at its prime. Since 1978, however, the wine has been lighter and less substantial, certain to be ready for drinking at 10 years even in great years such as 1989, 85, 83 and 82. It took a decade for this new style to find its feet but since 1988, the softer, spicier, but well-structured wine is winning admiration again. Best years: 1991 90 89 88 86 85 82 81 79 76.

MORELLINO DI SCANSANO DOC *Tuscany, Italy* Morellino is the local name for Sangiovese in Scansano, a small town in southwest Tuscany. The red has an attractive chunky character, but none of the finesse found further north in CHIANTI. The Riservas can age well for up to 5–7 years. Best producers: Erik Banti, Le Pupille. Best years: 1990 88 85 82.

MOREY-ST-DENIS AC *Côte de Nuits, Burgundy, France* Morey has five Grands Crus (BONNES-MARES, Clos des Lambrays, CLOS DE LA ROCHE, CLOS DE TART and Clos St-Denis) as well as some very good Premiers Crus. Nowadays much basic village Morey wine is dilute and dull. But from a good grower the wine has a good strawberry or redcurrant fruit and acquires an attractive depth as it ages. A tiny amount of startling, nutty white wine is also produced. Best producers: Castagnier-Vadey★★, Charlopin★★, DROUHIN, DUJAC★★, Georges Lignier★★, Marchand★, Perrot-Minot★, Ponsot★, J TARDY. Best years: 1990 89 88 85 83 80 78.

MORGON AC *Beaujolais, Burgundy, France* Most wine from this BEAUJOLAIS Cru has a soft, cherry fruit which makes for very easy drinking but from a good grower and from the slopes of the Mont du Py the wine can be thick and dark, acquiring a perfume of cherries as it ages. Best producers: Aucoeur, Brun, La Chanaise, Charvet★, Descombes, Janodet★, Lapierre★, Longuepierre, Savoye★, Vincent. Best years: 1991 90 89 88 85.

MORRIS *Rutherglen, Victoria, Australia* Historic winery, ORLANDO-owned but Mick Morris-run, making traditional regional favourites like liqueur Muscat ★★ and Tokay ★★ (Old Premium is ★★★), 'ports', 'sherries' and robust table wines from Shiraz ★, Cabernet ★, Durif and Blue Imperial (Cinsaut).

MORTON ESTATE *Katikati, North Island, New Zealand*   Katikati is the tiny town where Morton Estate built their winery in Dutch Cape of Good Hope style and established a small vineyard. Best wines are the robust, complex Black Label Chardonnay★, nectarine/tropical fruit Black Label Fumé Blanc ★, intense berries and cedar Black Label Cabernet Sauvignon/Merlot ★, as well as a highly successful fizz★★. Best years: 1992 91 90 89.

MOSCATO D'ASTI DOC *Piedmont, Italy*   The Muscat or Moscato grape comes in a seemingly infinite number of styles, but not one is as beguiling as this delicately scented and gently bubbling version from Moscato Bianco grapes from the hills between Asti and Alba in north-west Italy. The DOC zone is the same as for ASTI SPUMANTE, but the best grapes go into this wine, which is only Frizzante (semi-sparkling) rather than Spumante (fully sparkling). The best are thrillingly grapy and, low in alcohol. Drink the wines while still bubbling with youthful fragrance. Best producers: ASCHERI★★, Braida★, Chiarlo★, FONTANAFREDDA★, Viticoltori dell'Acquese★, VOERZIO★.

MOSCATO PASSITO DI PANTELLERIA DOC *Sicily, Italy*   The Muscat of Alexandria grape is used to make this powerful dessert wine. Pantelleria is a small island south-west of Sicily, closer to Africa than it is to Italy. The grapes are picked in mid-August and laid out in the sun to dry and shrivel for a fortnight. They are then crushed and fermented to give an amber-coloured, intensely flavoured sweet Muscat that is one of the best produced. Best drunk within 5–7 years of the vintage, though they can age gracefully for a decade or more. Best producers: De Bartoli (Bukkuram ★★), Murana (Martingana ★).

MOSEL-SAAR-RUWER *Germany*   Not a coherent wine region, but a collection of vineyard areas on the Mosel and its tributaries, the Saar and the Ruwer. The Mosel river itself rises in the French Vosges before forming the border between Germany and Luxembourg. In its first German incarnation in the upper Mosel the fairly dire Elbling grape holds sway but with the middle Mosel begins a series of villages responsible for some of the world's very best Riesling wines: Piesport, Wintrich, Brauneberg, Bernkastel, Graach, Ürzig and Erden. The wines are not big or powerful, but in good years they have tremendous 'slaty' breed and an ability to blend the greenness of perfumes and fruits with the golden warmth of honey. Great wines are rarer in the lower part of the valley as the Mosel swings round into Trier. South of Trier is the Saar which can produce wonderful, piercing wines in villages such as Serrig, Okfen and Wiltingen. The Ruwer stream is north of Trier and produces slightly softer wines; if no village names stand out here there are a few estates (MAXIMIN GRUNHAUS, KARTHAUSERHOF) which are on every list of the best in Germany. See also Ayl, Bernkastel, Brauneberg, Erden, Graach, Ockfen, Urzig, Wehlen.

LENZ MOSER *Rohrendorf-bei-Krems, Kamptal-Donauland, Austria*
Important merchant buying growers' wines and bottling them as 'Selection'. Also fine Burgenland wines from the Klosterkeller Siegendorf and Weinviertel wines (including Cabernet Sauvignon!) from the Malteser Ritterorden estate.

MOSS WOOD *Margaret River, Western Australia* Outstanding silky smooth, rich but structured Cabernet ★★. The Chardonnay ★★ can be rich and peachy and the Pinot Noir ★ erratic but magical at best. Sémillon ★★, both oaked and unoaked, is a consistently fascinating wine. Best years: (reds) 1990 89 87 85 83 80 75.

J P MOUEIX *Bordeaux, France* As well as owning PETRUS, LAFLEUR-PETRUS, MAGDELAINE, TROTANOY and other properties, the Moueix family runs a thriving merchant business specializing in the wines of the right bank, particularly POMEROL and FRONSAC. Christian Moueix (son of Jean-Pierre) also runs a California winery called DOMINUS. The quality of the Moueix wines is generally high. Best years: 1990 89 88 86 85 82.

MOULIN-À-VENT AC *Beaujolais, Burgundy, France* The BEAUJOLAIS Cru that resembles a full, chocolaty Burgundy, if you leave the wine to mature for 6–10 years. Best producers: Brugne, Champagnon★, Charvet★, Chauvet★, Ch. du Moulin-à-Vent, DUBOEUF (single domaines★), Ch. des Jacques, Janodet★, Siffert, la Tour de Bief★★, Trichard. Best years: 1991 90 89 88 87 85 83.

MOULIS AC *Haut-Médoc, Bordeaux, France* The smallest of the specific ACs within the HAUT-MEDOC area. Much of the wine is excellent – delicious to drink at 5–6 years old, though good examples should age 10–20 years – and not over-priced. Best producers: Brillette★, CHASSE-SPLEEN★★, Duplessis-Fabre, Dutruch-Grand-Poujeaux, Gressier-Grand-Poujeaux, MAUCAILLOU★, Moulin-à-Vent★. POUJEAUX★★. Best years: 1990 89 88 86 85 83 82 81 79 78.

MOUNT LANGI GHIRAN *Great Western, Victoria, Australia* Relative newcomer turning out extraordinary powerful, peppery Shiraz ★★★, fine Cabernet ★ and increasingly good Chardonnay ★.

MOUNT MARY *Yarra Valley, Victoria, Australia* Classic property using Bordeaux as a model, with dry white★ blended from Sauvignon Blanc, Sémillon and Muscadelle, and 'Cabernets' ★★ from all five Bordeaux red grapes that ages beautifully. The Pinot Noir ★★ is almost as good. Best years: 1991 90 88.

MOUNTADAM *Adelaide Hills, South Australia* David Wynn and his Bordeaux-educated son Adam, selected this high-altitude and high-flying property in the Adelaide Hills and planted the vineyards from scratch. The rich, buttery Chardonnay ★★ has a world reputation. There is also sumptuous Pinot ★★ and leaner Cabernet ★. The second label David  Wynn wines are fresh and fruity, as are the organic wines labelled Eden Ridge. Best years: 1991 90 89 87 84.

MOUNTARROW *Hunter Valley, New South Wales, Australia*
Revitalized by Nick Whitlam and part-owned by a Japanese company, this Upper Hunter winery grows some of its own grapes and buys in from other regions, notably Cowra. Many labels include Arrowfield, Carisbrook Estate, Simon Whitlam ★ and Simon Gilbert ★★. The emphasis is on oaky whites from Chardonnay and Sémillon and some nice tasty reds from Shiraz and Cabernet. Best years: 1991 90 88 87.

MOURVÈDRE One of the best southern French varieties, currently enjoying a return to fashion. Mourvèdre needs lots of sunshine to get fully ripe, which is why it performs so well on the Mediterranean coast at BANDOL, producing wines that can age for 20 years or more. It is increasingly important as a source of colour, body and tarry, pine-needle flavour in the wines of CHATEAUNEUF-DU-PAPE and the Midi. In Australia and California it is often known as Mataro, and is only just beginning to make a reputation for itself.

MOUSSEUX French for sparkling wine, as in Vin Mousseux. Seldom used for Champagne-method wines, the term is usually associated with sparkling wines of lesser quality.

MOUTON-CADET *Bordeaux AC, Bordeaux, France* The most widely-sold red Bordeaux in the world was created by Baron Philippe de Rothschild in the 1930s. The wine is blended and comes from the entire Bordeaux region, and not from MOUTON-ROTHSCHILD. The wine is perfectly correct, but uninspiring, and never cheap. There is also a white Mouton-Cadet.

CH. MOUTON-ROTHSCHILD ★★★ *Pauillac AC, 1er Cru Classé, Haut-Médoc, Bordeaux, France* Baron Philippe de Rothschild died in 1988 after 65 years of managing Mouton-Rothschild, raising it from being a run-down Second Growth to promotion to First Growth status in 1973 and a reputation as one of the greatest wines in the world. The most magnificently rich and indulgent of the great Bordeaux reds when young, the wine takes 15–20 years to open up fully to its brilliant blackcurrant and cigar box best. Best years: 1990 89 88 86 85 83 82 81 78 75 70.

MUGA *Rioja DOC, Rioja, Spain* A fairly small, very traditional family winery making high quality, elegant, rich red RIOJAS ★, especially the Gran Reserva, Prado Enea ★. In very recent years, the whites and rosés have been good and fruity, too. Best years: (reds) 1987 85 82 81 78 75.

MÜLLER-CATOIR *Neustadt-Haardt, Rheinpfalz, Germany* Clearly one of the best estates in Germany today, Müller-Catoir is an eye-opener for those who are sceptical about Germany's ability to make wines in a more international idiom. From vineyards in unsung corners of the warm Rheinpfalz region he produces wine of a piercing fruit flavour and powerful structure unmatched in

Germany – or anywhere else for that matter, including Riesling ★★★, Grauburgunder ★★★, Scheurebe ★★★, Rieslaner ★★ and Müller-Thurgau ★★. Best years: 1990 89 88.

MÜLLER-THURGAU The great workhorse grape of Germany, largely responsible for LIEBFRAUMILCH, Müller-Thurgau is a crossing of Riesling and Sylvaner. When yields are low it produces pleasant, floral wines; but yields are hardly ever low – it was bred for productivity, not restraint. It is rarely that much better in England where it is also common – though occasional good examples, with a slightly sharp green edge to the vaguely grapy flavour come from Austria, Switzerland, Luxembourg and northern Italy. New Zealand used to pride itself on making the world's best Müller-Thurgau in a light, off-dry, aromatic style – and it probably still does, but in terms of wine achievement that's like boasting to a 3-star chef that you boil a great egg.

G H MUMM *Champagne AC, Champagne, France* Mumm's top-selling non-vintage brand, Cordon Rouge, is one of the least impressive Grande Marque Champagnes, frequently out-performed by its Californian counterpart, DOMAINE MUMM. The deluxe cuvée, René Lalou, is slightly better, but the best wine is the elegant Mumm de Cramant ★★. Best years: 1985 82.

MUSCADET AC *Loire Valley, France* Basic Muscadet from vineyards at the mouth of the Loire near Nantes. This is usually pretty dull stuff, but if you drink the wine very young, even as Muscadet Nouveau released as early as November, it may have a modicum of freshness. The better vineyards to the south of the Loire can use the superior AC, MUSCADET DE SÈVRE-ET-MAINE.

MUSCADET DES COTEAUX DE LA LOIRE AC *Loire Valley, France* Muscadet from a large area on the right bank of the Loire between Nantes and Ancenis. It usually lacks the fresh zip of the better MUSCADET DE SÈVRE-ET-MAINE wines.

MUSCADET DE SÈVRE-ET-MAINE AC *Loire Valley, France* The Maine and Sèvre rivers converge south of Nantes and give their name to the area where 85% of MUSCADET is made. A lot of Muscadet can be dry and rather acid but a good example should have a creamy softness with just enough prickle to make your tongue tingle. It's a delightful wine to drink with the seafood of the region. You should really drink Muscadet within the year, but good examples can age for several years, becoming quite full and nutty. Look out for the term *sur lie* on a label as it describes the traditional method of bottling the wine is bottled directly off its sediment or lees, retaining a creamy, yeasty flavour and a slight prickle of carbon dioxide. Best producers: Michel Bahuaud★ (estate bottlings), Bossard★, Chasseloir, Chéreau-Carré★, Dimerie, Dorices, Marquis de Goulaine, Luneau★, Martin, Métaireau, Sauvion★, Touche★, Tourmaline. Best years: 1991 90 89 .

181

MUSCAT

It's strange, but there's hardly a wine grape in the world which makes wine that actually tastes of the grape itself. Yet there's one variety which is so joyously, exultantly grapy that it more than makes up for all the others – the Muscat, generally thought to be the original wine vine. In fact there seem to be about 200 different branches of the Muscat family, but the one that always makes the most exciting wine is called Muscat à Petits Grains (the Muscat with the small berries). These berries can be crunchily green, golden yellow, pink or even brown, and the wines they make can be either really pale and dry, fresh, rich and golden or as dark and sweet as treacle.

WINE STYLES

France Muscat is grown from the far north-east right down to the Spanish border, yet is rarely accorded great respect there. This is a pity because the dry, light, hauntingly grapy Muscats of Alsace are some of France's most delicately beautiful wines. (These are sometimes blended with the crossbreed Muscat Ottonel.) It pops up sporadically in the Rhône Valley, especially in the sparkling wine enclave of Die. Mixed with Clairette, the Clairette de Die Tradition is a dry but fragrant grapy fizz that should be better known.

Muscat de Beaumes-de-Venise could do with being less well-known because the quality of this deliciously fresh fortified wine has suffered in recent years, but its success has encouraged the traditional fortified winemakers of the Languedoc-Roussillon, especially in Frontignan and Rivesaltes, to make fresher, more perfumed wines rather than the flat and syrupy ones they've produced for generations.

Italy Muscat is grown in Italy both for dry table wines in the north and for fortified wines (though the less fine Muscat of Alexandria makes most of the rich southern Muscats). Yet the greatest Muscat à Petits Grains in Italy are those of Asti, where it is called Moscato Bianco. As either Asti Spumante or Moscato Naturale this brilliantly fresh, grapy fizz can be a blissful drink.

Other regions Elsewhere in Europe, Hungary still grows some Muscat, Crimea has shown how good it can be in the Massandra fortified wines, and Greece's finest wines are the rich, golden Muscats of Samos and Patras. California does grow Muscat à Petits Grains, often calling it Muscat Canelli, and Mondavi's Moscato d'Oro is a fair example, but South Africa and Australia make far better use of it. With darker berries, and called Brown Muscat in Australia and Muskadel in South Africa, they make some of the world's most intense, luscious, headily pungent fortified wines, especially in the North-East Victoria areas of Rutherglen and Glenrowan.

BEST PRODUCERS

Sparkling Muscat
France (Clairette de Die
Tradition) Clairette de Die
co-op, Achard-Vincent.

Italy (Moscato d'Asti)
Ascheri, Rivetti, Vietti,
Viticoltori dell'Acquese.

Dry Muscat
France (Muscat d'Alsace)
Cattin, Dirler, Kreydenweiss,
Trimbach, Zind-Humbrecht.

Italy (Goldenmuskateller)
Conti Martini, Tiefenbrunner;
(Rosenmuskateller)
Tiefenbrunner.

Sweet Muscat
Australia (Liqueur Muscat)
Bailey's, Morris, Seppelt,
Yalumba.

France (Muscat de
Beaumes-de-Venise)
Coyeux, Durban, Paul
Jaboulet; (Muscat de
Frontignan) Peyrade;
(Muscat de Rivesaltes)
Cazes, de Jau.

Greece Kourtakis.

Italy (Moscato di Strevi
Passito) Ivaldi; (Rosen-
muskateller) Graf Kuenberg;
(Valle d'Aosta DOC) Voyat.

South Africa Cavendish
Vintage.

183

MUSCAT OF ALEXANDRIA Not to be confused with the superior Muscat Blanc à Petits Grains, Muscat of Alexandria rarely shines in its own right but performs a useful job worldwide, adding perfume and fruit to what would otherwise be dull neutral white wines. It is common for sweet and fortified wines throughout the Mediterranean basin, and as a fruity, perfumed bulk producer in Australia and South Africa.

MUSCAT DE BEAUMES-DE-VENISE AC *Rhône Valley, France*
Some of the best Muscat Vin Doux Naturel in France comes from the attractive village of Beaumes-de-Venise in the southern Rhône. In the 1980s the wine achieved phenomenal success as a 'sophisticated' dessert wine though the locals sup it on the way home from work. It is certainly sweet but with a fruity acidity and a bright fresh feel to it. Best drunk young to get all that lovely grapy perfume at its peak. Best producers: Beaumes-de-Venise co-op★, Coyeux★, Durban★★, JABOULET★, Vidal-Fleury.

MUSCAT BLANC À PETITS GRAINS See Muscat.

MUSCAT DE FRONTIGNAN AC *Languedoc, France* The leading Muscat Vin Doux Naturel on the Mediterranean coast. Varying between bright gold and a deep orange colour, it is sweet and quite impressive but can seem rather cloying. Best producers: la Peyrade, Robiscau.

MUSCAT DE MIREVAL AC *Languedoc, France* Vin Doux Naturel a little further inland to the much better-known MUSCAT DE FRONTIGNAN. The wines, while still sweet and ripe, can have a little more acid freshness, and quite an alcoholic kick as well. Best producers: La Capelle, Mas des Pigeonniers.

MUSCAT DE RIVESALTES AC *Roussillon, France* Rivesaltes, a small town north of Perpignan, makes good COTES DU ROUSSILLON but its reputation is based on Muscat de Rivesaltes. Made from Muscat Blanc à Petits Grains and Muscat of Alexandria, the wine can be very good indeed, especially since several go-ahead producers are now allowing the skins to stay in the juice for longer periods, thereby gaining perfume and fruit. Best producers: CAZES★★, Destavel★, de Jau★★, de Chênes★, Laporte★, Mas Rous★, de Pena★, Sarda-Mallet★, le Vignon★★.

MUSCAT DE ST-JEAN-DE-MINERVOIS AC *Languedoc, France*
Vin Doux Naturel, made from the Muscat Blanc à Petits Grains in the north-east corner of the MINERVOIS region. The wines are pleasantly sweet but not that concentrated. Drink young. Best producers: Barroubio, Cave de St-Jean-de-Minervois, Sigé.

MUSIGNY AC *Grand Cru, Côte de Nuits, Burgundy, France* This Grand Cru, directly above CLOS DE VOUGEOT, can produce some very fragrant red Burgundies, yet the wines are often sweet and thick and very expensive. The tiny amount of nutty white Musigny also sells for a whopping price. Best producers: DROUHIN★★, JADOT★, LEROY★, de Vogüé★.

ANDRÉ MUSSY *Pommard, Côte de Beaune, Burgundy, France* A traditional, family-owned domaine, producing rich, ripe BEAUNES and POMMARDS that owe little to modern techniques and which are always marked by a beautiful concentration of fruit. The wines are good young, but even better after 6–8 years in bottle. Mussy's top wines are his Pommard Les Épenots ★★ and Beaune Épenottes ★★, but his considerably cheaper BOURGOGNE Rouge ★ is worth looking out for. Best years: 1990 89 88 87 86 85 83.

NAHE *Germany* Wine region named after the River Nahe which rises below Birkenfeld and joins the Rhine by Bingen, just opposite Rüdesheim in the Rheingau. Riesling, Müller-Thurgau and Silvaner are the main grapes and the Nahe Rieslings are considered some of the best of all. The finest stretch of vineyards are in Bereich Kreuznach around the town of Bad Kreuznach.

CH. NAIRAC★★ *Barsac AC, 2ème Cru Classé, Bordeaux, France* A rising star in BARSAC which, by dint of enormous effort and considerable investment, produces a wine on a par with the First Growths. The influence of aging in new oak casks, adding spice and even a little tough tannin, makes this sweet wine a good candidate for aging 10–15 years. Best years: 1990 89 88 86 83 82 81 80 76.

NAPA COUNTY *California, USA* By virtue of presenting a united front and being home to some of California's best traditional wineries as well as many of its more determined newcomers, Napa has made itself synonymous with quality California wine. The county itself is viticulturally diverse, with about 20 major sub-areas already identified, but no proof as yet that they offer 20 genuinely diverse styles. Napa's reputation rests on its Cabernet Sauvignon, Merlot and Chardonnay, with Pinot Noir important in the Carneros district. Many feel that in the long run, Chardonnay will become less important in Napa and plantings of Cabernet and Merlot will increase, except in Carneros. Best producers: BERINGER, Bouchaine, Burgess, Cain Cellars, Cakebread, Carneros Creek, Clos Pegase, CLOS DU VAL, Conn Creek, CUVAISON, DIAMOND CREEK, FLORA SPRINGS, Girard, Groth, The HESS COLLECTION, William Hill, Robert Keenan, La Jota, Mayacamas, MONDAVI, Mont St John Cellars, MONTICELLO, NEWTON, Niebaum-Coppola Estate, Joseph Phelps, Raymond, St Andrew's, St Clement, Smith Madrone, Spottswoode, Stonegate, Stony Hill, ZD.

NAPA VALLEY AVA *California, USA* This sprawling AVA was designed to be so inclusive that it is almost completely irrelevant. It includes vineyards that are actually outside of the Napa River drainage system – such as Pope Valley and Chiles Valley. Because of this an ongoing system of sub-AVAs have been and are in the process of being created, but few of them have any real claim to being discernibly different to their neighbours, and many fear, with justification, that these sub-AVAs will simply serve to dilute the magic of Napa's name.

NAVARRA DO *Navarra, Spain*   Navarra is fast becoming one of Spain's star wine regions for good, fruity young reds and rosés, and simple but fresh whites. The traditional Garnacha (which made good rosés but heavy reds) is steadily being replaced by Tempranillo, plus a little Cabernet Sauvignon and Merlot to use in blends. Best producers: Cenalsa, Julian CHIVITE★, Hergabia, Magaña, Malumbres, OCHOA★, SENORIO DE SARRIA★.

NEBBIOLO   The sole grape of BAROLO and BARBARESCO in Italy's Piedmont, this great red variety produces some of the most complex and longest-lived red wines in the world. Its name derives from the Italian for fog, *nebbia*, because it ripens late when the hills are shrouded in autumn mists. It needs a thick skin to withstand this fog, so gives wines with a very tannic character. Seldom deep in colour, it has a wonderful array of perfumes and an ability to develop great complexity with age that is rivalled only by the Pinot Noir. In sandier soils, like the ROERO and Nebbiolo d'Alba DOCs, it tends to produce a more perfumed style of wine for earlier drinking, while a promising trend in Barolo is for wines from younger vines to be bottled earlier as Nebbiolo delle Langhe.

NEDERBURG *Paarl, South Africa*   Once a private estate, now owned by Stellenbosch Farmers Winery, Nederburg produces a sound but unexciting range of blended wines and a more characterful Private Bin range, sold only through the annual Nederburg auction. The honey-saturated, botrytized Edelkeur ★★ is regularly outstanding.

NÉGOCIANT   French term for a merchant who buys and sells wine, usually under his own name. Many of the best *négociants* also have vineyards and make wine in their own right. A *négociant-éléveur* is a merchant who buys, makes, ages and sells wine.

NELSON *South Island, New Zealand*   A range of mountains separates Nelson from Marlborough at the northern end of the South Island. Unlike the flat Marlborough plains Nelson is made up of a series of small hills and valleys, with a wide range of mesoclimates. The Nelson climate supports most of the grape varieties grown in New Zealand. Best results are from Chardonnay, Riesling and Sauvignon Blanc. Best producers: NEUDORF, SEIFRIED (Redwood Valley★★).

NEUCHÂTEL *Switzerland*   Swiss canton with high-altitude vineyards, mainly Chasselas for whites and Pinot Noir for reds. Three small areas (Schloss Vaumarcus, Hôpital Poutalès and Domaine de Champrevèyres) have the right to a special appellation. Best producers: Ch. d'Auvernier, Porret.

NEUDORF *Nelson, South Island, New Zealand*   Owners Tim and Judy Finn make stylish and often innovative wines and have resisted the temptation to expand production, preferring instead to fine-tune the quality of their wines by careful vineyard and winery management. Best wines are Chardonnay★★, Sauvignon Blanc★ and Riesling ★★. Best years: 1992 91 90 89.

NEW SOUTH WALES *Australia* Australia's most populous state. The Riverina, a vast hot irrigated area of 4700ha (11,600 acres) grows 14% of Australia's grapes and makes oceans of basic quality table wine but is definitely showing signs of improvement. The Hunter Valley, Mudgee and Cowra-Hilltops are smaller, premium quality regions hugging the coastal highlands. South of Sydney, the Canberra district is a burgeoning area of tiny vineyards trying to make fine cool-area wines at chilly altitudes. See also Hunter Valley.

NEW YORK STATE *USA* Wine grapes were first planted on Manhattan Island in the mid-17th century but it wasn't until the early 1950s that a serious wine industry began to develop in New York as vinifera grapes were planted to replace natives such as *Vitis labrusca*. The most important region is Long Island where the maritime climate seems ideal for Chardonnay, Merlot and Pinot Noir, along with a scattering of Riesling sometimes made into a very successful sweet version. The wines, in general, have well developed varietal fruit character and show good balance but the erratic weather patterns of the East Coast can still pose ripeness problems. Best producers: (Long Island) Banfi, BRIDGEHAMPTON, Hargrave, Lenz, Palmer, Peconic Bay, Pindar; (others) Benmarl, Brotherhood, Four Chimneys Farm Winery, Heron Hill, Vinifera Wine Cellars, Wagner.

NEWTON VINEYARDS *Napa Valley, California, USA* Spectacular winery and vineyards set into steep mountain slopes above St Helena. Estate Cabernet Sauvignon ★★ and Merlot ★★ are some of California's most balanced and ageworthy examples of the varietals. Recent vintages of Chardonnay ★★ show beautiful perfume and structure. Newtonian★ is the excellent second label for Cabernet blend and Chardonnay. Best years:1991 90 89 87.

NGATARAWA *Hawkes Bay, North Island, New Zealand* One of Hawkes Bay's top estates. Chardonnay ★ and botrytized Riesling ★★ have produced the best results to date. Cabernet Sauvignon/Merlot can also be very good but lacks consistency. Special Selections are bottled under the Alwyn ★★ (Chardonnay) and Glazebrook ★★ (Cabernet/ Merlot) labels and are generally delicious.

NICOLAS *Paris, France* A large French merchant with its own chain of wine shops. Nicolas has been an important influence in the Midi, where it has encouraged growers and co-ops to raise the quality of their wines. Nicolas' other wines tend to be on the expensive side, given the adequate but unmemorable quality.

187

NIERSTEIN *Rheinhessen, Germany* Both a small town and a large Bereich which includes the famous Grosslage Gutes Domtal. The town of Nierstein boasts 23 individual vineyard sites and the top ones (such as Ölberg, Orbel and Hipping) are some of the best in the whole Rhine Valley. Best producers: GUNDERLOCH, GUNTRUM, HEYL ZU HERRNSHEIM, Rappenhof, Zittmann.

NIKOLAIHOF *Wachau, Niederösterreich, Austria* The Saahs family of Mautern make some of the best wines in the Wachau as well as in nearby Krems-Stein in Kamptal-Donauland, including minute amounts of one of Austria's most highly prized Rieslings from their small plot in the famous Steiner Hund vineyard ★★★. Best years: 1990 86 83 79 77.

NOBILO *Huapai, Auckland, North Island, New Zealand* A family winery which produces a wide range of wines from a popular Müller-Thurgau to single-vineyard varietals. Dixon Vineyard Chardonnay ★★, a lush and intensely flavoured wine, is Nobilo's best known 'prestige' label. Sleek Sauvignon Blanc ★ and Chardonnay ★ from Nobilo's newly developed Marlborough vineyard are rapidly moving towards centre-stage. Nobilo exports two-thirds of its total production. Best years: 1991 89.

NOBLE ROT English term for *Botrytis cinerea*, which the French call *pourriture noble* and the Germans *Edelfäule*, the beneficial fungus which attacks grapes under certain climatic conditions, shrivelling the bunches and intensifying their sugar through dehydration. Noble rot is a vital ingredient in the world's finest dessert wines, such as SAUTERNES and TROCKENBEERENAUSLESES.

NUITS-ST-GEORGES AC *Côte de Nuits, Burgundy, France* This large AC for mainly red wine is one of the few relatively reliable 'village' names in Burgundy. Although it has no Grands Crus many of its Premiers Crus (it has 38!) are extremely good. The red can be rather slow to open out, often needing at least 5 years. There are also minuscule amounts of white made by Gouges from a strange white mutation of Pinot Noir. Best producers: Chauvenet★, Chevillon★★, Confuron★, Dubois★★, FAIVE-LEY, Gouges★, GRIVOT★★, JAYER★★★, LABOURE-ROI★★, Michelot★★, Moillard★, Remoriquet★. Best years: (reds) 1990 89 88 85 83 80 78.

OC, VIN DE PAYS D' *Languedoc-Roussillon, Provence and Rhône Valley, France* The regional Vin de Pays for the whole of southern France. Consequently it used to be a bit of a dustbin title, but exciting new wines, especially from RYMAN and SKALLI, drawing on fruit from a wide area, will make it much more respected. Drink the wines young. Best producers: RYMAN, SKALLI.

OCHOA *Navarra DO, Navarra, Spain* Javier Ochoa has clearly taken his own advice as chief winemaker of the experimental wine research station, and completely modernized the family bodega. The resulting wines are fresh, clean and fruity, with particularly good Cabernet Sauvignon ★ and Tempranillo ★. Best years: (reds) 1990 89 87 85.

OCKFEN *Saar, Germany* Village with two famous individual vineyard sites, Kupp and Bockstein. The wines can be superb in a
sunny year, never losing their cold steely streak but packing in a
delightful full flavoured fruit as well. Best producers:
Dr Fischer, Heinz Wagner.

OECHSLE German scale measuring must weight based on specific
gravity. This scale is more familiar to beer fanatics in Britain
and the USA. To get the Oechsle figure you take the specific
gravity of water, 1000, and for every unit of specific gravity
above that – in the case of grapes this refers to units of sugar in
the grape's juice – you add 1. So grape juice with a specific
gravity of 1130 (130 parts of sugar over and above the basic
1000) has the first 1000 lopped off and we're left with a Oechsle
of 130, indicating a fairly ripe, sugar-filled grape, likely to give a
full, potentially quite alcoholic wine.

OESTE *Portugal* The geographical designation for Alcobaça,
Alenquer, ARRUDA, Encostas d'Aire, Obidos and TORRES, the IPR
regions near the coast between the BAIRRADA DOC and Lisbon.
More wine is produced here than in any other Portuguese
region, though only in Torres, Arruda and Alenquer are standards worthy of demarcation at present. Most wine is cherry-
scented red, with a few decent, creamy whites.

OISLY-ET-THÉSÉE, CONFRÉRIE DES VIGNERONS D' *Touraine,*
Loire Valley, France Founded in 1960, this innovative co-op
established itself as one of the leading names in TOURAINE under
the directorship of the late Jacques Choquet. Choquet's vision
lives on in the fresh, but richly flavoured wines especially the
Sauvignon-based whites ★, Gamay-based reds and CREMANT DE
LOIRE★ . The best wines are sold under the Baronnie d'Aignan ★
label. Best years: 1990 89.

OLOROSO See Jerez y Manzanilla DO.

OLTREPÒ PAVESE DOC *Lombardy, Italy* There were, at last
count, 14 different styles of wine permitted under the DOC
umbrella in this huge zone in south-east Lombardy. Though
potential is great, there is little of interest so far. Instead, it is the
source of good base wine for the Spumante industry and of
Milan's favourite quaffers. The best wines tend to be from
Barbera, Pinot Nero and Pinot Grigio, though Bonarda can be
delicious. Best producers: Frecciarossa, Monsupello.

OMAR KHAYYAM *Maharashtra, India* Champagne-method
sparkling wine produced from a blend of Chardonnay, Ugni
Blanc, Pinot Noir, Pinot Meunier – and Thompson Seedless. The
Thompson is being used less and less as plantings of the other
varieties come on stream. Technology, thanks to Champagne
consultants PIPER-HEIDSIECK, together with high-sited vineyards,
generally produce a firm, fresh, chunky sparkler – though
advances in New Zealand, Australia and California have meant
its achievement no longer seems remarkable.

OPPENHEIM *Rheinhessen, Germany* Village whose reputation has suffered from the sale of much inferior wine under the Oppenheimer Krötenbrunnen label, but in its best sites, such as Sackträger, it can be one of the best villages in the Rheinterrasse or 'terrace' of vineyards which lines the left bank of the Rhine, giving relatively earthy, but nonetheless full-flavoured wines. Best producers: Baumann, Dahlem, GUNTRUM, Koch.

OPUS ONE *Napa Valley AVA, California, USA* Widely publicized joint venture between Robert MONDAVI and the late Baron Philippe de Rothschild of MOUTON-ROTHSCHILD. The first vintage (1979) was released in 1983. At that time, the $50 price was the most expensive for any California wine, though others have reached beyond it now. The various Opus bottlings since 1979 have all been in the ★★ range but have rarely reached the standard of the Robert MONDAVI Reserve Cabernet Sauvignon and the price does seem too high. Best years: 1987 84 80.

OREGON *USA* Oregon shot to international stardom in the early 1980s following some perhaps overly generous praise of its Pinot Noir but the state has failed to consolidate on this position. Not that Oregon Pinot Noir can't be attractive but, at its best (like the 1988 vintage) it offers a bright black cherry fruit generally without much complexity or depth. Oregon Chardonnay can be quite good in an austere, understated style. The new rising star is Pinot Gris which, in Oregon's cool climate can be a very delicious wine with surprising complexity . The Willamette Valley, a cool east-west valley between Portland and the Pacific Ocean, is considered the best growing region and the Dundee hills area the best sub-region. Best producers: ADELSHEIM, Amity, Argyle, Arterberry, Bethel Heights, CAMERON, Drouhin, Elk Cove, Eola Hills, EYRIE, Henry Estate, KNUDSEN-ERATH, PONZI, Rex Hill, Sokol-Blosser, Tualatin, Yamhill Valley.

ORLANDO *Barossa Valley, South Australia* Australia's second-biggest wine company now owned by Pernod-Ricard, encompassing MORRIS, Wickham Hill, Gramps and the WYNDHAM ESTATE group. Top wines under the Orlando name are consistent Coonawarra reds St Hugo ★ and Jacaranda Ridge ★; individualistic Eden Valley Rieslings St Helga ★ and Steingarten ★★; and spicy Flaxmans Traminer ★. Jacobs Creek basics are deservedly Australia's most successful brand abroad.

ORNELLAIA, VINO DA TAVOLA *Tuscany, Italy* This beautiful property was developed by Lodovico Antinori, brother of Piero, after he left the family firm, ANTINORI, to strike out on his own. The red Ornellaia★★★, a Cabernet/Merlot blend, can be favourably compared with neighbouring SASSICAIA, while the white Poggio alle Gazze★, made solely with Sauvignon as from the 1991 vintage, is one of the most successful Tuscan versions of this grape. An outstanding Merlot★★, Masseto is produced in small quantities.

ORVIETO DOC *Umbria, Italy* Traditionally a lightly sweet, abboccato white wine, Orvieto is usually now a dry white wine of little character. In the superior Classico zone, however, the potential for broader, richer and more biscuity wines exist. Not generally a wine for aging, Palazzone's Riserva ★★ is an exception. Best producers: Barberani, Bigi, CASTELLO DELLA SALA, Decugnano dei Barbi★, Palazzone★.

OSBORNE *Jerez y Manzanilla DO, Andalucía, Spain* The biggest drinks company in Spain, Osborne do most of their business in brandy (Magno and Veterano) and other spirits. Their sherry arm in Puerto de Santa María specializes in the light Fino Quinta. Amontillado Coquinero★, rich, intense Bailén Oloroso ★★ and PX 1827★★ are very good indeed.

PACHERENC DU VIC BILH AC *South-West France* Small amount of individual whites from an area overlapping the MADIRAN AC in the Vic Bilh hills in north-east Béarn. The wines are sometimes medium-dry or sweet but usually dry and are best drunk as young as possible. Best producers: Aydie, Crampilh, Damiens★.

PADTHAWAY *South Australia* This fairly young region is the alter-ego of nearby Coonawarra, growing whites to complement Coonawarra's reds. HARDY's Eileen Hardy★★ and Collection★★ Chardonnays and LINDEMANS' Padthaway Chardonnay★★ are the best examples. Padthaway Sauvignon Blanc is also some of Australia's tastiest. Best producers: HARDY's, LINDEMANS, SEPPELT.

PALETTE AC *Provence, France* Tiny AC just east of Aix-en-Provence. Even though the local market pays high prices for the wines I find the reds and rosés rather tough and charmless. However, Ch. Simone, the only producer of white Palette, has managed to achieve a white wine of some flavour from basic southern grapes (Clairette, Grenache Blanc and Ugni Blanc). Best producers: Crémade, Ch. Simon.

CH. PALMER★★ *Margaux AC, 3ème Cru Classé, Haut-Médoc, Bordeaux, France* Named after a British major-general who fought in the Napoleonic Wars, Palmer was the leading property in the MARGAUX AC during the 1960s and 1970s until the Mentzelopolous family took over at Ch. MARGAUX in 1977. Although only a Third Growth, the wine, with its wonderful perfume and irresistible plump fruit, usually manages to be as good as the top Second Growths. Second wine: Réserve-du-Général. Best years: 1990 89 88 86 85 83 82 79 78 75 70.

PALOMAS *Rio Grande do Sul, Brazil* Winery just north of the Uruguay border, in the one area of Brazil where the climate at least tolerates the cultivation of classic vinifera varieties. Its simple, ramshackle wines satisfy curiosity rather than titillate.

CH. PAPE-CLÉMENT ★★ *Pessac-Léognan AC, Cru Classé de Graves, Bordeaux, France*   This expensive and famous GRAVES Classed Growth has not been as consistent as it should be – but things have looked up since the exciting 1985 vintage. In style, it is mid-way between the refinement of HAUT-BRION and the firmness of La MISSION-HAUT-BRION. Second wine: Clémentin. Best years: 1990 89 88 87 86 85.

PARELLADA   This Catalan exclusivity is the most characterful of the trio of simple white grapes that go to make CAVA wines in northeastern Spain. It also makes still wines, light, fresh and gently floral, with good acidity and (for Spain) lowish alcohol (between 9 and 11%). Drink it as young as possible – and I mean *young* – while it still has the benefit of freshness.

PARKER ESTATE *Coonawarra, South Australia*   Very recent arrival on the premium market, a red specialist impressing with its first efforts made by the experienced Ralph Fowler at Leconfield. The top label is the cheekily named Terra Rossa First Growth ★★.

PARRINA DOC *Tuscany, Italy*   On the coast in south-west Tuscany, the Sangiovese/Canaiolo red is minty and robust, the white is from Trebbiano and Ansonica. Drink within 3–5 years. Best producer: La Parrina. Best years: 1990 88 85.

PASSITO   Italian term indicating that the wine is made from dried grapes. The result is usually a sweet wine with a raisiny intensity of fruit. See also MOSCATO PASSITO DI PANTELLERIA, RECIOTO DI SOAVE, RECIOTO DELLA VALPOLICELLA, VIN SANTO.

LUIS PATO *Bairrada, Beira Litoral, Portugal*   Leading 'modernist' in BAIRRADA, passionately convinced of the Baga grape's ability to make great reds★ on clay soil. Best years: 1991 88 85.

PATRIMONIO AC *Corsica, France*   Good, underrated wines from the northern end of the island. The reds and rosés, based on the local Nielluccio grape, are your best bet, but look out for the fresh Vermentino whites and the fortified Muscat. Best producers: Arena, Gentile, Leccia. Best years: 1991 90 89.

PAUILLAC AC *Haut-Médoc, Bordeaux, France*   The deep gravel banks around the town of Pauillac in the HAUT-MEDOC are the true heartland of Cabernet Sauvignon. For many wine lovers, the king of red wine grapes finds its ultimate expression in the three Pauillac First Growths (LATOUR, LAFITE-ROTHSCHILD and MOUTON-ROTHSCHILD). The large AC also contains 15 other Classed Growths, including world-famous PICHON-LALANDE, PICHON-LONGUEVILLE, and LYNCH-BAGES. The uniting characteristic of Pauillac wines is their intense blackcurrant fruit flavour and their heady cedar and pencil-shavings perfume. These are the longest-lived of Bordeaux's great reds. Best producers: BATAILLEY★★, Fonbadet★, GRAND-PUY-DUCASSE★, GRAND-PUY-LACOSTE★★, HAUT-BAGES-LIBERAL★★, HAUT-BATAILLEY★, LAFITE-

ROTHSCHILD★★★, LATOUR★★★, LYNCH-BAGES★★★, MOUTON-ROTHSCHILD★★★, PICHON-LALANDE★★★, PICHON-LONGUEVILLE★★★. Best years: 1990 89 88 86 85 83 82 81 79 78.

CH. PAVIE ★★ *St-Émilion Grand Cru AC, 1er Grand Cru Classé, Bordeaux, France* The second biggest of the ST-EMILION Premiers Grands Crus (after FIGEAC), Pavie is one of the most improved properties in the AC. The wines will happily evolve for a decade yet never lose the soft, unctuous charm of the fruit and the sweet oak. Best years: 1990 89 88 85 83 82 81 79.

PÉCHARMANT AC *South-West France* Lovely red wines from a small AC north-east of BERGERAC. The wines are quite light in body but have a delicious, full, piercing flavour of blackcurrants and a most attractive grassy acidity. Good vintages will easily last 10 years and end up indistinguishable from a good HAUT-MEDOC wine. Best producers: Clos Peyrelevade★, Corbiac, Haut-Pécharmant★★, la Métairie, Tiregand★. Best years: 1990 89 88 86 85 83 82 81.

PEDROSA *Ribera del Duero DO, Castilla-León, Spain* Delicious, elegant reds★, both young and oak-aged, from a small family winery in the little hill village of Pedrosa del Duero. They are not cheap, but far less pricey than many stars of this fashionable region. Best years: (reds) 1989 86.

PENEDÉS DO *Catalonia, Spain* The wealthy CAVA industry is based in Penedés, and the majority of the still wines are white, made from the Cava trio of Parellada, Macabeo and Xarel-lo, clean and fresh when young, but never exciting. Better whites are made from foreign grapes, principally Chardonnay. The reds are variable, the best made from Cabernet Sauvignon and/or Tempranillo and Merlot. Best producers: Cavas Hill, Ferret, Hisenda Miret, Jean LEON★★, Masía Bach★, Naverán, TORRES★★.

PENFOLDS *Barossa Valley, South Australia* Part of Australia's biggest wine group, SA Brewing, Penfolds proves that quality *can* go in hand with quantity and is regarded as the dominant force in Australian wine at the moment. Makes the country's greatest red wine, Grange Hermitage ★★★, and a welter of superbly rich, structured reds from Magill Estate ★★ through St Henri★, Bin 707 Cabernet ★★★, Bin 389 Shiraz Cabernet ★★, Bin 28 Kalimna ★★ and Bin 128 Coonawarra Shiraz ★ to Koonunga Hill ★. Still very much a red wine name, although toasty Chardonnay★★ and lemony Sémillon-Chardonnay★ are attractive and well-made, especially under the Koonunga Hill label. Best years: (reds) 1991 90 88 86 84 83 82 79 78 76 71.

PENLEY ESTATE *Coonawarra, South Australia* Launched in 1991, the first wines are from bought grapes, but Penley's large but unproven Coonawarra vineyard will eventually be the source. The intention is to focus on concentrated, structured Cabernets. First red releases are good★ but the Chardonnay ★★ is beautifully dry, yet round and spicy.

PERLWEIN   German for lightly sparkling wine.

PERNAND-VERGELESSES AC *Côte de Beaune, Burgundy, France*

The little-known village of Pernand-Vergelesses contains a decent chunk of the great Corton hill, including much of the best white CORTON-CHARLEMAGNE Grand Cru vineyard. The red wines sold under the village name are very attractive when young with a nice raspberry pastille fruit and a slight earthiness, and will age for 6–10 years. As no-one ever links poor old Pernand with the heady heights of Corton-Charlemagne, the whites sold under the village name can be a bargain – quite a rarity in Burgundy. The wines can be a bit lean and dry to start with but fatten up beautifully after 2–4 years in bottle. Best producers: (reds) Besancenot-Mathouillet★, Bonneau du Martray★, Chandon de Briailles★, Denis★, Dubreuil-Fontaine★, Laleure-Piot★, Rapet★, Rollin★; (whites) Bonneau du Martray★★, Dubreuil-Fontaine★★, GERMAIN★, Guyon★, JADOT, Laleure-Piot★, Pavelot★, Rapet★, Rollin★. Best years: (reds) 1990 89 88 85 83; (whites) 1990 89 88 86 85

PERRIER-JOUËT *Champagne AC, Champagne, France*   The best of the Champagne houses owned by the Canadian multi-national Seagram, Perrier-Jouët makes a good, creamily elegant non-vintage ★★ as well as a richer vintage wine ★★ and a de luxe cuvée, Belle Époque ★★★, famous for its embossed Art Nouveau label but, for once in the image-obsessed world of Champagne, with an exciting flavour to match the exterior fol-de-rols. The Belle Époque rosé ★★ is excellent too. Best years: 1985 82.

PESQUERA *Ribera del Duero DO, Castilla-León, Spain*   Viña Pesquera wines, richly coloured, firm, fragrant and plummy-tobaccoey, are among Spain's most expensive – and best – reds. Made by the small firm of Alejandro Fernández, they are almost totally from Tempranillo, and sold generally as Crianzas★★, with Reservas★★ in the best years. Best years: (reds) 1989 86 85.

PESSAC-LÉOGNAN AC *Bordeaux, France*   A new AC, created in 1987, for the northern (and best) part of the GRAVES region and including all the Graves Classed Growths. The supremely gravelly soil tends to favour red wines over the rest of the Graves. Now one of the most exciting areas of France for top class whites, the standard is fast improving thanks to the advent of cool fermentation, controlled yeast selection and the use of new oak barrels. Best producers: (reds) DOMAINE DE CHEVALIER★★★, de FIEUZAL★★★, HAUT-BAILLY★★, HAUT-BRION★★★, la LOUVIERE★★, MALARTIC-LAGRAVIERE★, la MISSION-HAUT-BRION★★, PAPE-CLEMENT★★, de Rochemorin, SMITH-HAUT-LAFITTE★, la Tour-Haut-Brion, la TOUR-MARTILLAC★; (whites) DOMAINE DE CHEVALIER★★★, Couhins-Lurton★★, de FIEUZAL★★★, HAUT-BRION★★★, LAVILLE-HAUT-BRION★★★, la LOUVIERE★★, MALARTIC-LAGRAVIERE★, de Rochemorin★, SMITH-HAUT-LAFITTE★★★, la TOUR-MARTILLAC★★. Best years: (reds) 1990 89 88 86 85 83 82 81 79 78; (whites) 1990 89 88 87 86 85 83 82.

PETALUMA *Adelaide Hills, South Australia* Run by Brian Croser, probably Australia's most influential winemaker and teacher. Champagne-method Croser ★ is fine but very dry and lean. The Chardonnay★★ and Coonawarra Cabernet Merlot ★★★ are constantly improving and Clare Riesling ★★ is fuller and longer lasting than most of its peers. Best years: 1991 90 88 87 .

PÉTILLANT French for a slightly sparkling wine, often one which has been purposefully bottled with a bit of carbon dioxide.

PETIT CHABLIS AC *Chablis, Burgundy, France* Uninspired, rather green, unripe Chardonnay wine from the least good, outlying areas of the CHABLIS vineyards. Since the authorities have cynically 're-scheduled' most 'Petit Chablis' land as proper 'Chablis', you can imagine how feeble what's left must be.

PETIT VERDOT A rich, tannic red variety, grown mainly in Bordeaux's HAUT-MEDOC to add depth, colour and a fabulous fragrance of violets to a few top wines. Late-ripening and erratic yield limits its popularity. Experimental warmer climate plantings in Australia, Chile and California are giving exciting results.

CH. PETIT-VILLAGE★★ *Pomerol AC, Bordeaux, France* This top POMEROL wine, much sterner in style than its neighbours, is now made by Jean-Michel Cazes who also owns PICHON-LONGUEVILLE in PAUILLAC. In general it is worth aging the wine for 8–10 years at least. Best years: 1990 89 88 85 83 82 81 79 78 75.

PETITE SIRAH Long used as a blending grape in California but used also for varietal wines, Petite Sirah is supposed to be the Durif of southern France. At its best, the wine has great depth and strength with some complexity; at worst it can be monstrously huge, misshapen and unfriendly. Best producers: Inglenook, Preston, RIDGE★, Stags' Leap Vintners.

CH. PÉTRUS ★★★ *Pomerol AC, Bordeaux, France* Now the most expensive red wine in the world, but only 30 years ago Pétrus was virtually unknown. The powerful, concentrated wine is the result of the caring genius of Pétrus' co-owners since 1962, the MOUEIX family, who have maximized the potential of the vineyard of almost solid clay and remarkably old vines, in places up to 70 years of age. Drinkable for its astonishingly rich, dizzy-

ing blend of fruit and spice flavours after a decade, but top years will age for much longer, developing exotic scents of tobacco and chocolate and truffles as they mature. Best years: 1990 89 88 87 86 85 83 82 81 80 79 75 71.

CH. DE PEZ★★ *St-Estèphe AC, Cru Bourgeois, Haut-Médoc, Bordeaux, France* One of ST-ESTEPHE's leading non-Classed Growths, de Pez makes mouthfilling satisfying claret with sturdy fruit. Slow to evolve, good vintages need 15–20 years to mature. Best years: 1990 89 88 86 85 83 82 79 78 75.

PFEFFINGEN *Bad Dürkheim, Rheinpfalz, Germany* Riesling makes up 60% of this top Rheinpfalz estate, and the grape gives good results on the Ungsteiner Herrenberg site★. In good years there is also remarkable Gewürztraminer and Scheurebe. Best years: 1990 89 88.

PIAT D'OR An inexorably popular, off-dry Vin de Table. Piat d'Or is one of the bestselling wine brands in Britain, but is virtually unknown in France. The red and white are equally dull and ludicrously over-priced – but then someone has to pay for the extremely effective advertising. A masterpiece of marketing over matter.

PIAVE DOC *Veneto, Italy* The Piave plains, the flatlands north of Venice, churn out vast quantities of Merlot, Cabernet, Rabosa and Tocai. There are 8 different varieties permitted for use under the DOC umbrella, but while so much is bought up by Veronese merchants and sold simply as Merlot del Veneto, there is little incentive to reduce quantity and aim for quality. Best producers: Castello di Roncade, Collalto, Rechsteiner.

FRANZ PICHLER *Wachau, Niederösterreich, Austria* A leading Wachau superstar whose Dürnsteiner Kellerberg Rieslings★★ are superbly structured. There are also excellent Grüner Veltliners★ from the Loibnerberg. Best years: 1990 86 75.

CH. PICHON-LALANDE★★★ *Pauillac AC, 2ème Cru Classé, Haut-Médoc, Bordeaux, France* With vineyards on excellent land on the borders of PAUILLAC and ST-JULIEN, Pichon-Lalande has been run since 1978 by the inspired, messianic figure of Mme de Lencquesaing who has led the property ever upwards on a wave of passion and involvement, and on superlative vineyard management and wine-making sensitivity from her long-time *maître de chai* M. Godin. Though wonderful at 6–7 years due to their heavenly scent and round lush fruit, the wines will usually last for 20 at least. Second wine: Réserve de la Comtesse. Best years: 1989 88 87 86 85 83 82 81 80 79 78 75.

CH. PICHON-LONGUEVILLE★★★ *(since 1988) Pauillac AC, 2ème Cru Classé, Haut-Médoc, Bordeaux, France* Despite its superb vineyards with the potential for making great PAUILLAC, Pichon-Longueville (called Pichon-Baron until 1988) wines have been also rans for a long time. In 1987 the management was taken over by the talented Jean-Michel Cazes of LYNCH-BAGES and there has been a remarkable change in fortune. Recent vintages have been of First Growth standard, packed with firm, tannic structure and a dark rich fruit as exciting as any in Bordeaux. Best years: 1990 89 88 87 82.

PIEDMONT *Italy*   This large region, in north-west Italy is, as its name suggests, ringed by mountains. It is the most important Italian region for the production of quality wines. In the north, there is CAREMA, GHEMME and GATTINARA, while to the south of Turin in the Langhe hills, BAROLO and BARBARESCO from Nebbiolo, and a host of lesser wines from the Dolcetto and Barbera grapes make this the zone with the greatest concentration of fine producers of any in Italy. Further to the east, in the Monferrato hills, around the town of Asti, the Barbera, Moscato and Cortese grapes hold sway, and signs are that quality there is soon set to rival that already attained in the Langhe. ROERO is also beginning to produce a flow of highly attractive reds and whites. See also Asti Spumante, Erbaluce di Caluso, Gavi, Moscato d'Asti, Spanna.

PIEROPAN *Veneto, Italy*   Nino and Teresita Pieropan produce excellent SOAVE Classico ★, and, from two single vineyards, Calvarino ★★ and La Rocca ★★, the definitive wines of this zone. In addition, there is an excellent RECIOTO DI SOAVE Le Colombare ★★ and a good Riesling Italico. The key lies as much in the quality of the fruit as in the scrupulous care the grapes receive once they arrive in the cellar.

PINOT BIANCO   See Pinot Blanc.

PINOT BLANC   There is a great deal of confusion between Pinot Blanc and Chardonnay, but they are not actually related at all. Pinot Blanc wine has a clear, yeasty, appley taste and good examples can age to a delicious, honeyed fullness. In France its chief power-base is in Alsace where it is taking over the 'workhorse' role from Sylvaner and Chasselas and most CREMANT D'ALSACE now uses Pinot Blanc. It is important in northern Italy as Pinot Bianco, in Germany and Austria as Weissburgunder and is also successful in Hungary and Czechoslovakia.

PINOT GRIGIO   See Pinot Gris.

PINOT GRIS   Found mainly in France's Alsace where it is also called Tokay d'Alsace. With a low acidity and a deep colour the grape produces fat, rich wines that will often mature wonderfully. It is occasionally used in Burgundy to add fatness to a wine. Called Pinot Grigio it is also grown in northern Italy, where from far higher yields it produces some of the country's most popular dry white and sparkling wines. Also successful in Germany's southern regions as Ruländer or Grauer Burgunder, and as Malvoisie in the Swiss Valais. There are some fine, rich Romanian and Czechoslovakian examples as well as good spirited examples in Hungary (as Szurkebarat).

PINOT NERO   See Pinot Noir.

PINOT NOIR

There's this myth about Pinot Noir that I think I'd better lay to rest. It goes something like this. Pinot Noir is an incredibly tricky grape to grow, in fact Pinot is so difficult to grow that the only place that regularly achieves magical results is the thin stretch of land between Dijon and Chagny in France known as the Côte d'Or, where microclimate, soil conditions and 2000 years of experience weave an inimitable web of pleasure.

This just isn't so. The thin-skinned, early-ripening Pinot Noir is undoubtedly more difficult to grow than other great varieties like Cabernet or Chardonnay, but it isn't impossible to grow elsewhere – you just have to work at it with more sensitivity and flexibility. And although great red Burgundy is a hauntingly beautiful wine, most Burgundians completely fail to deliver the magic, and the glorious thing about places like New Zealand, California, Australia and Germany is that we are seeing an ever increasing number of wines that are thrillingly different to anything produced in Burgundy yet with flavours that are unique to the Pinot Noir.

WINE STYLES
France All France's great Pinot Noir wines do come from Burgundy's Côte d'Or. Rarely deep in colour, they should nonetheless possess a wonderful fruit quality when young – raspberry, strawberry, cherry or plum that becomes more scented and exotic with age, the plums turning to figs and pine, and the richness of chocolate mingling perilously with truffles and well-hung game. Strange, challenging, hedonistic. France's other Pinots – in north and south Burgundy, the Loire, Jura, Savoie and Alsace – are lighter and milder, and in Champagne its pale, thin wine is used to make sparkling wine.
Other European regions The great 1990, 89 and 88 vintages have allowed German winemakers to produce impressive, perfumed wines (generally called Spätburgunder). Italy and Switzerland both have fair success with the variety, Austria and Spain have produced a couple of good examples, and Romania, Czechoslovakia and Hungary produce significant amounts of variable quality.
New World Light, fragrant wines have bestowed upon Oregon in America's Pacific Northwest the greatest reputation for being 'another Burgundy'; but I get more excited about the marvellously fruity, erotically scented wines of California's Carneros region, and the startlingly original offerings from the outposts south of San Francisco. New Zealand is the most important southern hemisphere producer, with wines of thrilling fruit and individuality while Australia is slowly finding its way and even South Africa has one fine producer.

BEST PRODUCERS

France (Burgundy growers) Barthod-Noëllat, Henri Jayer, Lafarge, Lignier, Méo-Camuzet, de Montille, Perrot-Minot, Ponsot, Dom. de la Romanée-Conti, Rossignol-Trapet, Tollot-Beaut; (merchants) Drouhin, Faiveley, Camille Giraud, Jadot, Jaffelin, Labouré-Roi, Leroy; (co-ops) Buxy, Caves des Hautes Côtes.

Australia Briagolong, Coldstream Hills, Delatite, Moorilla, Mountadam, Moss Wood, Pipers Brook, Yarra Yering.

New Zealand Martinborough, St Helena, Waipara Springs.

South Africa Hamilton Russell Vineyards.

USA (California) Acacia, Au Bon Climat, Calera, Chalone, Dehlinger, Mondavi, Rasmussen, Saintsbury, Sanford; (Oregon) Domaine Drouhin.

PINOTAGE A Pinot Noir x Cinsaut cross, achieved in South Africa in 1925. It was not widely planted until the 1950s, and it received a mixed critical reception due to an estery or pear-drop smell that often appeared in its wines. The best producers, however, hold this character at bay to produce powerful, flavoury, opulently plummy wines that may yet prove to be South Africa's most characterful reds. Also found in New Zealand, California, Germany and Zimbabwe. Best producers: BACKSBERG, KANONKOP.

PIPER-HEIDSIECK *Champagne AC, Champagne, France*   One of Champagne's least distinguished Grandes Marques. The Piper non-vintage tends to be raw in its youth, but can develop complexity in bottle. The best wine here is the de luxe cuvée, Champagne Rare ★. Piper-Heidsieck also has a California outpost, Piper-Sonoma. Best years: 1985 82 79.

PIPERS BROOK VINEYARDS *Northern Tasmania, Australia*   Keenly sought wines combining classy design, clever marketing and skilled wine-making by Andrew Pirie. Steely Riesling ★★, classically reserved Chardonnay ★★, serious Pinot Noir ★ and tasty, barrel-fermented Sauvignon Blanc ★ are the highlights. The quality leader in Tasmania. Best years: 1992 91 90 88 86 84 82.

PIRRAMIMMA *Southern Vales, South Australia*   Traditional winery owned by the Johnston family with Geoff Johnston as wine-maker. The best wines are full-bodied peachy Chardonnay, gooseberry-like Sauvignon Blanc★ and smooth reds from Cabernet Sauvignon★ and Shiraz★. Best years: 1991 90 88 87.

PLAIMONT, L'UNION DES PRODUCTEURS *Madiran AC and Vin de Pays des Côtes de Gascogne, South-West France*   This grouping of three Gascon co-ops is the largest, most reliable, and increasingly most go-ahead producer of COTES DE GASCOGNE. The white wines★ full of crisp fruit, are reasonably priced and are best drunk young. The reds, especially under the COTES DE ST-MONT ★ label, are also very good.

PLANTAGENET *Lower Great Southern, Western Australia*   In an unglamorous apple-packing shed in chilly Mount Barker, Tony Smith and John Wade make a fine range of table wines. Noted for peppery Shiraz★, melony/nutty Chardonnay ★★, fine limy Riesling ★ and elegant Cabernet Sauvignon ★. Best years: 1991 90 88 86 85.

POL ROGER *Champagne AC, Champagne, France*   Makers of Winston Churchill's favourite Champagne and increasingly challenging for the title of Champagne's leading quality producer. The non-vintage White Foil ★★ is a gentle, light and consistently classy Champagne. Pol Roger also produce a Vintage ★★, a Rosé ★, a Vintage Chardonnay ★ and a Vintage Réserve Spécial ★★★. Their top Champagne, called Cuvée Sir Winston Churchill ★★ in his honour, is a deliciously refined drink. Best years: 1985 82 79.

POLIZIANO *Vino Nobile di Montepulciano, Tuscany, Italy* One of the leading lights in improving quality in Montepulciano. Vino Nobile★ is far better than average, while the Vino da Tavolas, Elegia★★ (Sangiovese) and Le Stanze★★ (Cabernet Sauvignon) are packed with fruit and sweet oak. Vin Santo★★ is unctuous.

POMEROL AC *Bordeaux, France* Now one of the most famous and expensive of the Bordeaux ACs, and the home of the world's most expensive red wine – PETRUS. The AC's unique quality lies in its deep clay in which the Merlot grape flourishes. The result is seductively rich, almost creamy wine with wonderful mouth-filling fruit flavours. Best producers: Bonalgue★, BON-PASTEUR★★, Certan-de-May★★, Clinet★★, Clos du Clocher★, CLOS RENE★, la Conseillante★★, l'EVANGILE★★, GAZIN★★, LAFLEUR★★, LAFLEUR-PETRUS★★, PETIT-VILLAGE★★, PETRUS★★★, le Pin★★, de SALES★, TROTANOY★★, VIEUX-CH.-CERTAN★★★. Best years: 1990 89 88 87 86 85 83 82 81 79 78.

POMINO DOC *Tuscany, Italy* This small zone, north-east of Florence in the hills above CHIANTI Rufina, is noted for its histori-cal use of French varieties in both the red (where Merlot and Cabernet are blended with Sangiovese) and the white (where, unusually, the Trebbiano plays a supporting role to that of Pinot Bianco and Chardonnay). FRESCOBALDI's Pomino Il Benefizio ★ (a barrique-fermented Chardonnay) was the trendsetting new wave Tuscan white. Best producers: FRESCOBALDI, Petrognano.

POMMARD AC *Côte de Beaune, Burgundy, France* The first village south of Beaune. At their best, the wines should have full, round, beefy flavours. When good they age well, often for 10 years or more. There are no Grands Crus but Les Rugiens Bas, Les Épenots and Les Arvelets (all Premiers Crus) occupy the best sites. Best producers: Clerget★, Garaudet★, Gaunoux★, Lehaye★, Lejeune★, Monnier, de MONTILLE★★, MUSSY★★, Parent★, Ch. de Pommard★, Pothier-Rieusset★, Pousse d'Or★. Best years: 1990 89 88 87 85 83 80 78.

CH. PONTET-CANET ★★ *Pauillac AC, 5ème Cru Classé, Haut-Médoc, Bordeaux, France* Until the mid-1970s Pontet-Canet was one of the most popular and widely available HAUT-MEDOC Classed Growths but the wine wasn't château-bottled and you never quite knew what you'd be finding in your bottle. The result was cheap, but hardly authentic claret in considerable quantities. Since 1979 when the Tesserons of LAFON-ROCHET bought Pontet-Canet we are gradually seeing a return to form – big, chewy and oaky claret that develops a beautiful blackcur-rant fruit. Best years: 1990 89 88 86 85 83 82.

PONZI *Willamette Valley AVA, Oregon, USA* A minty Pinot Noir ★ in both a regular and reserve bottling gets the attention but Ponzi was also one of the first in Oregon to make Pinot Gris. The Riesling ★ is usually successful, and Ponzi also brews great beer ★★ if wine-tasting has given you a thirst.

PORT DOC

Douro, Portugal

The Douro region, where the grapes for port are grown, is one of the wildest and most beautiful wine regions in the world. Steep hills covered in vineyard terraces plunge dramatically down to the Douro river. Grapes are one of the only crops that will grow in the inhospitable climate, which gets progressively drier the further inland you travel. But not all the Douro's grapes qualify to be made into port. A quota is established every year, and the rest are made into table wines.

Port grapes are partially fermented, and then pure alcohol is added – fortifying the wine, stopping the fermentation and leaving sweet, unfermented grape sugar in the finished port.

PORT STYLES

Vintage Finest of the ports matured in bottle, made from grapes from the best vineyards. Vintage port is not 'declared' every year, but only after two years in cask, if the shipper thinks the standard is high enough. It is then bottled, and should be kept at least 10 years before drinking, to soften its aggressive fiery youth into something cedary and sweet. Young vintage port is terrifyingly tannic, but softens to a cedary sweetness with age.

Single quinta Made in lesser years, and bottled after two years in cask. It is often made from the grapes grown on a single quinta or estate, and usually released only when ready to drink.

Aged tawny Matured in cask for 10, 20 or 30 years before bottling and sale. Older tawnies have delicious flavours of nuts and figs.

Colheita Tawny from a single vintage, matured in cask for at least 7 years – potentially the finest of the aged tawnies.

Late Bottled Vintage/Late Bottled Port matured for 4–6 years in cask then usually filtered to avoid sediment forming in the bottle. Traditional unfiltered port has much more flavour.

Crusted A blend of good ports from 2–3 vintages, bottled without filtration after 3–4 years in cask. 'Crusted' (or 'crusting') port forms a deposit ('crust') in the bottle and should be decanted.

Vintage Character Usually little more than expensive ruby, with no vintage character at all, though maybe a bit more age.

Ruby The youngest red port. Ruby port should be bursting with young, almost peppery fruit but it often isn't.

Tawny Cheap tawny is usually made by blending ruby with white port and is both dilute and raw.

White Almost always coarse and alcoholic, and best drunk chilled and diluted with tonic water.

See also CALEM, CHURCHILL GRAHAM, COCKBURN, CROFT, DOW, FERREIRA, FONSECA, GRAHAM, QUINTA DO COTTO, QUINTA DO NOVAL, RAMOS PINTO, SANDEMAN, SMITH WOODHOUSE, TAYLOR FLADGATE & YEATMAN, WARRE.

BEST YEARS

1985 83 80 77 70 66 63 60

BEST PRODUCERS

Vintage Cockburn, Croft, Dow, Fonseca, Graham, Niepoort, Quinta do Noval Nacional, Smith Woodhouse, Taylor, Warre.

Single quinta Churchill (Agua Alta), Dow (Quinta do Bomfim), Fonseca-Guimaraens, Graham (Malvedos), Taylor (Quinta de Vargellas), Warre (Quinta da Cavadinha).

Aged tawny/colheita Cálem, Cockburn, Dow, Ferreira, Fonseca, Niepoort, Ramos Pinto, Sandeman, Taylor.

WARRE'S
1983
VINTAGE PORT
BOTTLED 1985
WARRE & C.º L.º OPORTO
ESTABLISHED 1670
20% vol. PRODUCE OF PORTUGAL   e 75 cl.

Traditional late bottled vintages Fonseca, Ramos Pinto, Smith Woodhouse, Warre.

Crusted Cockburn, Churchill, Dow, Warre.

CH. POTENSAC ★★ *Médoc AC, Cru Bourgeois, Bordeaux, France*
Potensac's fabulous success is based on quality, consistency and value for money. Owned and run by Michel Delon, the genius of LEOVILLE-LAS-CASES, the wine can be drunk at 4–5 years old, but fine vintages will improve for at least 10, the 1982 for up to twice that. Best years: 1990 89 88 86 85 83 82 81 80 79 78 76.

POUILLY-FUISSÉ AC *Mâconnais, Burgundy, France* Dry white Chardonnay from 5 villages around the spectacular rocky outcrop of Solutré in the southern Mâconnais, including Pouilly and Fuissé. For years high prices and low quality meant this was a wine to avoid but now it is beginning to find a sensible price level and there are some committed growers producing wonderful buttery, creamy wines that can be delicious at 2 years, but will often age beautifully for up to 10. Best producers: Corsin★, Feret★★, Ch. FUISSE★★★, Guffens-Heynen★★, Léger-Plumet★, Luquet★, Noblet★. Best years: 1991 90 89 88 86 85.

POUILLY-FUMÉ AC *Loire Valley, France* *Fumé* means 'smoky' in French and a good Pouilly-Fumé has a strong, pungent smell which is often likened to gunflint. The only grape allowed is the Sauvignon Blanc and what gives these wines their extra smokiness is that many of the vineyards, on slopes near Pouilly-sur-Loire, are planted on a particularly flinty soil called silex. This is an AC of great potential, but many of the wines are rather ordinary given their exalted prices. Best producers: Bailly Père et Fils★, Didier DAGUENEAU★★, Guyot, de Ladoucette★, Pabiot, Redde★, Saget, Seguin★, Tracy★. Best years: 1990 89 88 86 85.

POUILLY-LOCHÉ AC *Mâconnais, Burgundy, France* Loché is a village to the east of Fuissé which has added the name of Pouilly to its own. The wines are no better than many MACON-VILLAGES and certainly not a patch on POUILLY-FUISSE, but the magic name of Pouilly commands higher prices. The wine can also be labelled as POUILLY-VINZELLES but not vice versa. Best producer: Caves des Grands Crus Blancs. Best years: 1991 90 89 88.

POUILLY-SUR-LOIRE AC *Loire Valley, France* Light, rather tasteless wines made from the Chasselas grape from vineyards around Pouilly-sur-Loire, the town which gave its name to POUILLY-FUME, one of the world's leading Sauvignon Blanc white wines. Drink as young as possible.

POUILLY-VINZELLES AC *Mâconnais, Burgundy, France* Like POUILLY-LOCHE, the village of Vinzelles has added the name of Pouilly to its own. Best producers: Cave des Grands Crus Blancs, Ch. de Vinzelles. Best years: 1991 90 89 88.

CH. POUJEAUX ★★ *Moulis AC, Cru Bourgeois, Haut-Médoc, Bordeaux, France* Poujeaux is one of the reasons why the MOULIS AC is attracting more and more attention – the wines have a delicious chunky fruit and new-oak sweetness. Attractive at only 6–7 years old, good vintages can easily last for 20–30 years. Best years: 1990 89 88 86 85 83 82 81 78.

PRÄDIKAT The grades which define quality wines in Germany and Austria. These are (in ascending order) Kabinett (not considered as Prädikat in Austria), Spätlese, Auslese, Beerenauslese, the Austrian-only category Ausbruch, and Trockenbeerenauslese. Strohwein and Eiswein are also Prädikat wines. The drawback of such a system which grades wine according to the amount of sugar in the unfermented grape juice or must, is that it implies that the sweeter the wine, the better it is. Some Spätleses and even a few Ausleses are now made as dry wines.

FRANZ PRAGER *Wachau, Niederösterreich, Austria* One of the Wachau pioneers with top Rieslings from the Achleiten and Klaus vineyards ★★. Also good Grüner Veltliners from the Steinriegl vineyard ★. Best years: 1990 86 81 79.

PREDICATO An attempt by a consortium of Tuscan producers to impose some discipline on the mass of table wines being produced in Tuscany. There are four categories: Predicato di Biturica (mainly Cabernet); di Cardisco (mainly Sangiovese); del Selvante (mainly Sauvignon); and del Muschio (mainly Chardonnay or Pinot Bianco).

PREMIER CRU The quality level below Grand Cru in the French appellation system. Premier Cru vineyards are usually less well-sited than the Grands Crus, although in the hands of a good winemaker, a Premier Cru wine can be exceptional.

PREMIÈRES CÔTES DE BLAYE AC *Bordeaux, France* An improving AC mainly for reds on the right bank of the Gironde. The fresh, Cabernet-based reds are ready at 2–3 years but will age for more. The whites are usually sold as COTES DE BLAYE AC. Best producers: Bourdieu, Charron, l'Escadre, Grand-Barrail, Jonqueyres, Peybonhomme, Segonzac. Best years: 1990 89 88.

PREMIÈRES CÔTES DE BORDEAUX AC *Bordeaux, France* A lovely hilly region with views across to GRAVES and SAUTERNES across the Garonne. For a long time the AC was best known for its Sauternes-style sweet wines, particularly from the communes of Cadillac, LOUPIAC and STE-CROIX-DU-MONT but in recent years the attractive, juicy reds and rosés have forged ahead. These are usually delicious at 2–3 years old but should last for 5–6. Best producers: (reds) Brethous, Cayla, Fayau, Grand-Mouëys, du Juge, du Peyrat, Reynon★, la Roche, Tanesse; (whites) Birot, Cayla, Grand Mouëys, du Juge, Lamothe★, Reynon★, Tanesse. Best years: (reds) 1990 89 88 86 85 83 82; (whites) 1990 89 88.

CH. PRIEURÉ-LICHINE ★ *Margaux AC, 4ème Cru Classé, Haut-Médoc, Bordeaux, France* Owned by Alexis Lichine, possibly the greatest promoter and apostle of French wines this century, until his death in 1989. This extraordinary man virtually single-handedly created the American market for high-quality, estate-bottled wines from France. The wine has a gentle, perfumed style, though it does not lack tannin and keeps well for 10–15 years. Best years: 1990 89 88 86 85 83 82 78.

PRIMEUR French term for a young wine, often released for sale within weeks of the harvest. BEAUJOLAIS NOUVEAU is the best-known example.

PRINZ ZU SALM-DALBERG *Wallhausen, Nahe, Germany* Germany's oldest wine estate producing good wines, including Scheurebe ★ and a very pale Spätburgunder (Pinot Noir). In 1989 the estate made weird and wonderful Spätburgunder Beerenauslese ★★. Best years: 1990 89 88.

PRIORATO DO *Catalonia, Spain* The wines (mostly red) from this lovely, wild, mountainous region are dark, concentrated and very alcoholic, thanks to baking summers and very low yields. But cool summer nights can make for high quality nevertheless. The usual grapes are Garnacha and Cariñena. Best producers: René Barbier Fil★ (his wines are not DO because of unauthorized grape varieties), Masía Barril★, Scala Dei★.

PROSECCO DI CONEGLIANO-VALDOBBIADENE DOC *Veneto, Italy* Prosecco is the all-purpose sparkling wine of Venice. Grown in the hills north of Venice, the Prosecco grape gives soft, scented wine made sparkling by a second fermentation in tank. Though not for aging, it can be a delicious sipping Spumante. Best producers: Adami, Cardinal, Carpene Malvolti, Case Bianche, Mionetto, Zardetto.

PROVENCE *France* Provence is the home of France's oldest vineyards but, with the possible exception of BANDOL, the region is better known for its nudist beaches and arts festivals than its wines. Things are changing, however, and Provence is caught up in the revolution which is sweeping through the vineyards of southern France. Provence has four small, high-quality ACs (BANDOL, BELLET, CASSIS and PALETTE), but the majority of its wines comes from the much larger areas of the COTES DE PROVENCE, COTEAUX VAROIS, Coteaux de Pierrevert, COTEAUX D'AIX-EN-PROVENCE and COTEAUX DES BAUX-EN-PROVENCE. Provençal reds and rosés are generally of better quality than its whites.

PRÜFUNGSNUMMER In Germany and Austria literally the 'test number' or 'official examination' which all quality wines must undergo. In Germany it is also called *Amtliche Prüfung*, and on labels is generally shortened to AP and followed by a number. In reality the test does not really appear to be strenuous enough.

J J PRÜM *Bernkastel, Mosel, Germany* Estate making some of Germany's best Riesling in vineyard sites like the Sonnenuhr★★★ in Wehlen, Himmelreich★★ in Graach and Lay★★ and Badstube★★ in Bernkastel, and one of the few Mosel producers to be just as happy making the modern dry styles as well as the great, traditional sweeter styles. Best years: 1990 89 88 86 85 83.

S A PRÜM *Wehlen, Mosel, Germany*   There are a confusing number of Prüms in the Mosel of which the best known is J J Prüm; but Raimund Prüm of S A Prüm comes a decent second. The estate's most interesting wine is Riesling from Wehlener Sonnenuhr★★, but it also makes good wine from sites in Bernkastel★, Graach★ and Zeltingen★. Best years: 1990 89 88.

PRUNOTTO *Barolo, Piedmont, Italy*   One of the great BAROLO producers, whose winemaker Giuseppe Colla pioneered the concept of single vineyards in the zone, Prunotto was bought by ANTINORI in 1989. Since the sale, quality has, if anything, improved. Highlights include their Barbera Pian Romualdo★, Nebbiolo Occhetti★ and Barolo from the Bussia★★ and Cannubi★★ vineyards. Best years: 1990 88 85.

PUIATTI *Collio DOC, Friuli-Venezia Giulia, Italy*   Impressive whites, made without any oak. Pinot Grigio★, Pinot Bianco★★, Chardonnay★★, Sauvignon★★ and Tocai★ have a clearly defined varietal character, great concentration, a rich but never unctuous texture, superb balance and marvellous length, good to drink young but better with age. Their Archetipi★★ range is reserved for those wines that will develop with age, so are not released until 3 years after the vintage. Under the Enofriulia label, they produce a less expensive but good range of varietals.

PUISSEGUIN-ST-ÉMILION AC *Bordeaux, France*   Small ST-ÉMILION satellite AC. The wines are usually fairly solid but with an attractive chunky fruit and usually make good drinking at 3–5 years. Best producers: Beaulieu, Bel-Air, Guibeau, des Laurets, Vieux-Ch.-Guibeau. Best years: 1990 89 88 85 83 82.

PULIGNY-MONTRACHET AC *Côte de Beaune, Burgundy, France*   Puligny is one of the greatest white wine villages in the world and long ago added the name of its greatest Grand Cru, Le MONTRACHET to its own. There are three other Grands Crus which are almost as good (BATARD-MONTRACHET, Bienvenues-Bâtard-Montrachet and Chevalier-Montrachet), and no fewer than 11 Premiers Crus. Wines from the flatter vineyards use the simple Puligny-Montrachet AC. Good vintages really need 5 years' aging, while the Premiers Crus and Grands Crus may need 10 years and can last for 20 years or more. Only about 3% of the AC is red wine. Best producers: CARILLON★★, CHARTRON ET TREBUCHET, Clerc★★, DROUHIN, JADOT, LABOURE-ROI, Laguiche★★, LATOUR, Dom. LEFLAIVE★★, Olivier LEFLAIVE, Ch. de Puligny-Montrachet★, RAMONET★★★, RODET, Sauzet★★, THENARD★★. Best years: 1990 89 88 86 85 83 82 79 78.

PYRÉNÉES-ORIENTALES, VIN DE PAYS DES *Roussillon, France*   The largest Vin de Pays in Roussillon, mainly producing robust red wines. Increased plantings of Cabernet Franc, Merlot, Cabernet Sauvignon and Syrah have improved the quality in recent years, but most wines are best drunk young. Best producers: Vignerons CATALANS, CAZES★, Chichet.

QbA (QUALITÄTSWEIN BESTIMMTER ANBAUGEBIETE) German for 'quality wine from designated regions'. These wines are permitted to add sugar to the juice when natural ripeness has not produced enough, and permitted yields are high. Usually pretty ordinary, but some estates downgrade good wines when necessary, and many fine 'experimental' wines are only QbA. In Austria *Qualitätswein* is equivalent to the German QbA.

QmP (QUALITÄTSWEIN MIT PRÄDIKAT) German for 'quality wine with distinction'. A higher category than QbA: with controlled yields and no sugar addition. QmP covers six levels based on the ripeness of the grapes (in ascending order): Kabinett, Spätlese, Auslese, Beerenauslese, Eiswein and Trockenbeerenauslese.

QUARTS DE CHAUME AC *Grand Cru, Loire Valley, France* The Chenin grape, the most raspingly acidic of all France's great grape varieties, finds one of its most special microclimates in the Layon Valley around the village of Chaume. Quarts de Chaume is a 40ha (100 acre) Grand Cru within the larger COTEAUX DU LAYON AC and here, as the mists of autumn begin to curl off the river Layon, the magic noble rot fungus attacks the grapes. The result is intense sweet wines which, thanks to Chenin's acidity, can last for longer than almost any in the world. Production is not high and prices are now rising fast. Best producers: Baumard★★, de Belle Rive★★, Écharderie★★, de Suronde★★. Best years: 1990 89 88 85 83 82 81 78 76 70 69 66 64 59 47.

QUINCY AC *Loire Valley, France* Intensely flavoured, dry white wine from Sauvignon Blanc vineyards west of Bourges. You can age the wine for a year or two but it will always keep its rather aggressive gooseberry flavour. Best producers: Mardon, Pichard, Pipet★, Rouzé. Best years: 1990 89 88.

QUINTA Portuguese for 'farm' or 'estate'.

QUINTA DA BACALHÔA *Setúbal Peninsula, Portugal* Estate near Azeitão growing Cabernet Sauvignon and Merlot grapes. These are made into rich, oaky, long-lived wine by Australian Peter Bright at J P VINHOS, yet never lose their Portuguese personality. Best years: 1989 85 82.

QUINTA DO CÔTTO *Douro DOC and Port DOC, Douro, Portugal* Table wine is the speciality at this family-owned Lower Douro estate. Basic red and white Quinta do Côtto ★ are good, and Grande Escolha ★★ is one of Portugal's best reds, oaky and powerful when young, rich and cedary when mature. Best years: (table wines) 1987 85 82 80.

QUINTA DO NOVAL *Port DOC, Douro, Portugal* An immaculate property perched above Pinhão and the source of an extraordinary port made from ungrafted vines, Quinta do Noval Nacional ★★★, probably the best vintage port made but it is virtually unobtainable except at auction. Other Noval ports (including vintage Quinta do Noval ★) are acceptable rather than great. Best years: (vintage ports) 1985 78 70.

QUINTARELLI *Valpolicella DOC, Veneto, Italy* Giuseppe Quintarelli's distinctive handwritten labels herald some of the most remarkable wines in VALPOLICELLA. His Classico★, AMARONE★★ and RECIOTO★★ Valpolicellas are all of massive proportions, and when good, can be truly outstanding. His artisanal approach, however, can lead to some alarming variation between bottles.

QUIVIRA *Dry Creek Valley, California, USA* The best of the new-wave Zinfandel★★ producers. Under former winemaker Doug Nalle (now at Nalle Vineyards★) the mid-1980s Zinfandels quickly established the trend for bright, fruity wine made for short-term consumption. The wines are quite delicious and will age well because of their balance, but California Zin purists are offended by their easy drinkability. Best years: 1991 90 88 87 86.

CH. RABAUD-PROMIS★★ *Sauternes AC, 1er Cru Classé, Bordeaux, France* Under-valued estate producing rich SAUTERNES that are occasionally lacking in finesse, but have been on good form recently. Second label: Ch. Jauga. Best years: 1990 89 86 83 79.

CH. RAHOUL *Graves AC, Bordeaux, France* Property at the unfashionable southern end of the GRAVES transformed by its erstwhile Danish winemaker, Peter Vinding-Diers, who ran the estate for 10 years until 1988. It has now lost some of its lustre, but continues to make good red and white Graves. Enjoyable at 3 years old, the Merlot-dominated red wine will age for 10, but production is tiny. White Rahoul is lovely young but ages well for 5 years or more. Best years: (reds) 1990 89 88 86 85 83 82 81 79; (whites) 1990 89 88 87 86 85.

RAÏMAT *Costers del Segre DO, Catalonia, Spain* Owned by the CAVA company, CODORNIU, this large, irrigated estate near Lérida in the west of Catalonia makes good to excellent wines from both Spanish and foreign grapes such as Cabernet Sauvignon★, Merlot★, Pinot Noir★ and Chardonnay. Best years: (reds) 1989 86 85.

RAMONET *Chassagne-Montrachet, Côte de Beaune, Burgundy, France* The Ramonets (father André and sons Noël and Jean-Claude) produce some of the most complex of all white Burgundies from three Grands Crus (BATARD-MONTRACHET ★★★, Bienvenues-Bâtard-Montrachet ★★★ and Le MONTRACHET ★★★) and five Premiers Crus (Les Ruchottes ★★★, Les Caillerets ★★, Les Vergers ★★, Morgeot ★★ and Les Chaumes ★★). The wines are extremely expensive, so if you want to inflict the minimum of damage on your wallet try the ST-AUBIN ★★ or the CHASSAGNE-MONTRACHET ★★. The reds here are good but not in the same league as the whites. Best years: 1990 89 88 86 85 83 82 81.

RAMOS PINTO *Port DOC, Douro, Portugal* Innovative port company now controlled by ROEDERER, the Champagne house and making complex, full-bodied Late Bottled Vintage ★ and marvellous aged tawnies (Quinta Ervamoira ★ and Quinta Bom Retiro ★★). Best years: (vintage ports) 1985 83 82.

RANCIO A fortified wine that has been deliberately exposed to the effects of oxidation. Most common in France's Languedoc-Roussillon and in southern Italy.

KENT RASMUSSEN *Carneros AVA, California, USA* Tightly structured Burgundian-style Chardonnay★★ capable of considerable bottle age and a fascinating juicy Pinot Noir★★ are made by ultra-traditional methods. Best years: 1991 90 89 88.

RASTEAU AC *Rhône Valley, France* Rasteau is one of 16 villages entitled to the COTES DU RHONE-VILLAGES AC. The Rasteau AC is for a fortified wine which can be either red or white. There is also a Rancio version which is left in barrel for two or more years. Best producer: Cave des Vignerons. Best years: (reds) 1991 90 89.

CH. RAUSAN-SÉGLA ★★★ *Margaux AC, 2ème Cru Classé, Haut-Médoc, Bordeaux, France* A dynamic change of ownership in 1983 brought about a startling change for the better. Now the wines are marked by a rich blackcurrant fruit, almost tarry, thick tannins and weight, excellent woody spice and superb concentration. Second wine: Ch. Lamouroux. Best years: 1990 89 88 86 85 83.

JEAN-MARIE RAVENEAU *Chablis AC, Burgundy, France* The outstanding grower in CHABLIS producing beautifully nuanced wines from three Grands Crus (Blanchot ★★, Les Clos ★★★ and Valmur★★★) and four Premiers Crus (Montée de Tonnerre ★★, Vaillons ★★, Butteaux ★★ and Chapelots ★★), using a combination of oak and stainless steel fermentation. The wines can easily age for a decade or more. Best years: 1990 89 88 86 85 84.

CH. RAYAS *Châteauneuf-du-Pape, Rhône Valley, France* The most famous estate in CHATEAUNEUF-DU-PAPE. The eccentric Jacques Reynaud produces big, alcoholic, exotically rich reds★★★ and whites★★ which also age well. Prices are not cheap, but at its best Rayas is worth the money. The red is made entirely from low-yielding Grenache vines – the only such wine in the AC – while the white is a blend of Clairette, Grenache Blanc and (so rumour has it) Chardonnay. Reynaud's COTES DU RHONE, called Ch. de Fonsalette ★, is also wonderful stuff. Best years: (reds) 1990 89 88 86 84; (whites) 1989 86.

RECIOTO DELLA VALPOLICELLA DOC *Veneto, Italy* The great sweet wine of VALPOLICELLA, made from a careful selection of grapes picked a week earlier than usual and left to dry on straw mats until the end of January. The wines are deep in colour, with a rich, bitter-sweet intensely cherryish fruit. They will age well for 5–8 years, but I think they're best drunk young and slightly chilled and are excellent at the end of the meal, or with strong cheeses. As with Valpolicella, the Classico tag is all important. Best producers: Serègo Alighieri★★, ALLEGRINI★, MASI★, QUINTARELLI★★, Tedeschi★. Best years: 1990 88 85.

210

RECIOTO DI SOAVE DOC *Veneto, Italy*   Sweet white made from dried grapes like RECIOTO DELLA VALPOLICELLA. Garganega grapes give wonderfully delicate yet intense wines that age well for up to a decade. Best producers: ANSELMI★★, Cantina Sociale di Soave★, PIEROPAN★★. Best years: 1990 88.

REDWOOD VALLEY See Seifried.

REGNIÉ AC *Beaujolais, Burgundy, France*   In 1988 the village of Regnié and its neighbour Durette were promoted to BEAUJOLAIS' 10th Cru. The wines are generally light and attractive but in poor years not up to Cru standard. Best producers: Cinquin, Crêt des Bruyères, DUBOEUF, Magrin, Trichard. Best years: 1991 90 89.

REGUENGOS IPR *Alentejo, Portugal*   One of the most promising of the Alentejo would-be DOCs with good, flavoursome reds epitomizing the excitingly juicy flavours of southern Portugal. Best producers: Esporão★, Reguengos de Monsaraz co-op★, J S Rosado Fernandes★★ (owned by FONSECA SUCCESSORES).

REMELLURI ★★ *Rioja DOC, País Vasco, Spain*   Organic RIOJA estate producing wines with far more fruit than usual and good concentration for aging. Best years: 1990 89 87 86 85 82.

RESERVA   Spanish wines of above average quality that have fulfilled certain aging requirements: reds must have at least three years' aging before sale, of which one must be in oak barrels, whites and rosés must have at least two years' aging, of which six months must be in oak.

RÉSERVE   French for what is, in theory at least, a winemaker's finest wine. The word has no legal definition in France.

BALTHASAR RESS *Eltville-Hattenheim, Rheingau, Germany*   Stefan Ress has cleared all the wood out of his cellar and replaced all his casks with stainless steel and fibre glass. Although his wines continue to exhibit some of the cleanest, purest fruit of any producer in the Rheingau, I wonder whether recent vintages have lost a little of their individuality. Basically a Riesling★ producer he also produces delicious Scheurebe★. Best years: 1990 89 88.

RETSINA *Greece*   Resinated white and rosé wine common now all over Greece. The best retsinas are deliciously oily and piny, while the resin provides (as mint does) a mild cooling effect on the tongue. For this reason, retsina need not be overchilled. The younger the better is a good rule here – and I've found a splash of lemonade is pretty tasty when the sun is high in the sky. Best producers: Achaia-Clauss, Botrys, Cambas, Kourtakis.

REUILLY AC *Loire Valley, France*   Extremely dry but attractive Sauvignon from vineyards west of the world-famous SANCERRE. Some pale Pinot Noir red and Pinot Gris rosé. Best producers: Beurdin★, Cordier, Lafond, Martin. Best years: 1990 89 88.

CH. REYNON *Premières Côtes de Bordeaux AC, Bordeaux, France*   Leading PREMIERES COTES château, owned by the brilliant Denis Dubourdieu. The reds★ are stylish, but the dry whites ★ (sold as Bordeaux Blanc) are the real stars. Best years: 1990 89 88 86 85.

RHEINGAU *Germany*   Germany's most aristocratic wine region, both in terms of the racy, slow-maturing 'breed' of the wines and because of the number of noble estate owners. The Rheingau occupies a south-facing stretch of the Rhine flanking the city of Wiesbaden and includes some of Germany's top wine names. See also Eltville, Geisenheim, Hattenheim, Hochheim, Johannisberg, Kiedrich, Rüdesheim, Winkel.

RHEINHESSEN *Germany*   Large wine region to the south and west of Mainz. On the Rheinterrasse between Mainz and Worms are a number of very famous, top quality estates, especially at Nackenheim, NIERSTEIN, OPPENHEIM and Bodenheim. BINGEN to the north-west also has a fine vineyard area along the southern banks of the Rhine.

RHEINPFALZ *Germany*   Germany's most productive wine region makes a lot of poor to middling wine but the best estates – both those in the well-established Mittelhaardt in the north, and increasingly among the young Turks further south – are capable of matching anything Germany has to offer. The Mittelhaardt has a considerable reputation for Riesling, especially round the villages of Wachenheim, FORST and Deidesheim, though Freinsheim, Ungstein, Kallstadt, Hambach and Haardt also produce fine Riesling, as well as Scheurebe, Pinot Gris and Dornfelder. Further south, in the Südliche Weinstrasse the warmer climate makes the area an ideal testing ground for the so-called Burgunders (Pinot Noir, Pinot Blanc and Pinot Gris), as well as Gewürztraminer, Scheurebe, Muscat and Dornfelder, often made dry but rich and often with an oak barrique influence. See also Bad Dürkheim.

RHÔNE VALLEY *France*   The Rhône starts out as a Swiss river, ambling through Lake Geneva before hurtling southwards into France. South of Lyon, between Vienne and Avignon, the valley becomes one of France's great wine regions. In the northern part where vertigo-inducing slopes overhang the river, there is not much wine produced but the little that is made is of remarkable individuality. The Syrah grape reigns here in COTE-ROTIE and on the great hill of HERMITAGE. ST-JOSEPH, CROZES-HERMITAGE and CORNAS also make excellent reds while the white Viognier grape yields perfumed, delicate wine at CONDRIEU and at the tiny AC CHATEAU-GRILLET. In the southern part the steep slopes give way to wide plains where the vines swelter in the hot sun with hills both in the west and east. Most of these vineyards are either COTES DU RHONE or COTES DU RHONE-VILLAGES, reds, whites and rosés, but there are also specific ACs. Best known of these are CHATEAUNEUF-DU-PAPE and the luscious, golden dessert wine, MUSCAT-DE-BEAUMES-DE-VENISE. See also Clairette de Die Tradition, Coteaux du Tricastin, Côtes du Luberon, Côtes du Vivarais, Gigondas, Lirac, St-Péray, Tavel, Vacquéyras.

RIAS BAIXAS DO *Galicia, Spain* By far the best of the three DOs of Galicia, Rias Baixas is making increasing quantities of Spain's best whites (apart perhaps from a few Chardonnays in the north-east). The magic ingredient is the characterful Albariño grape, making creamy-rich, fruity whites with a glorious fragrance. Best producers: Adegas las Eiras, Bodegas de Mollina, Lagar de Cervera, Morgadío, Santiago Ruiz.

RIBERA DEL DUERO DO *Castilla y León, Spain* The best reds in this DO are delicious, dark yet elegant, and aromatic too, made mostly from Tinto Fino (Tempranillo), sometimes with Cabernet and Merlot. Best producers: Ismael Arroyo, Victor Balbás, Hijos de Antonio Barcelo, Felix Callejo★, Alejandro Fernández (PESQUERA★★), Perez Pasquas (PEDROSA★), VEGA SICILIA★★★, Yllera★.

RICHEBOURG AC *Grand Cru, Côte de Nuits, Burgundy, France* Rich, fleshy wine from the northern end of VOSNE-ROMANEE. Most domaine-bottlings are exceptional. Best producers: Gros★★★, JAYER, Noëllat★★, Dom. de la ROMANEE-CONTI★★★. Best years: 1990 89 88 87 85 83 82 80 78.

RICHOU *Anjou, Loire Valley, France* Founded in 1550, this is one of the leading domaines in the Loire, producing a large consistently good range of wines. The best wines are the ANJOU-VILLAGES Vieilles Vignes★★ and the sweet COTEAUX DE L'AUBANCE Cuvée Les Trois Demoiselles★★. Best years: 1990 89 88.

MAX FERD RICHTER *Mülheim, Mosel-Saar-Ruwer, Germany* The genial Dr Richter makes Riesling wines in some of the best sites in the Mosel, including Wehlener Sonnenuhr★★ and Brauneberger Juffer★★★. His wines are marked out by splendid racy acidity but this is always balanced by a beautifully fragrant Riesling fruit. His Mülheimer Helenenkloster vineyard is unique in Germany for producing a magical Eiswein★★★ virtually every year, although in 1991 his entire crop got eaten by a very discriminating family of wild boar. Best years: 1990 89 88 85.

RIDGE VINEYARDS *Santa Clara, California, USA* Established as a Zinfandel-only winery in 1962, winemaker Paul Draper moved into Cabernet Sauvignon★★ and Petite Sirah★ in the late 1960s. The Zinfandels★★★, made with grapes from various sources, are noted for their great intensity, concentration and long life, and indeed all the reds display great ageability, impressive concentration of fruit and – above all, originality of flavour. There is now some pretty original Chardonnay★, too. Best years: 1991 90 88 85 84.

RIECINE *Chianti Classico DOCG, Tuscany, Italy* John Dunkley's small estate in Gaiole makes some of the most exquisite CHIANTI. Yields are low, so there is a great intensity of fruit and a superb definition of spiced cherry flavours. Both the Chianti Classico★★ and Riserva★★★ are outstanding, while the barrique-aged Vino da Tavola, La Gioia★★, is equally impressive. Best years: 1990 88 85.

RIESLING

I'm sad to have to make this bald statement at the beginning of the entry on Riesling, but I feel I must. If you have tasted wines with names like Laski Riesling, Olasz Riesling, Welsch Riesling, Gray Riesling, Riesling Italico and the like and found them unappetizing – do not blame the Riesling grape. These wines have filched Riesling's name, but have nothing whatsoever to do with the great grape itself.

Riesling is Germany's finest contribution to the world of wine – and herein lies the second problem. German wines have fallen to such a low level of general esteem through the proliferation of wines like Liebfraumilch, that Riesling, even true German Riesling, has been dragged down with it.

So what is true Riesling? It is a very ancient German grape, probably the descendant of wild vines growing in the Rhine Valley. It certainly performs best in the cool vineyard regions of Germany's Rhine and Mosel Valleys, but also does well in New Zealand and cool parts of Australia; yet it is widely planted in California, South Africa and Italy, and the warmer parts of Australia also grow it to good effect.

WINE STYLES

Germany These wines are based on a marvellous perfume and an ability to hold on to a piercing acidity, even at high ripeness levels, so long as the ripening period has been merely warm and gradual rather than broiling and rushed. German Rieslings can be bone – indeed bone-shiveringly – dry, through to medium and even lusciously sweet, but if they are dry, they must be made from fully ripe grapes, otherwise the acidity is excessive and the wine's body insufficient.

Young Rieslings often show a delightful cool floral perfume, sometimes blended with the crispness of green apples, often a splash of lime, sometimes even raisin or honey, depending upon the ripeness of the grapes. As the wines age, the lime often intensifies, and a flavour perhaps of slate, perhaps of petrol/kerosene intrudes.

Other regions The rather heavier, petrolly style is typical of Australia's warmer areas, while California generally produces a rather soft-edged grapy style which is best when sweet. The mountain vineyards of northern Italy, and the cool vineyards of Czechoslovakia and Switzerland can show a nice floral sharp style, but almost all the most fragrant wines come from Germany, from France's Alsace, and from New Zealand, with some success from America's Pacific Northwest and New York State, and from the odd cool spot in Australia.

In general Rieslings are best drunk young, but dry Alsace wines can improve for many years, and the truly sweet German styles can age for generations.

214

BEST PRODUCERS

Dry Rieslings
France (Alsace) Blanck, Kreydenweiss, Mader, Ostertag, Zind-Humbrecht.

Germany von Buhl, Diel, Guntrum, Dr Heger, Heintz, Heitlingen, Jost, Juliusspital, von Kesselstatt, Landgraf Hessisches Weingut, Lingenfelder, Loosen, Maximin Grünhaus, Messer, Müller-Catoir, Ress, Richter, Schloss Schönborn, Staatsdomäne Niederhausen.

Non-dry Rieslings
Germany Dr Becker, Guntrum, Jost, von Kesselstatt, Lauerburg, Lingenfelder, Loosen, Müller-Catoir, Paulinshof, J J Prüm, Ress, Richter, Schäfer, Schloss Reinharts-hausen, von Schubert, Staatsweingut Eltville, Thanisch, Villa Sachsen.

New World Rieslings
Australia Jim Barry, Delatite, Hardy, Henschke, Hill-Smith, St Huberts, Knappstein, Mitchell, Orlando, Petaluma, Seville Estate.

New Zealand Collards, Cooks, Giesen, Montana, Neudorf, Redwood Valley, Rongopai.

RIESLING ITALICO Known as the Welschriesling in the rest of Europe, and not in any way related to the great Riesling of the Rhine, this variety is widely planted in Italy, especially in the north, where it produces decent dry whites of moderate perfume. Best producers: Gravner, PIEROPAN.

CH. RIEUSSEC ★★ *Sauternes AC, 1er Cru Classé, Bordeaux, France*
Apart from the peerless and scarcely affordable YQUEM, Rieussec, bought by LAFITE-ROTHSCHILD in 1984, used often to be the richest, most succulently self-indulgent wine of SAUTERNES. However recent vintages have displayed a rather 'correct' style for what was always a wine that walked on the wild and wonderful side. The dry white wine, called 'R', is pretty dull. Second wine: Clos Labère. Best years: 1990 89 88 86 85 83 81 79 76 75.

RIOJA DOC *Rioja, Navarra, País Vasco and Castilla y León, Spain*
Rioja, in the centre of northern Spain, is not all oaky, creamy whites and elegant, barrel-aged reds, combining savoury oak flavours with wild strawberry and prune fruit. Over half Rioja's red wine is sold young, never having seen the inside of a barrel, and most of the white is fairly anonymous modern stuff. But this famous region has cause to celebrate as it has finally become the first one to win Denominación de Origen Calificada (DOC) status. This brings slightly tougher rules on yields, alcohol levels and the like, and should lead to greater consistency and quality. Grape prices have come down and 1989 and 90 were bountiful vintages after the meagre crop of 1988. Hopefully Rioja can now regain the place in the affections of wine drinkers that it lost through inconsistency and overcharging during the 1980s. Best producers: (reds) Amézola de la Mora, BARON DE LEY★, Beronia, CAMPILLO★★, CAMPO VIEJO (Marqués de Villamagna★★), CONTINO★★, El COTO★, CVNE★★, LOPEZ DE HEREDIA★★, MARQUES DE CACERES★, MARQUES DE MURRIETA★★, MARTINEZ BUJANDA★★, MUGA★, Navajas, REMELLURI,★★ La RIOJA ALTA★★★, RIOJANAS★; (whites) CVNE★, LOPEZ DE HEREDIA★, MARQUES DE CACERES★, MARQUES DE MURRIETA★, MARTINEZ BUJANDA, Navajas, La RIOJA ALTA★, RIOJANAS★.

LA RIOJA ALTA *Rioja DOC, Rioja, Spain* One of the very best of the old-established RIOJA producers, almost entirely making Reservas and Gran Reservas. Their only Crianza, Viña Alberdi ★, fulfils the minimum age requirements for a Reserva anyway. There is a little good, lemony-oaky Viña Ardanza Reserva ★ white. Their red Reservas, Viña Arana ★ and Viña Ardanza ★★, age splendidly, and their Gran Reservas, Reserva 904 ★★ and Reserva 890 ★★★ (only made in exceptional years) are among Rioja's best. Best years: (reds) 1989 85 83 82 81 78 76 73.

RIOJANAS *Rioja DOC, Rioja, Spain* This quality winery makes Reservas and Gran Reservas in two styles, elegant Viña Albina ★ and richer Monte Real ★. The white, Monte Real Blanco Crianza ★, is one of Rioja's best. Best years: (reds) 1987 83 82 78 73 64.

DANIEL RION *Nuits-St-Georges, Côte de Nuits, Burgundy, France*
One of Burgundy's most consistent performers, producing supple, concentrated but sometimes slightly 'serious' reds from Pinot Noir and a little bit of crisp, white Aligoté. The best wines are the VOSNE-ROMANEE Les Beaux Monts★★, and Les Chaumes★★, NUITS-ST-GEORGES Clos de Argillières★★ and the village level VOSNE-ROMANEE★. Best years: 1990 89 88 87 86 85.

RISERVA An Italian term, recognized in many DOCs and DOCGs, for a special selection of superior quality wine that has been aged longer before release. Quite often, it is also destined for longer aging. It is only a promise of a more pleasurable drink if the wine had enough fruit and structure in the first place. Discredited in BAROLO, it is still important in CHIANTI.

RIVERA *Castel del Monte, Puglia, Italy* One of southern Italy's most dynamic producers. In the traditional mould, the CASTEL DEL MONTE Riserva Il Falcone★ is an excellent, full-blooded southern red. There is also a series of varietals sold under the Vigna al Monte label, best of which are Pinot and Sauvignon.

RIVERLAND *South Australia* Vast irrigated region along the Murray River producing 27% of the national grape crush. Mainly given over to bulk and cheaper bottles of table and fortified wine, although BERRI RENMANO can produce some high quality special selections. Best producers: Angoves, BERRI RENMANO, YALUMBA (Oxford Landing).

RIVESALTES AC *Languedoc-Roussillon, France* Vin Doux Naturel from a large area of Roussillon around the town of Rivesaltes and including some of the Aude department in Languedoc. These fortified wines are some of southern France's best and can be made from an assortment of grapes, mainly white Muscat (when it is called MUSCAT DE RIVESALTES) and Grenache, both Noir, Gris and Blanc. There is also a Rancio style which ages well. Best producers: Ch. Cap de Fouste, Vignerons CATALANS, CAZES★★, Ch. de Corneilla, Ch. de Jau★, Mas Rancoure★, Sarda-Mallet★; also co-ops at Rivesaltes, Terrats and Troillas.

RIVIERA DEL GARDA BRESCIANO DOC *Lombardy, Italy* Though the largest DOC zone in Lombardy, stretching from the western shore of Lake Garda halfway to Brescia, it is not noted for the quality of its wine. A decent red and a Chiaretto (both from Gropello, Sangiovese and Cabernet) are seldom as good as LUGANA, the small white enclave in the zone. Best producers: Bottarelli, Ca' dei Frati, Comincioli, Costaripa, Pasini Produttori.

RIVIERA LIGURE DI PONENTE DOC *Liguria, Italy* This DOC zone stretches from Genoa westwards through stunning scenery to Ventimiglia on the French border, and north to Piedmont. The major grapes are the white Pigato and the more delicate Vermentino, and the red Ormeasco (Piedmont's Dolcetto, producing soft, plummy wines) and more fragile Rossese. Best producers: Feipu, Lupi, Maccario, Terre Rosse.

217

CH. LA RIVIÈRE ★ *Fronsac AC, Bordeaux, France*   This large estate is owned by self-promotion ace Jacques Borie. Luckily the wines are good too and they do age remarkably well, helped by at least one-third new oak barrels each year and a fair number of very old vines. Best years: 1990 89 88 85 83 82 78.

ROCKFORD *Barossa Valley, South Australia*   Wonderfully nostalgic wines from the stone winery of Robert 'Rocky' O'Callaghan, who has a great respect for the old vines so plentiful in the Barossa, and delights in using antique machinery. He produces masterful Basket Press Shiraz ★★, 1886 Vineyard Rhine Riesling ★, Dry Country Grenache and red sparkling cult wine, Black Shiraz ★★. Best years: 1991 90 88.

ANTONIN RODET *Mercurey, Côte Chalonnaise, Burgundy, France*   Merchant specializing in the Côte Chalonnaise wines, but produces an excellent range from throughout Burgundy. Now controlled by LAURENT-PERRIER, Rodet owns or co-owns four domaines – Ch. de Rully ★★, Ch. de Chamirey ★, Ch. de Mercurey ★★, and Jacques Prieur ★★ – and these are the source of their best wines. Don't miss the BOURGOGNE Vieilles Vignes ★, one of the most impressive, inexpensive Chardonnays on the market. Best years: 1990 89 88 85.

LOUIS ROEDERER *Champagne AC, Champagne, France*   Good-quality firm making some of the best, full-flavoured Champagnes around. As well as the excellent non-vintage ★★ and pale rosé ★ they also make a big, exciting Vintage ★★, and the famous Roederer Cristal ★★, a de luxe cuvée which is usually but not always delicious. Best years: 1985 82 79.

ROEDERER ESTATE *Anderson Valley, California, USA*   Californian off-shoot of French Champagne house Louis ROEDERER. The Brut ★★ is somewhat austere, a step back from the upfront fruit of many California sparklers but should age well if you have the patience.

ROERO DOC *Piedmont, Italy*   The Roero hills are over the River Tanaro from the Langhe hills, the home of BAROLO and BARBARESCO. The emphasis here has traditionally been on white grapes, like Arneis, but the Nebbiolo-based red can be attractively scented and supple. The whites should be drunk young, and though the reds can age well for 3–5 years, they are best drunk while still fresh and zesty. Best producers: Cornarea, Correggia, Deltetto★, Malvira★, Negro, Rabino.

ROMAGNA *Emilia-Romagna, Italy*   Romagna's wine production is centred on 4 DOCs and 1 DOCG east of Bologna. The whites are from Trebbiano (ineffably dull), Pagadebit (showing promise as both a dry and sweet wine) and Albana (ALBANA DI ROMAGNA was upgraded to DOCG in 1987 and is available in dry or gently sweet versions), the reds are dominated by the Sangiovese grape, which ranges in style from young and fresh through wines that can rival a good CHIANTI for structure and prestige. Best producers: Castelluccio★ (outstanding Sangiovese), Cesari, Ferrucci, Paradiso, Pasolini dall' Onda, San Patrignano, Spalletti, Zerbina.

LA ROMANÉE-CONTI AC★★★ *Grand Cru, Côte de Nuits, Burgundy, France* For many extremely wealthy wine lovers this is the pinnacle of all red Burgundy. It is an incredibly complex wine with great structure and pure, clearly-defined fruit flavour but you've got to age it a dozen years to see what all the fuss is about. The vineyard covers only 1.8ha (4 $^1/_2$ acres), which is one reason for the high prices. Wholly owned by Dom. de la Romanée-Conti. Best years: 1990 89 88 85 82 78 76.

DOM. DE LA ROMANÉE-CONTI *Vosne-Romanée, Côte de Nuits, Burgundy, France* One of the most famous red wine estates in the world. The domaine owns a string of Grands Crus in VOSNE-ROMANEE (LA TACHE ★★★, RICHEBOURG ★★★, ROMANEE-CONTI ★★★, ROMANEE-ST-VIVANT ★★, ECHEZEAUX ★★ and Grands-Échézeaux ★★) as well as a small parcel of Le MONTRACHET ★★★. The wines are ludicrously expensive but they can be quite sublime – full of fruit when young, but capable of aging for 15 years or more to an astonishing marriage made in heaven and hell of richness and decay. Recent vintages seem to show a necessary return to consistency. At these prices they'd better! Best years: 1990 89 88 87 86 85 83 80 78.

ROMANÉE-ST-VIVANT AC *Grand Cru, Côte de Nuits, Burgundy, France* By far the largest of VOSNE-ROMANEE's six Grands Crus. At 10–15 years the wines should reveal the keenly balanced brilliance of which the vineyard is capable but a surly, rough edge sometimes gets in the way. Best producers: Arnoux★, JADOT, LATOUR, Noëllat★★, Dom. de la ROMANEE-CONTI★★. Best years: 1990 89 88 87 85 84 83 80 78 76.

RONGOPAI *Te Kauwhata, Auckland, North Island, New Zealand* Small winery whose greatest success has been with bunch and berry-selected sweet botrytis styles which include Riesling, Müller-Thurgau and Chardonnay★★. There is also distinctive dry Sauvignon Blanc ★, Chardonnay★, Riesling and Cabernet Sauvignon. Best years: 1991 90 89.

ROSADO Spanish for pink wine or rosé.

ROSÉ French for pink wine. In effect, rosés range in colour from washed-out orange to vibrant day-glow pink.

ROSÉ D'ANJOU AC *Loire Valley, France* Cheap ANJOU rosé that is usually somewhere between off-dry and reasonably sweet. Produced predominantly from the Groslot grape, which doesn't give much colour or flavour. From a good producer the wine can be fresh, not too sweet with a lovely pale pink colour. Drink young. Best producer: Vignerons de Saumur co-op.

ROSÉ DE LOIRE AC *Loire Valley, France* AC for dry rosé wine that can come from SAUMUR and TOURAINE as well as ANJOU. It can be a lovely grassy drink but drink as young as possible and chill well. Best producer: Daheuiller.

ROSEMOUNT ESTATE *Hunter Valley, New South Wales, Australia*
Model winery now buying grapes from several regions to produce some of Australia's best and most popular wines. Top wines are complex, weighty Roxburgh ★★★ and Show Reserve ★★ Chardonnays; blackcurranty Coonawarra Cabernet ★★ and sappy perfumed Show Reserve Pinot Noir ★. New single-vineyard wines★ are pricy but promising. Basic Sémillon-Chardonnay and Shiraz-Cabernet ★ blends are among Australia's best simple gluggers. Best years: 1991 90 89 87 86 84.

ROSSESE DI DOLCEACQUA DOC *Liguria, Italy* A small area producing wines from the Rossese grape. Styles range from light and fresh to more structured wines. Drink within 3–5 years. Best producers: Cane, Lupi, Maccario.

ROSSO Italian for red.

ROSSO CONERO DOC *Marche, Italy* The best wines in this zone, on the Adriatic coast just south of Ancona, are those made solely from Montepulciano, for they have a wonderfully spicy richness undiluted by the addition of Sangiovese. Wine-making has improved greatly in recent years. Best producers: San Lorenzo★, Le Terrazze★, Villa Bonomi★. Best years: 1990 88 86.

ROSSO DI MONTALCINO DOC *Tuscany, Italy* The little brother of BRUNELLO DI MONTALCINO DOCG seems destined to become more important as sales of the grander wine peak. This is good news, since Rosso, made solely from younger Sangiovese vines in the same zone as Brunello, spends much less time in wood so retains a wonderful exuberance of flavour that Brunello loses through a protracted period of cask-aging. It is like a CHIANTI with oomph. Best producers: Casanova, Ciacci Piccolomini, Col d'Orcia★, Poggione★, Talenti★. Best years: 1990 88.

ROSSO DI MONTEPULCIANO DOC *Tuscany, Italy* This DOC was only created 1989, giving producers the option of honing production of their grander VINO NOBILE DI MONTEPULCIANO DOCG by diverting some of the younger, juicier vats into bottle at an earlier stage, so the style has yet to be clearly defined. Some producers turn out a fresh, jammy, rather innocuous style, while the best producers give the drinker a mouthful of plummy, chocolaty flavours that is pure delight. Best producers: Le Casalte★, Contucci★, POLIZIANO★. Best year: 1990.

ROSSO PICENO DOC *Marche, Italy.* The poor relation of ROSSO CONERO, due primarily to the increased element of Sangiovese in the blend. A minimum of 60% Sangiovese is required by law, though this can be greatly improved upon by using up to 40% of Montepulciano. Stick to Rosso Conero, unless you can find an example from one of the best producers. Best producers: Cocci Grifoni, Villa Pigna, Villamagna. Best years: 1990 88 86.

ROTHBURY ESTATE *Hunter Valley, New South Wales, Australia*
Len Evans is founder and chairman of this successful vineyard and winery now also buying grapes from Cowra and Upper

Hunter for their burgeoning Chardonnay★ (Reserve ★★) production. Rothbury also make what is possibly the Hunter's best
Sémillon ★★★ and good Shiraz ★★. Best years: (whites) 1991 90
86 84 79; (reds) 1991 89 87 86 83 81 79.

ROUGE French for red.

ROUPEIRO The main white grape of Portugal's Alentejo, the
Roupeiro makes honeyed, fresh wine when picked early, even in
the parched south of the country.

ROUSSANNE The Rhône Valley's best white variety, Roussanne is
frequently blended with Marsanne. Roussanne is the more aromatic and elegant of the two, less prone to oxidation and with
better acidity, but growers usually prefer Marsanne on account
of its higher yields.

ROUSSILLON *France*   The snow-covered peaks of the Pyrenees
form a spectacular backdrop to the ancient region of Roussillon,
now the Pyrénées-Orientales department. The vineyards produce
a wide range of fairly priced wines, mainly red, ranging from the
ripe, raisin-rich Vins Doux Naturels to light, fruity-fresh Vins de
Pays. See also Banyuls, Collioure, Côtes du Roussillon, Côtes du
Roussillon-Villages, Maury, Muscat de Rivesaltes, Pyrénées-
Orientales, Rivesaltes.

RUCHOTTES-CHAMBERTIN AC   See Chambertin AC.

RÜDESHEIM *Rheingau, Germany* Village producing full-flavoured
aromatic wines from some famous sites (Schlossberg, Berg
Rottland, Berg Roseneck and Bischofsberg). Not to be confused
with the Nahe village of the same name. Best producers: Georg
BREUER, Klosterkeller St Hildegard, Staatsweingut Eltville.

RUEDA DO *Castilla y León, Spain*   The Rueda DO is currently limited to crisp, grassy Verdejo-based whites and unexciting sherry-
type creations though there are good Sauvignons too. Best
producers: Ivarez y Diez, Castilla La Vieja (Mirador), Cerro Sol
(Doña Beatriz), MARQUES DE GRINON★, MARQUES DE RISCAL, Angél
Rodríguez Vidal (Martinsancho), Viños Sanz.

RUFFINO *Tuscany, Italy*   Huge wine-making concern, based in
Pontassieve to the east of Florence. Though at least 65% of their
business is still based on cheap CHIANTI, they have succeeded in
establishing some fine wines (Chianti Classico from estates at
Zano ★ and Nozzole ★ and Vino da Tavolas, Chardonnay Cabreo
La Pietra ★★, Cabernet Cabreo Il Borgo ★★ and Pinot Noir Nero
del Tondo ★).

RUINART *Champagne AC, France*   One of the oldest Champagne
houses, Ruinart has a surprisingly low profile, given the quality
of its wines. The non-vintage ★★ is very good, but the top wines
here are the excellent, classy Dom Ruinart Blanc de Blancs ★★★
and the Dom Ruinart Rosé ★★. Best years: 1985 83 82.

RULLY AC *Côte Chalonnaise, Burgundy, France* One of Burgundy's most improved ACs with good quality, reasonably priced wine. Originally famous for sparkling wines, it is now best known for its still whites, increasingly aged in oak. Red Rully is light, with a fleeting, strawberry and cherry perfume. Best producers: (whites) Belleville, Brelière, Chanzy, Delorme, Duvernay, FAIVELEY★★, La Folie, JAFFELIN★, Olivier LEFLAIVE★★, RODET★★; (reds) Chanzy, Cogny, Delorme, Duvernay, La Folie, Jacqueson. Best years: (whites) 1990 89 88 86 85; (reds) 1990 89 88 87 85.

RUSSE *Northern Region, Bulgaria* This Danube winery is an up-and-coming star, achieving vibrant, zesty results with Cabernet Sauvignon ★. The low-priced 'country' blends are good.

RUSTENBERG *Stellenbosch, South Africa* This beautiful farm, now a national monument, makes mostly red wines, particularly Cabernet Sauvignon★ that can exhibit lead-pencil perfume reminiscent of good Bordeaux. Best releases are under the Gold★ and Reserve★ labels. There is also good clove-charged Chardonnay.

RUTHERFORD *Napa Valley AVA, California, USA* This as-yet unde-fined viticultural area in mid-Napa Valley has inspired endless hours of argument and acrimony. The heart of the area – known as the Rutherford Bench – does seem to be a prime Cabernet Sauvignon production zone and many of the tradi-tional old Napa Cabernets have come from Rutherford and exhibit the 'Rutherford Dust' flavour.

RUTHERGLEN *Victoria, Australia* This district in North-East Victoria is the home of heroic reds from Shiraz, Cabernet and Durif, and luscious, world-beating fortifieds from Muscat and Tokay. There are also good sherries and ultra-ripe vintage ports. The whites from Chardonnay and Sémillon are tasty but unsub-tle. Best producers: Campbells, CHAMBERS, MORRIS, St Leonards (whites), Stanton & Killeen.

HUGH RYMAN *Bordeaux, France* One of the most important influ-ences on wine-making in the south and south-west of France, Hugh Ryman, a young English-born winemaker, trained in Australia and Bordeaux, who makes large quantities of keenly priced wine for the British market. He manages to bolt a fine Australian-type technique on to dry, lean, snappy-flavoured French fruit. Ryman set up his own consultancy and travelling wine-making operation after a spell at la JAUBERTIE, his father's BERGERAC property. He now makes wine all over the south of France and, since 1991, in Hungary, too. Ryman produces sharply fruity wines under a variety of different labels. His Vin de Pays d'OC Chardonnay★ and COTES DE GASCOGNE Dom. Le Puts ★ white are particularly good value for money, as are his Gyöngyös Estate Hungarian Sauvignon ★ and Chardonnay. There is also excellent MONBAZILLAC Ch. Hebras ★★ as well as good southern reds including Vin de Pays d'OC Cabernet ★.

SAALE-UNSTRUT *Germany* Region in former East Germany, near the city of Halle on the Saale river and its tributary, the Unstrut. In the old days Saale-Unstrut wines were virtually reserved for Party members and their chief reputation was for rarity.

SAAR See Mosel-Saar-Ruwer.

SACHSEN *Germany* Until recently one of Europe's forgotten wine regions, Saxony's vineyards lie on the river Elbe between Dresden and Meissen in former East Germany. The wine (mainly Müller-Thurgau) was always vinified at two co-ops at Meissen and Radebeul and there was certainly room for improvement.

CH. ST-AMAND ★★ *Sauternes AC, Bordeaux, France* One of the few non-Classed Growth properties which regularly manages to produce big, rich, classic SAUTERNES although the price is verging on the high side. The wine is also sold as Ch. la Chartreuse. Best years: 1990 89 88 86 83 81 80.

ST-AMOUR AC *Beaujolais, Burgundy, France* What a lovely name for the northernmost BEAUJOLAIS Cru, producing juicy, soft-fruited wine which lasts well for 2–3 years. Best producers: Billards, Dom. du Paradis, DUBOEUF, Patissier, Poitevin, Revillon, Saillant, Ch. de St-Amour. Best years: 1991 90 89 88.

ST-AUBIN AC *Côte de Beaune, Burgundy, France* Some of Burgundy's best-value wines. Good, cherry-fruited reds, especially from Premiers Crus like Les Frionnes and Les Murgers des Dents de Chien. Also high-class reasonably priced, oak-aged whites. Best producers: Bachelet, Clerget★, COLIN, Duvernay,  JADOT★★, JAFFELIN, Lamy★, Lamy-Pillot★, Olivier LEFLAIVE, Albert Morey★, Prudhon, Roux★, Thomas. Best years: (reds) 1990 89 88 87 85; (whites) 1990 89 88 86 85.

ST-CHINIAN AC *Languedoc, France* Large AC for strong, spicy red wines with more personality than the run of the Hérault mill, especially when carbonic maceration has been used. Best producers: Cazals-Viel, Clos Bagatelle, de Coujan, de Jougla; also Berlou and Roquebrun co-ops. Best years: 1991 90 89 88.

ST-DÉSIRAT-CHAMPAGNE, CAVE CO-OPERATIVE DE *St-Joseph, Rhône Valley, France* The largest single producer of ST-JOSEPH and one of the best co-ops in the Rhône Valley. The intense, smoky red St-Joseph ★★ is a fantastic bargain, as are local Vins de Pays. Best years: 1991 90 89 88.

ST-ÉMILION AC *Bordeaux, France* The Roman hill town of St-Émilion is the centre of Bordeaux's most historic wine region. The finest vineyards are on the Côtes or steep slopes around the town although a second large area to the west, called the Graves, contains two of St-Émilion's most famous properties, CHEVAL-BLANC and FIGEAC. It is a region of smallholdings, with over 1000 different properties and consequently the co-op is important. The dominant Merlot grape gives wines with a come hither softness and sweetness rare in red wine. Best producers: Bellefont-Belcier, Fombrauge, Laroque, Monbousquet, Union des Producteurs. Best years: 1990 89 88 86 85.

ST-ÉMILION GRAND CRU CLASSÉ AC *Bordeaux, France* St-Émilion's top quality AC. This is divided into the unofficial categories of Grand Cru Classé and Premier Grand Cru Classé. The 1985 classification lists 63 Grands Crus Classés. Top wines in this category are better value than Premiers Grands Crus Classés and can age for 10–15 years. Best producers: l'ANGELUS★★, l'ARROSEE★★, BALESTARD-LA-TONNELLE★, Canon la Gaffelière★★, Fonplégade★, Pavie-Decesse★, Tertre Rôteboeuf★★, Troplong-Mondot★★. Best years: 1990 89 88 86 85 83 82 79 78.

ST-ÉMILION PREMIER GRAND CRU CLASSÉ *Bordeaux, France* St-Émilion élite divided into two categories – 'A' and 'B', with only the much more expensive CHEVAL-BLANC and AUSONE in category 'A'. There are 9 'B' châteaux, FIGEAC and CANON are the outstanding names. Best producers: AUSONE★★, CANON★★, CHEVAL-BLANC★★★, FIGEAC★★, la Gaffelière★, MAGDELAINE★★, PAVIE★★. Best years: 1990 89 88 86 85 83 82 79.

ST-ESTÈPHE AC *Haut-Médoc, Bordeaux, France* Large AC north of PAUILLAC with 5 Classed Growths. St-Estèphe wines have high tannin levels but given time (10–20 years' aging for full development) those sought-after flavours of blackcurrant and cedarwood do peek out. Best producers: Andron-Blanquet, CALON-SEGUR★, COS D'ESTOURNEL★★★, Cos Labory★, HAUT-MARBUZET★★, LAFON-ROCHET★★, Lilian-Ladouys★, MEYNEY★, MONTROSE★★, les Ormes-de-Pez★, de PEZ★★. Best years: 1990 89 88 86 85 83 82 78 75.

ST-GEORGES-ST-ÉMILION AC *Bordeaux, France* The best satellite ST-EMILION with lovely soft wines that can still age for 6–10 years. Best producers: Bélair-Montaiguillon, Calon Cap d'Or, Ch. St-Georges★, Maquin St-Georges★, Tour-du-Pas-St-Georges★. Best years: 1990 89 1988 85 83 82.

ST HALLETT *Barossa Valley, South Australia* Larger than life Bob McLean manages this revitalized winery which makes Old Block Shiraz ★★, one of the valley's best reds, using very old vines and open fermenters. Sémillon-Sauvignon Blanc ★★ and Chardonnay ★ are excellent modern whites. Best years: 1991 90 89 88.

ST HELENA *Canterbury, South Island, New Zealand* This winery achieved fame with New Zealand's first outstanding Pinot Noir in 1982. Finally found form again with 1989★★ and 90★★. Also good Pinot Blanc ★ and Pinot Gris ★. Best years: 1990 89.

ST HUBERTS *Yarra Valley, Victoria, Australia* Ex-SEPPELT winemaker Brian Fletcher turns out a delightful range of table wines at this reborn property, famous in the 19th century. Today, crystal-clean Chardonnay★★, fragrant Pinot Noir ★ and elegant, modern Cabernet-Merlot ★★ stand out. Best years: 1991 90 88 87.

ST-JOSEPH AC *Rhône Valley, France* Large mainly red AC, on the opposite bank of the Rhône to HERMITAGE. Made from Syrah, the red wines have a rich, mouthfilling fruit and an irresistible blackcurrant richness. Brilliant at only 1–2 years they can last for up to 8 years. There is only a little white made and with up-to-date wine-making these are usually pleasant, flowery wines for chilling and drinking without too much ceremony at a year old or so. FLORENTIN makes a rare, hefty, old-style gobsmacker. Best producers: (reds) CHAPOUTIER, CHAVE★★, COURSODON★★, Gonon★, GRAILLOT, Gripa★, Grippat★, JABOULET★★, Marsanne, ST-DESIRAT-CHAMPAGNE co-op★★; (whites) FLORENTIN★, Grippat★, Trollat★. Best years: (reds) 1991 90 89 88 85; (whites) 1991 90 89 88.

ST-JULIEN AC *Haut-Médoc, Bordeaux, France* For many, St-Julien produces perfect claret, with an ideal balance between opulence and austerity and between the brashness of youth and the genius of maturity. It is the smallest of the HAUT-MEDOC ACs but almost all is first-rate vineyard land and quality is high. Best producers: BEYCHEVELLE★★, DUCRU-BEAUCAILLOU★★★, GLORIA★★, GRUAUD-LAROSE★★★, LAGRANGE★★, LEOVILLE-BARTON★★★, LEOVILLE-LAS-CASES★★★, LEOVILLE-POYFERRE★★, ST-PIERRE★★, TALBOT★★. Best years: 1990 89 88 86 85 83 82 81 79 78.

ST-NICOLAS-DE-BOURGUEIL AC *Loire Valley, France* An enclave of just under 500ha (1250 acres) within the larger BOURGUEIL AC. Almost all the wine is red and with the same piercing red fruit flavours of Bourgueil, but a little less weight. They are drinkable at 2–3 years, but especially in warm vintages are much better after 7–10 years. Best producers: Audebert, Jamet★★, Mabileau★, Taluau★, Vallée★. Best years: 1990 89 88 86 85 83.

ST-PÉRAY AC *Rhône Valley, France* Mainly rather hefty, Champagne-method sparkling wine from Marsanne and Roussanne grapes from vineyards across the river from Valence in the northern Rhône. There is a little still white which is usually dry and stolid. Best producers: Chaboud, CLAPE, DELAS, Juge, Thiers, Voge. Best years: 1991 90 89.

CH. ST-PIERRE ★★ *St-Julien AC, Haut-Médoc, Bordeaux, France* Small ST-JULIEN property making wines which have become much lusher and richer since 1982, with far more new oak spice. Drinkable early, but top vintages can improve for 20 years. Best years: 1990 89 88 86 85 83 81 79 75.

ST-ROMAIN AC *Côte de Beaune, Burgundy, France* Out-of-the-way village producing red wines with a firm, bitter-sweet cherrystone fruit and flinty-dry whites which can vary between the austerely acid and the quirkily old-style. Both are usually good value by Burgundian standards, and may take at least 5 years to open out. Best producers: (reds) Bazenet, Buisson, Thévenin-Monthélie★; (whites) Bazenet★, Buisson, Gras★, JAFFELIN★, Olivier LEFLAIVE★, Taupenot, Thévenin-Monthélie★. Best years: (reds) 1990 89 88 87 85 83 82; (whites) 1990 89 88 86 85.

ST-VÉRAN AC *Mâconnais, Burgundy, France*   Often thought of as a POUILLY-FUISSE understudy. This is gentle, fairly fruity, and normally unoaked Mâconnais Chardonnay at its best and the overall quality is good. The price is fair too. Drink young. Best producers: Chagny, Corsin★, Duperron, DUBOEUF★, Grégoire, Loron, Lycée Agricole de Davayé, Prissé co-op, Tissier★, Vincent★ (a bigger, weightier style). Best years: 1991 90 89 88.

DOM. STE-ANNE *Côtes du Rhône AC, Rhône Valley, France*   Top-notch COTES DU RHONE and COTES DU RHONE-VILLAGES produced by Burgundian ex-patriate, Guy Steinmaier. There are several reasonably priced, and marvellously full throttle reds – COTES DU RHONE ★, COTES DU RHONE-VILLAGES ★, Cuvée Notre Dame des Cellettes ★★ and Cuvée St-Gervais ★★ – as well as an extremely successful Viognier ★★. Best years: 1991 90 89 88 86 85 83 82.

STE-CROIX-DU-MONT AC *Bordeaux, France*   The best of the 3 sweet wine ACs which gaze jealously at SAUTERNES and BARSAC across the Garonne (the others are Cadillac and LOUPIAC). Usually the wine is mildly sweet, rather than splendidly rich, and is best as an aperitif or with hors d'oeuvres. The top wines can age for at least a decade. Best producers: Loubens, Lousteau-Vieil★, de Tastes★. Best years: 1990 89 88 86 85 83.

SAINTSBURY *Carneros AVA, California, USA*   New wave, deeply committed winery only using Carneros fruit. Their Pinot Noir wines are brilliant examples of the perfume and fruit quality of Carneros. The Reserve ★★ is deeper and oakier and Garnet ★ is a delicious, fragrant, lighter style. Chardonnay ★ and Reserve Chardonnay ★★ are similarly impressive. Best years: 1991 90 88 87.

CH. DE SALES ★ *Pomerol AC, Bordeaux, France*   This is POMEROL's largest property and most attractive château. Tucked away in the north-western tip of the AC, where the soil is sandier, the wines never have the tingling excitement of the best Pomerols but they are reasonably priced. Quick to mature they are still capable of aging for 10 years in bottle. Best years: 1990 89 88 85 83 82 81.

SALICE SALENTINO DOC *Puglia, Italy*   Probably the best of the DOCs in the Salento peninsula, turning out wines that are deep-coloured, ripe and chocolaty, acquiring hints of roast chestnuts and prunes with age. The wine is made from the ubiquitous Negroamaro, tempered by a dash of the perfumed Malvasia Nera. Best producers: Candido, De Castris, Taurino, Vallone.

SAN LUIS OBISPO COUNTY *California, USA*   Central Coast county best known for Chardonnay, Pinot Noir and Cabernet Sauvignon. There are four AVAs – Edna Valley, Paso Robles, Santa Maria Valley and York Mountain, each of which has already grown some outstanding grapes and will surely grow a lot more. Best producers: Chamisal, Clairborne & Churchill, Corbett Canyon, Creston Manor, Eberle, Edna Valley, Maison Deutz, Martin Brothers, RIDGE, Tobias.

SANCERRE AC *Loire Valley, France*   Sancerre mania broke out in the 1970s, firstly with the white wine which can provide the perfect expression of the bright green tang of the Sauvignon grape, then with the reds and rosés which are made from Pinot Noir. Consequently the wine is rather expensive. The whites, from a good grower in one of the best villages like Bué, Chavignol, Verdigny or Ménétréol, can be one of the most deliciously refreshing white wines of France, but the reds and rosés are less good as the Pinot Noir doesn't always ripen fully this far north. Drink the wines young. Best producers: Bailly-Reverdy★, Bourgeois★, Cotat★★, Crochet★★, Daulny, Alain Dezat★, Pierre Dezat, Dupuy-Chavignol, Foussier, Lalone, Merlin, Migeon, Millérioux★, Natter, Picard, Reverdy, Jean-Max Roger★, Vacheron★, Vatan★. Best years: 1990 89 88.

SANDEMAN *Port DOC, Douro, Portugal*   No longer one of the 'first growths' of port, Sandeman say they are trying to improve quality. We'll wait and see. Best at the moment are their aged tawnies, Royal 10-year-old ★ and Imperial 20-year-old ★★. Best years: (vintage ports) 1980 77 67 66 63.

SANFORD *Santa Barbara, California, USA*   Richard Sanford was one of the first Californians to appreciate the importance of matching specific vineyard sites with suitable grape varieties, and one of the first to seek out cool, slow-ripening conditions especially for Pinot Noir. He planted the great Benedict vineyard in the Santa Ynez Valley in 1971, thus establishing Santa Ynez and Santa Barbara as potentially top quality vineyard regions. It has taken a fair while for it to become established, but Sanford is now one of the leading Santa Barbara wineries making sharply focused, green-edged Pinot Noir★, Chardonnay★★ and Sauvignon Blanc★ mostly from Santa Maria fruit. And that Benedict vineyard, after a distinctly chequered existence, is finally back under Sanford's control – and may yet produce California's greatest Pinot Noir.

SANGIOVESE   The Sangiovese rivals Barbera and Trebbiano Toscano as the most widely planted grape variety in Italy. It is grown from Lombardy in the north through Romagna, the Marche and Umbria in central Italy to Puglia and Sicily in the deep south, but reaches its greatest heights in central Tuscany. Basically there are two types of Sangiovese grape: the large berried Sangiovese Grosso, grown in Montalcino (where it is known as Brunello), Montepulciano (Prugnolo) and Romagna; and the smaller berried Sangiovese Piccolo, which predominates in CHIANTI, where it is sometimes referred to as Sangioveto. Styles range from pale, lively and cherryish through the vivacious, mid-range Chiantis to the top Riservas and super-Vino da Tavolas. At the latter level, Sangiovese shows itself to be one of the great grapes of the world.

227

SANTA BARBARA COUNTY *California, USA*   Central Coast county just north of Los Angeles best known for Chardonnay, Riesling and Pinot Noir. The main AVAs are Santa Ynez Valley and a portion of the Santa Maria Valley, both leading areas for Pinot Noir. Best producers: AU BON CLIMAT, Babcock, Byron, Firestone, Qupé, SANFORD, Zaca Mesa.

SANTA MADDALENA DOC *Alto Adige, Italy*   Light, delicate wine from the Schiava grape grown in Santa Maddalena, a small village on the outskirts of Bolzano. It has an attractive perfume of black cherries, cream and bacon smoke, and can be improved no end with the legal addition of up to 10% of Lagrein. The best wines are generally from the original Classico zone. Ideally drink the wine really young but it can age. Best producers: Gojer, LAGEDER, Plattner, Hans Rottensteiner★, Heinrich Rottensteiner★.

SANTA RITA *Maipo/Curicó, Chile*   Having produced superb initial releases in Cabernet Sauvignon and Chardonnay, the standard became incredibly patchy and though the latest signs are of a return to quality, I'm still not totally convinced. Medalla Real wines can be ★ and the 120 reds provide reasonable gluggers.

SANTENAY AC *Côte de Beaune, Burgundy, France*   Santenay is best known for its therapeutic hot springs and casino but there are some good wines too. Though the reds often promise a good ripe flavour, the end result is usually just a little disappointing. It is worth aging Santenay for at least 4–6 years in the hope that the wine will open out. The best Santenay whites, as with the reds, come from Les Gravières Premier Cru on the border with CHASSAGNE-MONTRACHET, one of Burgundy's top white wine villages. Best producers: (reds) Belland, Clair, Fleurot-Larose, Girardin★, Lequin-Roussot, Mestre, Bernard Morey★, Pousse d'Or★, Prieur-Brunet, Roux★; (whites) JAFFELIN, Lequin-Roussot, Maufoux, Prieur-Brunet. Best years: (reds) 1990 89 88 87 85 83 82; (whites) 1990 89 88 86 85.

SARDINIA *Italy*   This huge, hilly Mediterranean island has been conquered by successive hordes of invaders over the centuries, yet it retains a uniquely Sardinian flavour. Grapes of Spanish origin, like the white Vermentino and Torbato and the red Monica, Cannonau and Carignano, dominate production, but they vie with a Malvasia of Greek origin and natives like Nuragus and Vernaccia. The cooler, northern part favours whites, especially Vermentino, while the southern and eastern parts are best suited to reds from Cannonau and Monica. Traditionally, the wines were powerful, alcoholic monsters, but the current trend is for a lighter, more drinkable style. See also Anghelu Ruju, Monica di Sardegna, Vernaccia di Oristano.

SASSICAIA, VINO DA TAVOLA ★★★ *Tuscany, Italy*   This Cabernet Sauvignon/Cabernet Franc blend from the Tuscan coast has perhaps done more than any other wine to gain credibility abroad for Italy. The vines were originally planted in 1944 to satisfy

Marchese Incisa della Rochetta's thirst for fine red Bordeaux, something which was in short supply during the war. The wine remained for family consumption until nephew Piero Antinori (of ANTINORI) and his winemaker, Giacomo Tachis, persuaded the Marchese to refine his production practices and release several thousand bottles from the 1968 vintage. Since then, its fame has increased as it consistently proved itself, in numerous blind tastings, to be one of the world's great Cabernets, combining a fine blackcurrant power of blistering intensity with a heavenly scent of cigars kept cool and moist in caskets of sandalwood. Best years: 1990 88 85 82 81 78 75 71 68.

SAUMUR AC *Loire Valley, France*   Dry white wines from the market town of Saumur. They can be rather harsh, but crisp and fruity wines come from the St-Cyr-en-Bourg co-op. The reds are light and rather sharp but refreshing in warm vintages. There is a little not bad off-dry Cabernet rosé. Best producers: Fourrier, Pérols, St-Cyr-en-Bourg co-op. Best years: 1990 89 88.

SAUMUR-CHAMPIGNY AC *Loire Valley, France*   Saumur's best red wine. Cabernet Franc is the main grape and in hot years the wine can be superb, with a piercing scent of blackcurrants and raspberries easily overpowering the earthy finish. Delicious young, it can age for 6–10 years. Best producers: Chaintre★, Duveau★, FILLIATREAU★★, Legrand★, St-Cyr-en-Bourg co-op, Sanzay★. Best years: 1990 89 88 85.

SAUMUR MOUSSEUX AC *Loire Valley, France*   Inexpensive Champagne-method sparkling wines made mainly from Chenin Blanc. Adding Chardonnay and Cabernet Franc makes Saumur Mousseux softer and more interesting. Usually non-vintage. Small quantities of rosé are also made. Best producers: ACKER-MAN-LAURANCE, BOUVET-LADUBAY★, GRATIEN & MEYER★, Langlois-Château★, St-Cyr-en-Bourg co-op★.

SAUTERNES AC *Bordeaux, France*   The name Sauternes is synonymous with the best sweet wines in the world. Sauternes and neighbouring BARSAC both lie on the banks of the little river Ciron north of the town of Langon and are two of the very few areas in France where noble rot occurs naturally. Production of these intense, sweet, luscious wines from botrytized grapes is a risk-laden and extremely expensive affair and the wines are never going to be cheap. From good producers (most of which are Crus Classés) the wines are worth their high price – with 14% alcohol they have a deep, mouth-coating richness full of flavours of pineapples, peaches, syrup and spice. Good vintages should be aged for 5–10 years and often twice as long. Best producers: BASTOR-LAMONTAGNE★★, de FARGUES★★, GILETTE★★, GUIRAUD★★, les Justices★, LAFAURIE-PEYRAGUEY★★, Lamothe-Guignard★, de Malle, RABAUD-PROMIS★★, Rayne-Vigneau★, RIEUSSEC★★, ST-AMAND★★, SUDUIRAUT★★, d'YQUEM★★★. Best years: 1990 89 88 86 83 81 80 76 75 71 70. See also Noble Rot.

SAUVIGNON BLANC

Of all the world's grapes, the Sauvignon Blanc is leader of the 'love it or loathe it' pack. It veers from being wildly fashionable to totally out of favour depending upon where it is grown and which country's consumers are being consulted. But Sauvignon is always at its best when full rein is allowed to its very particular talents because this grape does give intense, sometimes shocking flavours, and doesn't take kindly to being put into a straitjacket.

WINE STYLES

Sancerre-style Sauvignon Although initially used largely as a blending grape in Bordeaux where its characteristic green tang injected a bit of life into the blander, waxier Sémillon, Sauvignon first became trendy as the grape used for Sancerre, a bone-dry Loire white whose green gooseberry fruit and slightly smoky perfume inspired the winemakers of other countries to try to emulate, then often surpass the original model.

But Sauvignon is only successful where it is respected. The grape is not as easy to grow as Chardonnay, and the flavours are not so adaptable. Yet the range of styles Sauvignon produces is as wide, if less subtly nuanced, as Chardonnay. It is highly successful when picked not too ripe, fermented cool in stainless steel, and bottled early. This is the Sancerre model followed by growers elsewhere in France, in Italy and Eastern Europe, in South Africa and Chile up to a point, but above all in New Zealand.

Using oak Sauvignon also lends itself to fermentation in barrel and aging in new oak, though less happily than does Chardonnay. This is the model of the Graves region of Bordeaux, although generally here Sémillon would be blended in with Sauvignon to good effect.

New Zealand again excels at this style, though there are good examples from California, Australia, Italy and South Africa. Here the acidity that is Sauvignon's great strength should ideally remain, but there should be a dried apricots kind of fruit and a spicy, biscuity softness from the oak. These oaky styles are best drunk either within a year or so, or after aging for 5 years or so, and can produce remarkable, strongly individual flavours – that you'll either love or loath.

Sweet wines Sauvignon is also a crucial ingredient in the great sweet wines of Sauternes and Barsac from Bordeaux, though it is less susceptible than its partner Sémillon to the sweetness-enhancing 'noble rot' fungus or botrytis.

Sweet wines from the USA, South Africa, Australia, and, inevitably, New Zealand range from the interesting to the outstanding – but the characteristic green tang of the Sauvignon should stay in the wine even at ultra-sweet levels.

BEST PRODUCERS

Top class Sauvignons

France (Pouilly-Fumé) Bailly, Didier Dagueneau, André Dezat; (Sancerre) Bourgeois, Cotat, Crochet, Jean-Max Roger; (Pessac-Léognan) Couhins-Lurton.

New Zealand Cloudy Bay, Collards, Hunters, Matua Valley, Vavasour, Villa Maria, Waipara Springs, Wairau River.

Other good Sauvignons

Australia Jim Barry, Cullens, Hill-Smith, Pike, Schinus Molle, Taltarni.

Chile Caliterra, Errázuriz (from 1992).

France (Bergerac) la Jaubertie; (Touraine) Oisly-et-Thésée.

Hungary Gyngyos Estate.

New Zealand Montana, Rothbury, Selaks, Stoneleigh, Te Kairanga.

South Africa Neil Ellis (Whitehall), Far Enough, Oak Village, Van Loveren.

SAVENNIÈRES AC *Loire Valley, France*   Wines from Chenin Blanc,
produced on steep vineyards above the Loire south of Anjou and
which have always been thought of as steely and dry. They also
used to appear in semi-sweet and sweet styles, and with the
great 1989 and 90 vintages, we've seen a revival of these. The
top wines usually need about 8 years to mature, and can age for
longer. There are two extremely good Grand Cru vineyards with
their own ACs, La Coulée-de-Serrant and La Roche-aux-Moines.
Best producers: Baumard★★, Bizolière★, Brincard, Cham-
boureau★, Clos de la Coulée-de-Serrant★★, Closel★, d'Épiré★★.
Best years: 1990 89 88 85 83 82 78 76 71 70 69 66.

SAVIGNY-LÈS-BEAUNE AC *Côte de Beaune, Burgundy, France*
Large, mainly red wine village. The reds are usually fairly light
and are best drunk after 2–4 years, although the top Premiers
Crus are more substantial yet rarely shed their rather earthy
core. The whites manage to show a bit of dry, nutty class after
3–4 years. The wines are generally reasonably priced. Best producers: Bize, Camus-Bruchon★, Écard, Fougeray★, Girardin★,
Guillemot, LEROY, Maréchal★, Pavelot★, TOLLOT-BEAUT★. Best years:
(reds) 1990 89 88 87 85 83 82 80 78; (whites) 1990 89 88 86.

SAVOIE *France*   Savoie's high alpine vineyards, scattered between
Lake Geneva and Grenoble and on the banks of the Rhône and
Isère rivers, produce fresh, snappy white wines with loads of
taste, mainly due to the Altesse (or Roussette) grape. There are
some attractive light reds and rosés too, mainly from a group of
villages south of Chambéry and in hot years some positively
Rhône-like reds from the Mondeuse grape. Most of the better
wines use the VIN DE SAVOIE AC. See also Crépy, Seyssel.

SCHEUREBE   Very popular Silvaner x Riesling crossing most widespread in Germany's Rheinhessen and Rheinpfalz. Also planted
in Austria. Scheurebe is suitable for higher Prädikat wines such
as Trockenbeerenauslese and Eiswein. When ripe it has a marvellous flavour of honey and the pithiest of pink grapefruit.

SCHIOPETTO *Friuli-Venezia Giulia, Italy*   Mario Schiopetto is one of
the legends of Italian viniculture. Pioneering the development of
scented varietals and above all high quality, intensely concentrated white wines from Friuli and in particular COLLIO. Most
outstanding are his Tocai★★ and Pinot Bianco★★, both of
which begin life as intense but closed wines, opening out with
age to display a myriad range of flavours.

SCHLOSS BÖCKELHEIM *Nahe, Germany*   Both the name of a
Bereich and a village. The village's best known vineyard is the
Kupfergrübe but there are good wines from Felsenberg,
Mühlberg and Königsfels too. Best producers (in the village): Paul
ANHEUSER, CRUSIUS, Hermann Dönnhof, Staatlichen Weinbaud-
omänen Niederhausen-Schlossböckelheim.

SCHLOSS REINHARTSHAUSEN *Erbach, Rheingau, Germany*
Estate formerly wholly owned by the Hohenzollern family which ruled Prussia and then Germany until 1918. There are several fine vineyard sites, including the Erbacher Marcobrunn. There is an interesting Weissburgunder/Chardonnay blend from its vines in Erbacher Rheinhell, an island in the middle of the Rhine. Superb classic Rieslings★★ (some ★★★) were made in both 1989 and 90. Also good Sekt. Best years: 1990 89 88 85 83 79.

SCHLOSS SAARSTEIN *Serrig, Saar, Germany*   This estate makes some of the best wines in the Saar. The Riesling Dry can taste a little austere; better balanced are wines like the Serriger Riesling Kabinett ★★ or Spätlese ★★ which keep the startling acidity but coat it with fruit. Saarstein makes an occasional Eiswein ★★★. Best years: 1990 89 88 86 85.

SCHLOSS VOLLRADS *Oestrich-Winkel, Rheingau, Germany*
Schloss Vollrads is owned by Graf Matuschka-Greiffenclau, who has been making it his business for some years now to tell people how to drink his wines with food. To anyone brought up in France his ideas would sound decidedly weird, but Matuschka does have his followers, though few live outside his native Germany. Most of his wines are angular, austere and lean, but he occasionally produces Spätlese and Auslese beauties as good as any in the Rhine Valley. Best years: 1990 89 88 85 83.

SCHLOSSGUT DIEL *Burg Layen, Nahe, Germany*   Armin Diel used to attract a lot of publicity by making unconventional wines on his Nahe estate, and he was in the vanguard of the move towards 'dry' wines in Germany. Diel was possibly the first man in Germany to play the new oak fermentation card and he continues to use it for wines like his Tafelwein Grauburgunder 1988. Some may find the oakiness exaggerated. Diel has returned to making more traditional wines on his Dorsheimer Goldloch site where in 1990 he made excellent Spätlese ★★ and Auslese★★ wines . Best years: 1990 89 88.

SCHRAMSBERG *Napa Valley, California, USA*   The first Californian winery to make Champagne-method sparkling wine from the classic Champagne grapes. Though all releases do not achieve the same heights, the best wines can be unequalled in California – and in most of Champagne too. The Crémant ★ is an attractive sweetish sparkler, the Blanc de Noirs ★★ and the Blanc de Blancs ★★ stand out. Top of the line is the Reserve Brut ★★★ which is frequently world class. There is also a more basic sparkler called Mirabelle .

SEAVIEW *Southern Vales, South Australia*   Best known for good, mass-market fizz★ but, along with commercial quality reds and whites occasionally produces super export selection Cabernet★.

SEC French for dry.
SECCO Italian for dry.
SECO Spanish for dry.

SEIFRIED ESTATE *Nelson, South Island, New Zealand* Established in 1974 by Austrian, Hermann Seifried and his New Zealand wife Agnes. The best wines include botrytized Riesling ★★ and Gewürztraminer ★★ and Sauvignon Blanc ★★ made from Marlborough grapes. The Redwood Valley label is used in export markets. Best years: 1992 91 90 89.

SEKT German for sparkling wine. The wine will be entirely German only if it is called 'Deutscher Sekt' or 'Sekt bA'. The best wines are Champagne method and will occasionally be 100% Riesling. Best producers: Deutz & Gelderman, DEINHARD (Lila), SCHLOSS REIN-HARTSHAUSEN.

SELAKS *Kumeu, Auckland, North Island* A long-established winery making very slow-developing Sauvignon Blanc/Sémillon★★ as well as good Sauvignon Blanc ★, Chardonnay★ and Riesling . Best years: 1992 91 89.

SELBACH-OSTER *Zeltingen, Mosel, Germany* Very good estate in the middle Mosel with excellent vineyards in Zeltingen, Bernkastel, Graach and Wehlen. Best years: 1990 89 88 85.

SÉLECTION DE GRAINS NOBLES *Alsace AC, Alsace, France* This term is used for late-harvest wines made exclusively from super-ripe Muscat, Riesling, Gewürztraminer or Pinot Gris grapes. Usually sweet or medium sweet and often affected by noble rot, they are among Alsace's finest, but are very expensive to produce (and to buy). Best producers: HUGEL★★★, Schlumberger★★, TRIMBACH★★, ZIND-HUMBRECHT★★. Best years: 1990 89 83 76.

SÉMILLON Found mainly in south-west France especially in the sweet wines of SAUTERNES and BARSAC where, because of its thin skin, it is prone to the noble rot fungus. Sémillon is also blended with Sauvignon Blanc to make dry wine and almost all the great GRAVES Classed Growths are based on this blend. Performs well in Australia (aged Sémillon, particularly from the Hunter Valley, can be quite wonderful) on its own or as a useful blender with Chardonnay. It is blended with Sauvignon in New Zealand, California and Washington State. Sémillon is undistinguished in Chile and Argentina and slightly better in South Africa.

SEÑORÍO DE SARRÍA *Navarra DO, Navarra, Spain* The wines from this extensive and beautiful NAVARRA estate have recently improved greatly after massive investment. The whites and rosés are now fresh and fruity and recent reds ★ (mostly Tempranillo with some Cabernet Sauvignon) are rich and flavourful.

SEPPELT *Barossa Valley, South Australia* Leading Australian bubbly producer, from mass-produced Great Western 'champagne' up to excellent Fleur de Lys ★, Jean Trouette ★★ and Salinger ★★, all made by the Champagne-method from Pinot Noir and Chardonnay. These wines are pristine and fruity without much yeast influence. The table wines are generally extremely good, especially Great Western Hermitage (Shiraz) ★★ and Chardonnay ★★, Dorrien Cabernet ★, Partalunga Riesling ★, and the wines from super-cool Drumborg. Seppelt also makes wild and wonderful sparkling red Shiraz ★★.

SETÚBAL DOC *Setúbal Peninsula, Portugal* Undistinguished fortified wine from the south of Lisbon, originally based on Moscatel, but now containing so little that the grape name is banned from the label. **Best producers:** FONSECA SUCCESSORES, J P VINHOS.

SETÚBAL PENINSULA *Oeste, Portugal* Area south of Lisbon with two IPR regions, Arrábida and Palmela. SETUBAL – decent enough fortified wine – is the local celebrity but is fast being outstripped by excellent table wines, particularly red from Periquita with Cabernet and Merlot. **Best producers:** FONSECA SUCCESSORES, J P VINHOS.

SEYSSEL AC *Savoie, France* Known for its feather-light, sparkling wine, Seyssel Mousseux. With the lovely sharp, peppery bite of the Molette and Altesse grapes smoothed out with a creamy yeast, it is an ideal summer gulper. The still white is light, and florally. **Best producers:** Mollex, Varichon & Clerc★.

SEYVAL BLANC Hybrid grape (Seibel 5656 x Rayon d'Or) whose disease resistance and ability to continue ripening in a damp autumn makes it a useful variety in England and New York State. Gives clean, sappy, grapefruit-edged wines that sometimes give a very passable imitation of bone-dry Chablis.

SHAFER *Stags Leap, California, USA* One of the best of the newer Napa wineries making unusually fruity Cabernet★ and Merlot ★, and crisp, appley Chardonnay★.

SHERRY See Jerez y Manzanilla DO, page 146.

SHIRAZ See Syrah, page 242.

SICILY *Italy* It is very hot on the island, and the best wines are the high-strength examples that make use of these conditions and those that are fortified (MARSALA).  Yet classy table wines can be produced in the cooler uplands. Grillo and Inzolia are the best white grapes, followed by Catarratto, but the boring Trebbiano is becoming far too common in Sicily. The best Sicilian reds come from Calabese, Perricone and Nerello Mascalese. See also Alcamo, Corvo, Moscato Passito di Pantelleria, Vecchio Samperi.

SILVER OAK WINE CELLARS *Napa Valley, California, USA* One of California's best Cabernet Sauvignon producers with bottlings from Alexander Valley ★★ grapes and Napa Valley ★ as well as a superlative limited release Bonny's Vineyard ★★★. They are forward, wonderfully generous, fruity wines, impossible not to enjoy young, yet with great staying power. **Best years:** 1991 90 88 87 86 85 84 83 82.

SIMI *Sonoma Valley, California, USA*   Historic winery which has been revitalized by the current owner, Moët-Hennessy, also owner of DOMAINE CHANDON. The major turning point came when Zelma Long arrived as winemaker in 1981. Long has brought the Cabernet Sauvignon★, Chardonnay★★ and Sauvignon★ Blanc up to high standards, and some of the Reserve bottlings of Cabernet and Chardonnay achieve ★★★ heights.

SION *Valais, Switzerland*   Considered one of the top wine villages in the Valais and best known for its pure Chasselas Fendant. Best producers: Michel Clavien★, Domaine du Mont d'Or★.

CH. SIRAN★★ *Margaux AC, Cru Bourgeois, Haut-Médoc, Bordeaux, France*   Consistently good claret, approachable young, but with enough structure to last for as long as 20 years. Second wine: Ch. Bellegarde. Best years: 1990 89 86 85 83 82.

ROBERT SKALLI *Languedoc-Roussillon, France*   An increasingly important name in the south of France, Robert Skalli produces modern, varietal wines under the catch-all Vins de Pays d'OC label. The oak-influenced Chardonnay★, Sauvignon Blanc★ and Cabernet Sauvignon★, all sold under the name Fortant de France, are Skalli's best wines, but look out, too, for his ILE DE BEAUTE wines★. Skalli also owns the St Supéry winery in California. Best years: 1991 90 89.

SLIVEN *Southern Region, Bulgaria*   This pioneering winery is now proving its potential with some of Bulgaria's best, most cleanly varietal Chardonnay. The reds, like the juicy Merlot/Pinot Noir Country Wine, deliver the goods, too.

CH. SMITH-HAUT-LAFITTE *Pessac-Léognan AC, Cru Classé de Graves, Bordeaux, France*   Large property best known for its reds★ even though these have never been terribly exciting. However since the mid-1980s there have been distinct signs of improvement. There is only a little white ★★★ (from 100% Sauvignon) but it is a shining example of tip top modern white Bordeaux. Best years: (reds) 1990 89 88 86 85 83; (whites) 1990 89 88 87 86 85.

SMITH WOODHOUSE *Port DOC, Portugal*   Underrated but consistently satisfying port shipper. The Smith Woodhouse vintage ★★ is worth looking out for, and their Late Bottled Vintage Port ★★ is the rich and characterful, figgy, unfiltered type rarely made now. Best years: (vintage ports) 1985 83 80 77 70 63.

SOAVE DOC *Veneto, Italy*   One of the most abused of all Italian wine names but from the Classico region in the hills above Verona, the Garganega and Trebbiano di Soave grapes can produce ripe, nutty scented wines of great quality. However 70% of all Soave comes from the flat fertile plains and much of this is cynically blended by merchants into a limp, tasteless white. Luckily the dominant local co-op can produce excellent wine. Best producers: ANSELMI★, Bertani, Cantina Sociale di Soave, Gini, MASI, PIEROPAN★★, Pra, Suavia, Tommasi.

CH. SOCIANDO-MALLET★★ *Haut-Médoc AC, Cru Bourgeois, Haut-Médoc, Bordeaux, France* Owner Jean Gautreau has made Sociando-Mallet one of Bordeaux's rising stars. The wine is dark and tannic with every sign of great classic red Bordeaux flavours to come if you can hang on for 10–15 years. Best years: 1990 89 88 86 85 83 82 78 76 75.

SOGRAPE *Portugal* Sogrape proves that it is possible to be the biggest *and* among the best and can be credited with revolutionizing quality in some of Portugal's most reactionary wine regions. Mateus Rosé was (and still is) the company's golden egg, but Sogrape makes good to excellent wines in BAIRRADA, DAO, DOURO and VINHO VERDE as well, and subsidiary FERREIRA provides top-flight ports. From Bairrada the Reserva Branco ★★ is a nutty, oaky white, previously unparalleled in Portugal. First signs from the new winery in Dão are hopeful; Grão Vasco is set to improve, Quinta dos Carvalhais Branco ★ is oaky, marmalady and characterful, and the Duque de Viseu red ★★ is crammed with ripe, oaky mulberry fruit that one had no idea Dão had the potential to produce.

SOLERA A traditional Spanish system of blending fortified wines, especially sherry and MONTILLA-MORILES. About a third of the wine from the oldest barrels is bottled, and the barrels are topped up with slightly younger wine from another set of barrels and so on, with a minimum of three sets of barrels. The idea is that the younger wine takes on the character of older wine left in the barrels, as well as keeping the blend refreshed.

SOMONTANO DO *Aragón, Spain* In the foothills of the Pyrenees, this region is an up-and-coming star. Reds and rosés from the local grapes (Moristel and Tempranillo) can be light, fresh and flavourful, the whites fresh and pleasant, and new plantings of French varieties are already yielding promising wines. Best producers: COVISA★, Somontano de Sobrarbe co-op★.

SONOMA COUNTY *California, USA* Unlike the compact growing area in Napa, Sonoma is a big, sprawling county with dozens of microclimates and soil types ranging from the fairly warm Sonoma Valley/Alexander Valley region to the cool western reaches of the county and the Green Valley and lower Russian River Valley areas. Best grape varieties are Chardonnay, Cabernet Sauvignon, Sauvignon Blanc and Zinfandel. Overshadowed for many years by Napa, Sonoma is rapidly catching up in terms of wine quality and originality of flavours. Best producers: Alexander Valley Vineyards, B R Cohn, BUENA VISTA, CARMENET, CHATEAU ST JEAN, CLOS DU BOIS, De Loach, Domaine Michel, Dry Creek Vineyards, Duxoup Wine Works, Ferrari-Carano, Fisher Vineyards, Geyser Peak, Gundlach-Bundschu, LAUREL GLEN, Lyeth, Murphy-Goode, Nalle, J Pedroncelli, A Rafenelli, Ravenswood, St Francis, Seghesio, SIMI, Robert Stemmler, Rodney Strong, SONOMA-CUTRER, William Wheeler, Williams Selyem.

SONOMA-CUTRER *Sonoma, California, USA*   Crisp, pleasant but often overrated Chardonnay from three vineyards: Les Pierres is the most complex and richest of the three, often worth ★★. Cutrer ★ can also have a complexity worth waiting for but the Russian River Ranches is rather flat and ordinary.

SOUTH AUSTRALIA   Australia's biggest grape-growing state, with 25,000ha (62,000 acres) of vineyards. South Australia covers many climates and most wine styles from bulk wines to the very best. Old established areas are Barossa, Clare and Eden Valleys, Southern Vales, Langhorne Creek, Coonawarra and Riverland. Newer districts creating excitement are Adelaide Hills and Padthaway. See also Adelaide Hills, Barossa Valley, Clare Valley, Coonawarra, Padthaway, Riverland, Southern Vales.

SOUTH-WEST FRANCE   As well as the world-famous wines of Bordeaux, the south-west of France is the source of a large variety of lesser-known, inexpensive ACs, VDQS and Vins de Pays, covering no fewer than 10 different departments from the Atlantic coast to the Languedoc-Roussillon.
Bordeaux grapes (Cabernet Sauvignon, Merlot and Cabernet Franc for reds; Sauvignon Blanc, Sémillon and Muscadelle for whites) are common, but there are lots of interesting local varieties as well, such as Tannat (in MADIRAN), Petit Manseng (in JURANCON) and Mauzac (in GAILLAC). See also Bergerac, Cahors, Côtes de Duras, Côtes du Frontonnais, Côtes de Montravel, Gaillac, Monbazillac, Montravel, Pacherenc du Vic-Bihl.

SOUTHERN VALES *South Australia*   Warm, sunny maritime region just south of Adelaide, with about 45 mainly small wineries, and big boys, HARDY and SEAVIEW. Once a 'port' area, nowadays it is good for full-bodied whites and reds from Chardonnay, Sauvignon Blanc, Shiraz and Cabernet. Best producers: Chapel Hill, Chateau Reynella, Coriole, HARDY, Geoff MERRILL, Normans, PIRRAMIMMA, SEAVIEW, Wirra Wirra, Woodstock.

SPANNA, VINO DA TAVOLA *Piedmont, Italy*   I used to drink Spanna, from the northern Piedmont hills of Novara and Vercelli, for its round soft flavours of plum, chocolate and smoke, the only examples I knew of the fearsome Nebbiolo grape making a wine remotely approachable for a northern European. But then the new wave of consumer-aware producers began to influence the flavours of BAROLO and BARBARESCO and the other red wines of Roero and the Langhe hills, and in consequence Spanna began to lose importance. Sadly quality faded too. The neighbouring area of GHEMME and especially GATTINARA now far outclass it. Best producers: Traversagna, Vallana, Villa Era.

SPÄTBURGUNDER See Pinot Noir.

SPÄTLESE German for literally 'late-picked' and therefore riper grapes, but as in all Prädikat wines this is a question of must weight of the juice. In Germany the Oechsle level runs from 76 for a Mosel Riesling to 92 for a Baden Ruländer. In Austria a Spätlese must be 19 KMW or 94 Oechsle.

SPUMANTE Italian for sparkling.

SQUINZANO DOC *Puglia, Italy* The name today evokes memories of deep-coloured, high-strength wines, for it was the Italian blending wine par excellence. A blend of Negroamaro and Malvasia Nera grapes, the wines are too often clumsy, though the potential undoubtedly exists. Best producer: Villa Valletta.

STAG'S LEAP WINE CELLARS *Stags Leap, California, USA* The winery's fame was made when the 1973 vintage of Cabernet Sauvignon took first place at the Paris tasting in 1976. At its best, Stag's Leap Cabernet Sauvignon ★★ can be a stunning wine, particularly the SLV Reserve ★★ from estate vineyards; the Cask 23 Cabernet Sauvignon ★ is a good, sometimes very good but overhyped red. Recent vintages haven't seemed to measure up to earlier standards. A lot of work has gone into the Chardonnay and from the 1989 ★★ vintage the style is one of Napa's most successful. Best years: 1991 90 89 88 84 81 79 78.

STAPLE ST JAMES *Kent, England* A small but well-run vineyard near the Kent coast, whose vibrantly fruity Huxelrebe ★ is consistently one of England's best bone-dry whites.

STEIERMARK *Austria* Also known as Styria, this wine region in south-east Austria formerly covered much of Slovenia's vineyards too. The best wines are Morillon (or unoaked Chardonnay), Sauvignon Blanc and Gelber Muskateller.

STERLING VINEYARDS *Napa Valley, California, USA* Winery on an upswing at the moment. The Reserve Cabernet Sauvignon ★★ is good to very good while the regular bottling is consistently ★. Winery Lake Pinot Noir ★ is now beginning to hit its stride. The Chardonnay ★ is rich and intense but balanced. Best years: 1991 90 88.

STONYRIDGE *Waiheke Island, Auckland, North Island, New Zealand* The best winery on Waiheke Island, Stonyridge specializes in reds made from Cabernet Sauvignon, Merlot and Cabernet Franc. The top label, Larose ★★ is a remarkably Bordeaux-like red of real intensity. Best years: 1990 89 87.

CH. SUDUIRAUT ★★ *Sauternes AC, 1er Cru Classé, Bordeaux, France* Together with RIEUSSEC, Suduiraut is regarded as a close runner-up to D'YQUEM. Although the wines are delicious at only a few years old, the richness and excitement increase enormously after a decade or so and it really is worth the wait. The wine is expensive and some of the 1980s vintages, while definitely good, seem to have lacked a little of the magic needed for this kind of outlay. Best years: 1990 89 88 86 83 82 79 76.

SUHINDOL *Northern Region, Bulgaria*   The old warhorse among Bulgarian wineries, unusual in having control over its own vineyards. It has perfected the creamy, curranty, throat-soothing style of Cabernet Sauvignon now synonymous with Bulgaria, but its popularity sometimes stretches supplies a bit thin.

SUPÉRIEUR French for a wine with a higher alcohol content than the basic appellation. Bordeaux Supérieur, for example, has a minimum of 10.5% alcohol by volume, compared with 10% for straight Bordeaux. The wine is not necessarily of better quality.

SUPERIORE Italian for wines with higher alcohol and maybe more aging too.

SUTTER HOME *Napa Valley, California, USA*   Now known for White Zinfandel, Sutter Home still makes a very drinkable Amador County Zinfandel, although it doesn't achieve the intensity and richness of its Zins of the 1970s and early 1980s.

SWAN VALLEY *Western Australia*   The original Western Australian wine region, spread along the torrid, fertile silty flats of Perth's Swan River and the hottest stretch of vineyards in Australia – except for a doughty example at Alice Springs. It used to special-ize in fortified wines, but South Australia and North-East Victoria both do them better. In general the whites are rather coarse and the reds porty. Best producers: Jane Brook, Paul Conti, EVANS & TATE, HOUGHTON, Moondah Brook.

SYRAH See page 242.

LA TÂCHE AC★★★ *Grand Cru, Côte de Nuits, Burgundy, France*   Along with La ROMANÉE-CONTI, La Tâche is the greatest of the great VOSNE-ROMANÉE Grands Crus and it is similarly owned by Dom. de la ROMANÉE-CONTI. The wine has the rare ability to pro-vide layer on layer of flavours – I find it the most sensuous and emotional of all the great red wines. Keep it for 10 years or you'll only experience a fraction of the pleasures in store. Best years: 1990 89 88 87 85 84 83 82 80 79 78.

TAFELWEIN German for table wine.

TAITTINGER *Champagne AC, Champagne, France*   One of the few large independently owned Champagne houses. The top wine, Comtes de Champagne Blanc de Blancs ★★, used to be memo-rable for its creamy, foaming pleasures, but hasn't been so hot recently. Ordinary non-vintage ★ is soft and honeyed and shows the relatively high percentage of Chardonnay used by Taittinger. The rosé ★ is elegant and always enjoyable. The de luxe cuvée called Vintage Collection ★, is certainly good, but sells at a silly price. Best years: 1985 82 79.

CH. TALBOT ★★ *St-Julien AC, 4ème Cru Classé, Haut-Médoc, Bordeaux, France*   A superb Fourth Growth which really should be upgraded to a Second. The wine is chunky, soft-centred but sturdy, capable of aging extremely well for 10–20 years. Second wine: Connétable Talbot. Best years: 1990 89 88 86 85 83 82 81 79 78.

TALTARNI *Pyrenees, Victoria, Australia* Biggest winery in this region, specializing in classic, deep-flavoured, rather European-style Cabernet ★★, Syrah ★★, Merlot and Malbec; also good and improving fizz ★. Fumé Blanc ★★ is full yet tangy and gooseberry-like. Best years: (reds) 1990 88 86 84.

TASMANIA *Australia* A tiny state viticulturally with only 200ha (500 acres) of vines. The very cool climate has attracted seekers of greatness in Pinot Noir and Chardonnay, but doesn't always deliver. Even the best wineries are erratic. Top Pinots are great but they're a minority, Chardonnay is usually good and often superbly refined, and there is some delicious Riesling. Best producers: Delamere, Freycinet, HEEMSKERK, Moorilla, Notley Gorge, PIPERS BROOK, Rochecombe.

TAURASI DOC *Campania, Italy* Remarkably, a single producer – MASTROBERARDINO – and a single vintage, 1968, created the reputation for this red. The 1968 was a fabulous, deep autumnal wine, never again repeated, and showing the great potential of the Aglianico grape. But the wines do need 5–10 years aging. Best producers: MASTROBERARDINO (single-vineyard Radici★), Sruzziero. Best recent years: 1990 88 86.

TAVEL AC *Rhône Valley, France* Big, alcoholic rosé from north-west of Avignon. Grenache and Cinsaut are the main grapes. Drink Tavel at one year old if you want it cheerful, heady, yet refreshing. Best producers: Aquéria, Genestière, Trinquevedel, Vieux Moulin. Best years: 1991 90 89.

TAYLOR FLADGATE & YEATMAN *Port DOC, Douro, Portugal* The aristocrats of the port industry, 300 years old and still going strong. Their vintage ports ★★★ are always among the longest-lived and highest priced and generally among the best. Their second string wine is Quinta de Vargellas ★★, an elegant, cedary, single-Quinta vintage port made in the best of the 'off-vintages' and released when it is mature. Taylor's 20-year-old ★ is an excellent aged tawny, and Taylor's Late Bottled Vintage has improved recently – at long last – and is reasonably figgy and complex for a filtered port. Best years: (vintage ports) 1985 83 80 77 75 70 66 63.

TE MATA *Hawkes Bay, North Island, New Zealand* Hawkes Bay's glamour winery which, in quality terms, towers above all others in the area. Best known are the Te Mata reds; Coleraine ★★★ and Awatea ★; both based on Cabernet Sauvignon with varying proportions of Merlot and Cabernet Franc. Also outstanding Elston Chardonnay ★★★, a superbly crafted, toasty, spicy wine, capable of long aging. Best years: 1991 90 89 87 85 83 82.

DOM. TEMPIER *Bandol AC, Provence, France* Leading BANDOL estate, run by the dynamic Péyraud family and making rich, ageworthy reds made from a high percentage of Mourvèdre. The top wines are Migoua ★★ and La Tourtine ★★. The rosé ★ is one of Provence's best. Best years: 1990 89 88 85 84 83 82 81 79.

SYRAH

Syrah so far produces world-class wines in only two countries. In France, where Hermitage and Côte-Rôtie are two of the world's great reds; and in Australia, where, known as Shiraz, it produces some of the New World's most remarkable reds. And wherever Syrah appears it trumpets a proud and wilful personality based on loads of flavour and unmistakeable originality.

Perhaps it is exactly this proud and wilful personality that has thus far limited its spread round the warmer wine regions of the world, but there may be another reason. Syrah's heartland – Hermitage and Côte-Rôtie in the Rhône Valley – comprise a mere 270ha (670 acres) of steeply terraced vineyards producing hardly enough wine to make more than a very rarefied reputation for themselves. Growers in countries like Italy, Spain, California or Eastern Europe simply had no idea as to what kind of flavour the Syrah grape produced, so didn't copy it.

WINE STYLES
France The flavours of Syrah are most individual, but with modern vineyard practices and modern wine-making techniques they are far less daunting than they used to be. Traditional Syrah had a savage, almost coarse, throaty roar of a flavour. And from the very low-yielding Hermitage vineyards, the small grapes often showed a bitter tannic quality.

But better selections of clones in the vineyard, and the replacement of old, dirty equipment and antediluvian wine-making practices with stainless steel, clean, new wood, and scientifically correct wine-making, have revealed that Syrah in fact gives a wine with a majestic depth of fruit, all blackberry and damson, loganberry and plum, some quite strong tannin, and some tangy smoke, but also a warm creamy aftertaste, and a promise of chocolate and occasionally a scent of violets – it is these characteristics that have made Syrah increasingly popular throughout the south of France as an 'improving' variety for their rather rustic red wines.

Australia Syrah/Shiraz is Australia's most widely planted red variety, and is often used for light soft bulk wines. But it can give spectacularly good results when taken seriously – especially in the Clare, Eden Valley and Barossa regions of South Australia, in Victoria's warmer vineyards especially near Great Western, and in New South Wales' Hunter Valley. The flavours are rich, intense, thick sweet fruit coated with chocolate, and seasoned with leather, herbs and spice. It is frequently blended with Cabernet Sauvignon to add a little richness to Cabernet's more angular frame.

Other regions So far only California and South Africa elsewhere are taking Syrah seriously but results are excellent.

BEST PRODUCERS

Top Syrahs
France (Rhône Valley)
Allemande, Chapoutier
(since 1988), Chave,
A Clape, Courbis, Guigal,
Jaboulet (since 1988),
Jamet, Jasmin.

Top Shiraz
Australia Tim Adams,
Coriole, Henschke (Hill of
Grace, Mount Edelstone),
Mount Langi Ghiran,
Penfolds (Grange), Rockford,
Yarra Yerring.

Other good Syrahs
France (Languedoc) Skalli;
(Provence) Triennes; (Rhône)
Cuilleron, Cusson,
Desmeures, Graillot, B Gripa,
St-Désirat-Champagne co-
op, Vignerons Ardèchois.

USA (California) Qupé.

Other good Shiraz
Australia Bailey's, Best's,
Cape Mentelle, Henschke
(Keyneton Estate),
Lindemans, Mitchell,
McWilliams, Penfolds (Bin
28), Rothbury, Seppelt,
Taltarni, David Wynn.

South Africa Fairview Estate,
Spier Estate.

TEMPRANILLO Spain's best quality native red grape can make wonderful red wine, with wild strawberry and spicy, tobaccoey flavours. It is important in RIOJA, PENEDES (as Ull de Llebre or Ojo de Liebre), RIBERA DEL DUERO (as Tinto Fino or Tinto del País), La MANCHA and VALDEPENAS (as Cencibel), NAVARRA, SOMONTANO, UTIEL-REQUENA and TORO (as Tinto de Toro). In Portugal it is found in the DOURO and DAO (as Tinta Roriz or Aragonez). The wines can be made deliciously fruity for drinking young, but Tempranillo also matures well, and its flavours blend happily with oak.

TERLANO DOC *Alto Adige, Italy* Primarily white wine DOC zone, to the south and east of Bolzano, especially good for Chardonnay, Pinot Bianco and Sauvignon. Best producers: LAGEDER (Sauvignon Lehenhof), Schloss Schwanburg.

TEROLDEGO ROTALIANO DOC *Trentino, Italy* Teroldego is a native Trentino variety producing deep-coloured, grassy, blackberry-flavoured wine on the gravel soils of the Rotaliano plain. Best producers: Foradori, Zeni★.

CH. DU TERTRE ★★ *Margaux AC, 5ème Cru Classé, Haut-Médoc, Bordeaux, France* Obscure MARGAUX property at last gaining the recognition it deserves. With lots of fruit and tannin, the wine is usually delicious at 5–6 years old, but will happily age for 10–15 years. Best years: 1990 89 88 86 85 83 82 80 79 78.

THAMES VALLEY *Berkshire, England* No less than 18 grape varieties planted over 9.7ha (24 acres) from which two Australians, viticulturist Jon Leighton and winemaker John Worontschak produce a range of firm, full-flavoured wines, many showing cunning antipodean-style use of oak. In particular, the Thames Valley Fumé★ is a remarkable GRAVES-lookalike. Worontschak is also mad keen on sweet wine ★ and fizz and my feeling is – we ain't seen nothing yet.

H THANISCH *Bernkastel, Mosel, Germany* This is the rump of the original Thanisch estate. The labels remain substantially the same, so look out for the VDP eagle, which will tell you that you have the wine which is still in family hands. The Thanisch heirs have kept a chunk of the famous Doctor vineyard too. Quality has improved of late in both the Doctor ★★★ and Lay ★★ sites. Best years: 1990 89 88 76 75 71.

DOM. THÉNARD *Givry, Côte Chalonnaise, Burgundy, France* Estate making some of the best reds in GIVRY, particularly the red Cellier aux Moines ★, and a new oak-influenced white. This domaine also has one of the largest holdings in Le MONTRACHET ★★, as well as smaller parcels of Grands-Échezeaux ★★ and CORTON Clos du Roi ★★. Best years: 1990 89 88 85.

THERMENREGION *Niederösterreich, Austria* This region, to the south of Vienna, derives its name from the thermal spa towns of Baden and Bad Vöslau. Just south of Vienna is the village of Gumpoldskirchen with its rich, and often sweet wines. The red wine area around Baden produces large amounts of Blauer Portugieser plus attempts at Pinot Noir and Cabernet Sauvignon.

THREE CHOIRS *Gloucestershire, England*   Tom Day and his wine-maker, Martin Fowke make an impressive range of wines including a zingy New Release blended from Huxelrebe and Reichensteiner – a sort of white English BEAUJOLAIS NOUVEAU offered to the brave at the same time – and a pungently dry Bacchus ★.

TICINO *Switzerland*   Italian-speaking, southerly canton of Switzerland. The most important wine is Merlot del Ticino, usu-ally soft and highly gluggable, but sometimes made fuller and more serious with some oak barrel-aging. Best producers: Cantina Giubiasco, Delea, Valsangiacomo fu Vittore, Vinattieri Ticinesi.

TIGNANELLO, VINO DA TAVOLA★★ *Tuscany, Italy*   The wine that broke the mould in Tuscany. Piero ANTINORI took control of his family company in the 1960s at a time when CHIANTI's reputa-tion was rock bottom. Aware of the great reputation of Bordeaux reds, he set out to imitate them, with advice from Bordeaux's leading winemaker Professor Peynaud. In particular he employed the previously unheard of practice of aging in small French oak barrels. Since this was against Chianti regulations, the wine had to be labelled as simple Vino da Tavola, but the quality was superb and Tignanello's success sparked off the Vino da Tavola movement outside DOC regulations that has produced many of Italy's most exciting wines. Originally from the Tignanello vineyard the grapes are now from several sources and the blend is 80% Sangiovese and 20% Cabernet Sauvignon. Top vintages are truly great wines: lesser vintages are of decent Chianti Classico quality. Best vintages: 1990 88 85 82.

TINTA BAIRRADA   See Baga.

TINTO   Spanish for red.

TOCAI FRIULANO   Unrelated to Hungary's or Alsace's Tokay, the Tocai Friulano is a north-east Italian grape producing dry, nutty, oily whites of great character in COLLIO and COLLI ORIENTALI and good wines in the Veneto's Colli Euganei as well as lots of neutral stuff in Piave. Best producers: Dorigo★, Livio Felluga★, PUIATTI, Russiz Superiore★, SCHIOPETTO★★.

TOKAJI *Hungary*   Strange, fascinating and unique, Tokaji wine, with its sweet-sour-sweet, sherry-like tang, was reputed to revive Russian Tsars on their death beds. It comes from a small hilly area in north-east Hungary that straddles the Czechoslovakian border. Here mists from the river Bodrog ensure that noble rot or botrytis on the Furmint, Hárslevelü and Muscotaly (Muscat Ottonel) grapes is fairly common. Old, single-vineyard Museum wines ★★ from the Tokaji Wine Trust

245

demonstrate the area's potential. Tokaji should be sold ready to drink, though the oxidized style of some releases makes you think they've missed the boat a bit.

TOLLOT-BEAUT & FILS *Chorey-lès-Beaune, Burgundy, France*
High quality COTE DE BEAUNE reds with lots of fruit and a pronounced new oak character. The village-level CHOREY-LES-BEAUNE ★, ALOXE-CORTON ★★ and SAVIGNY-LES-BEAUNE ★ wines are all excellent, as is the top-notch BEAUNE Premier Cru Clos du Roi ★★. Best drunk between 5 and 10 years old. Best years: 1990 89 88 87 85.

TORGIANO DOC & DOCG *Umbria, Italy*   A zone near Perugia dominated by LUNGAROTTI. In the 1960s and 1970s while most central Italian red was harsh and fruitless, LUNGAROTTI's Rubesco Torgiano was always ripe and plummy – an oasis of friendliness in a pleasure-seeker's desert. The basic Rubesco Torgiano is no longer so good but the Riserva Vigna Monticchio ★★ is a fine black, cherry-flavoured wine. Torgiano Riserva wines have just been accorded DOCG. Best producer: LUNGAROTTI.

TORO DO *Castilla y León, Spain*   Toro makes mainly reds, strong, robust, full of colour, tannin and pretty high in alcohol. The main grape, Tinto de Toro, is a local deviant of Tempranillo, and there is some Garnacha. Whites from the Malvasía grape are generally heavy. Best producers: Fariña★ (reds), MARQUES DE GRINON (Durius rosé and white).

TORREBIANCO *Puglia, Italy*   Southern Italian estate important for its outstanding Chardonnay, Preludio No. 1 ★. Owned by the northern Italian Spumante giant Gancia.

TORRES IPR *Oeste, Portugal*   Region around the town of Torres Vedras producing more wine than any other in Portugal. Patchy results so far, except for fruity young reds and good Reservas ★ from the co-op, and buttery whites ★ from Quinta da Folgorosa. Best producers: Quinta da Folgorosa, Torres Vedras co-op.

TORRES *Penedés, Catalonia, Spain*   Large family winery led by visionary Miguel Torres, making good wines with local grapes, Parellada and Tempranillo, but also renowned for their plantings of French varieties. Viña Esmeralda ★ (Muscat d'Alsace and Gewürztraminer) is grapy and spicy, Fransola ★ (Parellada and Sauvignon Blanc) is richly grassy, and Milmanda ★★ is a delicious, expensive Chardonnay from a CONCA DE BARBERA vineyard. Successful reds are Gran Coronas ★, soft, oaky and blackcurranty (Tempranillo and Cabernet), fine, deliciously rich Mas la Plana ★★ (Cabernet Sauvignon), floral, perfumed Mas Borras★ (Pinot Noir) and raisiny Las Torres★ (Merlot). Best years (Mas la Plana): 1987 83 81 76 75 73.

MIGUEL TORRES *Curicó, Chile*   The wizard of PENEDES arrived in Chile in 1979, seduced by its lack of phylloxera and near-perfect viticultural conditions. Torres led the way technically for many years, helping other producers by example, and introducing stainless steel, cool fermentation and new oak barrels to Chile. He showed what could be achieved with Riesling (soft but reasonably varietal), Gewürztraminer (plump and easy) and with his rather too dry but correct Chardonnay-Pinot Noir sparkling Brut Nature. There's a good Cabernet-based rosé★, too. Minty Cabernet Sauvignon and the firmer, leaner, oak-aged Manso de Valasco Cabernet★ (from 80-year-old vines) complete the range.

CH. LA TOUR-MARTILLAC *Pessac-Léognan AC, Cru Classé de Graves, Bordeaux, France*   A GRAVES Classed Growth that for many years positively cultivated an old-fashioned image but which is now a property to watch. Organic practice is strictly followed in the vineyard which has many ancient vines. In the past, the reds★ were deep, dark and well-structured but somehow they lacked charm. Things improved considerably in the 1980s. Since 1986 new-style vinification has also transformed the whites ★★. Best years: (reds) 1990 89 88 86 85 83 82; (whites) 1990 89 88 87 86.

TOURAINE AC *Loire Valley, France*   The general AC for Touraine wines in the central Loire. Altogether there are 6140ha (15,170 acres) of AC vineyards, divided half and half between red or rosé and white. Most of the reds are from the Gamay grape and in hot years these can be juicy, rough-fruited wines. Yet there is a fair amount of Cabernet too, both Sauvignon and Franc. The reds are best drunk young. Fairly decent white wines come from the Chenin Blanc grape but the best wines are from Sauvignon Blanc. These can be a good SANCERRE substitute at half the price. Drink at one year old, though Chenin wines can last longer. There are also three more specific ACs, Touraine-Amboise, Touraine-Azay-le-Rideau and Touraine-Mesland mainly for reds and rosés. Best producers: (reds and rosés) Charmoise, Corbillières, Octavie, OISLY-ET-THESEE co-op; (whites) Barbou, Baron Briare★, Aimé Boucher, Bougrier, Charmoise★, Marcadet★, Octavie★, OISLY-ET-THESEE co-op★. Best years: (reds) 1990 89 88; (whites) 1991 90 89 88.

TOURAINE MOUSSEUX AC *Loire Valley, France*   A comparatively unimportant sparkling wine AC covering the entire Touraine region. The wines are rarely as good as the best VOUVRAY and CREMANT DE LOIRE. Best producer: Monmousseau★.

CH. TOURTEAU-CHOLLET *Graves AC, Bordeaux, France*   Full dry red wines with good fruit from the southern, less fashionable part of the GRAVES. Ready at 3–4 years old, they are much better after 6–7 years. Best years: 1990 89 88 86 85 83 82 81.

TRAPICHE *Mendoza, Argentina*   The quality arm of Peñaflor, Argentina's biggest wine producer, exports a sound range of wines. Firmly stated reds from Malbec and Cabernet Sauvignon and some improving nutty Chardonnay.

TRAS-OS-MONTES *Portugal* Impoverished north-eastern province traditionally a supplier of grapes for Mateus Rosé, but with three IPR regions, Valpaços, Chaves and Planalto-Mirandês still producing pretty rustic stuff. Best producer: Valle Pradinho.

TREBBIANO The most widely planted white Italian grape variety – far too widely, in fact, for Italy's good. As the Trebbiano Toscano, it is used as the base for GALESTRO and any number of other neutral, dry whites, as well as in VIN SANTO. But there are also a number of grapes choosing to masquerade under the Trebbiano name that aren't anything like as neutral. The most notable are the Trebbiano from Lugana and Abruzzo – both grapes capable of full-bodied, fragrant wines. Called Ugni Blanc in France, and primarily used for distilling, as it should be.

TREFETHEN VINEYARDS *Napa Valley, California, USA* An off-dry Riesling ★ is one of the best wines from this Napa estate, although the Chardonnay has won more praise. The Cabernet is haphazard, but recent bottlings of Hillside ★ grapes show better form. Two good value wines, Eshcol White and Eshcol Red are frequently the most attractive wines made by Trefethen.

TRENTINO DOC *Italy* This northern Italian region is officially linked with its neighbour to the north, the Alto Adige, but they are completely different. The wines rarely have the verve or perfume of ALTO ADIGE examples, but can make up for this with riper softer flavours, where vineyard yields have been kept in check. The regional Trentino DOC covers 20 different types or styles of wine, in particular white Pinot Bianco, Pinot Grigio, Moscato Giallo, Müller-Thurgau and Nosiola, and red Schiava, Lagrein, Marzemino, Teroldego and Cabernet. Best producers: Bossi Foradori, Gaierhof, Mezzacorona, Mezzalombardo, Simoncelli.

DOM. DE TRÉVALLON *Coteaux-des-Baux-en-Provence AC, Provence, France* An iconoclastic Parisian called Eloi Dürrbach is the force behind this domaine's brilliant reds ★★★, mixing the wildness of the Mediterranean herb-strewn hills with a sweetness of blackberry, blackcurrant and black, black plums. Dürrbach's tradition-busting blend of Cabernet Sauvignon and Syrah, now grudgingly accepted by the French AC authorities, is the finest wine to come out of Provence in the last decade. The wines age extremely well, but are surprisingly drinkable in their youth. Best years: 1990 89 88 86 85 83 82 81 80.

F E TRIMBACH *Alsace AC, Alsace, France* Excellent grower/merchant whose trademark is a beautifully structured, subtly perfumed elegance. Riesling and Gewürztraminer are the specialities, but the Pinot Gris and Pinot Blanc are first-rate too. Top wines are the superb Gewürztraminer Cuvée des Seigneurs de Ribeaupierre ★★★, the Riesling Cuvée Frédéric Émile ★★★ and the Riesling Clos St-Hune ★★★. Best years: 1990 89 88 85.

TROCKEN German for dry. In most parts of Germany Trocken means less than 9g per litre residual sugar. In Austria the figure is half this: 4.5g. Trocken wines have become something of a fashion in Germany, but have not made great strides in other countries that have a wider range of wine styles to choose from.

TROCKENBEERENAUSLESE A long German word which says that the grapes were 'dry berry selected'. This generally means that they were affected by noble rot or *Botrytis cinerea* (*Edelfäule* in German) and the wines will be lusciously sweet. Whereas the Oechsle scale for most Prädikat wines varies from region to region in Germany, there is little room for manoeuvre for Trockenbeerenauslese: 150 Oechsle for a Mosel Riesling or 154 for a south Baden Ruländer. An Austrian Trockenbeerenauslese must be 30 KMW or 156 Oechsle.

CH. TROTANOY ★★ *Pomerol AC, Bordeaux, France* Another POMEROL estate (along with PETRUS, LAFLEUR, LATOUR-A-POMEROL and others) which has benefited from the brilliant touch of the MOUEIX family. The wine has lost some of its flair recently, but is still great Pomerol. Best years: 1990 89 88 85 83 82 81 79 78 76 75.

TUSCANY *Italy* Tuscany evokes Italy and Italian wine as no other region does. Its rolling hills, clad with vines, olive trees and cypresses, have produced wine since at least Etruscan times, and today, Tuscany leads the way in promoting the new image of Italian wines. Its 20-odd DOCs are led by CHIANTI, BRUNELLO DI MONTALCINO and many others based on the red Sangiovese grape and there are, as well, countless famous Vino da Tavolas like SASSICAIA, ORNELLAIA and TIGNANELLO. White wines, despite sweet VIN SANTO, and the occasional excellent Chardonnay and Sauvignon, do not figure highly in Tuscany. See also Carmignano, Galestro, Pomino, Rosso di Montalcino, Rosso di Montepulciano, Vino Nobile di Montepulciano.

TYRRELL'S *Hunter Valley, New South Wales, Australia* Large family-owned and run company with prime Lower Hunter vineyards but with an infuriatingly lackadaisical approach to some of its wines with a consequent effect on their consistency. Superb Vat 1 Sémillon ★★, intermittently excellent Vat 47 Chardonnay ★, Vat 5 and 9 Shiraz can be fine. Vat 6 Pinot Noir is variable despite achieving international acclaim with early vintages. Best years: (Sémillon) 1991 86 79 76 74 72; (Chardonnay) 1991 86 84 80 79 77; (reds) 1991 87 85 83 75 65.

UGNI BLANC See Trebbiano.

UMBRIA *Italy* Wine production in this land-locked, central Italian region is dominated by ORVIETO, which accounts for almost 70% of Umbrian DOC production. However some of the most characterful wines are the reds from TORGIANO and MONTEFALCO. Other zones, like Colli del Trasimento, Colli Altotiberini and Colli Perugini produce mainly forgettable reds and whites.

249

ÜRZIG *Mosel, Germany*   Middle Mosel village with a very famous vineyard site – the Würzgarten (spice garden) that tumbles spectacularly down to the river banks and produces marvellously spicy Riesling wines. Best producers: LOOSEN, Mönchhof.

UTIEL REQUENA DO *Valencia, Spain*   An hour's drive inland from Valencia, Utiel-Requena is renowned for its rosés, mostly made from Bobal. A lot of Tempranillo has been planted recently, making better, more lasting reds. Best producer: Casa Lo Alto.

VACQUEYRAS AC *Rhône Valley, France*   The most important and consistently successful of the COTES DU RHONE-VILLAGES communes was promoted to its own AC in 1989. The reds have a lovely dark colour, a round, warm, spicy bouquet and a rich deep flavour that seems infused with the herbs and pine dust of the south. They are lovely to drink at 2–3 years. Good producers' wines from good vintages will age for 10 years or more. Best producers: Clos des Cazaux, Combe★, Couroulu★, la Fourmone★, JABOULET, des Lambertins, de Montmirail★, Pascal★, des Roques, Vacqueyras co-op★. Best years: 1991 90 89 88 86 85 83 81.

VAL D'ORBIEU, LES VIGNERONS DU *Languedoc-Roussillon, France*   A dynamic growers' association that sells in excess of 20 million cases a year from the Midi. Its membership includes several, but by no means all, of the Midi's best co-ops (Cucugnan, Ribauté and Montredon) and individual producers (Dom. du Révérend, Dom. de Fontsainte, Ch. la Voulte-Gasparets and Ch. St-Auriol). Best years: 1991 90 89 88.

VALAIS *Switzerland*   Swiss canton and wine region flanking the Rhône above Lake Geneva. The Valais is, in general, very dry. Between Martigny and Sierre – Switzerland's driest spot – the valley turns north east creating an Alpine suntrap, and this short stretch of intensely cultivated vineyard land provides the majority of Switzerland's most individual wines.

VALDEPEÑAS DO *Castilla-La Mancha, Spain*   Valdepeñas offers some of Spain's best inexpensive oak-aged reds, but these are a small drop in a sea of less exciting stuff. In fact there are more whites than reds, at least some of them now modern, fresh and fruity. Best producers: Los Llanos★, Luís Megía, Félix Solís.

VALDESPINO *Jerez y Manzanilla DO, Andalucía, Spain*   Very old-fashioned, very high-quality family sherry business. Delicious wines include Fino Inocente ★, Tio Diego Amontillado ★★, the expensive but wonderfully concentrated Palo Cortado Cardenal ★★, dry amontillados Coliseo ★★★ and Don Tomás ★★, Don Gonzálo Old Dry Oloroso ★★ and Pedro Ximénez Solera Superior ★★.

VALENCIA DO *Valencia, Spain*   The best wines from Valencia in the south-east of Spain are the inexpensive, sweet, grapy Moscatels. Simple, fruity whites, reds and rosés are also good. Best producers: Cherubino Valsangiacomo (Marqués de Caro), Schenk (Los Monteros), Vincente Gandía Pla.

VALLE D'AOSTA DOC *Italy* Tiny Alpine valley sandwiched between Piedmont and the French Alps in northern Italy. The regional DOC covers 17 wine styles, referring either to a specific grape variety (like Gamay or Pinot Nero) or to a delimited region like Donnaz, a northern extension of Piedmont's CAREMA, producing a light red from the Nebbiolo grape. Perhaps the finest wine from these steep slopes is the sweet Chambave Moscato. Best producer: Ezio Voyat★.

VALLÉE DE PARADIS, VIN DE PAYS DE LA *Languedoc, France* With a name like the valley of paradise, the wines from this area to the south-west of Narbonne around Durban ought to be heavenly. In fact, they're good, basic quaffers made principally from Carignan, Cinsaut and Grenache.

VALLET FRÈRES *Gevrey Chambertin, Burgundy, France* Merchant, making small amounts of Burgundy in a highly traditional manner. The wines can seem tough and dense when young, but the best – especially their Premier Cru and Grand Cru wines from GEVREY-CHAMBERTIN ★★ – can age to a sultry but satisfying maturity over many years. Also good VOSNE-ROMANEE ★ and MOREY-ST-DENIS ★. The wines may be labelled Pierre Bourée.

VALPOLICELLA DOC *Veneto, Italy* This Veronese red wine can range in style from a light, cherryish red to the rich, port-like RECIOTO and AMARONE Valpolicellas. Most Valpolicella from the plains is pale and insipid, and bears little comparison with Valpolicella Classico from the hills. Made from Corvina (the best grape), Rondinella and Molinara (eliminated from the blend when a more structured wine is required), Valpolicella Classico can be either a light, cherryish red of great appeal, for drinking within 18 months of the vintage, or a fuller wine of considerable bitter-sweet complexity, made either from a particular vineyard (like ALLEGRINI's La Grola), or by  refermenting the wine on the skins of the Amarone (as QUINTARELLI does), a style called Ripasso. Best producers: Serègo Alighieri, ALLEGRINI★★, MASI,★ QUINTARELLI★, Le Ragosse★. Best recent years: 1990 88 86 85.

VALTELLINA DOC *Lombardy, Italy* Red wine produced on the precipitous slopes of northern Lombardy, closer to Switzerland than to Milan. There is a basic, light red, made from at least 70% Nebbiolo (here called Chiavennasca), but the best wines are made under the Valtellina Superiore DOC. From top vintages the wines are attractively perfumed and approachable examples of the Nebbiolo grape. Sfursat is a dense, high-alcohol red (up to 14.5%) made from semi-dried grapes. Best producers: Enologica Valtellinese, Negri★. Best years: 1990 88 85.

VASSE FELIX *Margaret River, Western Australia* One of the originals responsible for this district rocketing to fame, with decadently rich, profound Cabernet Sauvignon ★★ and rare but very special Shiraz ★★. Best years: (reds) 1989 86 84 83 79.

VAUD *Switzerland* With the exception of the canton of Geneva, the Vaud accounts for the vineyards bordering Lake Geneva, forming a seemingly unbroken line from Nyon to Montreux. There are 5 regions: La Côte, Lavaux, Chablais, Côtes de l'Orbe-Bonvillars and Vully. Most of the production is Dorin (Chasselas) and it can be a delightful light summer white. Reds are made from Gamay and Pinot Noir. Best producers: Badoux, Conne, Delarze, Grognuz, Massy, Obrist, Pinget, J & P Testuz.

VAVASOUR *Marlborough, South Island, New Zealand* An exciting new winery in the Awatere Valley near Marlborough's main viticultural region, enjoying spectacular success since the first release of the 1989 wines. One of New Zealand's best Chardonnays ★★★, a superb Cabernet Sauvignon/Franc Reserve★★ and fabulous Sauvignon Blanc ★★★, already the envy of other Marlborough winemakers. Best years: 1991 90.

VDP Recognizable on the label by a Prussian eagle bearing a bunch of grapes, the VDP or Verband Deutscher Prädikats-und Qualitätsweingüter is a German organization dating back to 1910. Membership extends to all quality regions of Germany but is only granted to consistently good estates. All the wines undergo an examination that is separate from the general Amtliche Prüfung testing, and, luckily, rather more exacting.

VDQS (VIN DÉLIMITÉ DE QUALITÉ SUPÉRIEURE) The second highest classification for French wines, behind AC (Appellation Contrôlée) but ahead of Vin de Pays and Vin de Table. Indications are that the authorities would like to phase out VDQS, making me wonder whether they'll upgrade all the wines however unworthy, or risk the fury of the farmers by downgrading undeserving candidates.

VECCHIO SAMPERI *Sicily, Italy* Vecchio Samperi is a dry but unfortified MARSALA-style wine produced by Marco De Bartoli, being his version of what he believes Marsala was before the first English merchant, John Woodhouse, fortified it for export. Released as 10★-, 20★★- and 30-year old★★ wines – these are dry, intense and redolent of candied peel, dates and old, old raisins. Some of the finest wines of this style in the world.

VEGA SICILIA *Ribera del Duero DO, Castilla y León, Spain* Spain's most expensive red wines, rich, fragrant, complex and very slow to mature, and by no means always easy to appreciate. This estate was the first in Spain to introduce French varieties, and over a quarter of the vines are now Cabernet Sauvignon, two-thirds are Tempranillo and the rest Malbec and Merlot. Vega Sicilia Unico ★★★ – the top wine – has traditionally been given about 10 years' wood aging, but this is now being reduced and a certain volatility evident in some vintages should now no longer occur. The second wine, Valbuena ★ will from now on be sold with a vintage, rather than as a vague 'third year' and 'fifth year' wine. Best years: 1982 79 76 75.

VENEGAZZÙ *Veneto, Italy*   Estate in north-east Italy known primarily for its red Vino da Tavola, Venegazzù della Casa, based on red Bordeaux varieties. Though a pacesetter in the field, it has faded somewhat as more convincing versions have come on the scene. The black label version – their equivalent of a Riserva – can still pack a smoky, aggressive black-fruited punch. Best years: 1988 85 83 82.

VENETO *Italy*   The Veneto region takes in the wine zones of SOAVE, VALPOLICELLA, BARDOLINO and PIAVE in north-east Italy. Its huge production makes it the source of a great deal of inexpensive wine, but the Soave and Valpolicella hills are also capable of producing small quantities of high-quality wine. Other hilly areas like COLLI BERICI and Colli Euganei which at the moment only produce large quantities of dull staple varietal wines, really ought to be turning out more decent wines but the producers do not appear to be so inclined.

VERDICCHIO   This white grape, related to the Trebbiano of Soave and Lugana, produces crisp, sometimes moderately perfumed dry white wines in the Matelica and Castelli dei Jesi DOC zones on Italy's eastern, Adriatic coast. The grape is also used for various Vino da Tavolas in the Marche and as a base for sparklers.

VERMENTINO   The best dry white wines of Sardinia generally come from the Vermentino grape. Light, dry, perfumed and nutty, the best wines tend to be from the north of the island, where it is DOC in Gallura. Liguria also grows a Vermentino, but this is thought to be a different variety.

VERNACCIA DI ORISTANO DOC *Sardinia, Italy*   Outstanding oxidized, almost sherry-like wines from the west of the island. The wines acquire complexity and colour through long aging in wood. They are amber coloured and dry, nutty and long on the finish. Best producer: Contini.

VERNACCIA DI SAN GIMIGNANO DOC *Tuscany, Italy*   The dry white wine made from the Vernaccia grape grown in the hills around the beautiful Tuscan town of San Gimignano gained fame as Italy's first DOC in 1966. This fame was perhaps justified then when every other Tuscan white wine was made with Trebbiano, but today, with imports like Chardonnay and Sauvignon turning out impressive wines, it rarely looks better than a decent dry quaffing white for drinking 6–18 months after the vintage. Best producers: Le Colonne, Cusona, Montenidoli, Teruzzi e Puthod (especially Terre di Tufi ★).

253

NOËL VERSET *Cornas AC, Rhône Valley, France* Massive, concentrated reds ★★ from some of the oldest, and best-sited vines in CORNAS. Yields are tiny here and it shows in the depth and power that Verset achieves in his wine. Worth aging for 10 years or more. Best years: 1990 89 88 85 83 81.

VEUVE CLICQUOT *Champagne AC, Champagne, France* These Champagnes in general still live up to the high standards set by the original Widow Clicquot at the beginning of the 19th century although many are released too young. The non-vintage ★★ is full, toasty and satisfyingly weighty yet still refreshing; the vintage ★★ is that bit fuller than the non-vintage Champagne; and the de luxe, called Grande Dame ★★ after the original widow, is hefty but impressive stuff. Best years: 1985 82 79.

VEUVE DU VERNAY A best-selling French sparkling wine brand of no particular quality whose popularity is deservedly on the wane as other better-made, low-priced fizz comes on the market.

VICTORIA *Australia* Despite its small area, Victoria has arguably more land suited to quality grape-growing than any other state, with climates ranging from hot Sunraysia and Rutherglen on the Murray River to cool Mornington Peninsula and Gippsland in the south. The range of flavours is similarly wide and exciting. Victoria, with more than 170 wineries, has experienced more of the boutique winery boom than any other state. See also Rutherglen, Yarra Valley.

VIDE This acronym on a label indicates that the producer belongs to the Association of Italian Wine Producers, a quality-oriented group of growers and producers. The wines must be analysed and tasted and if they don't pass muster, they cannot use the VIDE symbol even if the producer is a member.

LA VIEILLE FERME ★ *Côtes du Ventoux AC, Rhône Valley, France* A brilliantly spicy, concentrated red produced in a lesser AC by the owners of the world-famous Ch. de BEAUCASTEL in CHATEAUNEUF-DU-PAPE. If only all COTES DU VENTOUX were as exciting. Best years: 1990 89 88.

VIEILLES VIGNES French term for a wine made from old vines, which should mean at least 20 years old if not twice that. Old vines give more concentrated wine.

CH. VIEUX-CHÂTEAU-CERTAN ★★★ *Pomerol AC, Bordeaux, France* Slow-developing and tannic red (because of the use of 50% Cabernet) which after 15–20 years finally resembles more a fragrant refined 'Médoc' than a gushing, hedonistic POMEROL. Best years: 1990 89 88 87 86 85 83 82 81 75.

VIEUX TÉLÉGRAPHE *Châteauneuf-du-Pape AC, Rhône Valley, France* One of the top names in the AC, less tannic than BEAUCASTEL perhaps but with just as much aging potential. The vines are some of the oldest in Châteauneuf and this Grenache-based red ★★ is among the best modern-style wines produced in the

Rhône Valley even if it has lost a little of its magic in recent vintages. There is also a small amount of white ★ which is heavenly to drink at the youngest possible stage. Best years: 1990 89 88 86 85 83.

VILLA BANFI *Tuscany, Italy*   The audacity of this venture is to be admired, even if the wines do not always live up to expectations. In the late 1970s, the Mariani brothers, New York wine importers, wanted to invest in an estate in Italy. They enlisted the services of Ezio Rivella, one of Italy's premier winemakers, who carved out an estate in the southern part of the BRUNELLO DI MONTALCINO zone. They built a high-tech winery, and planned to sustain the premium wines like Brunello, Chardonnay and Cabernet with a range of inexpensive wines, but the premium wines have turned out to be more buoyant, and the market for the inexpensive wines a difficult one. Their Brunello ★ can be good and the Chardonnay and Cabernet are fair enough but I often get most fun out of their light, frothy, rose-petal-scented Brachetto.

VILLA MARIA *Auckland, North Island, New Zealand*   George Fistonich, founder and co-owner of Villa Maria, also owns the Hawkes Bay wineries, Vidal and Esk Valley. Together the group crush around 10% of New Zealand's grape crop. Villa Maria Reserve Cabernet ★★ or Cabernet Sauvignon/Merlot ★ are good. Reserve Chardonnay from Vidal★★ or Villa Maria ★★ are power-packed complex wines. Villa Maria also score well with extremely focused dry Marlborough Sauvignon Blanc ★★, and at the sweeter end with a stunning 1991 Late Harvest Riesling ★★★ from Marlborough. Best years: 1991 90 89 87.

VILLA SACHSEN *Bingen, Rheinhessen, Germany*   One of the first companies to work out how to make bone-dry Trocken wines without taking the enamel off your teeth. Also makes lovely sweeter wines ★★ from their Binger Kirchberg and Scharlachberg sites. Best years: 1990 89 88.

VILLARD *Maipo, Chile*   A partnership between globe-trotting Frenchman Thierry Villard (formerly of ORLANDO in South Australia), Viña Santa Emiliana and two local growers. First releases of Maipo Chardonnay, Aconcagua Sauvignon Blanc and Chimbarongo Cabernet Sauvignon have been full of bright fruit wrapped in coconutty oak.

VIN DU BUGEY VDQS *Savoie, France*   Scattered vineyards in the Ain department, halfway between Lyon and Savoie. The best wines are definitely the whites, from Chardonnay, Pinot Gris, Mondeuse Blanche, Altesse and Jacquère. Roussette du Bugey is usually a blend of Altesse with a little Chardonnay. Best producers: Bel-Air, Crussy, Monin, Peillot.

VIN DE CORSE AC *Corsica, France* The overall AC for Corsica with 5 superior sub-regions (Calvi, Cap Corse, Figari, Porto Vecchio and Sartène). PATRIMONIO and AJACCIO are entitled to their own ACs. Things are improving on this lovely island but slowly. The most distinctive wines, mainly red, come from local grapes (Nielluccio and Sciaccarello for reds and Vermentino for whites). There are some rich sweet Muscats – especially from Cap Corse and Patrimonio. Best producers: Cantone, Couvent d'Alzipratu, Gentile, Leccia, Péraldi★, UVAL, SKALLI★, Torraccia.

VIN DE L'ORLÉANAIS VDQS *Loire Valley, France* Mainly rosé wine from Pinot Meunier, here called Gris Meunier d'Orléans. There is some delightful Chardonnay too (here called Auvernat Blanc). Best producers: Clos St-Fiacre★, Legroux.

VIN DE PAILLE A sweet wine found mainly in the Jura region of eastern France. Traditionally, the grapes are left to dry for 2–3 months on straw (*paille*) mats before fermentation. This process dehydrates the grapes and concentrates their sugar content. The wines are a cross between SAUTERNES and amontillado sherry – sweet but slightly nutty, too. Vins de Paille can be found in COTES DU JURA, ARBOIS and L'ETOILE, and occasionally in the Rhône Valley. Best producers: CHAPOUTIER★★, Rolet★, Tissot★.

VIN DE PAYS *France* The phrase suggests a traditional wine from the country districts of France but the reality is a little different as many Vins de Pays are impressively modern and forward-looking and are now the source of some of France's best-value flavours. This category of wine was created in 1968 to give a geographical identity and quality yardstick to wines which had previously been sold off for blending. It is a particularly useful category for adventurous winemakers (such as RYMAN and SKALLI) who want to use good quality grapes not allowed under the frequently restrictive AC regulations. Many Vin de Pays wines are labelled with the grape variety.

VIN DE SAVOIE AC *Savoie, France* The general AC for the scattered vineyards in the Alpine region of Savoie. The 15 best villages, including Abymes, Apremont, Arbin, Chignin, Cruet and Montmélian, can add their own name to the AC name. The best wines are white and to enjoy the thrilling snap of their tangy fruit drink them young. Occasional good Pinot Noir and excellent beefy Mondeuse reds. Best producers: Belluard, Boniface★, Cavaillé★, Monin, Monterminod★, Neyroud, Perret, Perrier, Quénard, de Ripaille★, Rocailles★. Best years: 1990 89 88 87 86.

VIN DE TABLE French for a table wine, the lowest rung on the Appellation Contrôlée ladder.

VIN DOUX NATUREL French for a fortified wine, where fermentation has been stopped by the addition of alcohol, leaving the wine 'naturally' sweet, although you could argue that stopping fermentation with a slug of powerful spirit is distinctly unnatural, but there you go.

VIN JAUNE *Jura, France* A Jura speciality made from the Savagnin grape. In CHATEAU-CHALON it is the only permitted wine style. The wine is made in a similar way to fino sherry but is not fortified. Vin Jaune usually ages well, too. Best producers: Clavelin★, Courbet★, Macle★, Perron★.

VIN SANTO *Trentino,Tuscany and Umbria, Italy* The 'holy wine' of Tuscany can be one of the world's great sweet wines – just occasionally, that is, for it is also one of the most wantonly abused wine terms in Italy. Made from grapes that are laid on mats after harvest to dry, the resulting wines, fermented and aged in sealed barrels for up to 7–8 years, should be intensely nutty, oxidized, full of the flavours of dried apricots and crystallized orange peel, concentrated and long. Vin Santo is also produced in Umbria and in Trentino (where it is called Vino Santo) but the best comes from Tuscany. Best producers: AVIGNONESI★★★, Cappezzana★, Castell'in Villa★, Castello di Cacchiano★, ISOLE E OLENA★★★, POLIZIANO, Selvapiana★.

VIÑA CANEPA *Maipo, Chile* South America's most modern winery produces a surgically clean range of whites – especially the nettly Sauvignon Blanc and the lean and hungry Oaked Chardonnay. The reds can lack flesh, though the spicy Oaked Cabernet Sauvignon is not too anorexic. Best years: 1992 91 90.

VINHO VERDE DOC *Minho and Douro Litoral, Portugal* 'Vinho Verde' is a region, a wine and a style of wine. 'Green' only in the sense of being young, Vinho Verde can be red *or* white, and in a restaurant the term often refers simply to the younger wines on the wine list. The demarcated Vinhos Verdes, however, come from north-west Portugal. The reds are an acquired taste, and drunk by few outside the region – though I do claim to be one of those few. Both red and white are strongly acidic, usually with a prickle of fizz, and best drunk young and chilled with the local cuisine. The whites range from sharply lemony to aromatically flowery (when made from the Loureiro and Trajadura grapes) and extravagantly fruity (the Alvarinho grape). Because the climate is damp and mild, vines have to be trained high, sometimes even up trees, to protect them from fungal infections. Best producers: Casa de Cabanelas, Casa de Compostela, Paço do Cardido, Palacio da Brejoeira, Passo de Teixeró, Ponte de Lima co-op, Quinta do Tamariz, Solar das Bouças★, Tormes.

J P VINHOS *Setúbal Peninsula, Portugal* The name has changed since the João Pires Muscat brand was sold to IDV, but the wine-making is as forward-looking as ever. Australian Peter Bright is winemaker, and uses Portuguese and foreign grapes with equal ease. QUINTA DA BACALHOA★ is an oaky, meaty Cabernet Sauvignon/Merlot blend, Tinto da Anfora★ lean and figgy, Quinta da Santo Amaro★ light, aromatic and raisiny, white Herdade de Santa Marta★ rich, greengagy and mouthfilling, and Cova du Ursa★★, a stunning, toasty rich Chardonnay.

VINO DA TAVOLA

Italy

Vino da Tavola, meaning 'table wine', is the lowest quality category in Italian wine. There are virtually no regulations controlling quality at all, yet this lowly rank has been the vehicle for the biggest revolution the Italian wine world has ever seen. Italy is the world's largest producer of wine, yet any international reputation it has for quality is extremely recent. Abuse of its famous wine names had become so widespread by the 1960s that a control system was introduced – the Denominazione di Origine Controllata (DOC). It did bring some order to the chaos, but regrettably enshrined bad practices rather than encouraging innovations that might improve quality.

ITALIAN RENAISSANCE

The 1960s and '70s were a time when enormous strides were being made in Bordeaux, Australia and California yet this change threatened to bypass Italy completely. A group of winemakers, led by Piero Antinori, realized that Italy would never establish an international reputation if it couldn't produce wines of international appeal – employing international grapes like Cabernet Sauvignon, Merlot and Chardonnay and international methods, in particular the use of new small oak barrels for aging the wine, followed by bottling early after only one or two years. Yet the DOC laws specifically forbade such innovations.

So, quite simply, these men told the law to go hang, and trusting to their wines finding a market through their flavours and their individuality, they vowed to create the necessary modern international styles regardless of the law, and label them as plain Vino da Tavola.

The 'Super Tuscan' Vino da Tavolas, as they were quickly dubbed, were a phenomenal success, brilliant in flavour, and able to command far higher prices than Chianti ever could. Soon it was not just Tuscany that was leaping into the fray. Piedmont was another region with old-fashioned laws stifling innovation. Soave and Valpolicella were other wines whose laws condoned all sorts of abuse. All over the north-west and north-east – and, later, indeed, in the south as well – winemakers broke free from hide-bound tradition and created exciting individualistic wines to satisfy the new wave of wine drinkers.

And now, not only do the Vino da Tavolas prosper as never before, but as DOC regulations are reformed, the lawmakers themselves are incorporating many of the Vino da Tavola practices that they have spent a generation trying to suppress.

See also ORNELLAIA, SASSICAIA, SPANNA, TIGNANELLO.

BEST PRODUCERS AND WINES

Barbera/Nebbiolo Voerzio (Vignaserra).

Cabernet Ruffino (Cabreo Il Borgo); Gaja (Darmagi); Capezzana (Ghiaie della Furba); Ruffino (Nozzole); Ornellaia; Sassicaia.

Chardonnay Gaja (Gaia and Rey); Torrebianco (Preludio no.1).

Merlot Ornellaia (Masseto); Castello di Ama (L'Apparita); Avignonesi.

Sangiovese Boscarelli; Isole e Olena (Cepparello); Fontodi (Flaccianello); Felsina Berardenga (Fontalloro); Riecine (La Gioia); Monte Vertine (Il Sodaccio); Castellare (I Sodi di San Niccolí); Monte Vertine (Le Pergole Torte); Vinattieri (Vinattieri Rosso).

Sangiovese/Cabernet Altesino (Alte d'Altesi); Caparzo (Ca' del Pazzo); Avignonesi (Grifi); Castello dei Rampolla (Sammarco); Antinori (Tignanello); Antinori (Solaia).

Syrah Fontodi, Isole e Olena.

VINO NOBILE DI MONTEPULCIANO DOCG *Tuscany, Italy* The 'noble wine' from the hills around the town of Montepulciano is made from the Sangiovese grape, known locally as the Prugnolo, with the help of a little Canaiolo and Mammolo. At its best, it combines the power and structure of BRUNELLO DI MONTAL-CINO with the finesse and complexity found in the best CHIANTI. Unfortunately, the best was a rare beast until recently, though the rate of improvement in the past 5 years has been impressive. Best producers: AVIGNONESI★, Boscarelli★★, Le Casalte★, La Casella, Contucci★, Del Cerro, POLIZIANO★. Best years: 1990 88 85 (anything older should be approached with caution).

VIOGNIER Planted only in tiny amounts mainly in the northern Rhône at CHATEAU-GRILLET and CONDRIEU, Viognier is a poor yielder and also markedly prone to disease. But the wine is delicious – peachy and apricotty with a soft, almost waxy texture, usually a fragrance of spring flowers and sometimes a taste almost like crème fraîche. It is now found in Languedoc-Roussillon and the southern Rhône as well as in California and Australia.

VOERZIO *Piedmont, Italy* Roberto Voerzio is one of the best of the younger generation of BAROLO producers, emphasizing fruit and minimizing tannin. His Dolcetto ★★ is particularly successful, as is his barrique-aged Nebbiolo/Barbera blend, Vigna Serra ★★. He took a bit of time to work out how to adapt Barolo to his philosophy, but his 1987 ★★ is remarkably good for a difficult year and his 88 ★★ is marvellously dark and bitter-sweet, only beaten by his single-vineyard La Serra ★★★. Best years: 1990 88 85.

VOLNAY AC *Côte de Beaune, Burgundy, France* There are two main styles of Volnay – one is light and perfumed in a delicious cherry way, for drinking at 3–4 years, the second has tremendous, juicy, plummy power and benefits from 7–10 years' aging. No Grands Crus, but the top Premiers Crus (Clos des Chênes, Les Caillerets, Les Champans) are some of Burgundy's best vineyards. Best producers: Bitouzet-Prieur★, Blain-Gagnard★, Clerget★, Glantenay★, Lafarge★★, LAFON★★, Marquis d'Angerville★★, de MONTILLE★★, Potinet-Ampeau★, Pousse d'Or★ Vaudoisey-Mutinde★★. Best years: 1990 89 88 87 85 83 82 80 78.

VOSNE-ROMANÉE AC *Côte de Nuits, Burgundy, France* The greatest village in the Côte de Nuits with a clutch of 5 Grands Crus and 13 Premiers Crus (the best of these are Les Malconsorts and Les Suchots) which are often as good as other villages' Grands Crus. The quality of the village wine is also high. In good years the wines should have at least 6 years' aging and 10–15 would be better. Best producers: Arnoux★, Cacheux★, GRIVOT★★, Gros★★, JADOT, JAYER★★★, Lamarche★★, MEO-CAMUZET★★, Moillard★, Mongeard-Mugneret★★, RION★, Dom. de la ROMANEE-CONTI★★. Best years: 1990 89 88 87 85 83 82 80 78 76.

VOUGEOT AC *Côte de Nuits, Burgundy, France* The 12.5ha (32 acres) of vines outside the walls of CLOS DE VOUGEOT only qualify for Vougeot AC. The wine, mainly red, is not bad and a lot cheaper than any Clos de Vougeot. Best producer: Bertagna★, Chopin-Groffier★. Best years: 1990 89 88 85.

VOUVRAY AC *Loire Valley, France* Dry, medium-dry, sweet and sparkling wines from Chenin grapes grown in picturesque vineyards east of Tours. The dry wines acquire beautifully rounded flavours after 10 years or so. Medium-dry wines, when properly made from a single domaine, are worth aging for 20 years or more. Spectacular noble-rot affected sweet wines were produced in 1990 and 1989 with an intense peach and honey soft sweetness but also an ever-present acidity. The fizz is some of the Loire's best. Best producers: Aubuisières, Bourillon D'Orléons, Brédif★, Champalou★, Foreau★★, Fouquet, Freslier, Huet★★, Mabille. Best years: 1990 89 88 85 83 82 78 76 75 70.

WACHAU *Niederösterreich, Austria* Stunningly beautiful stretch of the Danube between Krems-Stein and the monastery of Melk, the Wachau is Austria's top region for dry whites. Riesling is the grape here, followed by Grüner Veltliner.

WAIPARA SPRINGS *Canterbury, South Island, New Zealand* Winemaker north of Christchurch in the Waipara/Amberley region who has shot to stardom with first releases. Zesty Sauvignon Blanc ★ and Rhine Riesling ★, but the real stars are a toasty, cool-climate Chardonnay★★ and a juicily plummy Pinot Noir ★★. I believe we'll see some really top wines from here before long. Best years: 1991 90.

WARRE *Port DOC, Douro, Portugal* Top quality vintage ports ★★, and a good 'off-vintage' port from their Quinta da Cavadinha ★. Nimrod ★, a 10- to 15-year-old tawny, is also delicious, and their Crusted ★★ and Late Bottled Vintage ★ wines are both very welcome traditional, full-bodied ports. Best years: (vintage ports) 1985 83 80 77 75 70 66 63.

WASHINGTON STATE *USA* Washington is the second largest premium wine-producing state, with over 4452ha (11,000 acres) of vinifera grapes planted. The chief growing areas are in irrigated high desert, east of the coastal Cascade Mountains. Although the heat is not as intense as California, the long summer days with extra hours of sunshine due to the northern latitude seem to deepen the intensity of fruit flavours. This has led to wines of great depth and flavour, both white and red. Cabernet Sauvignon, Merlot, Chardonnay, Sauvignon Blanc and Sémillon produce very good wines here. There are some who believe that in the long run, the wines of Washington State will come to be regarded as the best in the US. Best producers: Champs de Brionne, CHATEAU STE MICHELLE, Covey Run, Hogue Cellars, KIONA, L'École No 41, Leonetti Cellars, Preston Wine Cellars, Salishan Vineyards, Snoqualmie, Staton Hills, Paul Thomas, WOODWARD CANYON.

WEGELER-DEINHARD *Bernkastel, Mosel; Oestrich-Winkel,*
Ⓨ *Rheingau; Deidesheim, Rheinpfalz, Germany* Huge estate with
vast holdings in Germany's top vineyards. Over the years
Deinhard has been pulling its hair out to find a means of marketing all these separate strands of German viticulture. In
Germany they spin money with Sekt and their still wines are
only a minute section of their portfolio. Outside Germany they
have led the way in introducing new dry styles. One idea was
the village series of Piesport, Bernkastel, Deidesheim, Nierstein,
Hochheim and Johannisberg called the Heritage Selection. Their
best marketing concept to date has been the range of generic
Mosel-Saar-Ruwer, Rheingau, Rheinpfalz Kabinetts and Spätlesc
wines ★. Deinhard continue to market a few top village sites
such as Forster Ungeheuer, Rüdesheimer Berg Rottland,
Winkeler Hasensprung, Wehlener Sonnenuhr, and Bernkasteler
Doctor. These are generally of Spätlese quality, sometimes, as in
1990 of Auslese or even Beerenauslese ripeness and all merit
★★ with the very best Doctor and Sonnenuhr Rieslings meriting
★★★. Best years: 1990 89 88 86 85 83 81 79 76 75.

WEHLEN *Mosel, Germany* Village whose steep Wehlener
Ⓨ Sonnenuhr vineyard produces some of the most powerful yet
fragrant Rieslings in Germany. Best producers: J J PRUM, RICHTER,
WEGELER-DEINHARD.

WEISSBURGUNDER See Pinot Blanc.

WEISSHERBST German rosé wine, a speciality of Baden. The wines
are often dry. The label must state the grape variety.

WELSCHRIESLING See Riesling Italico.

WENDOUREE *Clare Valley, South Australia* Small winery making
Ⓟ enormous, ageworthy reds from tiny yields off their own very
old Shiraz, Cabernet, Malbec and Mataro (Mourvèdre) vines.
Old-fashioned methods and limited output spell cult following
and thickly textured palate-blasters ★★ in the bottle. There are
tiny amounts of sweet Muscat ★. Best years: 1990 89 86 83.

WENTE BROS *Livermore Valley, California, USA* Pioneering
Ⓟ California winery with a wide range, including pleasant fattish
Chardonnay★, an excellent Livermore Valley Sauvignon Blanc ★
and decent fizz. Recent vintages show great progress.

WERNER *Hochheim, Rheingau, Germany* Classy estate with well-
Ⓟ sited bits of the Domdechaney, Hölle and Kirchenstück vineyards
in Hochheim that made especially good wines in 1990★. Best
years: 1990 89 88 86.

WESTERN AUSTRALIA Only the south-west corner of this vast
state is suited to vines: the Swan Valley and Perth environs
being the oldest and hottest district, with present attention
focused on Lower Great Southern, Margaret River, South-West
Coastal Plain and most recently, Pemberton/Manjimup. Quality
and individuality rival the best of the eastern states but it lags
behind in consistency.

WHITE ZINFANDEL Pink, sweetish Californian wine made from the red grape, Zinfandel, but given minimal skin contact. The wines range from awful to really attractive no-frills gluggers.

WIEN *Austria* Wine region within the city limits of Wien or Vienna. The best vines come from the south-facing sites in Grinzing, Nussdorf and Weiden; and the Bisamberg hill north of the Danube. Best producers: Bernreiter, Mayer, Wieninger.

WINKEL *Rheingau, Germany* Rheingau village whose best vineyard is the large Hasensprung Einzellage but the most famous one is SCHLOSS VOLLRADS – an ancient estate that does not use the village name on its label. Best producers: Johannishof, Landgraf Hessisches Weingut, von Mumm, Ress, WEGELER-DEINHARD.

WINZERGENOSSENSCHAFT A growers' co-op in Germany or Austria. The quality of wine varies enormously.

WIRRA WIRRA *Southern Vales, South Australia* Run with panache by celebrated eccentric Greg Trott who consistently makes white wines with more finesse than customary in the region. Well-balanced Sauvignon Blanc★, ageworthy Sémillon blend★, buttery Chardonnay★ and soft reds. Also a good value W W label.

WOLFF-METTERNICH *Durbach, Baden, Germany* Leading Baden estate with a preponderance of Klingelberger★ (Riesling) unusual in Baden, but also a sure hand in making full, impressive Traminer★ and Spätburgunder★ wines. Best years: 1990 89 88.

WOODWARD CANYON *Walla Walla AVA, Washington State, USA* Big barrel-fermented Chardonnay★★ with layers of new oak is the trademark wine. Also good Charbonneau Red (Cabernet Sauvignon/Merlot) and Charbonneau White (Sémillon/Sauvignon Blanc).

WOOTTON *Somerset, England* Owner Colin Gillespie produces well-focused varietals including a fine Schönburger and a stylish, salty Auxerrois★ as well as consulting to many local vineyards. Best years: 1991 90 89.

WÜRTTEMBERG *Germany* Southern German wine region centred on the river Neckar and its tributaries. Most of the wine is drunk in the cities of Stuttgart and Heilbron. More than half the wine made is red and the best comes from the Lemberger, Dornfelder or Blaufränkisch grapes, the rest mostly from the Trollinger of the Südtirol. These red wines can be very light indeed due to massive yields. Isolated steep sites on the Neckar produce fine Riesling too.

WYNDHAM ESTATE *Hunter Valley, New South Wales, Australia* This reliable brand, ingeniously marketed in the 1980s by Brian McGuigan, is now part of Pernod-Ricard's ORLANDO group. It is the Hunter's biggest winery and an active exporter. Top wines are juicy Bin 888 Cabernet Merlot★, even juicier Bin 827 Shiraz★, and fruity salady Oak Cask Chardonnay★ as well as Verdelho and Traminer. Subtle they are not, but their upfront flavours seem to make an awful lot of people happy.

WYNNS *Coonawarra, South Australia* The greatest name in Coonawarra, yet one which is struggling to hold on to its own character after takeover by PENFOLDS. Only the stunning John Riddoch Cabernet ★★★ of recent releases has been really exciting. 'Hermitage' (Shiraz) ★ is top value at a price kept low by large volume. Also indulgent Chardonnay ★ in big, oaky style and oceans of cheap quaffing Riesling, but Wynns Riesling used to be a classic till recently. Not any more. Ovens Valley Shiraz was short on elegance but long on flavour and satisfaction; it has now been discontinued. Why? Best years: 1990 88 86 84 82 76 66 62 55.

YALUMBA *Barossa Valley, South Australia* Large, distinguished old firm, owned by the Hill-Smith family, makes a wide range of wines including estate wines Heggies ★★ (oustanding Riesling, red Bordeaux blend and botrytis Riesling), Hill-Smith Estate ★ (racy Sauvignon Blanc, fine Chardonnay and citrusy botrytis Sémillon) and Pewsey Vale ★ (fine Riesling and Cabernet Sauvignon). The Yalumba range are Barossa-based blends (the Signature ★ series stands out). Oxford Landing Chardonnay and Cabernet Shiraz are both highly successful Riverland quaffers. Yalumba is also the pioneer of remarkably good 2-litre casks. Angas Brut is huge-selling, enjoyable fizz for the masses (me included); Yalumba D ★★★ has recently leapt to the fore showing delicious toasty, creamy style and is now one of Australia's best premium sparklers. The fortifieds are also excellent, particularly Liqueur Muscat ★★.

YARRA VALLEY *Victoria, Australia* Yarra wine was famous last century but virtually died out until the early 1970s when Mount Mary, Seville Estate, Yarra Yering and Yeringberg rekindled it. With its cool maritime climate it is shaping up as Australia's best Pinot Noir region. Exciting also for Chardonnay and Cabernet Merlot blends and as a supplier of base wine for sparklers. Best producers: COLDSTREAM HILLS, De Bortoli, DOMAINE CHANDON, MOUNT MARY, Oakridge, ST HUBERTS, Seville Estate, Tarrawarra, Yarra Ridge, YARRA YERING, Yeringberg.

YARRA YERING *Yarra Valley, Victoria, Australia* Bailey Carrodus uses quaint wine-making methods to create extraordinary wines from his exceptional vineyard. Chardonnay ★★, after a pedestrian start, is now showing exciting form too. The reds, labelled Dry Red No.1 ★★★ (Cabernet-based) and No.2 ★★★ (Shiraz-based), are profound, concentrated, structured for aging, packed with unnervingly self-confident fruit and memorable perfume. The Pinot Noir ★★ is expensive but very fine, and getting finer and wilder by the vintage. Best years: 1991 90 88.

YELLOWGLEN *Ballarat, Victoria, Australia* Big Champagne-method fizz producer owned by MILDARA. The quality is good but the wines are often released too young. Basic, high-volume lines are Brut NV, Brut Crémant and Brut Rosé.

YGREC *Bordeaux AC, Bordeaux, France* The dry wine of YQUEM, the world-famous SAUTERNES estate. Ygrec ★★ was first made in 1959 and created something of a vogue among Sauternes producers for releasing a dry wine in addition to a sweet one. An equal blend of Sauvignon Blanc and Sémillon it displays something of the concentration and power of YQUEM as it ages, but the shock is – it's bone dry. Best years: 1990 89 86 85.

YONNE, VIN DE PAYS DE L' *Chablis, Burgundy, France* Light, rather tart wine usually from young vines in the Chablis region or from Chardonnay or other varieties that don't qualify for anything more prestigious. Best producer: Fèvre.

CH. D'YQUEM ★★★ *Sauternes AC, Grand 1er Cru Classé, Bordeaux, France* Often rated as the most sublime sweet wine in the world, no-one can question Yquem's total commitment to quality. Despite the large vineyard (100ha/250 acres) production is tiny. Only fully noble-rotted grapes are picked, often berry by berry, and the low yield means each vine produces only a glass of wine! This precious liquid gold is then fermented in new oak barrels and left to mature for $3\frac{1}{2}$ years before bottling. The wine is one of the world's most expensive but is in constant demand because of its richness and exotic flavours – loony prices or not. Best years: 1990 89 88 86 83 81 80 76 75 71 67 62.

ZIND-HUMBRECHT *Alsace AC, France* Olivier Humbrecht is one of France's outstanding young winemakers, producing a brilliantly nuanced range of wines from his family's large estate. The Humbrechts own vines in four Grand Cru sites – Rangen, Goldert, Hengst and Brand - and these wines (Riesling ★★, Pinot Gris ★★★, Gewürztraminer ★★★ and Muscat ★★) are excellent. It is hard to find a single uninspiring wine here – even the basic Sylvaners ★ and Pinot Blancs ★★ are fine. The three splendid vintages of 1990, 89 and 88 produced a heady array of delights. Best years: 1990 89 88 85 83.

ZINFANDEL California's grape, probably the Primitivo from Italy. Zinfandel is a very versatile red grape that can be used to make anything from an insipid blush wine to a big, bruising, late-harvest-style dessert wine with in-between stops at both light and hefty dry styles with fruit always to the fore. Best producers: GRGICH HILLS★★, KENDALL-JACKSON (DuPratt-DePatie Vineyard★★), Nalle★, QUIVIRA★★, Ravenswood★★, RIDGE★★★.

ZWEIGELT High-yielding Austrian grape developed by a Dr Zweigelt in 1922. It needs vigorous pruning to bring out all its cherry fruit. Best producers: Breyer, Fischer, Gisperg, Kollwentz, Müller (vines planted by Dr Zweigelt), Pitnauer, Wagentristl.

And if anyone can think of a more exciting entry starting Zx, Zy or Zz – we'll put it in next year!

MAKING THE MOST OF WINE

Most wine is pretty hardy stuff and can put up with a fair amount of rough handling. Young red wines can knock about in the back of a car for a day or two and be lugged from garage to kitchen to table without too much harm. Young white wines can cover up all kinds of ill-treatment with a couple of hours in the fridge. Even so, there are some conditions that are better than others for storing your wine – especially if they are on the mature side. And there are certain ways of serving wines which will emphasize any flavours or perfumes they have.

STORING

Most wines are sold for drinking soon, and it will be hard to ruin them in the next few months before you pull the cork. Don't stand them next to the central heating or the cooker, though, or on the sunny windowsill.

Light and extremes of temperature are also the things to worry about if you are storing wine long-term. Some wines, Chardonnay for instance, are particularly sensitive to exposure to light over several months. The warmer the wine, the quicker it will age, and really high temperatures can spoil wine quite quickly. Beware in the winter of garages and outhouses, too. A really cold snap might freeze your wine, push out the corks and crack the bottles. An underground cellar is ideal, with a fairly constant temperature of between 10° and 12°C (50° and 53°F). And bottles really do need to lie on their sides, so that the cork stays damp and swollen, and keeps out the air.

TEMPERATURE

The person who thought up the rule that red wine should be served at room temperature certainly didn't live in an efficient, modern, centrally-heated flat. It's no great sin to serve a big beefy red at the temperature of your central heating, but I prefer most reds just a touch cooler. Over-heated wine tastes flabby, and may lose some of its more volatile aromas. In general, the lighter the red, the cooler it can be. Really light, refreshing reds, such as Beaujolais, are nice lightly chilled. Ideally, I'd serve Burgundy at larder temperature, Bordeaux a bit warmer, Australian Cabernet at the temperature of a draughty room.

Chilling white wines makes them taste fresher, emphasizing their acidity. White wines with low acidity benefit especially from chilling, and it's vital for fizzy wines if you don't want exploding corks and a tableful of froth. Drastic chilling also subdues flavours – a useful ruse if you're serving basic wine, but a shame if the wine is very good.

A good guide for whites is to give the cheapest and lightest a spell in the fridge, but serve bigger and better wines – Australian Chardonnays or top white Burgundies – perhaps half way between fridge and central heating temperature. If you're undecided, err on the cooler side, for whites or reds.

OPENING THE BOTTLE

There's no corkscrew to beat the Screwpull and the Spinhandle Screwpull is especially easy to use. Don't worry if bits of cork crumble into the wine – just fish them out of your glass. Tight corks that refuse to budge might be loosened if you run hot water over the bottle neck to expand the glass. If the cork is loose and falls in, push it right in and forget about it.

Opening sparkling wines is a serious business – point the cork away from people! Once you've started, never take your hand off the cork until it's safely out. Loosen the wire, hold the wire and cork firmly and twist the bottle. If the wine froths, hold the bottle at 45 degrees, and have a glass at hand.

AIRING AND DECANTING

Scientists have proved that opening young to middle-aged red wines an hour before serving makes no difference whatsoever. The surface area of wine in contact with air in the bottle neck is too tiny to be significant. Decanting is a different matter, because sloshing the wine from bottle to jug or decanter mixes it up quite thoroughly with the air. The only wines that really need to be decanted are those that have a sediment which would cloud the wine if they were poured directly – mature red Bordeaux, Burgundy and vintage port are the commonest examples. Ideally, if forewarned, you need to stand the bottle upright for a day or two to let the sediment settle in the bottom. Draw the cork extremely gently. As you tip the bottle, shine a bright light through from underneath, so that you can see the sediment as you pour, all in one, steady movement. Stop pouring when you see the sediment approaching the bottle neck.

Contrary to many wine buffs' practice, I would decant a mature wine only just before serving. Elderly wines often fade very rapidly once they meet with air, and an hour in the decanter could kill off what little fruit they had left.

KEEPING LEFTOVERS

Leftover white wine keeps better than red, since the tannin and colouring matter in red wine is easily attacked by the air. Any wine, red or white, keeps better in the fridge than in a warm kitchen. And most wines, if well made in the first place, will be perfectly acceptable if not pristine after two or three days re-corked in the fridge. But for better results it's best to use one of the gadgets sold for this purpose. The ones that work by blanketing the wine with heavier-than-air inert gas are much better than those that create a vacuum in the air space in the bottle.

VINTAGE CHARTS

FRANCE	91	90	89	88	87	86	85	84	83
Alsace	5	10	9	8	5	5	9	4	8
Bordeaux									
Margaux	5	9	8	7	5	8	8	4	8
St.-Jul., Pauillac, St-Est.	5	9	9	8	5	8	8	4	8
Graves/Pessac-L. (R)	4	8	7	9	5	7	8	4	8
Graves/Pessac-L. (W)	5	8	8	9	6	8	7	4	8
St-Émilion, Pomerol	3	8	10	8	6	7	9	3	7
Sauternes	3	10	9	9	4	10	6	3	9
Burgundy									
Chablis	5	9	8	7	5	8	8	4	7
Côte de Beaune (W)	6	8	9	8	5	8	8	5	6
Côte de Nuits (R)	6	10	9	8	7	6	10	4	7
Beaujolais Cru	9	8	8	7	5	5	9	4	8
Loire									
Bourgueil, Chinon	4	9	10	8	5	6	9	3	7
Sancerre (W)	7	8	7	8	6	8	6	5	8
Loire Sweet	5	10	10	7	4	6	9	4	9
Rhône									
Hermitage (W)	6	10	9	9	5	6	8	6	9
Hermitage (R)	6	10	9	9	5	6	9	5	10
Côte-Rôtie	8	7	9	8	5	6	10	4	9
Châteauneuf (R)	5	10	9	8	4	7	8	6	7

The numerals (1–10) represent an overall rating for each year.

ITALY	91	90	89	88	87	86	85	84	83
Barolo, Barbaresco	6	10	9	8	6	7	9	6	6
Chianti Classico	6	10	6	9	6	7	10	4	8
Brunello, Vino Nobile	7	10	6	9	6	7	10	5	8
GERMANY									
Mosel Riesling	5	10	8	7	4	5	7	4	8
Rheingau Riesling	5	9	8	8	4	6	7	4	9
SPAIN									
Ribera del Duero	8	9	6	6	9	8	8	3	8
Rioja (R)	8	8	9	6	6	9	8	3	8
PORTUGAL									
Bairrada	6	7	7	6	6	5	10	4	7
Dão	7	6	6	6	7	4	8	5	8
Port	9	8	6	5	7	5	9	4	10
USA									
Napa Cabernet	9	8	7	7	8	9	10	9	6
Carneros Chardonnay	9	8	6	8	8	9	10	7	6
AUSTRALIA									
Coonawarra Cabernet	9	8	5	9	7	9	8	7	4
Hunter Chardonnay	10	5	8	7	8	9	7	6	5
NEW ZEALAND									
M'lborough Sauvignon	10	6	9	8	8	9	8	7	8
Hawkes Bay Cabernet	9	7	9	5	9	8	8	5	9

◗ *Not ready*   ● *Just ready*   ◉ *At peak*   ◖ *Past best*

INDEX OF MAIN PRODUCERS

ACKNOWLEDGMENTS

Editorial Director Sandy Carr; **Editor** Fiona Holman;
Editorial Assistant Lyn Parry; **Researcher & Proofreader** Wink
Lorch; **Art Director** Douglas Wilson; **Art Editor** Jason Vrakas;
Designer Stephen Moore; **Indexer** Naomi Good.

NOTES